A Year of Sundays

A Year of Sundays

TAKING THE PLUNGE
(AND OUR CAT)
TO EXPLORE EUROPE

EDWARD D. WEBSTER

VanderWyk & Burnham

Published by VanderWyk & Burnham
P.O. Box 2789, Acton, Massachusetts 01720

This book is available for quantity purchases. For information on bulk discounts, call (800) 789-7916 or write to Special Sales at the above address.

Library of Congress Cataloging-in-Publication Data
Webster, Edward D., 1947-
        A year of Sundays : taking the plunge (and our cat) to explore Europe / Edward D. Webster.
            p. cm.
        ISBN 1-889242-21-7
        1. Europe, Western—Description and travel. 2. Webster, Edward D., 1947–
—Travel—Europe, Western. 3. Webster, Marguerite—Travel—Europe, Western.
4. Blind—Travel—Europe, Western. I. Title.

D967.W45 2004
914.04'559—dc22

                                                                    2004041920

www.VandB.com

FIRST PRINTING
Manufactured in the United States of America
10 9 8 7 6 5 4 3 2 1

To Marguerite, companion *extraordinaire* for life's journey,
and to Felicia, Queen of the Traveling Cats

Contents

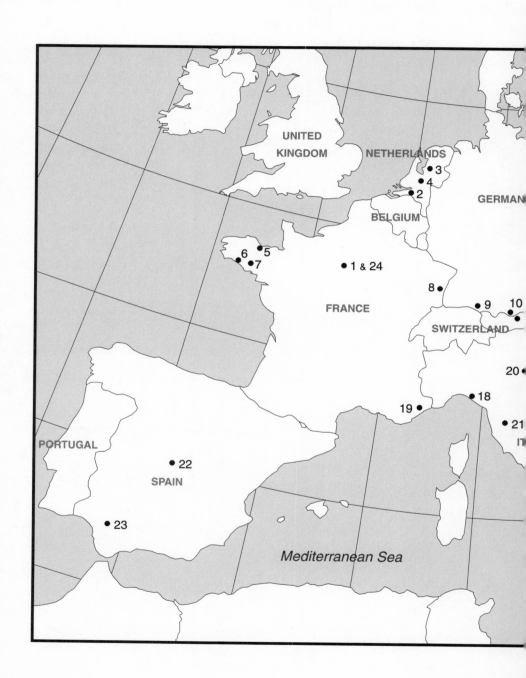

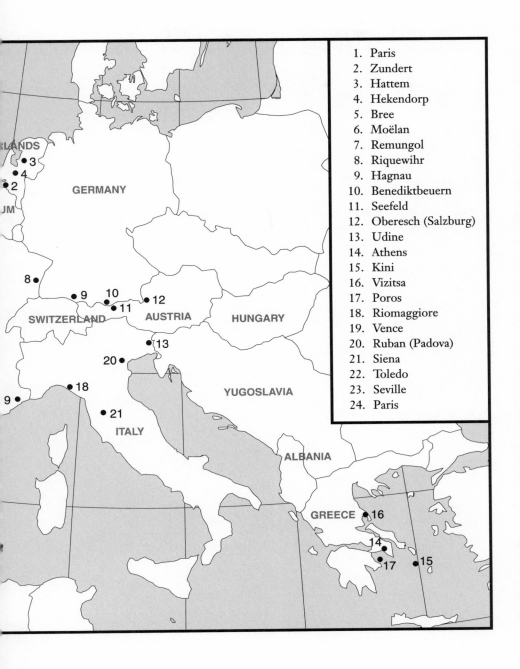

1. Paris
2. Zundert
3. Hattem
4. Hekendorp
5. Bree
6. Moëlan
7. Remungol
8. Riquewihr
9. Hagnau
10. Benediktbeuern
11. Seefeld
12. Oberesch (Salzburg)
13. Udine
14. Athens
15. Kini
16. Vizitsa
17. Poros
18. Riomaggiore
19. Vence
20. Ruban (Padova)
21. Siena
22. Toledo
23. Seville
24. Paris

Prologue

Perplexed

June 1997, Moëlan-sur-Mer, Brittany, France

We were thousands of miles from home, on a year of independent travel. The three of us—Marguerite, my blind, menopausal wife; our sixteen-year-old cat, Felicia; and I—had come on a quest for adventure. And adventure we had found—discovering cafés and museums during April in Paris, bicycling on a rented tandem for weeks in Holland, exploring medieval villages here in Brittany. Even renting this home by the Atlantic for three weeks, negotiating and signing contracts all in French, had been a feat.

But not all was joyful. We had also come to isolation. We had found pockets of sadness deep inside us.

Outside, rays from the sunrise ignited the sky and lit the tops of pine trees. The cadence of ocean waves drifted in through the French doors behind me. I hunched over the kitchen table and punched the keys of my computer, writing about my feelings, trying to make sense of them.

June 27

I brought Marguerite and Felicia here, but I haven't been able to guarantee a happy journey. Some hours are ideal, others so very lonely. We are separated from friends, family, and the English language. Sometimes a small chore becomes a big problem for no reason. Why do I let such minor things overwhelm me? I expect irrational reactions from Marguerite when she's in her menopausal madness, but forty-nine-year-old men don't have menopause. . . . Do they? I'm supposed to be the logical one, the stabilizing influence.

I keep reminding myself that I'm the luckiest man in the world, but I've begun taking something called Stabilium to ease my anxiety. As best as I can tell from the French-only information sheet, it's composed of the better parts of fish brains. Come on, little trout cerebrums, do your thing.

3

Good, I thought, there's humor in those words. If I could nurture that crumb of mirth, maybe I could regain my confidence. I walked to the opposite window and looked toward the sea—no answers there. A thump from somewhere behind startled me, and I turned.

Marguerite stood at the edge of the living room in a flannel nightgown, her hair tousled from sleep. She held Felicia in her arms and had a hopeful smile on her lips. "Eddie . . . I feel better. How about visiting that animal park after breakfast?"

The prospect of a joyous day cheered me. "That sounds *great*, honey."

Okay, maybe it was manic to feel that way, but that's how I felt; and how could I pass up a delight-filled day with her? Later that night, while she slept, I would think this over. I would reflect on the events that had brought us here.

The Dream

The Dream

A Year Before the Trip

When had the dream first come to life? Had it lain dormant since our visit to Europe in 1970, when we explored all those countries together in that little red VW? Had it been since our retreat to the woods in 1986, when we decided to change careers and take more time for ourselves?

The first time we spoke of it, a larger company was in the process of swallowing the one I worked for. I would get ten months' pay if they dropped me. I asked Marguerite, "What should I do if they lay me off?"

"We could go to Europe for a year," she smiled tentatively.

It may have been a serious suggestion . . . or not. We didn't explore it deeply, but it made me feel better about the possibility of getting canned. "We'll take off to Europe for a year" became our standard reply when asked about our contingency plans. The new company didn't fire me, but the dream gnawed at my thoughts and popped up in discussions with Marguerite from then on.

A few years later I met Lester and Esther in my writers' group. They took Marguerite and me under their wing and told us about their seasons in Europe twenty years ago. From then on, we'd known there would come a time for us to spend the year . . . but when?

I was getting itchy to go for it, but Marguerite held back. Even though she felt burned out after fourteen years as a marriage and family therapist, there were security issues for her—all that time away from family, all that time not earning money.

But the dream . . . the idea . . .

The realization that it wasn't a crazy idea was founded, for me, in my father's death when he was fifty-five and I was twenty. It was confirmed by the reminders our bodies were sending us—that things were changing and not for the better—that one or both of us, like my father, might not live to retire, might not be healthy enough to enjoy a trip in fifteen years. The chance to spend a generous portion of time in each other's company could vanish in a heartbeat or ebb away with the progression of a disabling illness. Marguerite might be lost to me or I to her, leaving one huge regret that we never created the opportunity.

I came to believe that this year away was one of the most sensible things we could do. It became out of the question for us to put it off.

It was early 1996, and we sat in the living room of our country home in southern California. Felicia rested on my lap as I read aloud from an issue of *International Travel News*. Marguerite snuggled into the couch beside me, a blissful look settling on her face. "It would be great to live without a schedule, wouldn't it? To explore Provence . . . the Greek islands . . . with absolutely no demands."

"Then I have a deal for you. . . ." I set the magazine on the end table. "We can spend this year planning and saving—read and research and enjoy the heck out of doing it—and then take off in '97."

"If we don't go pretty soon," she added, "I'll have to find a new career."

I felt nonsensical joy seeping into my heart as I hugged her.

She rested her head against my shoulder but then pulled back, her expression sober. "If we go that long, my blindness will be more of an issue. I won't have a support system, no drivers to take me places, no telephone. I won't be able to arrange things or do simple chores like laundry. I'll be so very dependent on you, and you may get tired of it."

"No one loves spending time together like you and I do. We'll do fine . . . better than fine."

"But . . ."

"We've been messing around with this idea for too long. It's like getting married. I'm ready to make a commitment. Are you?"

She frowned, but slowly a broad smile spread over her face. "Oh, yes! I want to go."

Felicia Had Always Wanted to Go to Europe

Our cat, Felicia, never said much about it, but we could tell by the subtle things she did: the way she paced the floor, the pleading looks she cast with golden eyes as we packed our bags before trips, her obsession with sleeping in our suitcases, the way she turned her back on us and pouted after we returned. "But you wouldn't like it, Effie," we told her. "The flights are a pain, and you couldn't really see anything."

"Try me," she answered silently, as she lay a champagne-colored cheek in my hand.

Then it came time for the grand journey that we'd discussed for years—our year in Europe. As we planned, Felicia listened eagerly to our discussions, laid for hours on my lap as I read travel magazines to Marguerite. Her furry face looked up at me, and she seemed to ask, "It's my turn now, right?"

Marguerite and I pondered the question, but not for long. Felicia was sixteen, an old, mellow cat, our constant companion at home. How could we leave her in California and maybe never see her again?

Felicia rolled onto her back, looked up at me with contentment, and purred her loudest purr. She knew it was a go.

A Year Is All I Ask

Ten Months Before the Trip

My armpits grew wet, my mouth dry, but I forced a smile as I entered Susan's office. She was a county supervisor, one of five officials elected to run our county in southern California. She was a strong woman who could stand up to developers, who spoke out for kids and the mentally ill. I was one of her three assistants who researched issues, recommended policies, represented constituents when they needed help with the county agencies, and generally tried to keep the agencies from going to war with each other.

As a boss she was usually a pussycat. Her dress code was, "You must dress." She let me cover any subject I wanted, as long as I kept her informed about air pollution, transportation, the fire department, and the child abuse center we were creating.

But this request was different.

I pulled a pile of papers from one of the chairs in her office and sat down. She was in one of her dress-down outfits—slacks and a T-shirt that said, "Kids Come First," with stick figures of playing children. She glanced at me and then resumed reading the report on her desk. "Yes?"

That was Susan's way. She did at least two things at a time. It was a habit that sometimes set me off balance.

"I have a request. Well, actually, it was Felicia's idea." Susan sat back. Her blue eyes locked on me. Susan loved cats.

"You know how Marguerite and I go off to Europe for a month or two at a time? Felicia doesn't like it. She also says we work too much."

"Right," Susan snickered, but her eyes narrowed. "What are you planning this time?"

"It's Felicia. She wants us to spend some quality time with her. A lot of quality time. . . . The three of us are heading to Europe for a year."

If we had been going away without Felicia, Susan would have seen it as cat abuse. She wouldn't have supported it. But we *were* taking Felicia. I thought I had a chance. "I'd like a leave of absence," I said, omitting the fact that without a leave I would resign and go anyway.

Susan looked away, appeared flustered. "Have you seen the proposed budget? There may not even be a job for you to come back to." She stood and strode around the end of her desk.

"That's why this is a good time." I followed her toward the door. "You could hire someone to fill in part-time and that would give us salary savings."

"Talk to me after the budget hearings."

That was all. Susan was out the door, moving on to the next

subject and the next person, clearly not wanting to discuss it further. I would have to wait two months for an answer.

Checklist:
   Research cheap flights to Paris.
   Obtain brochures on apartments in Paris and Salzburg.
   Check on requirements for taking a cat to the countries
      of Europe.
   Find out if we need any visas for this long a trip.

The Answer

Eight Months to Departure

The county budget was adopted, and the dust settled. I still had a position. But I delayed asking Susan about the leave, waiting for a day when she had no grueling meetings, no environmental disaster, no outright infighting between agencies, no petition drive to eliminate county government.

Finally, I forced myself to ask the big question, and Susan gave the big answer with no flourish or fanfare. Yes, I could have a leave.

I stopped for a special bottle of champagne on the way home. Marguerite and I clinked glasses and did a dance of joy.

Checklist:
   Rent and pay for apartments—April in Paris, August in Salzburg.
   Book flights to and from Paris.
   Reserve cabin space in plane for Felicia.
   Open joint checking account with Marguerite's sister Patricia.
   Arrange for Patricia to buy our car.
   Obtain debit cards (both Visa and MasterCard).
   Arrange for cars in Europe to cover the whole 11+ months.

Alternative Medicine

One Month Before the Trip

I led Marguerite into the almost-barren room we had visited five times during the past two months. We sat in straight chairs by a bare wooden table to wait for Dr. Wong. A pungent herbal smell suffused the room. On the wall hung a Chinese calendar, the only adornment except for a side table with white enameled pots and jars holding powders and dried leaves. Through the window, the orange-tiled rooftops of Malibu clashed with this austerity.

Dr. Wong—a chunky Chinese man with black hair touched by gray—strode in and settled on his stool. "Okay, Mrs. Wester, I hold your wrist." He took Marguerite's pulse in that very intense way he had. "Now the other." She extended the other arm, and he repeated.

I had decided that the doctor took the pulse from both wrists as part of some subtle Chinese methodology, the balancing of body energies, yin and yang.

"Now I look your eyes." Marguerite faced him, and the doctor stared at her. "Your symptoms?"

"I still have night sweats and hot flashes. I get exhausted some days."

"I will make new granules with more ginseng. I use American ginseng, not Korean or Siberian; those are too harsh." He turned to me, "Your wife has a fragile system, Mr. Wester."

It was a mistake to exclude Marguerite as if she were a child. She was blind, but that didn't make her foolish and certainly not submissive.

"There's something you need to know." My so-called fragile wife focused her energy on the doctor. "We are going away in a month."

"Yes, yes." The doctor's brow wrinkled.

"I can't be stranded in Europe feeling sick. Before we leave, I want you to have my system in shape."

"You must understand, this is Eastern medicine. . . ."

"I'm beginning to wonder how well this medicine works."

Marguerite kept her focus leveled toward him as I cringed. In my family, you didn't talk to doctors that way. "I have tried very hard with your herbs. I have brewed teas from roots and leaves, thistles and seashells; my kitchen has smelled like a swamp for two months. And now you have me taking these awful crystals mixed in hot water every day."

"Yes, Mrs. Wester. You are good patient."

"But when we leave for Europe, there will be no crystals. There will be pills."

Dr. Wong's eyes narrowed, like a boy with hurt feelings. "Pills not as effective." He swallowed, assessed her determination, and made an entry in his notes. "Okay, Mrs. Wester, we do crystals two, three more weeks. Then I get you tablets."

A few minutes later we left carrying a couple of pounds of crystals in a paper bag. I led Marguerite to the elevator and pushed the down button. "You're a difficult patient."

"Bull."

"Dr. Wong thinks you're stubborn."

"I'm assertive. . . . How do you know what Dr. Wong thinks, anyway?"

The elevator arrived, and I led her on. "I'm worried for you. You've been uncomfortable and moody. We'll be away from our doctor, in countries where we don't speak the language. Maybe you should try the hormones."

"No! It's like Dr. Wong said: I need a gentle remedy. I have too many friends with breast cancer to chance taking estrogen. I'll be okay once I stop working. . . . We'll have a great trip."

Checklist:
   Buy a soft-sided, under-the-seat carrier for Felicia.
   Type mailing labels to family and friends.
   Get health and vaccination certificates for Felicia and send to
      USDA for endorsement.
   Prepay bills (insurance, property tax, water, etc.).
   Make auto insurance dormant, effective April 1.

File forwarding address at post office, effective March 30.

Change address on credit-card and joint accounts.

Last-Minute Frenzy

Three Days to Departure

Marguerite had been—excuse the expression—demented during our preparations for the trip.

She felt guilty about taking off for a year from her counseling practice and felt compelled to work up to the last minute. She questioned if we were doing the right thing, if we could afford it. She changed her mind constantly and couldn't make the simplest decisions, like which music CDs to take along. In short, she was in the viselike grip of perimenopause.

We would leave for Paris in three days . . . or would we? Marguerite paced the living room floor. "Ed, I haven't been sleeping. The night sweats and headaches aren't getting better. How can we take a trip when I feel like this?"

I felt little shards of my heart break off and plunge into my stomach. "We've been planning all year. We can't chuck it. Not if there's any way . . ."

I put my hand on her shoulder to stop her movement, wrapped my arms around her, and felt some of the tension drain from her shoulders as she leaned against me.

"The herbal medicines aren't working, not enough anyway," she said. "But I'm not ready to take hormones. What if we're in Europe, and I can't . . ."

She couldn't pull out on me now. This trip was the most important thing we'd ever do. I touched her lips to silence her. "We talked about this before."

"We don't have to go to Europe, you know," she pleaded. "Not if we're sick."

"No. We don't have to, but we've paid for the tickets and the cars. I took leave from my job. I think we should take off in the plane on Monday and come back if . . ."

"What about my symptoms? Maybe these natural medicines aren't for me."

"That's not insoluble. We'll bring the herbs *and* the hormones. That way you're covered."

She pulled back and looked up at me. "I could have thought of that."

"Yeah. Why didn't you?"

"I wanted you to feel smart."

"Admit it. It's the 'pause. Rampant hormones are dithering your brain. I hope they let you into Europe. They may have prohibitions against confused, blind people."

"I don't care. *I'm going.*"

Marguerite marched into the kitchen and called Mary, her ob-gyn.

It took her a few minutes, and I could tell Mary wasn't making it easy. Marguerite was almost in tears.

Without the medicine, I could picture her refusing to take the trip. The least onerous result would involve a break-in at a local pharmacy, and I had no doubt who would have to drive the getaway car.

She hung up and turned to me. "Okay. She's giving me a prescription for Prempro, and I have to get a boar's-hair brush and disposable diapers."

"Interesting list. What are those for?"

"The hairdresser told me a boar's-hair brush will work best with my hair style."

"Are these brushes common? What if we can't find one?"

"Then we cancel the trip."

"That makes sense. So the boar's-hair brush is a must. What about the diapers?"

"Jamie told me. They're for the bottom of the cat carrier, just in case Felicia has an accident."

"How do you get these things to stay flat under the cat?"

"Don't worry. *I'll* handle it."

Fortunately, we found the boar's-hair brush and disposable diapers. We bought the Prempro and added it to our medical arsenal. By the time we left the country, we were toting everything from a first-aid kit to antibiotics to pounds of herbal pills. Counting Marguerite's cleansers and creams, our medicines weighed more than our clothing and took up almost as much room.

For better or worse, we were on our way.

Checklist:
　Boar's-hair brush
　Prempro
　Disposable diapers
　Pack everything for trip, including Effie's soft bed and baby sling.
　Repack into larger suitcases.

April Is Paris

Nous Sommes Arrivés (We Have Arrived)

Felicia was in trouble.

We were soaring somewhere over the Atlantic on our way to Paris. Marguerite slept beside me, her head cocked at an uncomfortable angle against the seat back.

I reached down to unzip the top of Effie's carrier. Inside I found something more like a pelt than a living, breathing cat. I prodded her furry chin with my fingers. Lethargically, she raised her head. I dabbed some water on her lips. The altitude and dryness were killing her. This trip was a disastrous mistake, but there was nothing to do until we arrived in Paris and no point in waking Marguerite.

The plane pulled up to our gate at Orly Airport. I slid Felicia's green nylon-and-leather carrier from beneath the seat, lifted her to eye level, and looked through the mesh side of the carrier. Still curled in a ball, she opened an eye! A glimmer of hope touched my heart. I helped Marguerite strap the computer onto her back and then hefted Felicia and our other carry-on bag. Marguerite clutched my elbow and followed me off the plane.

In the terminal, I set Effie atop a luggage cart. Something shifted—the carrier bulged on one side. A soft but insistent meow sounded . . . then a louder meow. Relief flooded me. I looked in to see a fully alive cat, alive and with an attitude. "She's okay. I was really worried on the plane."

The fatigue on Marguerite's face from the long flight gave way to a beaming smile. "I touched her during the flight, but she didn't move. I didn't want to upset you, but I thought she'd died."

We hugged, and then I grabbed two baggies of cat litter and the cardboard tray we'd brought and took our kitty to the men's room. The minute I set her feet in the litter there was another flood of relief.

"You did *great*," I told her. From the back of the case, I extracted the wadded-up heap of dry diapers Marguerite had spread in the carrier back in California. Felicia eyed them, sarcastically I thought.

❧

Our belongings formed a precarious mass on top of the luggage cart. I pushed as Marguerite shored up the sloping heap of suitcases and satchels, and protected our kitty.

The customs booths came into view. In my jacket pocket I fingered the packet with Felicia's health and vaccination certificates. Still, I worried that the customs official would say, "Take your cat and your papers and go back to where you came from," or worse, "We must lock your cat in a little cage for three months with only bread and water."

I slid our passports to the official. *"Bonjour."*

His eyes darted up at me and then back under his visor. He mumbled, *"Bonjour,"* and glanced at Marguerite's passport, then her face. My palms sweated. He leafed through and ca-chunked his stamp onto one of the pages, repeated the same with my document, and waved us to go ahead. But wasn't there something else we needed, a paper to legitimize Felicia's entry into France? Better face it now than not be able to take her home at the end of the trip.

"Et nous avons la chatte." I lifted the carrier to eye level. He nodded and swung his arm toward the door a second time. As I pushed forward, annoyance set in. "He didn't even want to see Felicia's documents."

"I told you this was no big deal. They love pets in France."

❧

On the way into the city, our cab driver pointed out some of the stadiums and squares to us. Then he asked in French, "Your cat, does she like to travel?"

"It was her first time in a plane," I said.

"Tell him she was very good," Marguerite directed.

"Elle était très bonne."

"Tell him she slept all the way, and she waited to pee until you took her to the restroom."

"That's a lot of French, and it might be more than he needs to know."

"I have a cat, too," the cabby volunteered. "His name is Beauregard. He is a fine cat, but he never travels farther than my neighbor's yard to see his girlfriend." (This being a loose translation based on my limited French.)

Our cab entered the traffic circle around the Arc de Triomphe. Cars rushed in from boulevards on all sides, but I focused on the monument with its sculpted battle scenes.

Adrenaline roused me as we veered down the Champs-Elysées, and I spied its symmetrical rows of trees, wide sidewalks, glitzy perfume shops, *brasseries*. Soon we would see our Paris home.

The cabby waited while I picked up the key for our apartment at the PSR rental office, one floor up from the Mercedes dealer on the grand avenue. Back inside the cab, Marguerite had unzipped the cat case. Felicia's cinnamon-colored head stuck out, scanning from side to side. The cabby observed as Marguerite told our kitty that this was the most glamorous street in the world.

The driver executed two U-turns and pulled to a stop in front of our building. *"L'avenue des Champs-Elysées, c'est très élégante,"* he remarked. He would never guess that we would pay only $63 a night for this prominent address.

As I paid, I offered, "Say *bonjour* to Beauregard."

"Meow," Felicia added genially.

❧

The next morning my eyes shot open before dawn. It was 6 AM, 9 AM California time. Marguerite slept on, but jet lag and excitement had pumped my mind full of adrenaline and questions: What goes on at 6 AM in Paris? What was I waiting for?

Five flights down at street level, our building housed an indoor arcade—a *brasserie*-style restaurant in the center, surrounded by shops, all closed and eerie at this hour. I peeked in windows and saw gold jewelry, women's clothing (way-too-bright yellows, chartreuses, and oranges—with shoes to match), a display of African statues, gems, and baubles.

Loud music assaulted my ears. Two men in denim overalls pulled a buffing machine from a closet by the elevator. Their boom box blasted American pop music at full volume as they prepared to clean floors. Fleeing the building, I passed the Planet Hollywood club, its windows displaying ultra-geeky mannequins in gaudy outfits and space glasses. So much for Paris fashion.

A thin fog drifted in as I walked along the deserted sidewalk—not just down any street but the most famous boulevard anywhere. I stopped at the window of the Brioche Dorée. Tasty-looking croissants, raisin wheels, apricot rolls, and strawberry tarts beckoned, but the sign said *Fermé* (Closed).

I heard a putt-putt sound and spotted first one, then another, spring-green contraption. Soon, several of them were buzzing along the sidewalk. Silly gizmos . . . no, ingenious. They were a cross between a street sweeper, a mini garbage truck, and a miniature bucket-truck that can lift a person. I watched as a fellow in an orange jumpsuit pulled his green truck in front of a darker green kiosk, elevated himself in his bucket, and began cleaning the structure with a jet of water.

I stopped at an ATM, requested 2000 francs ($350), and received it in a few seconds—a modern miracle. Everything was working great and feeling good. And this was Paris—too exciting to miss. Time to go wake Marguerite.

Half an hour later, still rubbing sleep from her eyes, Marguerite accompanied me along the grand avenue toward the Arc de

Triomphe. The sight of the imposing monument filled me with awe.

Marguerite wrapped herself tighter in her jacket and put her arm around my waist. "You got me out here. Now I need coffee."

I led her to a *brasserie*, just opening for the day, and checked the menu. "We're not getting it here. It's $10 for only two croissants and a coffee to share."

"That's crazy. We'll never make our budget." We had decided we could spend up to $50 a day on food, entertainment, and incidentals.

We hustled down rue Lincoln, a side street, to the Bar-Brasserie Saucisson, a little place with red leather booths and a bartender in black vest and bow tie. I helped Marguerite onto a stool and ordered croissants and *cafés au lait*.

"*Cafés crèmes*," the waiter corrected.

"Man, I don't even know how to order coffee."

The barman gestured toward a booth and rattled off some French, which I comprehended not at all. But I got the gist and said, "*Non, merci.*"

"The guidebooks were right," I told Marguerite. "If we follow his suggestion and sit at a table, the prices will double."

"This is a *lovely* stool." Marguerite shifted to get more comfortable, as the barman eyed us to see if we would reconsider.

The coffee and croissants arrived. I requested *confitures*. The barman—a laconic, short-haired, sharp-nosed fellow—understood my French just fine and set a bowl of rich peach preserves before me, but he replied with not a word that I could recognize. Was he a French Eliza Doolittle, or did he intentionally put on this accent to befuddle tourists?

I devoured two pastries to Marguerite's one, and then we shared another. "The best croissants in the world," I proclaimed. Indeed they were, but the four croissants and three large *crèmes* we consumed were all the more delicious because we spent less than half of what we would have at the other *brasserie*.

"I am satisfied beyond belief," Marguerite said, yawning. "But I feel a nap coming on."

23

"But . . . but . . . don't you want to see the city?"

"We have a month."

A whole month—learning about Paris . . . learning a little French . . . beginning to watch expenses. Outside, sidewalks glistened with the moisture of a recent washing. The fog was beginning to dissipate. Everything was new, bright, and thrilling.

Marguerite agreed to visit the tourist office first and to stop in at the Métro to buy monthly passes, but then I took her home and left her to nap with Felicia.

It was late in the morning as I walked along the Seine. I crossed the elaborate, gold-statued Alexander III Bridge and glimpsed the Eiffel Tower in the distance. It was all still sinking in.

From the riverbank near the Musée d'Orsay, I spotted the expansive palace of the Louvre farther down across the Seine, then the funky booksellers along the quay, and Notre Dame. I watched a juggler on a unicycle perform for a crowd on the bridge to the Ile Saint-Louis, and then I circled the island with its quaint, elegant apartment buildings.

Part of me longed to be with Marguerite, as she slept with Felicia curled against her chest . . . to share our first moments . . . in our Paris apartment . . . on the Champs-Elysées, our home for all of April.

We had dreamed and planned and hoped for so long. This couldn't be real. But with each street and each city square like a museum before me, I knew it was. We were really here, living our dream. Would it pass too quickly? Would I be back at work in the blink of an eye?

Our year of Sundays was beginning.

Settling In

April 4

Our sweet apartment has all the comforts we could want—plenty of light, French doors to a balcony overlooking Paris rooftops, washing

machine, bathroom with those wonderful heating tubes to dry our
towels, twin beds that we push together, the wicker love seat we asked
for, which Felicia loves. The compact kitchen is stocked with coffee
maker, microwave, two-burner stove, large cups for café crème, small
ones for espresso, lettuce spinner . . . a very well designed package. Oh,
we have a color TV, too, not that there are any shows we understand.
Although our building fronts the bustling Champs-Elysées, our
apartment is at the back, over a narrow one-way street, so our
balcony is peaceful.

Now, it's time to go shopping.

We stepped out onto the sidewalk. "Look at that," I said.
"We're taking a detour."

"Where?"

"You'll find out." (All right, it might be a little mean to treat a
blind person that way, but a wee bit of mystery is good for anyone.)

I led Marguerite to a crosswalk and waited for the light to
change. We walked to the safety island in the middle of the street
and turned to face uphill. "There. The boulevard is lined on both
sides with trees covered in new green leaves, all the way up to the
Arc de Triomphe."

"Aren't they the same trees from yesterday?"

"And the arch is in the center, grand against the morning sky,
the carved figures majestic."

"Yes?"

The traffic light turned, and motorcycles erupted into motion
on either side of us, followed closely by automobiles, all flying off
the mark like sprinters in a 100-meter dash from hell. The air filled
with acrid exhaust. Our narrow island seemed scant shelter.

When the racket subsided, I continued. "The difference is that
today there are French tri-colors—blue, white, and red—hanging
from poles all the way up the street, and one huge flag is rippling in
the breeze under the Arc." I turned her to face the opposite
direction. "Down this way, more tri-colors, scores of them, running
to the Egyptian obelisk at the Place de la Concorde."

"We are *so* lucky to be here!"

We headed to the Prisunic supermarket a couple of blocks from our building, picked up a basket, and began exploring. The store was much smaller than the supermarkets back in the States. I led Marguerite past some freezers. "Look over here. Frozen Coquilles Saint-Jacques—good-sized scallops sitting in their shells; and they have escargots, too, cozy in their spiral armor with a dab of green stuff on them."

She stuck out her tongue. "Did you have to mention the green stuff?"

"Don't want you to miss any of this. And up ahead . . ." Excited, I approached a refrigerated case, with Marguerite holding on. "All sorts of cold pastas. How about asparagus ravioli?"

"Mmmm."

"Across the aisle, canned *cassoulet* (a bean and sausage dish from southwest France). Oh, and let's get some Provençal-style sauce for the ravioli." I plopped a jar into our basket.

At the deli counter, we waited in line behind two women in business suits. I peeked between them to spot the delicacies in the cases. A catchy jingle came from speakers overhead, "Pris-un-ic, Pris-un-ic." A woman's voice sang the words, followed by an announcement in French—their version of "blue-light specials." The man behind the counter took my order for salmon pâté and a few great-looking stuffed *aubergines* (eggplant halves crowned with a mixture of onions, tomatoes, and herbs).

The smell of fresh bread lured us to the bakery counter, where we selected a baguette and a pear tart that looked and smelled about 3,000 percent better than anything back home.

The produce section, only a quarter of the size we were used to, was packed with a bright, plump harvest.

"These strawberries are from Spain. Take a sniff." I held a couple under Marguerite's nose.

"Mmmm. Pop them in."

"And these little onions with the long green tails look great . . . grown in Paris. And here are the ever-present *haricots verts*. They're skinnier than I remembered."

"I know. Green beans . . . this is sure fun." Marguerite smiled. "I feel like a Parisian."

Following the example of other shoppers, we bagged lettuce, onions, and a bunch of tomatoes still on the vine. I slipped the neck of each bag through a little gadget that sealed it with tape. In the tradition of the do-it-yourself French market, I tossed the tomatoes on the scale and pushed a button with their picture. It spit out a price tag to stick on the bag.

We picked up paper goods, wine, and, last but not least, cat food and litter. I carried the much-too-heavy basket, and Marguerite held packages of toilet paper and paper towels clutched to her chest, as we edged to the checkout.

The young brunette in a white smock who sat at the check stand looked as bored as any clerk could be. I showed my Visa card and asked, *"C'est bien?"* She nodded. We would charge our purchases in the American-market tradition, but here was where American customs evaporated. In the *supermarché*, the customer—not the clerk—bagged the groceries.

Despite the young woman's apathy, our purchases dashed past with surprising speed. While I tried to watch prices on the register, I handed Marguerite some plastic bags. "Would you open these?"

As the cashier took my credit card, Marguerite muttered, "They stick together. I can't get them open." I took a bag and began struggling with it. The woman handed me the credit slip to sign. Marguerite said, "I got one open. Where do I find our groceries?"

I picked up the pen. "Feel your way past me to the end of the counter." Marguerite patted her way by. I signed the slip and shoved my credit card into my shirt pocket.

As I was squidgying the top of a bag between my fingers to open it, the clerk began ringing up the next customer and flinging groceries down the ramp. "Oh, man. This is getting hairy."

Marguerite had filled her first bag and was trying to open another. "Take your time. The others will have to wait," she said.

I bulldozed our purchases to one side to separate them from

the new arrivals. Marguerite succeeded with another sack. While cramming things into my bag, I eyed the next customer—a stout woman in drab gray, who disdainfully observed our lack of progress. My lips were forming an embarrassed half-smile as I handed Marguerite the full sacks. I set the remaining paper goods on the floor, clutched the last of our groceries, and stood in the aisle trying to open one more bag. "How do zee French get zee damned leetle bags open?"

April 6

We're feeling good, getting to know our home, our neighborhood, and the French routine. Today we coined a couple of expressions. Pamplemousse, for example, already a perfectly good French word meaning "grapefruit," has an added significance for us. In the Métro, when we encounter someone without the benefit of deodorant, Marguerite might say, "At the grocery store, let's get some pamplemousse for breakfast." Translation: "P.U. That person stinks!" Voilà. Now we can comment without offending.

Haricots verts is also doing double duty. In a crowd, if Marguerite wonders about security precautions for our computer, she'll say, "The maids are coming today. Did you lock the haricots verts in the cabinet?" The thieves of Paris don't realize she's asking about our computer. (But now we live in constant fear of green-bean thieves.)

Marguerite is still exhausted in the evenings, but in the mornings she's an industrious beaver. She gets up at dawn, sending Felicia into a chorus of meows at the prospect of breakfast. They hustle into the kitchen and close the door. Marguerite cleans dishes from the night before, tidies the kitchen, makes coffee, and feeds Effie a snack— but not in that order. Effie comes first.

The Music of Paris

"I'd like to turn each painting into music, so you could feel it," I said.

28

"It's art, Eddie. It's not meant to be played on a violin."

"But I want you to enjoy this."

"Find me a seat, and I'll be happy. You're here for the art. I'm keeping you company."

I led Marguerite to a padded bench in the middle of the gallery, walked to a far corner, and looked back at her. Dozens of splendid paintings—crucifixions, nativity scenes, ascending angels, agonized demons—adorned the palace walls around her. Light filtered in through tall, sheer-curtained windows, illuminated the parquet floor, and glistened in the blonde highlights of her hair. She sat erect in her denim jumper and pink blouse, her white cane folded by her side, a serene look on her face. Other visitors lingered before paintings and moved thoughtfully around the room, adding occasional movement to the background. She's a piece of art herself, I thought—*Still Life, Marguerite at the Louvre, 1997*. I wished I had a daisy for her hand so the portrait would include the flower, since "daisy" is the French meaning of her name.

I wandered off for half an hour, visited similar rooms, arrays of like paintings, returned, and told her about the art. We walked to another hall, and she waited as I explored.

So this was the Louvre. At first I was thrilled by the magnificent works on the walls, but after a while, all the views of angels and Satan, all the bare-breasted Marys suckling the baby Jesus became too much. Couldn't any of these artists paint a regular child, a mountain, or a Marguerite? Of course, this was only one wing of the immense museum, a wing that reflected a time when artists were shunned for painting secular subjects. The volume and gravity of the works overwhelmed me. I needed rest and companionship.

We found a tranquil café in a former grand salon of the palace, where we ate a simple but delicious salad, some cheese, and bread. "Did you find things to enjoy?" I asked.

"Well, *this* is really nice." She gestured at the room around us. "I love the fact that we're dining in the Louvre, that it's a palace, and that it's the heart of French art. I love knowing that we have crystal chandeliers and crystal glasses around us, even if I can't see them."

"When you were waiting in the galleries, what were you thinking?"

"I was thinking how very different this was from our normal lives. I listened to the voices—so many languages, so cosmopolitan. When the room grew still, I had time to let it sink in. We're *really* in Paris." She grinned, and I knew she was thrilled.

🐾

From sharing life with Marguerite, I know that she can find unique ways to appreciate things. My descriptions might bring up mental images from before she lost her sight. Other times my descriptions are too tiring or not satisfying, or they bring back feelings of loss. I have learned to accept the limitations and move on to something else.

Marguerite said she was happy to visit the Louvre, and she obviously meant it. But there with her in the café, I vowed to find as much as possible for her to experience. During our month in Paris, *I* would see, feel, and taste so many things, and I wanted Marguerite to taste, touch, and hear as many as I could find for her.

The Fine Art of Feeling Paris

We had visited the Louvre first, not because it was the most famous museum but because admission was free the first Sunday of the month. When we stopped at the Musée Rodin, it turned out that admission was free for a blind person *and* her guide no matter what day it was. I liked that a lot, and so did Marguerite—she because it seemed thoughtful of them, and I, well, I love a deal. We found a more intimate collection at the Rodin, small enough so we could grasp it, take it in, comprehend its unity.

It was a gorgeous spring day, and Marguerite posed for a photo in the garden at the base of Rodin's masterpiece, *The Thinker*. Inside the stately mansion-turned-museum we wandered while I described.

I kept wanting to have her touch the pieces, but signs said *Ne Touchez Pas*. At the top of the regal staircase, I spotted a smaller version of *The Thinker*, less than two feet high. I couldn't resist.

A gray-haired guard in a navy sweater sat nearby, observing us closely, with his policeman's cap tilted to one side and his walkie-talkie resting on his lap.

"Monsieur," I said. "Madame is not able to see." I pointed to her cane. "Would it be all right for her to touch this piece?"

The man looked her over and nodded slowly. *"Oui, monsieur. This one time."*

I led her to the sculpture. She felt it and smiled.

"Notice the way his chin rests on his hand?"

"It's just the way a thinker should be. And the statue outside is the same?"

"It's on a massive pedestal, and *The Thinker* itself is ten feet tall."

"I like this little guy."

Moving outdoors, we ambled through a small forest where we found other statues, though they were too large for Marguerite to put her hands around, and the birds had been there first.

I felt good she'd had a chance to feel one famous piece, but frustrated, too. The experience whetted my appetite to show her more.

The Life of Leisure Isn't Always a Piece of *Gâteau*

Closing in on my fiftieth birthday with an elderly cat and a menopausal wife . . . nothing was easy. Even routine tasks in this foreign country proved to be downright *difficile*.

Felicia was in the midst of some sort of malaise. She complained, paced the floor, shunned my caress; and there were no "number twos" in the cat litter.

I was a little worried, but Marguerite seemed close to frenzied. "I knew it. We made her sick by taking her on the airplane. All of those people with germs. You have to find a cat emergency clinic."

"It could just be the French cat food. She's used to special stuff, for the 'mature cat'."

"Well . . . maybe."

"Let's find her some senior cuisine and a laxative."

We passed up a trip to Versailles with our friends Dave and Judy, who were visiting from Houston, so we could stay close to Felicia. I scanned the French dictionary looking for the proper phrases to say, "She does not move the bowels, *monsieur*." It turned out that the word *constipation* comes from the French. Does that surprise anyone?

We tracked down a pet store, bought senior cat food (at three times the U.S. price), and requested laxatives. "*Mais non, monsieur*," the clerk said. "For that you must go to the *pharmacie*."

"But it's for our cat." I meowed to make sure we were communicating.

"Yes, yes. At the *pharmacie*."

At the drugstore, we explained our problem again. "Oh, *monsieur*, I am sorry," the saleswoman said. "To get the medicines for the *animaux*, you must visit a *pharmacie* with both a green cross and a blue cross. We have only the blue cross, for the people's medicine."

We found the right kind of drugstore, delivered the laxative into our kitty's digestive tract in the evening, and then again in the morning. I looked up *vétérinaires* in the Yellow Pages and hiked over to one of their offices in case the laxative failed. When I returned, Felicia was fine, but the litter box needed some help.

We strolled down the Champs-Elysées one morning in search of a cybercafe. The woman at the Paris Tourist Office had directed us to something called a Virgin Megastore. The name sounded questionable, maybe even kinky. Inside the building we found three floors of music, from CDs and tapes galore to listening stations with headphones to hear the latest hits. Upstairs there was a café with food but no sign of a cybercafe.

We finally found the computers down in the basement, but they were all turned off. I waited in line to speak to a tattooed man wearing the store's red-vested uniform. "I do not do the computers," he said in French. "I do the movie tickets. You see the hours? They are on the board." Sure enough, the sign listed computer times—five days a week from 2 PM to 9 PM.

We returned the following day at 3 PM, to the same flock of dark screens and the tattooed man. "The computers are available at the times on the sign," he snapped.

"What time does the sign say for today?" Marguerite asked.

"It says 2 PM to 9 PM." To the tattooed man I said, "The time is now."

"Oh, right. The fellow didn't come to work today."

As we climbed the stairs, Marguerite demanded, "Don't they understand how important this is?"

"We'll come back on Monday."

"But I've already waited an extra day. I wanted to hear from Robyn and Lauraine today."

I would have told her to ease off, but Marguerite was surprisingly close to tears. "I didn't know this was so important to you."

"I didn't either. I'm missing my friends." She wiped a tear and smiled sheepishly. "It's the hormones again, isn't it? The herbal remedies aren't doing much good."

From Paws to the 'Pause

April 16

    Marguerite still has jet lag . . . but it can't *be that; we've been here two weeks . . . must be menopause lag. She starts early, cleans everything, begins rearranging. She finds "better" ways to use the fruit basket, turns an egg cup into a sugar bowl, shifts things from one cabinet to another. You wouldn't think a blind person would keep moving stuff around. But that's one of the little compulsions that makes her Marguerite.*

Exhaustion sets in by afternoon.

Another one of her compulsions is doing "her share." Our division of labor involves Marguerite doing everything she is readily able to do, because there are lots of things she can't do alone. Usually she chops the ingredients, and I read the recipe and do the cooking. That works fine here in Paris, as it did back home. At home she does the laundry, but our Paris washing machine doesn't have Braille labels on the knobs for hot or cold, normal or delicate. . . .

Each morning and each night she popped Dr. Wong's herbal pills. Still, she woke in the night to flashes and sweats. In bed I heard her listening to novels on the tape player—hour after hour of sleeplessness.

All the little things upset her, like e-mail postponements and her new travel hairdryer that fried itself and blew out the circuit breaker the first time she used it. Time and money would heal those things, but she stewed over each disappointment.

"Is there anything more we can do about the symptoms?" I asked.

"I'm *not* taking *hormones*," she half-shouted. "Not yet. I don't want to. . . . I'm afraid."

"I didn't mention hormones. I didn't even say the 'pause. How about something else that's natural?"

"Dr. Wong told me about progesterone made from yams."

We found yam cream (very reasonable) at the pharmacy where we'd bought the cat laxatives. The laxatives had done wonders for Felicia, and the yam cream would hopefully help her mother.

Something had to work, or Marguerite's trip might not be worth traveling.

I returned from one of my two-hour walks late one afternoon. "Look what I found—orange coffee from Fauchon."

"What's *Fauchon?*"

"It's a snooty gourmet shop on the . . ." I glanced at her and stopped short. "What's wrong?"

She was standing next to the washing machine with a garbage can in one hand and a dishtowel in the other. The vacuum cleaner was by her feet, its hose snaked around her ankles. "I spilled laundry powder all over back there." She pointed between the washing machine and the wall.

"Anything else wrong?"

"I tried to clean it up, but I couldn't find a plug for this." She jabbed a finger toward the vacuum. "Would you show me how to use this *crummy* machine?" Marguerite smacked her hand on top of the washer, her face crinkling in an almost-to-tears look.

"When I left the apartment, you were sound asleep with Felicia, looking like a kid with her teddy bear. What happened?"

"I wanted to surprise you and get the laundry done. I put in the clothes and the detergent, which I spilled. But then I was stuck. I didn't know where to set the dials or which buttons to push or . . ."

"Did you squeeze in the fabric softener?"

"Where would I find fabric softener? And if I did, how would I know where to put it?"

"The softener is down here . . . hmmm . . . it has a dusting of powder all over it." I hugged her and stroked her hair in hopes of warding off the tears, but I felt her sobbing against my chest. When she seemed a little better, I led her to the couch, slid Felicia aside, and sat with her.

"This is what I was afraid of before the trip," she said. "At home, I can get around and arrange for rides to go somewhere. I can do laundry. But here I'm helpless."

"You help me with the cooking."

"That's another thing. I don't know how to get the heat right on the stove."

"And you keep Effie company."

"Big help."

"It's all right."

"No. I bug you about too many things."

"Like the socks?"

She smiled for the first time. "I know you're kidding when you say, 'Blind people should only have one color of socks.' But you have to do so much for me."

"We're on vacation. It's not like my day is filled with work."

"Well, I hope I can get used to this. . . . Otherwise, we'll have to go home early."

I chewed on that as I showed her where to find the little bladder of French softener, where to pour it into the machine, and which button to push. I didn't want to cut our adventure short, but we couldn't stay if she felt this awful. What else could I do to make it better for her?

April 18

Our friend Robyn called, and Marguerite told her about her menopausal problems. Robyn came up with a theory. When Marguerite was losing her sight, she seemed intent on being cheerful about it, like it was just one of those things. Now, in the throes of menopause, she needs to feel the pain, to grieve this cruel thing that is happening to her.

Robyn might be right; she's a psychologist after all. But if this is some kind of delayed grieving thing, the timing could have been a little better.

Yes, Marguerite, There Is Accessible Art in the City

"I'd like you to pose for me," I said. I led Marguerite to a spot next to one of those great van Gogh farm scenes in the Musée d'Orsay, the grand old railroad-station-turned-museum on the banks of the Seine. I turned her toward me and backed away. "The house in the picture is molded in greens and browns all splotched together," I said, as I set my camera. "The building is charmingly off-kilter." I switched off the flash a second time to make sure.

"The hay pile by the barn seems to flow like water," I continued. "And the sky is vibrant, swirling blue and white. I don't think those effects are actually possible, but van Gogh must have been too crazy to know. Okay . . . smile." I snapped the photo and turned to spot a man with a very erect posture, an identity badge on his suit jacket, and a meticulously folded white handkerchief sticking out from his pocket. Had I been too loud? Was I not supposed to take pictures?

He nodded, and his light brown hair moved not a twitch. A hint of a grin creased his cheeks. He leaned close and murmured, "Sir, you speak English, I think?"

I wanted to protest that I hadn't been monopolizing van Gogh, but his smile kept me from it. I held my breath.

"*Monsieur*, they have a special exhibit for the people who cannot see. Did you know? If you go to the desk on the first floor, they will help you."

We descended to the ground floor of the museum and located the information desk. Behind it stood a fair-haired woman in her mid-forties, wearing a royal-blue suit and matching scarf. Her makeup, her bearing, her jewels, and the line of her clothes looked flawless. We asked her about the exhibit for the blind.

"Ah, yes. We have such a manifestation. It is not today."

I turned to see Marguerite's disappointment, looked back to Madame.

"But you can come another day during the week, yes?" she asked.

"I'm afraid not. We have plans," Marguerite said. "It's all right."

Madame gazed at Marguerite again, drew in a sad breath. "No. We cannot have this. I will find a way." She picked up the phone. "Please *attendez.*"

I stared at the glass panels of the huge arching ceiling of the museum as Madame spoke on the phone. I decided one way or another Marguerite would get to touch the exhibits. We would come back another day.

Madame nodded to me. "I think I have found a person."

Overhead the museum's famous rococo gold-and-white clock ticked off the minutes. Another phone call. I examined the exquisite form of a pair of alabaster nudes by Rodin fifty feet away and gazed at the terra-cotta Roman soldier way down at the end of the hall.

A dark-haired woman in a navy blazer approached. "I am Mademoiselle Renée," she said in French. "Please follow me."

Madame stood at her post wearing a happy grin. "You see? We make it happen."

We thanked Madame and followed Mademoiselle Renée to a stairwell. "You must be careful," she said, and began descending.

"It's all right. We walk everywhere," I replied. Then I translated for Marguerite.

"Yes, of course," our guide answered. "I said something silly, no?"

"Not at all." I brought my hand to the middle of my back. On cue, Marguerite stepped behind me. I let my hand indicate each step as she followed me down.

Mademoiselle Renée descended slowly and kept looking back. "You do very well." She unlocked a wrought-iron gate. "How long has your wife been blind?"

"It's a disease that keeps getting worse. Since she was sixteen."

"And now?"

"She sees nothing."

"*Quel dommage!* (Such a shame!)" Mademoiselle Renée's eyes appeared to flick back tears. She led us into a basement room set amid brick walls. Before us were fifty or sixty statues eerily staring—from perches atop walls, from alcoves, from upright positions beside pillars—into the empty room.

"Take as much time as you like. I will go back to my other duties and return for you."

I led Marguerite to a special statue. "It's the same one we saw upstairs—*Ballerina* by Degas."

I set her hands on the plaster woman's waist, and Marguerite slid them upwards, over the sides, the breast, the slender neck. She felt the fine features, the etched hair tied back in a twist. Her fingers slid down to the rippled skirt. She knelt and felt her way past the thighs, the calves. She lingered on a ballet slipper. Marguerite smiled up at me. "She's beautiful. And this is great—my own museum. It's so still and private."

"Here's another one you'll like over on this table. What do you think it is?"

"Smooth . . . ears . . . a chin . . . tail. It's a cat sitting up." She grinned with certainty.

"Right, but not just any feline. A golden emperor's cat from Egypt. Notice how long and sleek. Feel the necklace?"

She probed it. "Like Felicia. She *loves* her necklaces."

I continued showing statues to Marguerite one after another—lovers embracing, a donkey, busts and figurines of authors and kings, an iguana. After a while, I noticed Mademoiselle Renée standing back behind the gates watching. She dropped her eyes. Was I wrong or had she been fascinated by the ballet of Ed and Marguerite, slowly feeling their way through her museum?

When we finished, Mademoiselle Renée led us back to Madame. "I am sorry," Madame said. "It is such a small collection, and they are only reproductions. We hire artisans, and they make other statues for you. . . . We have not a way yet to show the paintings."

"This was wonderful," Marguerite exclaimed. "And *you* made it possible."

Madame beamed. "It is nothing."

"No, it's a great deal," Marguerite said. "It has made me happy."

I led my wife to the side where Mademoiselle Renée stood, brought Marguerite's hand to hers, and she shook it. "Tell her she's very generous," Marguerite said.

"*Vous êtes très gentille.*"

"*Oh, non, monsieur.*" Renée lowered her head, but she couldn't hide the glow of her joy.

They're Everywhere, and They're Great—Computer Geeks

I woke that Monday to hear Marguerite's voice, in a decidedly cheerful tone, coming from the kitchen. "You know, Felicia, you can't be walking in front of me the way you do with Ed. That's how you get trampled. . . . Oh. Are you rubbing my legs because you're out of food?" Sympathy crept into Marguerite's voice. She paused, and I pictured her feeling in the bowl. "No. You still have some." I heard a meow, and Marguerite continued. "Okay, granted, your bowl is a little low, but . . ." Another meow. "*All right*, I'll give you some more little crunchies."

Obviously, Effie would be in charge of the trip from then on. I hoped she wouldn't take too much advantage. But this little dialogue reminded me that Felicia was back to her lovable, healthy self, and Marguerite's energy seemed high. It would be a fun day.

A while later Marguerite was brushing her hair in preparation for our return to the cybercafe.

"What's this?" I peered into her cosmetics case. "Aren't you using your boar's-hair brush?"

"Yes."

"But here in your bag I see another just like it."

"Okay, so I have two."

"Correct me if I'm wrong, but weren't you going to cancel our trip if we didn't buy *this* brush that last day in California, because you needed to have *a* boar's-hair brush—*a* being singular and meaning 'one' brush?"

"Well, I made a mistake and brought two, but it's a good thing. This one's very different from the other. I need both."

"Let me see." I took the brush from her hand and compared it to the one in the bag. "Funny, they look the same. And you also have a couple of plain brushes. . . ."

"Yes, they're important, too. I let *you* use them."

❧

Once her hair was suitably coifed, using at least two of the implements from her fleet of hair-care apparatus, we headed off in search of e-mail.

It was on this lucky day that the Virgin Megastore's cybercafe was up and running. Down in the abode of the computers, a couple of teenagers sat before lit-up screens, happily clicking mice.

I approached a red-vested young man of perhaps twenty years, who was firing up one of the machines. "Monsieur."

He turned, and I recognized the prototype for a Hollywood computer geek—a little plump, thick glasses, hairline already receding.

"*Oui, monsieur.* Can I help you?"

I explained in French. "We would like to retrieve our e-mail from the United States."

"Certainly. You must first calculate the time you will use on the computer. Then you pay the cashier upstairs. . . ." The fellow shot out a few more French phrases that flew by way too fast. He smirked at my confusion and hit me with English. "You bring the receipt, I enter the password, and you have the Internet."

Marguerite and I pitched in the equivalent of $7 for half an hour and returned with the receipt. Monsieur Computer Geek entered the password and all the mumbo jumbo to fire the thing up, and then left us to it.

The Internet program was familiar—Netscape, in English—but the keyboard had some not-so-subtle differences. Most of the keys were the same, but some, such as the *a* and the *q*, had been interchanged; likewise for the *x* and the *w*; and the *m* was where one would hope to press the *;*.

Before this trip, I had visited a cybercafe twice, and, with help, had been able to retrieve my e-mail remotely. Now, a month after my last lesson, I couldn't get it to work. Our $7 was dribbling away, so I flagged down our new acquaintance, who ambled over, punched a few keys, told me to enter my password, and smirked again. *"Voilà, monsieur."*

I read aloud to Marguerite the messages from our friends, and she commented on the news from home as I took notes.

When we finished reading them all, she bubbled with enthusiasm. "Wasn't that *great?*"

"Well, yes . . . but I felt pressured to get it done in time."

"You worry too much. Let's go home and write up our replies. . . . I can't believe you got it to run."

"It was Computer Geek Man."

"Don't call him that. He's nice and smart; and it's really a miracle, isn't it?"

"What?"

"E-mail."

"A miracle, yes, but I'm not sure it's all a blessing."

"Thanks. You did this for me, and I loved it."

We breezed through Prisunic, buying bread, Camembert cheese, an unknown pâté with three layers, and a salad of *haricots verts*. We ate on the balcony with our kitty while composing a brief version of our adventures to date, including responses to the e-mails we'd received. The same long message would go to all of our cyber friends. My notes were full of arrows, and the margin full of scribbles, because of interjections from Marguerite like "Don't forget to tell Esther and Lester about the auto club."

The next day we were back at the cybercafe, with an hour of computer time. I began typing from the notes, constantly backspacing because, oh damn, that was a *q*, which should really be an *a*, and making sure I hadn't left anything out, like the story of our favorite little bar with the wonderful croissants. And, damn again, that's not where the *m* is.

Marguerite perched on the edge of her stool, popping in random thoughts like "Tell them how the supermarket works," or

"We left out a note to Genie," or . . .

As time clicked away, Marguerite sensed my tension and began to massage my shoulders.

Somehow, as the end of the hour neared, I had entered umpteen e-mail addresses—all precisely correct—typed everything, and fixed a few rough spots. Things were getting fairly legible. That's when the computer went into a coma. French words of impending finality flashed on the screen.

"Oh, God," I yelped. "We've run out of time."

"Don't panic."

"Easy for you to say. I've typed my fingers off and now it's history."

"It's okay to ask for help."

I located Computer Geek, whose face was pressed to a computer screen and whose brain was likely somewhere inside of it.

"You need assistance?"

"We've run out of time. I think everything is lost."

"Oh, I think not." Our red-vested helper strolled over and entered a few keystrokes. My letter reappeared on the screen, and my heart resumed beating. "Do you want to send what you have written?" I nodded, and he punched a key. *Voilà.* It is sent."

I wanted to hug him but didn't want to offend. The French, especially Parisians, can be quite formal.

We visited the cybercafe two more times during our Paris stay. By the last visit, Marguerite was clearly in love with Computer Geek, but by then I had learned to respect her feelings. He was absolutely the best thing that had ever happened to computer-stupid travelers like us. Marguerite spoke about setting him up with her sister, Patricia, but I doubted that sisterly betterment was really on her mind.

On our last stop, Computer Geek had a visitor and a dreamy, self-satisfied look on his pudgy, bespeckled face. A pretty young woman with long black hair flirted, chatted, and touched his arm whenever he wasn't with a customer. I explained to Marguerite and watched her beam. "Oh, I'm happy for him." Then she frowned. "What about Patricia . . . ?"

Music of the Night

We climbed the stairs from the Métro and reached the street, where a bone-chilling wind strafed us. Marguerite paused to fasten the top button of her coat. "The concert begins in half an hour," I said. "While *you* fiddle with your buttons, *other* people are getting the best seats."

"Just a minute." She took gloves out of her pocket, slid them on, and smoothed each finger. We headed toward the cathedral.

Tonight we would attend our first formal concert in Paris, the Lille Philharmonic performing inside Notre Dame.

The big, square towers of the cathedral, illuminated by spotlights, loomed through low-hanging mist. We joined the crowd making its way beneath the pointed arches lined in rows of saintly statues. We passed through the heavy wooden doors.

Inside, the lofty cathedral dwarfed the temporary stage at the back of the nave. Well-dressed Parisians in rich-looking coats—those who had paid a premium—sat in the pews or on folding chairs packed in the center. We edged along the periphery, following the mass of people away from the stage.

"This is fantastic," I said. "Remember the giant columns I had you touch the other day when we were here? Between each pair, a crystal chandelier is sparkling. It's magical."

"It sounds lovely. . . . Guess there's no heat in here."

"Lots of warm bodies."

We settled in folding chairs toward the back, and Marguerite nuzzled her forehead into my coat. I put my fingertips under her chin, tilted her face up, and kissed her. "Your nose is freezing."

"You can't kiss me in here. It's a church."

She shivered, and I wrapped my arm around her.

At the front of the cathedral, musicians took gleaming French horns, trumpets, and tubas from their cases. Violinists and bass players plucked strings and cranked tuning pegs. Along the walls I could make out intricate stained-glass designs—much less brilliant than they had been by daylight. Instead, in this lighting, the arcades stood out—patterns of light and shadow draped the undersides of arches, highlighted some nooks and obscured others. What a monumental task it had been to create this structure from blocks of stone. What loving care it had taken to chisel the arches, fluted pillars, and statues. "What are you thinking about?" I asked.

"Wondering if any igloos are in sight."

"Think of penguins carrying trombones and wearing bow ties. They're getting settled now." The audience hushed. I glanced at the people in our row—couples in their fifties or sixties, a mother with her twenty-something daughter—all focused on the stage. Musicians arranged pages and settled into readiness. "The head penguin is raising his baton."

Flutes, then strings, and then the entire orchestra encircled us in music. The organ boomed. The grand cathedral filled with sound. Granite walls seemed to shudder. I closed my eyes and tried to feel each note echoing among the stone pillars, rising up their flanks to the heights, to feel it as Marguerite would.

Throughout the concert, I watched the conductor and the musicians. My eyes were lured to radiant chandeliers, the huge window with petals of stained glass, converging arcs of stone that peaked at the top of the ceiling. The evening was filled with so much more than just sound.

From time to time I turned to Marguerite, sitting closed-eyed, wearing a smile that looked like satisfaction. The music was wonderful, but could she sense the majesty that surrounded her?

After the concert, we hurried on board a Métro train bound for

La Paella, the oldest Spanish restaurant in Paris, for our late-dinner reservations.

We left the Métro at the Gare de l'Ouest train station and hurried past an assortment of—shall we say—adult shops. Several blocks farther, with my arm around my wife's shoulder for warmth, we turned into a lonely alley between two decaying buildings. "Interesting neighborhood." It grew shabbier, and I toyed with the idea of turning back, until I spotted it. "There's a red-neon sign for La Paella, with a blue bullfighter on it. . . ."

"I'm not sure I like your tone. Think we ought to vamoose?"

I opened the door and peered inside. "The bar looks homey. Come on."

A fellow in red gaucho vest with black embroidery led us upstairs to a cozy room with Spanish decorations—a wooden bull on a shelf, a Don Quixote statue, crossed swords, a Spanish flag. We sat together on the same side of a booth (our usual way).

"There's a woman in a bright-chartreuse jacket—is that the right name for a greenish-yellow that threatens to blot out the color receptors in my eyes?"

"Don't mess them up. They're the only eyes we've got."

"She thinks she's the height of elegance with her black top and pearls."

"You said they're selling those bright colors in the stores. It could be 'in'."

"They're awful on mannequins and worse in person. . . . She's rolling her own cigarette. She's putting it into a long, gold holder and sticking it between shocking-red lips. There's a guy beside her— he's got to be twenty years younger—and she's staring into his eyes. She looks so self-assured. I can't believe this."

"Is he lighting her cigarette?"

"Yup."

"Stop staring. She'll think you want her."

"Okay. . . . I'm looking over to the other corner. I'd say those two sixty-year-old women are lesbians. They're dressed really nicely in blazers—one black, one royal blue—sitting on the same side of the table like you and me. One is pouring champagne for both, while the other is serving *tapas* from a big plate."

"What makes you think they're lesbians?"

"They look *very* comfortable together."

"That could be Bette and me out on the town."

"And their shoulders are in constant contact."

"Don't stare at *them*, either." She tried to look stern, but a little laugh broke through.

I described a giggling couple in their fifties. The woman was taking fruit from her Sangria and serving it to the man on a knife blade—she with wedding ring, he without. "*Yikes*, the chartreuse lady is sneaking looks at me."

"Probably commenting on the gorgeous blind woman and her dapper escort." Marguerite beamed at me and shrugged her coat onto the chair. "This is a delightful evening, and it's nice and toasty in here." Her silver and black necklace glinted against the deep blue velour of her dress.

The gaucho-waiter served us a pitcher of Sangria and our appetizer, *moules* (mussels) drenched in a savory broth, in little crockery cups.

"I hope you enjoyed the concert," I said. "I felt bad for you, shivering there in the cathedral."

"The beauty of the music . . . I appreciate it even more now that I'm back to warmth. I *really* loved it."

"Did you get a feel for Notre Dame?"

She nodded. "Before they began playing, the cold made me think about the dead people buried under the floor."

"Ugh! That's not what I had in mind."

She speared a *moule*, popped it into her mouth, and chewed thoughtfully. "That huge stone edifice has stood all this time. All the history . . . I thought about the French Revolution, mobs toppling statues and lopping off the stone heads of the kings of Israel. And I thought of Quasimodo, the hunchback, swinging from bell ropes, trying to save his love, what's-her-name. When the music began, I felt the space around me, so immense. I pictured chandeliers all shining. Music filled me, and I forgot the cold and the church. I thought of heaven."

I considered those images and the privilege of spending our evening in that setting, the joy of dining in this restaurant with my wife, whose insights once again added dimension to my own experience.

The *paella* was presented in a wide copper pan. Two *caballeros* sang and played guitars. As they strolled, the woman in icky-green sent me another glance, and I turned quickly back to my meal. The Simon and Garfunkel tunes they were singing lacked English, but that only deepened the ambiance, and then their music turned to flamenco. We sipped Sangria, tasted the savory seafood and roasted pepper-and-rice mixture, felt the Spanish soul of the music, and felt very silly and very content, and . . .

"Now that your lips are warm . . . ," I said.

"If we kiss, they'll talk about us."

I waited. She leaned closer, brought her lips to mine.

It was an evening *très romantique*.

So Much Music, So Little Time (and Stamina)

Music for the eye—the kind of music I longed to give Marguerite but could not—graced every square and *grande rue* of the city, adorned countless noble monuments, flowed from each majestic bridge that crossed the Seine. Every church was a gallery full of uplifting art.

We followed walking tours in our guidebooks through some of the quarters of the city, as I described statues, edifices, and exhibits. But we also detoured for church bells and church choirs, foreign voices, and bird songs.

We visited the Bois de Boulogne to breathe the scents and touch the petals of iris, lilac, and rose. A swan boat took us across a lake to an island, where we dined simply at an outdoor restaurant, watching real swans glide and feeling the cool breezes that rustled new spring leaves on the bushes.

We rode the Métro to the far side of the city, a North African section, in search of the open-air market Marché d'Aligre. Swarthy, gray-mustached shopkeepers sat on storefront steps awaiting customers. Women with heads wrapped in brown scarves passed in twos and threes, bearing tots and trailing wheeled baskets of produce. In the square, we listened to the rhythms of far-off lands in the patois of dialects and the percussion of sidewalk musicians. The aroma of unique spices and the scents of the people mingled to exotic dimensions. Under a covered, metal-roofed marketplace, right out of the nineteenth century, stood glass cases holding sausages, chickens, skinned rabbits, and cheeses—from Brie to Roquefort— their sharp scents blending into the medley. Outside, counters overflowed with produce. Shoulder-to-shoulder Parisians vied to make purchases. We selected onions, thyme, and basil by their pungent fragrance for use in our evening meal—coq au vin—to be prepared from one of the 10,000 recipes on the CD we'd brought for our computer.

At the far end of the square, one grand counter was flooded with blossoms—reds, blues, whites, yellows, purples. We bargained for a dozen pink roses with a tangy-sweet bouquet.

On other days, restaurants brought us the spices of India, Vietnam, Lebanon, Thailand, and more . . . three-course meals for under $10, nicely within our budget.

Late afternoons, we sometimes shopped with the locals at the supermarket. Along with fresh produce from all over Europe, we found native specialties, fresh and frozen. We discovered great Bordeaux, Rhone, Loire Valley, and Provençal wines for $3 or $4 a bottle.

In our compact kitchen we cooked light French cuisine or simple pasta dishes for dinner. Afterward, I would lead our threesome to the balcony overlooking the Paris rooftops and read aloud from the novels we never had time to read back home.

Whenever we splurged on an elaborate meal out, we compensated with a picnic the next day—this time with cheese crêpes purchased from a vendor and eaten on a bench in the Luxembourg Gardens. We dined among the students from the Sorbonne, as they discussed (we assumed) art, literature, and the nature of being, or looked longingly into each other's eyes.

We were smelling, tasting, and listening our way around the city, and Paris was playing enchanting music.

April 22

The time is slipping away, and now we must choose carefully. Shall we have breakfast at our little bar—just across the Champs-Elysées—with the best croissants and peach preserves in the known universe, or at the Brioche Dorée with those wonderful, warm pain aux raisins *and sugared croissants with apricots?*

We are staggered by the array of museums still unseen. There are the covered arcades with quaint little shops and eateries to try. Should we attend a concert at one of the grand cathedrals or spend time absorbing the feel of a lesser-known church? Whole districts remain unexplored. We've only been to Montmartre twice.

Our Métro pass expires in a week and a day, and with it, our visit to Paris. We will miss our apartment and its view of quaint rooftops, its convenience to the sights and sensations of the great capital, its well-planned efficiency. At our next stop, a colander may not be standard issue, a lettuce spinner unlikely. Will we have shutters that bang against the sill and talk to us in the wind? Will there be a comfortable love seat where the three of us can sit cozily or where Felicia can stretch out for a nap?

We entered the seventeenth-century mansion that housed the Picasso Museum through the courtyard and made our way from room to room, following the arrows and signs that read *Sens de la Visite.*

"Picasso drew an incredible picture of people when he did the standard thing," I said. "The woman in this painting has large, enchanting eyes and an expressive face. With some of his other pictures, I can't tell where the face is, let alone the eyes."

Marguerite indulged me while I viewed the paintings, which moved from traditional to pleasantly deranged to moderately grotesque. When she lagged, I practiced the old Louvre routine: I left her in one room while I visited others. As we moved on, we entered a chamber with central piers made of golden stone that curved up gracefully to support the ceiling. She sat down, looking more forlorn than serene, and I began to feel guilty.

I browsed but returned to her quickly. "This one's worth standing up for." I led her to Picasso's painting *Marguerite*, which was, happily, one of his more normal pieces. "Your namesake." I snapped her photo beside the portrait.

"There's one of his goat statues, made of old, raggedy slats of wood and stuffing that wants to fall out. It's cordoned off, so you can't touch it."

"Sounds *strange*."

"Picasso is *about* strange."

The next courtyard also held bizarre figures. "Guess what, Marguerite."

"Can I sit while you tell me?"

"You might want to stay upright. There are some really neat statues here, and I think it's all right to feel these babies." Images of the Musée d'Orsay flashed in my mind, Marguerite's brilliant smile on her lips as she explored with inquisitive fingers.

"I'm so tired."

"Touch a few." I tried to keep disappointment from my voice. "Check out this distorted face. You haven't felt anything like it."

I placed her hands on the statue of a woman's head. "Picasso was brilliant, don't you think?"

"What's this?"

"Has to be a nose."

"Are you sure? It's huge and off-center." A spark of energy seemed to ignite within her.

"If you think that's funny, wait until you see where he put the arms on this one. . . . And over there is a mother wheeling a baby carriage, but her head is like a weasel's, and her breasts look like gears or machine parts."

She ran fingers over the statue's head and chest. "Does it make you wonder if he liked his mother?"

"You're the counselor. Here's another question: Do you think he liked his mother's nose? Try this one."

"*Sorry.* I need to sit down."

I told myself not to feel bad. Being able to touch these figures was something I wanted for her, maybe not something she wanted . . . not something she had the strength for.

We left and ate in a little Indian restaurant, then headed homeward to nap.

The Métro isn't easy, especially for a blind person, and more especially for a tired blind person.

For anyone taking the subway, there are stairs that go up and down accompanied by the rumbling of trains echoing through underground halls. But the average person can descend the stairs with confidence, seeing the next step and all the steps ahead. The average person isn't listening for clues, isn't probing with a cane, isn't relying on someone else.

Marguerite, on the other hand, concentrates with other senses—the ones that are less efficient in this environment. Had the stairwell not been permeated by noise, she would have listened to the tapping of shoes on the stairs and the echoes from them to help orient herself. She would hold a railing. But in this case, it's more important for me to hold the railing. I am strong enough to keep her up if she falters, not the other way around, so she is suspended on these stairs with her feet on the steps and her safety in my hand.

Climbing takes energy. Concentration takes energy. And there must be some fear, especially with the earsplitting rumble of a train nearby. Fear takes energy.

We have a system. When there is room, we walk nearly side by side, with me a bit ahead, so she can feel the rise of my body through my hand. Descending, I am well placed to prevent a fall forward.

When we have to run down stairs to catch a train, I position her so her shoulder presses into mine. We run at an angle, a single unit of highly trained, stair-stepping machinery. It works, and she is safe, even if it doesn't sound so. But when she is tired, we wouldn't think of running down stairs.

Returning from the Picasso Museum, Marguerite's exhaustion set in with a vengeance. We stopped for rests along the streets, on the stairs to the Métro, in the lobby of our building. Back in the apartment, she sought out Felicia and sat beside her on the love seat. "Some motherly advice for you," she told our kitty. "Don't ever have menopause—it sucks." Effie rolled over and fell back to sleep, her head resting against Marguerite's thigh.

Each afternoon, Marguerite napped with Felicia while I explored. Afternoons brought the sidewalks of the Champs-Elysées to life. Mobs of people—many high-school or college aged with leather jackets and spiky hair, tourists staring at Parisians, Parisians walking their dogs and trying to ignore the tourists. . . . This mass of humanity sauntered collectively as one organism. Individuals broke off—paused to peer in windows; entered arcades, perfume stores, or the Virgin Megastore; stood in line at movie theatres; read menus outside ice-cream parlors or *brasseries*—before rejoining the organic current.

I sped past, bound for my destination, perhaps a neighborhood to wander, a church to experience. In Saint-Germain-des-Prés I ran my fingers over tombs with exquisite carvings of Elizabethan men in soldier gear, marble so translucent I could almost see myself inside. At Saint-Sulpice I reflected on the famous paintings by Delacroix, and the tender statue of Mary with the Child floating on a cloud.

Like the Church of the Madeleine, where I often walked, these places were like museums, huge open spaces to explore thoughts and dreams, with art, soaring columns, and, at least in Saint-Sulpice, streaming light to inspire and to guide.

Along Paris streets and in the gardens, I discovered more statues than I could appreciate in a year. And though I loved each hike and each discovery, the constant exploration fatigued me. I missed my companion and worried. She was tiring too easily and feeling dejected. Had it been the wrong time for our adventure?

Violins, Birds, and Elbow Macaroni

I woke at dawn, slipped out of bed, and went to make coffee. With cup in hand, I settled on the love seat facing the French doors and city rooftops. I spread a towel across my thighs, and Felicia hopped up. Light inched down the building walls as the sun rose. It was sweet . . . but thoughts poked around inside my head. I *wanted* to stay with my kitty, but I *needed* to write about my feelings. Pigeons flew by outside, and Felicia began those little chomping motions with her teeth. The birds circled, and her gaze circled with them. I finished my coffee, reluctantly moved Effie to the cushion, and took the computer out of the cupboard.

April 25

We are making extensive use of the little magazine called Pariscope, *which I purchased at a newsstand last Wednesday.* Pariscope *costs less than a dollar and lists museum exhibits, lectures, shows, and concerts galore—many for free.*

Violins, brightly colored birds, and elbow macaroni always remind me of Mom, and the concert we attended on Sunday really made me miss her. . . .

That afternoon at the Eglise Saint-Médard, three violinists and two cellists played Schubert to honor the bicentennial of his birth.

As the young women laid violins on their shoulders and lifted their bows, I wasn't noticing the beauty of the church. Instead, I was observing the serious looks on their faces and thinking of Mom—the sad sound of her violin music drifting down the stairway on summer afternoons when I was a boy. She practiced for hours up in her bedroom, and one of our cats would climb on the table next to her and rub his face against Mom's ear. She told us the cat thought she was crying, and he was offering kitty comfort.

As I watched the women play in this church, more memories filtered through. Mom had probably dreamed of playing like these women. They did a beautiful job. But it was the memories, not the music, that touched me that day.

After the concert, Marguerite still had energy, so we hopped on the Métro to the 5:30 PM organ concert at Saint-Eustache.

April 25, continued

I am amazed to have found a more perfect Gothic church than Notre Dame in Saint-Eustache. Before the concert, I admired its stained glass—the striking reds and blues of a nativity scene, the three tiers of colorful windows reaching to its heights. Saint-Eustache is a marvel of sixteenth-century talent. The slender arches to the roof, converging in geometric harmony impossibly high above, seemed much too delicate to support that weight—certainly not for 350 years.

We sat in a pew at Saint-Eustache, surrounded by pillars. I gazed up as organ music floated, skimmed, and reverberated among them. A choir commenced to sing a pious churchly song. Images came to me of the times Mom had taken Marguerite and me to midnight services at her unadorned church. The organ there was a toy compared to this.

For Mom, choir kept the music alive after she gave up the violin.

The organ's deep tones thudded in my chest and pulled me into its melancholy—to thoughts of her funeral.

When the music shifted to light melodies, serenity filled me. I rediscovered Marguerite and the beauty around me all at once.

April 25, rejoined

We've attended several free concerts around the city, each unique in its own way. None has brought the richness of that night at Notre Dame. I continue prowling for special experiences for M.

Roots of My Melancholy

April 28

After a month in Paris, we're both more than ready to move on. Has the great city become like the roses in our pitcher, wilted in our eyes? Still, I explore every afternoon.

Blind energy sent me out to pace the sidewalks. I walked past the opera house, so ornate with all its gold and bronze statuary. Had I come out to remind myself of the city's excesses? Was I trying to fall out of love with her? There was so much glitz, so much beauty, such extravagance—it was blending into sameness. Disappointment weighed heavily.

In the Tuileries Gardens, I saw lovers kissing passionately and thought about—no felt—the loss of that youth, those hormones, the lithe bodies—mine and Marguerite's—the energy, which Marguerite seemed to have left behind.

What had shifted to make me angry at the city? Why did I feel suddenly old in the presence of the lovers? Did it have to do with my thinking of Mom? Was it because of Marguerite's fatigue? Was it that we were moving one month closer to the end of our trip?

Back in the apartment, I found Marguerite cutting onions in the kitchen. She gave me a huge hug and called out, "Look, Felicia, your dad's home."

I felt instantly better. "What are we making?"

"We have to use these up." She pointed to the onions and a bell pepper. "And we still have three eggs and a couple of potatoes. Tonight we have zee omelette."

I popped the cork on a bottle of wine, poured two glasses, and said, "Are you ready to head for Holland?"

"Absolutely. The city's too noisy."

"And it's too beautiful."

She frowned.

I tried to explain. "Remember coming back from Montmartre, when we discovered that square with the colossal church? At first I felt excited, but then disappointed, because it was just one of many. At the Louvre, all those bare breasts, faces with pious expressions or hatred beyond reason, Christ crucified in fifty-eight flavors—each one was spectacular in its own right, but there were just so many! They became monotonous. Each street corner with its domed or trapezoidal, black roofs . . . each block is the epitome of France by itself, but it's too much."

"I take you to Paris for a month, and do you appreciate it?" Marguerite quipped.

"I know. I'm ungrateful. But Paris is like a museum full of crazy motorcyclists and litterbugs. They hose down the sidewalks each day to make it new, but then it's despoiled again by nightfall with trash and dog dung."

"It's okay, Eddie. We'll be gone in two days."

"But I'm not sure I want to go. There's so much we haven't seen."

A Daisy for Her Hand

April 30

We are becoming models of decadence. Each morning I head down to the Brioche Dorée for a bag of treats—those great, chocolate-filled croissants or some other Parisian pastry we have come to love. As we feast, I read from Pariscope *or from our guidebooks. We choose a concert, a museum, or an area to explore and take off on the Métro. Today, for our last concert, we go to the Sorbonne.*

According to *Pariscope*, the concert was supposed to take place in the Amphitheatre Quinet de la Sorbonne, but, for some reason, we were shown into a regular university classroom, while most of the audience stayed outside it. The woman at the door said a few sentences in French and stepped aside as I led Marguerite through the door.

We sat in cramped bench seats with folded-up desktops. I felt disappointed. I described the half-paneled walls, the overhead florescent tubes, and the blackboards as musicians entered with their instruments. "Here's some authentic French graffiti on this desk," I said. "A student from 1954 was bored to death by anthropology."

Marguerite laughed. "No surprise there."

Two flutists, a man and a woman dressed in fine, white shirts and black slacks, assumed places in front of the room. "I wonder why no one's coming in," I whispered. "There must be a couple hundred people waiting out in the hall and in the stairwell." The musicians played part of a number and stopped. A guitarist entered, joined one of the flute players, and ran through the beginning of a tune.

"I have a nagging feeling," Marguerite said. "Could this be the practice room?"

"The woman at the door said the concert was delayed, but it's going to be in here."

"Are you sure?"

Good question. My French was far from perfect. I got up and checked the lobby—still packed with our fellow concert-goers.

"I guess we were supposed to wait outside," I said, as I came back to my seat. "That makes us rehearsal thieves."

The audience started to file in. Murmuring, clunking, and shuffling sounds filled the room. The concert commenced with a guitar duo, then a flute and soprano. The musicians seemed quite ordinary; the concert seemed already too long.

Finally, a slender, dark-haired man entered, dressed in a jacket and tie. He was the pianist, David Saunier. Monsieur Saunier played a duet with one of the flutists. With the addition of the piano, the concert began to look up. The flute player departed, leaving us with only the intense, young pianist.

Monsieur Saunier addressed the piano. He grazed the keys with his fingers and produced the plinking sound of dripping snowmelt. He stroked the piano and brought forth the rhythm of a cascading stream, which grew to the roar of surging rapids. Music echoed in my chest and then rose still more thunderous. Music vanquished my vision of the room. The melody was everything. I closed my eyes, let it take and hold me. Finally, I felt it ebb, descend slowly, until it hovered in the near-silent hymn of a circlet of water, expanding in a still pond. I turned to observe my wife. At last, in this simple classroom at the Sorbonne, we had found an exquisite beauty she could perhaps feel best of all.

I wished once more that I had a daisy for her to hold, because her face, so full of rapture, was again a work of art.

April 30, continued
After our concert this afternoon, I have come full-circle from anger at Paris and its noise to elation over her loveliness and her music. Can such rapidly changing moods be healthy?

Sacre Bleu, There *Is* Life After Paris

It was May Day, time for a new beginning.

After breakfast, I stationed Marguerite by the elevator and brought out two bags at a time for her to guard. Soon she was surrounded by an awesome collection. There was one large rolling suitcase; a huge, green Boston Celtics duffel bag; a tote containing Felicia's supplies; two carry-on-size bags for our short-term clothes; and the miscellaneous shopping bags that we nicknamed the Beverly Hillbillies Collection, holding our kitchen wares, paper goods, and laundry supplies.

In three stages, we moved everything outside. Marguerite stood beside the Champs-Elysées, encircled by this cluttered pile, in full view of the fashion capital of the world. I returned to the apartment to get Felicia in her carrier and the computer in its backpack. Warm thoughts slipped through my mind—thoughts of returning after each day's exploration, cooking with Marguerite in this efficient kitchen, sipping champagne on our balcony. I picked up our kitty and headed out, my mind shifting from Paris and the past to our next adventure.

The cab driver rolled his eyes at the sight of us, but he wordlessly helped me load everything and then took us to Orly Airport. There we found the counter for a company called Sodexa, which manages Peugeot's purchase–buy-back program, to pick up the car we'd reserved from the U.S.

The Sodexa representative was a dark-featured, mustached man, who spoke fairly good English, with what I took to be a Middle Eastern accent. "You understand that you will own this car until you return it?"

We both nodded.

"It is not a rental. And you can keep it for no more than 175 days. Otherwise, you will have ownership forever."

Gulps and nods.

"If you do not return it to Nice by October 22, this agreement states that you will pay 17,726 American dollars. This is the loan document, which you have already signed in America. The percentage of interest is listed." He squidged a yellow highlighter across the figure that stated fifteen percent. "Please sign again for me here."

My pen was poised, but I hesitated. Why wouldn't I sign something I'd already approved before? "We've already paid, so we owe nothing as long as we return it on time. Right?"

"And the insurance is covered?" Marguerite asked.

"Yes, yes. If you have a problem, call this number." He pulled a card from an envelope, waved it in front of me, and slid it back inside.

I signed the document plus a few more, and then the fellow led us outside.

My last driving adventure in Europe using a standard transmission had left me with back pain for months, so we'd reserved an automatic. Air conditioning was also necessary so that we could drive in comfort, with the windows closed and our kitty safe. These two requirements dictated a plush, and more expensive, car than we might otherwise have chosen.

Through the purchase–buy-back program, our cost, including all insurance, was still a reasonable $28 per day. Sodexa would buy the car back from us in October. Then we would lease a Citroën for the rest of our trip.

We met our sleek, silver Peugeot 405, and the fellow explained its features, such as the security measures for the radio and the code to start the engine. Then he left us to it.

After stuffing the trunk, I had two leftover satchels for the back seat. The litter box fit on the floor behind Marguerite, and the water bowl behind me. We got in, offered soothing words and caresses for our kitty, and then I fired it up.

We bypassed Paris and took the main artery north. Ahead, an expanse of highway stretched over the hills toward Holland. My tension eased. Marguerite looked content with her head against the rest. Felicia tested sleeping positions—alternating between Marguerite's lap and atop our carry-on bags in the back seat.

"It's great to be in the country," I said.

Marguerite beamed. "I feel it, too."

"Green forests, fields of yellow flowers—it was getting too noisy in Paris, don't you think?"

"All that jumping on and off the Métro and climbing stairs."

"There's something to be said for driving around like vagabonds."

"But Paris sure was great," she sighed.

She was right, of course. "What did you like best?"

"The romance—sitting on that balcony with you, sipping champagne, and listening to our new French CDs."

Felicia sat up in the back seat and gave a little chirp.

"Oh, sure, Effie," Marguerite said. "You were with us on the balcony, too. We're the Three Musketeers."

"How about the music in the city?"

"Aahh." Her smile glowed. "My favorite was the piano solo at the Sorbonne, of course, but there were also the people at the Musée d'Orsay. . . . There was the music of joy and the music of kindness."

"I like that. There is music in relationships, too. Maybe that's what I missed in Paris. . . . That day at the *musée* was the closest we got to the people of the city."

"Yes. But we had each other, *mon amour.*"

Pannenkoeken in Holland

Dutch Feast, Balloons Included

That first day, we drove from Paris, through northern France and Belgium, to a point where a knuckle of Holland sticks down into its southern neighbor.

In Zundert, a village along a minor highway, I questioned the owner of a nondescript hotel located in the village center. We established the rental price, which fit our budget. Then I blurted out the big question. "We are traveling with a cat—is it all right?" I found myself holding my breath, *really* wanting him to accept our kitty.

"Oh, a cat. Yes," he said with a smile. "We have one of those here somewhere, and we get along very well with him." He scanned the floor but didn't spot the cat. "That's no problem at all. I will show you our rooms. You can choose one your cat will enjoy."

I followed him upstairs and chose a room on the third floor with a view of a cemetery in back. As I paid, the proprietor said, "We are the birthplace of the artist van Gogh in this township. You can visit the statue one street down."

From the car I collected my female and feline. Marguerite carried Felicia in her carrier as I toted cat litter and food. Next I went to retrieve the small suitcases from the back seat.

Still puffing from climbing the stairs a third time, I asked Marguerite, "Should I bring the stuff from the trunk?"

"It's a small town. It'll be all right there."

"The travel articles say to leave nothing in the car, but . . ." The prospect of climbing those stairs again and again sent spasms through my leg muscles. "All right, we'll leave it for the crooks."

We released Felicia, and she poked her nose into everything as I showed Marguerite the room. "Let's leave the windows open," I said.

"We can't. She'll get out."

"It's hot in here."

"When we decided to bring Felicia, we knew it might be inconvenient."

"There's a three-story drop. She's not suicidal."

Marguerite looked like she'd been struck, no doubt imagining our kitty spinning through the air and crashing to the earth—appropriately, into a cemetery.

"I'll wedge the windows open an inch and cover them with the curtains." I jammed a washcloth between the sill and the window frame and helped her feel how well it held.

"Are you sure?"

"Yes. Now let's go downstairs for a drink."

We settled in the sunshine on the glass-sided patio, and I surveyed the scene. "There's a group of teenagers at another table."

"Sounds like a busy day at McDonald's, only in Dutch."

"The waitress just brought them a huge platter of French fries and a plate with some deep-fried balls on it—croquettes, I'd guess. The hotelkeeper is coming out with a tray of ice-cream sundaes, three of them, no four. The kids are digging in."

We ordered a carafe of white wine and two three-course dinners. A block away, a church steeple stood majestic against the deepening blue sky. Puffy white clouds drifted by. Mothers wheeled shopping carts past, bound for a 1950s-looking grocery store on the main street. Each mom was accompanied by one or two blonde, red-cheeked children. Some of the children were sitting in the carts; some were walking beside, clutching their mother's arm. Six- or seven-year-olds followed close at hand.

"There's something touching about them all walking together," I said.

"Sounds like a scene from the last century, before mothers had to work to buy VCRs and camcorders."

"That's part of it. But the women are talking with their kids and vice versa, like they're giving serious advice as they walk, like they adore these little ones. And the kids think the world of their moms."

The entertainment continued. Besides the passing shoppers, a series of brilliantly colored, hot-air balloons drifted across the sky, one by one, past the church steeple and out of sight. We could hear the blasts of their burners from time to time, and I described the colors and the logos that advertised Sony, Shell, Heineken, and some others I didn't recognize.

"It's so peaceful . . . such a change from Paris." Marguerite sipped her wine and sighed.

"I'm really glad they accepted Felicia."

"Me, too. It was a long day of driving. I didn't want you to have to go on."

"It wasn't just that. As I waited for the owner to answer, I felt like it would hurt me if he rejected Effie."

Marguerite fixed me with an incredulous gaze. "Of course, *we* love her, but not everyone's going to feel that way."

"It felt like this was the first test of our game plan. We did all that planning and decided to bring Felicia, but I don't want to have to search all over for rooms. I want our trip to be easy."

"It doesn't do any good to worry."

"When we get home, and I write about the trip, I want to be able to say that taking Felicia was the right decision."

"Have another glass of wine and chill out."

It was well after eight o'clock, and the sun was finally down. We moved inside for dinner. Marguerite had the "surprise" appetizer, which turned out to be some sort of pâté. I ate the asparagus with bacon crumbles and smoked salmon. The main course arrived a few minutes later—a schnitzel for me and salmon for Marguerite, with bowls of spinach, broccoli, carrots, Brussels sprouts, fries, and little roasted potatoes. "This is fantastic," I said. "The table is covered with food."

"And delicious," Marguerite added, spearing a roasted potato-half and waving it in the air to punctuate her words.

"How can the Dutch eat so much?"

"They work it off by bicycling."

The waitress came by to get our dessert order, and I asked, "Is the tip included in the price?" It had been in most of the Paris restaurants.

"Tip? What is this?"

"Service charge . . . extra money for you."

"No. It is not any service charge."

Had she understood? Should I leave fifteen percent or something less, perhaps a token like they do in Paris? I opted for ten percent, but the matter of tips became a perpetual question as we traveled, never completely resolved.

The waitress returned with a huge peach melba for Marguerite and tiramisu for me. I abandoned the last part of my tiramisu so I could help Marguerite polish off the melba . . . not exactly an altruistic act. It finished us off, too, and sent us to bed with full, full, full stomachs.

What a delicious beginning to our Holland adventure.

Finding a Base

Our first day in the land of the Dutch was occupied by running from town to town, tourist office to tourist office, seeking houses for rent and, later, seeking lodging. We ended the evening at ten o'clock, exhausted, at a hotel just outside Zwolle (pronounced "SWOLE-uh") in northeastern Holland. Not willing to risk rejection, we decided to sneak Felicia in.

The clerk had explained, "The hotels are very full this part of year. May Day is holiday; that is yesterday. Tomorrow is Liberation Day from the War, and Friday is Queen's Day. Everyone travels this time in our country. No one works, except me."

In the morning, we left our kitty in the hotel, set out the Do Not Disturb sign, and made a beeline into Zwolle to renew our quest for lodging.

I parked and led Marguerite toward the town center. "We're crossing a bridge over what looks like a moat. Ahead is an old city gate, but it isn't just a rope and a few boards. It's a building made of dark-brown brick that soars fifty feet high with a couple of turrets and some steeples on top."

We joined a small crowd of pedestrians waiting for some cars to pass through the gate. Once the way was clear, we continued on.

"Along this street are little shops with old-time pane windows. This one has hefty disks of cheese, a foot and a half across, piled in a display."

"I'm glad they haven't run out."

"It's not the cheese I'm worried about, it's the lodging. We pretty well struck out yesterday."

"Take it easy. We'll be okay."

"We're coming into a cobbled square. There's a huge brick church with a neat steeple, and a dark, graceful statue of a man. Here, you can touch it."

"Some other time. We have to get back to Felicia before checkout."

"You may not want to miss this. It's a nude guy." I checked the inscription. "*Adam* by Rodin."

"I'm not touching a nude in front of all these Dutch people."

"Right. We'll sneak back at night when no one's around."

We headed across the square to the VVV, the Dutch tourist office. Inside, we found a long, narrow room with poster-covered walls and racks crammed with pamphlets. I approached a tall, robust woman with braided, blonde hair. "We would like a cottage or apartment to rent for three or four weeks."

"A cottage would be better," Marguerite said.

"We'd like a quiet place in the country," I added.

"For a month."

The woman's gaze shifted back and forth between us, and a frown settled in. Did she understand?

"I must sadly inform you, we do not the cottage have for rent in Holland. . . ."

She showed us brochures about hotels and resort communities, but we held out for something unique. Finally, a light lit in her eyes. "One moment." She thumbed through a file and pulled out an index card. "I have this, in forest, very comfortable. You would like."

"Do you have pictures? Can we go see it?"

"No pictures." We waited while she called the owner and then reported back. "You cannot go see, because there is a renter. But no problem. You will like. You can start on Sunday for one week."

We rented it sight unseen for 500 guilders ($260) a week and then returned to the hotel to reserve our room for two more nights. I led Marguerite back to the room to see how Felicia was doing. "Someone has been in here. They've put a letter on the desk."

"Where's Felicia?" Marguerite's voice was edged in panic.

I scanned the room. "She's curled up on a chair by the window." Effie began purring as soon as I scooped her up and brought her to Marguerite.

"They shouldn't have come in with the Do Not Disturb sign out. It must have startled Felicia. . . . What does the note say?"

Had the discovery of our kitty precipitated eviction proceedings? No, the note concerned a different topic. "Tonight all over Holland, we celebrate the liberation of our country during World War II. With gratitude and reverence we honor the men and women of other countries who gave their lives to free our people. Please observe a minute of silence at 18:00 hours."

As I read, I felt tears forming. Marguerite's tears formed, too. I brought her a tissue, and she dabbed her eyes.

In California, Memorial Day sometimes seems like just another holiday, but here we were among people who knew the meaning of Nazi domination. It was humbling to think that we had to come to Holland to appreciate our own land and the soldiers of our parents' generation.

A little before 6:00 PM, we went to the lobby and stood in a circle of silent remembrance with several of our Dutch brethren.

To Hattem We Will Go

I drove down a country lane lined by lush, green trees and then followed a long drive beside a meadow where brown-and-white cows grazed. Two buildings sat side by side in the woods—the first was a typical, brick, seventeenth-century Dutch house, with three stories and a bell-shaped gable; the second was a single-story, white house, with a thatched roof and red-and-gold shutters.

A tall, ruddy-cheeked woman of indeterminate age appeared in the doorway of the brick house. "Hello. I am Mrs. Von B. You are the Vebsters?"

She led us into the thatched cottage, our home for the week.

"This house was built in the 1800s," our hostess informed us. The slightly musty smell enhanced her credibility. "The caretaker of the estate lived here. The house next door, where I live, was the grain store from 1640. Molecaten is the mansion through the forest." She pointed out the window. "All of this was the estate of my late husband's family. The shutters beside the windows—the colors are of his family."

In the bedroom, lit by the ambient light of a small window, two not-very-sturdy-looking beds sat side by side, and the ceiling sloped down overhead. A rough, wooden beam jutted up by the foot of one bed to support the roof. A cabinet stood in the corner. "You can put your clothes in here," she said. "Plenty of space for two people. And across the hall . . ."

She showed us the second, bare-walled bedroom, with children's twin beds, and the bathroom. I carefully led Marguerite, gauging her height to see if she would have to duck coming out of the main bedroom. It was okay for her, potentially dangerous for me.

"Is there a place to do laundry?" Marguerite asked.

The woman fixed her with a what-a-dumb-question look. "Naturally, in the sink."

Marguerite returned a look that said, not in my world. "And how do we dry it?"

"In the *centrifugen*." Our landlady pointed to a white, cylindrical contraption, like an industrial, canister vacuum cleaner.

We stared at her in confusion. She gave us a look that said, these spoiled Americans will be trouble. "*Centrifugen?* This is the word, no?"

"Centrifuge . . . " I said. "How do we work it?"

She unlatched the top. "Clothes in this little barrel. It spins. The water falls out."

"But it's so humid here," Marguerite said. "Will they be dry enough?"

"Sure, sure. Just hang them up a little time."

We toured the large living room with its dining table; cushy, old armchairs; and wood-burning stove. The basic kitchen had a 1950s refrigerator and gas range. There was only one doorway that would threaten Marguerite's noggin, and three that might kill me.

"Oh, would you be wanting sheets for the bed?" Mrs. Von B. assessed our mood with a glance and added, "I will charge merely 50 guilders for washing the sheets and for cleaning house when you go—a very good price." That would be just over $25—a ten-percent bump from our 500 guilder rent. What could we do but agree?

After she left, Marguerite said, "So she plans to clean *after* we leave. It must be a new policy."

"You don't think she cleaned for us?"

She held her nose between her thumb and forefinger. "It's musty."

"A little bit," I conceded. "That's because the roof is made of branches and twigs. It's really a neat old place, a part of history."

"Did you feel the dirt on that counter?" Marguerite's touch test is generally more discriminating than my visual check.

"Ever think you'd get to live in a *real* thatched cottage?"

Marguerite spent the next hour cleaning the kitchen and storing the cooking supplies that we'd accumulated in Paris. I locked Felicia in the main bedroom, hauled our belongings from the car, and put them in the children's room. Then I let the kitty out and watched her sniff the corners along the hall. Her little nose came out draped in cobwebs, and she sneezed. I petted her face to clean it and left her to continue.

I carted some of our dirty clothes to the bathroom sink. After washing them, I threw a few items into the *centrifugen* and headed off in search of Marguerite to share the experience of starting it up. My progress halted abruptly when my forehead smacked the big, bare beam that topped the doorway from the hall to the living room. "Ow. Ow!"

"Are you okay?" Marguerite popped out of the kitchen and felt her way toward me.

"Yeah. Damn it. I hit my head. . . . I thought you might like to be here when I tried this thing."

"It's dangerous to let sighted people loose in these old houses."

"Thanks for your concern."

She stood in the doorway and waited.

I plugged the machine into an outlet in the hallway and stepped back. It began clanking, then wobbling. I wanted to grab it but hesitated. Water jetted out of a hose at the bottom onto the floor. The machine rotated in my direction, spit on my feet, pitched over on its side, and gyrated. I ripped the plug from wall. "Damn, I didn't think about that! The water has to go somewhere. It's all over the floor . . . and me."

She laughed and hugged me.

"I'll drag it into the bathroom and use it in there," I said.

"But you'll get the bathroom floor wet."

"Didn't I tell you? The bathroom and the shower are one and the same, like in a boat. It's all tiled, and there's a drain, so you don't have to worry about a shower curtain. Isn't that great?"

"What else haven't you told me?"

"Not much." I waited for the next question, but instead she asked me to take her to the suitcases.

Soon she was situated in the guest room with our luggage and some hangers. I went back to the centrifuge. The trick was to put one garment in at a time, point it at the drain in the bathroom floor, and hold on. The clothes came out almost dry. I hung two shirts on our inflatable hangers just above the electric heater and turned it on high to finish the job.

Outside the bathroom, I found evidence of Marguerite's efforts to protect me. Hanging down from the "killer beam," a fluffy, bright red sock warned me of danger. (And it must have worked, because by the end of the week I had only the one major bruise to show for our tenure in the cottage.)

Though the beam's threat had been diminished, the smell of

burning plastic informed me that my traumas hadn't ended. Back in the bathroom, black smoke puffed from the hanging clothes. I switched off the heater, grabbed the hangers, and found a hole melted into one.

I filled Marguerite in on the debacle, and she yelped, "Oh, no! I *loved* those hangers."

"It was an accident."

She looked as if she would cry.

"Why are they so important to you?"

"They are one of our travel gadgets that really work." She wiped a tear. "They're *better* than other hangers, because they don't take up space. And they puff up to make the front and back of a shirt separate, so things dry faster."

"Know what I think . . . ?"

"Those hangers were essential, and now you've ruined one. Don't think of touching the other one without permission."

"Which was worse? The melted hanger or my bruised skull?"

Her look implied I might not want to hear the answer.

We soon dubbed this "The Adventure of the Laundry Spinner" and stored it in our list of travel mishaps.

May 6, 2:00 AM

I am sitting in the living room of the original hobbit hut—truly. It has a thatched roof and stands next to a traditional, Dutch, three-story, brick house with a Hans Brinker front. We have just moved into this delight, which, for Marguerite, is a curse. Nothing is even or level in this place. One room's entrance isn't opposite another, the floor is wavy, the attic stairs jut out. It's cold, at least for her, but the wood-burning stove spews choking smoke unless you leave the stove doors closed and miss out on all the fun of the fire.

I see it in her face, the struggle between wanting to like what's unique, wanting to please me—because I obviously think it's pretty great—and the misery that creeps into her. Most of our clothes are still in suitcases. She touches spider webs in the corners. We have to duck to enter the kitchen or the living room or to go out the front door. A

*huge, old, wrought-wood beam in our bedroom keeps us from getting
to the armoire without climbing over the bed.*

*It's quirky and not practical, but it calls out for love. Felicia sees
it. She likes all the nooks and irregularities. She loves the worn
armchair in the living room, where she sits beside me now as I type.*

*I look forward to the peace of these surroundings, so welcome
after Paris. I look forward to walks in these woods, exploring Hattem,
and visiting the windmill I've seen from a distance. But peace may not
come for Marguerite here.*

Pannenkoeken

The next morning we followed Mrs. Von B's recommendation
for a restaurant a few miles down the road in the village of
Wapenveld. I led Marguerite through a light rain into the glassed-in
porch of the Pannenkoekhuis (pancake house) 't Mussennest, and we
settled in at a wooden, octagonal table. "I'm looking out at sheep
grazing on lush grass, and it's starting to really pour out there."

Marguerite somehow managed to smile and frown
simultaneously. "Great! I love rain and sheep. But do we have the
menu yet?" Though she likes to know about the scenery, Marguerite
sometimes has other priorities.

I opened the menu and turned to the English-language section.
"Whoa! Ham-and-cheese pancakes! Mushroom pancakes! Cherry or
apple or banana pancakes, with or without liqueur and whipped
cream." I glanced back and forth between the Dutch and English
pages. "'Whipped cream' in Dutch seems to be *slagroom*. . . . Who
would eat a pancake with mushrooms in it?"

"How big are these things? Are some of them supposed to be
the main course and others dessert?"

The plump, blonde waitress overheard. "You get one pancake
on a plate. They can be the meal. They can be dessert. Some people
eat them all together." She grinned irresistibly.

"Maybe we should each get two?"

"Oh, no. You should not."

Two couples at another table laughed, and one of the women told us, "They'll be big enough to fill you."

We ordered a banana pancake with liqueur and whipped cream, and a bacon-and-mushroom pancake. Each of us received one huge pancake that covered an oversized plate. They knocked our socks off. Not as thin as crêpes or as thick as the pancakes back home, they were pieces of art—but we didn't pause to admire them. We attacked with knife and fork.

"This is delicious," I opined.

"And very filling . . . how about giving me a turn at those banana cakes?"

The only problem we encountered as we swapped the plates back and forth was that we wanted to save some of the banana-liqueur cakes for dessert, but neither of us wanted to stop eating. We had fallen in love with *pannenkoeken*.

❦

A few days later on an early walk, I spotted the sails turning on the town windmill in Hattem, so I headed in that direction. A tall, white-haired man in denim overalls greeted me at the base of the mill and led me inside. I found myself in an octagonal room with posters explaining the workings of the mill; tables displaying grains and different types of flour; and a stout, wooden ladder leading to the next level. The room seemed alive with creaking and grinding sounds coming from overhead. We climbed one ladder, then another, up past the workings of the mill. My companion took me out on the deck.

As the big sails swished by overhead, I learned that my guide was a retired, oil-company engineer who volunteered to help maintain the mill. I wondered aloud, "The canvas is stretched only part way across the frames. Do you adjust it sometimes?"

"Surely, we do. Windmills are much like sailboats. When the winds are strong, we cut back a little. Today is a grand day, don't you think? In fact, today is officially Windmill Day in Holland."

He led me into the bowels of the machinery and showed me how the wooden shafts and gears adjusted automatically to the shifting wind speeds. Then he made his most important statement: "The flour from this mill is the best for making pancakes. You don't even need eggs."

I hurried home to Marguerite and brought her back to meet my friend. By now, two local women dressed in traditional, flowered skirts were frying small pancakes on a gas fire at the base of the mill. As each cake came out of the pan, a woman sprinkled it with powdered sugar, wrapped it in paper, and sold it to one of the people assembled. We shared one as the women discussed their recipe—just mix the flour and milk, and fry it. It sounded like something we could handle. We had another pancake.

"Want to try the recipe?" I asked. Marguerite nodded, and I purchased a kilo of flour. We were in business.

Creeping Melancholy

I stirred the batter with a fork, peeled an onion, and began slicing it into the frying pan.

From the back of the house I heard a wail, and I rushed to the bathroom. Inside, the mirror, the sink, and the floor were covered with beaded water. Marguerite sat on the toilet, a towel wrapped around her head like a turban and another around her body. "Can you get me some dry toilet paper?" She glared at the soggy sheets in her hand.

"You should have protected it before you took a shower."

"Thanks for the suggestion."

"There's another roll here somewhere. Let's see. . . . Oh, it's on the floor. . . . That's no good." I lifted the sodden mess and dropped it into the wastebasket.

"I'm getting moldy."

I tracked down a leftover roll from Paris and handed it over.

Marguerite joined me in the kitchen a few minutes later.

"I'm making pancakes the Dutch way." I shoved the spatula under the edge of the huge cake that filled the frying pan, skimmed it around to loosen the entire cake, lifted the pan, and began sliding the half-cooked pancake onto a plate.

"Would you check my outfit? Is this the blue top or the pink? Does it go with these pants?"

"Not right now."

"And which pair of socks would work? I brought three choices."

I glanced at her and then turned back to my work. "This is a critical point in the history of pancake making." I eased the large disk onto the plate and prepared to flip it back into the pan to cook the other side.

"My feet are freezing. And don't give me that bit that blind people should have only one color of socks."

"You're thinking of your feet, but I'm worried about the stove. If I flip this wrong, I'll cover the place with onion-yuck." I swept the plate into the air, aimed the pancake at the frying pan, and let fly. "Success. The eagle has landed. . . . So, what was that about the socks?"

I divided the pancake onto two plates. "You don't seem very lively."

"Dr. Wong's pills aren't working. I've been awake with the sweats."

"You could try the hormones. . . ."

"*No*, I won't! We'll find something at a Dutch drugstore."

"I'm worried about you." I saw the sulky look on her face and gave up. "How do you like the Dutch-style pancakes? I made them with the flour from the windmill."

"They're wonderful. Next time, let's try bell peppers."

That day we took the fifteen-minute walk to Hattem, and Marguerite was exhausted well before we got back. She napped away the afternoon, while I hiked in the forest by our home. When I returned, I woke her to help me cook supper and then read to her from *Jean de Florette* by Marcel Pagnol, but she only listened to a few pages before drifting off again. Felicia slept, too. They had both checked out on me.

May 7, 10:30 PM

It was fun exploring Hattem today. It's a pretty town with bakeries; butcher shops; a neat steepled gate that's a smaller version of the one in Zwolle; a really narrow, high-spired church; and a pretty windmill. But the best part was the chocolate factory. Marguerite and I chatted with the owner about the history of his family's chocolate works, while machinery spun and clunked, and a little conveyor belt churned along behind him.

It seems Marguerite and I are both having trouble sleeping. I lie in bed next to her, but the one window in the bedroom seems minuscule and very far away. Claustrophobia leads me to melancholy—the melancholy from Paris slipping back.

It starts with impressions of how Marguerite and I were twenty-seven years ago on our three-week sprint around Europe in the red VW. We had passed through Holland in three days, staying in Amsterdam and Haarlem. Truthfully, we were just twenty-three-year-old kids with no thoughts in our heads but having fun. Truthfully, we have everything now that we did then and more; everything, that is, except those twenty-seven years to look forward to. But now there are bits and pieces of our health that seem to be slipping, and she's exhausted. When she sleeps away the day like this, I feel like I'm on a solo tour of Europe, and this could be a very lonely month.

In the morning, I told Marguerite about my nostalgia for that first trip to Europe, but I didn't mention my disappointment over her lagging energy. She concluded, "You're turning fifty, my dear. It's natural to mourn your youth." I was mourning, not only my own youth but hers as well.

Beware the *Appen*

With our faithful kitty hung across my chest in her blue baby sling, I headed home from an early morning walk through the forest. The air felt crisp, the forest still, the soil springy underfoot. Felicia seemed content yet curious about the woods, her head rotating from side to side. Our thatched-roof cottage came into sight, and I quickened my pace.

I flipped off my shoes by the back door and peeked into the bedroom—no Marguerite. I carried Felicia down the hall, ducked to avoid a sock to the head (both kinds), passed through the living room, and located Marguerite in the kitchen. We hugged good morning with our "baby" wedged in between. Marguerite stroked Effie, who began to purr.

"What are you up to?" I asked.

"Just tidying, and I've made coffee."

"You must feel better this morning."

"Finally got some sleep."

I left her to the coffeepot as I thumbed through the travel brochures that Mrs. Von B. had left us in the living room. One had the caricature of a monkey on the cover.

Marguerite stepped in from the kitchen carrying two coffee mugs, dangling a bag of cookies from her teeth, and making sounds reminiscent of primordial human speech.

"Listen," I said. "This brochure says, 'Oog in oog in Apeldoorn.'"

Marguerite felt her way to the table, set a mug down for me, and then pulled her bag of cookies free. "That's nice, honey. Oog in oog to you."

"It's a leaflet for a place named Apenheul, and, fortunately, part of it is in English."

"What is it?"

"I'll give you a hint—the pictures have monkeys in them."

"Monkeys?" Marguerite took a sip, set down her mug, and focused on me. "Monkeys I can hold?"

"I'm reading. . . . The park has lots of apes—twenty breeds. It's near the town of Apeldoorn. Don't you love these Dutch names? The pictures show children with little yellow monkeys on their laps."

"If I can have monkeys on me, I want to go."

"Hold on. It might be just for kids. The brochure doesn't say."

"If we tell them I've come from America to see the monkeys, if we mention I'm blind, if I look pitiful, don't you think they'll let me?"

Marguerite is not above using her disability. "Sure, honey. How could they resist?"

We raised Marguerite's cane to eye level and asked the cashier about special rates for the disabled. "Yes, surely," the well-tanned brunette said. "You will pay just the one."

I paid my fee, and the woman warned, "Now you everything in a bag put, so the monkeys won't take. The missus must remove her . . ." The woman made a plucking motion at her ears.

"You have to take off your earrings," I said.

A stocky fellow handed us a black bag similar to a piece of carry-on luggage, with an extra clasp to hold the zipper closed.

Marguerite beamed. "See, it's not just for kids. We're going to touch monkeys, and they'll touch us."

With empty pockets and a bulging black bag, I led her to an area where stone and cement walls surrounded grassy sections with trees spaced well apart. A building with large observation windows stood to one side. "Let's sit on the wall and wait. There's a sign in English and Dutch that says, "Next feeding, 11:00." I unzipped the bag and checked my watch. "Fifteen minutes until feeding time."

"Why aren't the monkeys here?" She practically bounced up and down on the wall.

"Could be a no-show."

She shot me a dark look—one of her specialties.

Several people joined us, mostly teenagers or parents with smaller children, but no other types of primates. They chattered

81

in various languages, none of which was English—nor gorilla or chimpanzee, either.

I heard them before I spotted them, a multitude of high-pitched sounds, "scree, scree, scree," and a rustling in the trees. Marguerite turned to the noise and sang the words, "They're coming."

Little forms appeared, swinging from limb to limb, several, many, hundreds, all coming our way. Within a minute they poured over the roof of the observation building, swung into the trees, scampered past.

"They're all around us," I said.

"Eddie, catch one and put him on my lap."

"The little guys move too fast. They're mostly yellow with some brown on them, and they're fluffy and cute."

No staff members had arrived to feed them, but these little monkeys knew something was afoot. Some hung in the trees; others sprinted from place to place; a few ventured closer to the people, but all stayed nearby.

"A monkey has settled next to a girl over there," I reported. "He's climbing onto her lap. Now there's one walking by our feet."

"Please get him for me."

"I'm not grabbing one of these suckers. They aren't cats, you know."

"I wish one would come . . . YOW!" One tiny fellow had hopped onto her knee. She reached out to touch his arm, and the little guy leaped into the air, landed on the pavement, scampered across to a ten-year-old boy, and jumped onto his shoulder.

"Better not to seize him," I suggested. "He may have jagged incisors."

One walked across my legs and settled onto Marguerite's lap. A huge grin spread across her face. "I *love* this place." I snapped a picture as the little guy peered at her, moved his head in jerky motions, and reached up to tug at a drawstring on her coat. "Eddie, he's taking my coat apart."

"Smile," I said, but the direction wasn't necessary.

Two young men walked among us passing out handfuls of granola. Marguerite took chunks of the food and handed them to the monkey on her lap, who stored it in his puffy cheeks and chewed rapidly.

"They're so small," she giggled. "Ooh, did you feel their hands? They're tiny, very soft, and rubbery. *Whoa.*" A second one hopped onto her shoulder.

"I can't help you. This one's trying to eat my camera."

"I don't want help."

"Stop wiggling. I'm trying to take pictures." A monkey ran up my arm, stepped on the camera, and launched himself onto a woman across the sidewalk—wasted shot.

"How can I stay still? He's grabbed my ear."

Within a few minutes, the food was gone and the frenzy abated, but many of the little guys stayed close, hanging overhead in the trees. We began strolling, talking to the monkeys, offering them leaves or little sticks to lure them. Marguerite unfolded her white cane to its full length, and I noticed the way the monkeys looked at it. "Hold it out by this tree."

The minute her cane lodged against the tree, two yellow fellows skittered down to observe. One grabbed and tugged at it. When that didn't work, he stepped tentatively onto the cane, venturing out like a nimble, tightrope walker. The second primate tested it with his foot and climbed on, then he flipped down and hung by his hands. I lent a hand to help Marguerite support it. The first little fellow jumped onto her shoulder. Children flocked over to watch the scene, reaching out to try to divert the monkeys. Marguerite became an instant hit as monkeys hopped from shoulder to shoulder among the growing crowd.

When the little rascals tired of the cane, we moved on to the other apes. It began to sprinkle, then pour, so we hid under the canopy of a snack bar. Marguerite nibbled French fries, looking like a jubilant monkey herself. "This is one of the best days of my life." She paused and added, "After our wedding day, that is."

To Euphoria and Back

Lying in bed that night, the doorway seemed miles away. The modest window, my only other contact with the outside, was shrinking. Tons of thatch rested on hundred-and-fifty-year-old beams close overhead, poised to break through and smother me. I began climbing over Marguerite to make my escape. "Are you okay?" she asked.

"No. I'm getting sad again, and I feel closed in."

"Would you like to move closer to the door?"

We switched positions, but soon I had to get up and turn on the light. I needed to see that more of the world existed than just the inside of my head and that tiny window, to see that I wasn't inhabiting an ever-diminishing cave.

"Want to talk?"

"You sleep."

"I could get up with you."

"I'm okay." But somewhere inside my chest, sadness tightened like a python.

May 10, 1:00 AM

I write to make sense of this indefinable malaise.

Seeing Marguerite so sweetly delighted today at the monkey park made me just as happy. She is the love and substance of my life, and I told her that. I thought that once she felt better, I would, too. So I'm baffled and feeling cheated. It's amazing how I can go from melancholy to enchantment and now back again.

Am I missing other human companionship? The Dutch all speak English, but I have real conversations with only Marguerite. We are reading Manon of the Springs *together. It's the follow-up to* Jean de Florette *by Marcel Pagnol. It's a bit depressing but finely written. I shouldn't let a book affect my mood. Perhaps it's because I lack purpose.*

We leave this cottage the day after tomorrow, and we've called ahead to rent a place for three weeks near Gouda. Staying here only a week has given Marguerite enough time to learn her way around but not enough time to let her guard down. She walks carefully, feeling her way to avoid low beams and wrong turns. In her eyes I see the struggle—she's mad at herself for not having energy, for not being able to relax and enjoy the idiosyncrasies of this place. I feel the strain as she tries not to be so dependent on me, tries to get things unpacked and organized, wonders if we should even bother to unpack. We'll move on, and her familiarizing herself with the next place will start from scratch. The strain will come again and again as we travel.

To stop dwelling on these thoughts, I'm going to try to get back to work on my novel.

Good night.

Rijsttafel for Two, and a Touch of Gossip

After all the monkey fun, Marguerite seemed in better shape. We walked to Hattem the next afternoon and headed to a Chinese restaurant.

I showed her to a booth by the window. "It looks very Oriental in here. Lots of those rice-paper lamps, with paintings of little Chinese bridges and tassels hanging down."

"I love that stuff. Are the tassels red?"

The waiter arrived, brought menus, and left. "Of course. Red is the color for Chinese tassels. And they have those wooden screens with the dragons carved all over them."

"What's to eat?"

"There's the regular chop suey and stuff, *and* they have two types of feast—a Chinese feast and an Indonesian *rijsttafel* (pronounced 'RICE-taf-fel'). Don't let me influence you, but I could go with the *rijsttafel* again." We had eaten some in Zwolle the week before.

She nodded happily.

"The complete or the lesser *rijsttafel?* I bet they're both huge, but with the lesser we don't get the chicken satay, the fried bananas, or one of the beef dishes."

"I could live without the beef, but I'm not willing to give up the bananas."

I ordered white wine and the complete *rijsttafel* for two, and then sat back to wait for the show to begin.

Marguerite lifted my hand and kissed it. "I'm sorry I've been so out of it. I won't let you down today."

"It's not . . . it's okay that you're tired. I just want you to have a good time."

"You worry too much for me. Look at the fun I had with the monkeys."

"That was super . . . but when I go out hiking, I worry you might be bored."

"Felicia keeps me company."

The waiter set two raised, metal platforms in front of us and lit braziers underneath. He left but then immediately returned with two wide, stainless-steel trays covered with a multitude of delicacies, each in its own niche.

"Would you like the chicken satay, one of the beef dishes, or the sweet-and-sour pork first? Wait a minute. On the other tray there is another pork or chicken concoction. I *think* it's pork or chicken. It might be duck—it's crustier."

"Whatever you pick."

"I bet you'd like some of these string beans and pickled cabbage. How about a poached egg in sauce?"

"Forget the egg, but I'll take everything else as soon as you can plop it on the plate."

"Where would you like the raisins, grated coconut, and peanuts—on top of the meat dishes or on the side?"

I pointed out the locations of all the items on Marguerite's plate (rather than the three o'clock, six o'clock method, I usually take her hand with the fork in it and point at things so she can feel where they are). I gave her my best guess about the contents of each item, and then we began feasting.

When we were stuffed, half of the meat remained—leftovers for future meals in the hobbit hut.

We consumed this feast four or five more times while in Holland, and it always included way too much meat. (The first four times we hardly noticed, I guess.)

❧

In the center of Hattem we entered the tourist office. "Hey, this is cool," I said. "Our hut is on one of the postcards."

"Let's get some for Mom and my sisters."

The man behind the desk offered, "If you wish, I tell you where is this house out in the nature preserve."

"We live in it," I said.

"Oh. Oh, yes. A very interesting history of that place, very old estate, Molecaten. The woman did not be of the Von B. family, but she married him that was." He gave a knowing smirk.

"Our landlady seems like an interesting woman," Marguerite put in. "Know anything about her?"

"Well, you should hear *this.*" The man leaned in close, his brow creased tightly beneath his balding forehead, voice low. "When she married, she was young, and Herr Von B. was getting on, older than her father, I think. Now he is dead, and he was the last of the line. The whole estate she sold to an insurance company even before he died. Too much expense to keep up, they say. Rich widow, I say."

"But she's still living there."

"Yes. She made the bargain. She and her daughter are the last who can stay on, and then the insurance company has it all."

No need to buy *The National Enquirer* in this village.

❧

That evening, taking advantage of Marguerite's rejuvenation, I bundled Felicia into her baby sling and took the three of us out for a stroll. Walking along a lane, we came to a farm, carved out of the forest. "Come on over by this fence. I have something to show you and Effie."

87

Marguerite resisted. "What is it?" She knows my propensity to put her hand in the middle of "interesting" things. Before I could answer, a loud "baah" made her jump. "Whoa!"

"It's Effie's first sheep. What do you think of her, Felicia?" Our kitty declined comment, but she seemed pretty unimpressed. "Want to pet it, Marguerite?"

"Yes, but don't bring Felicia too close. She might get fleas or germs or something." The sheep spoke a few more times, and we walked on.

Soon the sky began to darken, and the wind came up. We turned around and rushed home. I gathered some of the wood and made a fire in the stove. "Outside the window," I said, "it's starting to hail."

"I can't hear it."

"The thatched roof is too thick."

I buckled Felicia's lavender harness around her, attached her matching leash to it, and secured her to the coffee table. I opened the door so Marguerite could hear.

"Are you sure Felicia's safe?" Marguerite asked. "I don't want her getting out."

"She's in the harness."

We stood by the open door with our arms around one another's waist. Hail rattled the leaves outside. I bent low and stepped through the doorway to gather hail pellets the size of peas for Marguerite. When I turned back, the harness lay empty on the floor. Felicia stood in the doorway next to us, sniffing the crisp air and watching the white grains dance on the hard earth.

I rushed to pick her up and then looked over at Marguerite, who was casually awaiting my return.

"Everything is all right," I said.

"What is? Is it Felicia?"

"I have her."

She plucked Felicia from me. *"Close the door,"* she said firmly. She cooed to Effie, "It's all right, baby. We'll never count on that harness again."

May 11

So what's become of my sadness? Touches of it creep back from time to time. In the night, I think of embarrassing moments in my life, like the day in eighth grade when Mrs. Fitzgerald called me chubby in front of the class. Marguerite says turning fifty is a bitch for almost anyone. There's necessary stuff to sort through. . . .

Yesterday, the young couple who are the next week's renters for the hobbit hut stopped by to leave some belongings in the shed out back. Their little kid cornered Felicia, and we started talking with them while keeping watch to make sure our kitty was all right.

Suddenly the man popped out a question for Marguerite. "So, how is Holland, not seeing?" She told him about eating rijsttafel *and visiting the monkeys at Apenheul. She said she was enjoying Holland because the people seemed so nice.*

She told me later she was charmed by the openness of the question. No one in the U.S. would dare ask something like that the first time they met her.

Marguerite is doing better with our home, too. She laughs now about the low, head-clunking beams; the hot water that gives out just when her hair is lathered; the light that fell from the guest-room ceiling; even the melted inflatable hanger. . . .

She asked if I wanted to leave a day early to be rid of my claustrophobia, but I declined. I want to stay in this area, in these woods. I like the hut— mostly, anyway. The bedroom still feels closed in but not as desperately so. The surrounding woods are calm and idyllic.

Hey, did I mention our place is on a postcard of Hattem? We bought five.

Good-bye, Old Hut

On Monday I walked to the bakery in town for our last warm *appelflaps* (turnovers, only better). The woman at De Echte Bakker Blom, whose sweet smile I had fallen for in the three previous visits, wasn't there. Alas, I trudged home a little disappointed but looking forward to sharing the treats with Marguerite.

After breakfast, Mrs. Von B. came by to check on the place. She walked from room to room with an envelope under her arm. I pointed out the light that had fallen down in the guest room, and she nodded.

When we got to the living room, she asked, "Did you write in the guest book?" Her voice sounded accusatory, and I was happy that I had jotted down a few words about the pleasant time we'd had, about the town and the lovely woods.

When she looked up from reading the book, her visage held unexpected warmth. "So, you had a good stay here?"

I thought back to our first day, to Marguerite's questions about where to do the laundry. Our hostess had assumed we were too spoiled to enjoy this rustic home, but we had shown her.

"I am glad." A wisp of a smile crossed her lips. "And I bring you something. Yesterday you asked questions about these houses and about the area."

"Yes, for an article I want to write."

From the envelope she extracted some papers. "This is a picture of the mansion at Molecaten early in the century. And this is today's view—very different, you see. Here I have written notes about the house you live in and my house, too. And last, this is a paper about the history of Molecaten."

I didn't mention that the article I planned to write was about pancake houses, and so there was no need for pictures of her estate. She was just beginning to warm up to us. Why wreck the mood? "Thank you. This will help me."

Our landlady reached into her skirt pocket. "And I brought you this." She handed me a can. "For your small companion."

"Cat food. That's very kind."

Our landlady followed as I picked up Felicia in her carrying case and led Marguerite to the car.

We climbed in, and I started the engine. "Thanks for the pictures and the information," I called through Marguerite's open window.

"*Tot ziens* (Good-bye)," said Marguerite.

"Good travels. Thank you for staying in my cottage." Mrs. Von B. stood in the driveway, waving until we were out of sight.

Marguerite unzipped Felicia's carrier and took her onto her lap. We passed by Hattem, and I turned toward the main highway south. "Mrs. Von B. really warmed up to us at the end, didn't she?"

"We *are* charming."

"Probably Felicia's the one who charmed her." Our kitty stopped washing her face, uttered a chirp, and went back to bathing.

On to Hekendorp

We drove an hour south on the highway, through flat farming country with occasional patches of water off to the right, past Utrecht, and then down a few narrow country roads to the hamlet of Hekendorp. I asked some teenagers outside the village café for directions to our landlord's home, a pretty green bungalow under a weeping willow beside a canal. Once we arrived, Marguerite and Effie waited in the car as I approached the house.

The man who opened the door was red-faced and wearing a broad grin. He was around sixty years old, I figured, and had short, dark hair that rimmed his forehead.

"Meester Vebster?" He ushered me in, introducing himself and his wife as Mr. and Mrs. Nederend—all in Dutch.

"Do you speak English?" I asked him.

"Eengleesh," he said. "No . . . Yes . . . Leetle, leetle." He looked pleased with himself for this linguistic achievement.

Back at the car, I introduced him to Marguerite. As she emerged from the Peugeot, he eyed her cane, his broad smile never wavering. He led us through a quick once-around of our new home, which was tucked between Mr. Nederend's house and a couple of little barn-shaped buildings. It was only a hundred steps from the back of the café we had stopped at. He unlocked the door, handed me the keys, and was gone.

"Are there any low beams to conk our heads on, or can I put the red socks away?" Marguerite asked.

"It's safe. And it's bright—lots of windows."

"Good, no claustrophobia then. . . . I heard quacking while I was waiting in the car."

"Yep. We have our own canal, fifty feet from the front door."

I brought in a few loads, put our luggage on the lower bunk in the guest room, and showed Marguerite the closets. She began rummaging through our suitcases as Felicia took inventory.

I entered the kitchen with two bags of supplies and put them on the counter. "Yikes!"

"What?"

"They must have unplugged the refrigerator after the last guests left."

"So, plug it in."

"We have company. . . . Tiny ants are running a caravan operation out of the refrigerator."

"You'll have to get rid of them if you want me to stay."

I had already figured that out—but how to get rid of them? With a knife, I carefully squished a couple of ants. I preserved the crumpled carcasses in a tissue and proceeded to kill as many as I could find. I plugged in the refrigerator and brought the tissue with its dead samples outside. Mr. Nederend was shoveling dirt from a pile into a blue wheelbarrow. "Halloo," he said.

I showed him the specimens. "We have *ants.*" I wiggled my fingers in front of him, hoping he would get the concept of tiny insect legs. I pushed the button on an imaginary spray can and said, "Pssst, pssst."

Our landlord poked at the black specks in the tissue and nodded. "*Ja. Ja.* Okay." At his house, he rummaged through a cabinet for a jar of white powder. Pointing at it, he clenched one hand around his throat, made a choking sound, and stuck out his tongue. As I retreated with the jar, he said something I took for "Kill 'em."

I sprinkled powder along the house's foundation and into any visible holes, and then I went inside. "Mr. Nederend gave me some poison to put around."

"Not where Effie can get into it."

"That's the problem. I need something for inside the house. There's a little store up the street. I'll go see if they have cinnamon." Back home in California, we had experienced limited success driving ants away with cinnamon powder—the operative word being *limited*.

May 16

I am sitting at the table in the "dining room" (a corner of the living room) of an ample little house in Hekendorp, Holland, our home for the next three weeks. (We've come to call it "the Dorp.") I look out to a weeping-willow tree and a red-roofed home across our own canal, with ducks and coots aplenty. It's early, and Marguerite is still sleeping. Beside me on a chair is my sweet cat, Felicia. She wants me to move to one of our two couches and put a comforter on my lap so she can sit on me, but I resist this temptation.

The house looks like an elongated gypsy wagon without wheels—I don't know why. I guess it's the way the planking forms the sides of the house. The house is dark green with burgundy trim.

The place is grand for us, complete with two bedrooms, a kitchen with a pine bar to separate it from the living room, a toilet room for us and another for Felicia, which is actually the shower room. There's a short-wave radio, which comes in handy when Marguerite can't sleep at night. She listens to the BBC and the Netherlands station, which is sometimes in English but often not.

The TV sometimes gets CNN, NBC, TNT, and a bunch of channels in Dutch, French, and Spanish. Movies are occasionally in English, and when we're lucky, we catch one near the beginning. Yesterday we savored an entire episode of Poirot *and watched the* Today *show. It made me feel less—and more—isolated, all at the same time. Katie and Matt were like our favorite niece and nephew coming to visit.*

We have a separate entryway to the house where we leave our shoes. We've come to call this "the cat-free zone." It's a great buffer, so we never have to worry about Felicia escaping.

Unfortunately, we have an ongoing problem with ants.

Out and About in the Dorp

It was my third visit to the town store in as many days. Inside, it was a one-room equivalent of an old general store, only with a freezer and modern packages of cereals, condiments, soaps, and paper goods. Everything was in small portions, but the portions added up so that the shelves were stuffed to the ceiling.

The forty-ish, brown-haired proprietress shared an alcove by the entrance with baskets full of breads and rolls, all stacked neatly behind the bare, wooden counter. The first day she made sure to let me know, "Any kind of bread I will provide if you tell me day before, from the bakery fresh next morning." We took advantage of her offer and ordered raisin bread, which turned out to be delicious.

But her help was limited when it came to my objective today. "I would like to buy cinnamon."

"What is this? I do not know."

"A powder . . . used in baking . . . kind of brown . . . a spice." Each phrase brought a blank look.

"I ask my supplier, and he will know. Come tomorrow."

The next day, I picked up the raisin bread and asked, "Did you find the cinnamon?"

"No. I do not know that word, but my daughter speaks better English. If you come when she is here, perhaps . . ."

For the next two days, ants continued coming into our kitchen but only in dribs and drabs, no caravans now that the refrigerator was running and the poison was dispersed outside.

I finally stopped in the store when "the translator" was present. The storekeeper led me through a door behind the counter to a modest dining room with a view through the kitchen window to a canal. A teenage girl, whose long hair matched the shopkeeper's, sat at the dining-room table, which was strewn with books and papers. "This is my daughter, who knows very good English. You tell her what you wish."

"Hello. I would like to buy some cin-na-mon." I thought back to the French and Spanish courses I had taken in school. Perhaps we had learned to say *salt*, but *pepper* was doubtful, and *cinnamon* didn't have a chance.

"I do not know what is cin-na-mon."

I went through the explanation again—a spice, used in baking, blah, blah.

"I do not still know. Unless . . . maybe . . . could it be *kaneel?*"

"Is it *kaneel?*" the storekeeper asked.

"What's *kaneel?*"

The woman led me through the store, reached up on a shelf, and took down one of those rectangular spice tins, like the ones we have at home. *"Kaneel,"* she said. "Is this the thing you want?"

"Maybe."

She opened the container and tapped a little into my hand. I sniffed and tasted it. "Yes! Cinnamon."

The woman grinned and turned toward her daughter. "Very good. You get it right."

"You get an A in English," I said. The girl giggled and retreated.

I went home and sprinkled it around the kitchen floor, but Dutch ants turned out to be immune to the repulsive force of *kaneel*.

May 17

Hekendorp is a charming place for us. There's a little store open once in a while, selling really fresh bread and really dried-out cheese. There is also a café that serves pancakes and schnitzels, but their main occupation seems to be serving drinks to teens and young adults on their patio. They serve fries, ice cream, croquettes, too—the fast food of Holland. Very friendly—the café owner waves to us when we walk by.

There's a small, unpretentious church and a place that makes

*wrought-iron weather vanes and lamps. The post office, run by an
elderly couple, sells toys, shoe polish, and postcards. It also sells and
repairs shoes, and closes for two hours midday. On Wednesday
afternoons, forget about getting stamps, or pretty much anything else
in Holland. These Dutch know how to live.*

*Oh, yes, and there's a guy who sells computer software in town.
Interesting.*

From Keukenhof to Haarlem to the Edge of Gloom

"What's that sound?" asked Marguerite.

I turned the TV lower and looked out the front window.
"Looks like an apparition, but I think it's Mr. Nederend, shoveling
sand from the pile by our house."

"It must be 10 PM. For all he knows, we could be sleeping."

The sound stopped, and the phantom wheeled the load away.
"He's taking advantage of the long days. There's still a trace of
light."

"Well, I'll give him points for diligence."

"He and the other men are always moving stuff here and there.
But this may be the last of it. The piles of dirt and sand are getting
depleted."

In the morning, a pair of dump trucks arrived and deposited
new piles farther down the driveway. Mercifully, the pile near our
home wasn't replenished.

What was the dirt for? I left the question for another day.
This day we would visit the famous Keukenhof gardens an hour
from home.

*

We spent several hours in Keukenhof. We explored the forested
park, filled with brilliant swaths of tulips and lilies; a jetting fountain;
a windmill; and greenhouses full of fragrant blooms, which surprised
Marguerite. She had come for me, but her energy was up that day,

and the feelings and scents satisfied her.

In the park's gift shop, while picking out a pair of red-tulip earrings for her, I asked casually, "Do you have any energy left? I'd like to drive up to Haarlem."

"Didn't we go there on our first trip to Europe?"

"I remember it as a pretty town, and I'd like to check my memory."

"Is it important?"

"I don't know why, exactly, but I want to go."

🐾

The old part of Haarlem, with its walking streets and well-preserved main square, was as delightful as I had hoped. We bought whipped-cream pastries at a bakery and pale-orange tulips for our home. Back in the car, we devoured the goodies and cleaned our messy lips with moist towelettes.

I had confirmed my memories of Haarlem, but what had it accomplished? Holland was full of pretty towns.

That evening in bed, we listened to the BBC radio droning on and on. I knew the room shouldn't feel claustrophobic with its large windows on two sides, but the feeling came anyway. When the same world news repeated for a third time, I crept out of bed.

My furry, four-footed girl followed me to the living room and joined me on the couch. I opened the book I had bought in Zwolle, *Sophie's World*, the story of a high-school girl who receives anonymous messages explaining the history of philosophy. It gave me something to read when I was alone, and I hadn't thought about philosophical theories in ages.

I paused to absorb some of the concepts and found myself wondering why it had been so important for me to see Haarlem again. I set the book aside as the sadness that had been fluttering inside me rose to the surface.

For some reason, Lucerne, Switzerland, came to mind. We had visited Lucerne in 1970 and had gone back in 1981, so now it was sixteen years since that last visit. If we didn't go to Lucerne on this trip, I might never see the city again. Back in 1981, I had gotten up at dawn, climbed a hill over the center of old Lucerne, and taken pictures of the church steeples misted in a rising fog. It was a rediscovering. It would be such a shame never to return there.

I was lucky, though. I could certainly go to Lucerne this year—but that wasn't the point. If I had to go back to every place I'd ever visited, and if I stopped in new places along the way, the number of required destinations would rise exponentially.

Why did I have to go back? It seemed that somehow this had to do with dying. I wanted to be able to go back and back and back to these places to prove that I'd lost nothing in life, to know there would always be a Lucerne, that I would always be able to go there . . . forever.

Folly! At some point I wouldn't be able to, or Marguerite wouldn't. I thought of my friend Lester, referring to his ailments and saying his upcoming trip to Greece would likely be his last. I repeated aloud, "You can't ever go back, you can't ever go back, you can't . . ." Felicia looked up to see what I was rambling about.

How selfish I was, with this wonderful year ahead and all of its new experiences.

"What's life about for me?" I said out loud to Felicia and to no one. "It should be about loving, not about going places. Maybe it comes down to my fear of losing Marguerite some day, not having my companion to share the adventure." Effie pushed her cheek against my fingers, accepted my petting, and snoozed.

Back in the bedroom, I slipped into bed and wrapped an arm around Marguerite, but the sadness strangled me. Then my thoughts shifted. What if we really have past and future lives, or for that matter, the Christian life everlasting?

I'm not religious, but, if I had to choose, I would pick reincarnation as my best guess for an unknowable reality. If any of those religions are right, my experiences would go on and on. Wouldn't all this worrying and moping be pretty dumb then? Miraculously, my sorrow lifted.

As I drifted off to sleep, I thought, So maybe I have to have faith in an afterlife to keep from melancholy. But that's not faith, it's a coping device. Ah-ha! The origin of religion . . .

In the morning, I reported to Marguerite, "I think I've solved the problem of my sadness. I'm becoming a Buddhist."

Success on All Fronts

I took my first sip of coffee. "It looks like another warm, gorgeous day. I hope it doesn't get too hot to eat out on the patio."

"Do you spend time worrying about that?"

"Not worrying, exactly, just wanting everything perfect."

Ten minutes later, I noticed Mr. Nederend, a rosy grin dimpling his cheeks, lugging an umbrella over to our patio table. He slid the umbrella into the hole and bent down to secure it to its base. I opened the window to greet him. "Good morning."

"*Goede morgen.*" He turned his face up to the sky. "*Zon.*" He stretched his arms wide. "*Goed . . . varm.*"

"Yes. Good, warm," I confirmed. We nodded at each other for a minute, and I closed the window.

"Our landlord is a real crackerjack," I reported. "He's anticipated my problem and abolished my worries."

On this day we drove to Gouda, with a few errands in mind. First we stopped at the railroad station, hoping to find a tandem bicycle to rent. Past experience told us that tandems were scarce in Europe, but surely the bicycle-loving Dutch would accommodate us. They did—we reserved a cycle to pick up the next day for 96 guilders ($51) a week. Our next goal was e-mail.

The tall, balding man in his early forties walked between computer-topped desks as he approached us. His wary look said, I don't think you're here to make a purchase.

After handshakes, I told him, "We've come from the VVV."

"We're looking for a cybercafe," Marguerite added.

"We are a computer store, not a cybercafe."

"The tourist agent says there's only one Internet place in the whole country. That's in Amsterdam, and they may be out of business."

The man nodded. "Maybe there is one there in the city."

"But this is a modern country," Marguerite argued. "There should be dozens."

"In Holland, you see, we use computers in business, not so much for personal."

"It's important." Marguerite's voice pleaded. "I haven't had mail in weeks. My friends will wonder. . . ."

"We don't want to go to Amsterdam," I added. "We spent a month in Paris, and now we're avoiding cities. And the place there may have closed."

The fellow scrutinized us and then eased into a generous smile. "I have a way. . . . You are welcome to use a computer in the store one Thursday night when I am open late."

"We'd be happy to pay."

"No, no. It costs me nothing, and I will make it a gift."

"I can't tell you how *wonderful* that is." Marguerite swelled with gratitude and moved a little closer to the man. Would she try to hug the fellow, maybe plant a big kiss on his lips? He watched, too, a little nervously I thought, but she held back. "You're saving my sanity," she said.

Not only that, he was saving me from figuring out how to deal with Amsterdam. "Let's celebrate with some Merlot and one of those great mozzarella, basil, and tomato salads at the Rimini Restaurant," I suggested to Marguerite. "We can sit out on the square and bask in the sunshine."

"We're on a roll. Let's enter the lottery."

Having no understanding of Dutch lotteries, we settled for the former suggestion and then returned home to our kitty.

The next morning we managed to buy bus coupons at the

Hekendorp post office—the only non-English-speaking establishment in town (besides our landlord if you count him as an establishment). We walked across the drawbridge to wait on the main road for the bus to Gouda.

"Do I hear horses?" Marguerite asked.

"Not just horses, a procession of carriages is coming—five of them, each with a driver and an attendant, decked in top hats and tails. They're waving to us." We returned their greetings.

The cavalcade turned down a dirt road and entered a farmyard. The line of automobiles, which had been following it at a crawl, accelerated toward normal speed.

"I bet they're picking up a bride for her wedding," Marguerite said. "Why didn't we do that? Now we'll have to get married again."

"Gee, I thought the limousine was nice."

We rode the bus into Gouda and took possession of our tandem, a sturdily built, three-speed, touring bicycle (like the English bicycles I rode as a child) and a carrier that had two shopping bags for straddling the back wheel. We paid for the week and left a deposit of 100 guilders (just over $50) in cash.

The bicycle seemed not too different from our two-seater back home, but we were still a little wobbly as we navigated the back streets of Gouda. Traffic patterns *were* different. In Holland, bicycles had status. At intersections, they sometimes had their own signal lights and sometimes had first priority. Eventually, I got the knack, and we joined the stream of cyclists of all ages, including mothers peddling with their children in front, protected by wee, plastic windshields.

We followed the canal and on our way home entered the hamlet of Haastrecht. There we came upon the carriages from the morning, waiting by the old, brown, step-gabled *stadhuis* (city hall). A bride and groom emerged to a hail of rice, ran down the steps, and climbed into their carriage.

They knew how to celebrate weddings in the Netherlands. Throughout our stay we saw several horse-drawn wedding carriages and wedding parties, formed up for pictures by a castle, at a *stadhuis*, in front of a windmill. It was a happy tradition that always cheered us.

Back in our home town we decided to stop by the café to see what was going on with the locals. With all of the outdoor tables full, we went inside, sat at the bar, and ordered some wine. I watched a few teens shooting darts and listened to the din of indecipherable Dutch conversations in the crowded, narrow barroom.

A well-tanned man in his mid-twenties, with dark, short-cut hair and prominent eyebrows, came in and settled next to me on a stool. After a moment he held out his hand and said, "I'm Alex. I live here in the town."

I introduced him to myself and to Marguerite, and he ordered a beer.

Our new acquaintance gestured toward the door. "If you'd like, you can join my friends outside. We have a place on the patio."

I felt momentarily overwhelmed by his hospitality and then overjoyed by the prospect of holding a social conversation in English. We accepted, and Alex told the bartender to bring us each another glass of wine outside.

Alex's friends ranged from late teens to mid-twenties, mostly guys and a couple of their girlfriends. They lounged in a quasi circle of chairs that surrounded two plastic tables covered by beer bottles, glasses, and empty plates from snacks they had devoured. Two more chairs were pulled over, and the circle spread wider. Suddenly, we had English-speaking comrades. We had joined the in-crowd.

Most of their names soon evaporated, but I remembered Rick, a bear-like man with pork-chop sideburns that merged into a not-so-recently-shaven chin; Alex's brother, what was his name?; and his wife, Yvonne, who arrived a few minutes later and flashed her bright, pretty smile.

We asked our new friends what they did for a living. They were high-school or college students, a truck driver, and a couple of young professionals, including Alex.

Two elderly women walked by, and one of our comrades called out to them.

"What's he saying?" Marguerite asked.

"It's his mother and his aunt walking there," Alex said.

"But they're ignoring him," I pointed out. "They look angry."

"Because he hangs out here and drinks with us. His mother thinks he should be studying or looking for a wife."

So we were part of the younger set all of a sudden, or at least part of the co-alcoholic set. Local headline might read: "Americans in Hekendorp Encourage Sloth in Youths."

Walking home, Marguerite said, "I felt great meeting them, didn't you?"

"They were so happy we came from the States. I feel like a celebrity."

"I can't believe how open they were to us. You know what Rick told me?"

"I *did* observe you talking intimately," I said.

"Everyone thinks he's weird, or so he says. I told him he seemed pretty normal, but he said that he was big and ugly, that he acts a little crazed to cover his shyness."

"He wasn't shy with you."

"He felt comfortable with me because I couldn't see him," she laughed. "And he said he wouldn't act crazy with me because I have enough problems with being blind and don't need him freaking me out."

"Do you think he wants a date?"

"No, but I think you're feeling pretty sassy today."

"Why shouldn't I? My wife is in high spirits. We have a brand new bicycle, new friends. And I have my cat here in Europe by my side."

Oudewater, Holland—Witch-Testing Center of the Universe

May 20

We stopped at the computer store today where the kind proprietor had offered to let us pick up our e-mail. Since meeting him two days

*ago, he apparently had been calculating the possibilities. When we
entered the store and asked if it would be a good time to use the
computers, he told us, "I have been thinking about this cybercafe idea.
It might be a good business."*

*"Well, then, would you like us to pay?" He scratched his head and
said no. We sat down at one of the computers, and I managed to bring
up our messages. I began reading them to Marguerite.*

*Again, the man tossed out his idea, "So I might begin a cybercafe
here." And again, I asked how much we should pay. He responded, "I
said I would not charge you, so you should not pay, but if you decide to
come back for another time, perhaps. . . ."*

*Marguerite asked me to reread several of our e-mail messages,
and by the end of our session, she wore a giant smile. Afterward, we
stopped at a candy store and brought the computer man back a big box
of chocolates. Then he was the one wearing the great big smile.*

We rode our tandem down the one-lane road along the main
canal. After a few hundred yards the lane dipped down off the bank
to become level with the farms below. We passed farmhouses built of
dark-brown bricks, with bell-shaped fronts. Cows mooed while goats
nibbled lush grass beside picture-book barns. Sheep baahed. Geese
and swans paddled in channels between homesteads.

After twenty minutes we pedaled into Oudewater (old water)
and locked our bicycle by the central square.

"The town is full of step-gabled buildings." (We later learned
that stepped gables were the signature style of the seventeenth
century roofline—with different shapes for other centuries.)

Marguerite's look begged for explanation. I took her hands and
held them far apart with the palms facing each other. Then I stepped
them inward and upward like two sets of stairs approaching each
other. They met at the top, and she smiled. "I get it."

"Red, brick facades like that are all around, and there's not a
car to be seen in the square. But I see an ominous, black-bottomed
cloud scudding this way."

The sky erupted just as I spotted two tables under the green awning of a bakery in one of the old brick buildings. We hustled to one and took up residence. Water dribbled off the awning and splashed next to my foot. I huddled close to Marguerite and pulled my leg away from the wetness. A waitress appeared, wearing a white apron and a royal-blue skirt beneath.

"We would like coffee—very hot," I said. "And what pastries are your best?"

"The *apelflaps* are nice, and we have the *slagroom* pastries."

"*Slagroom.*" Marguerite licked a corner of her mouth. "Great! Got any with *slagroom* and chocolate?"

"Chocolate éclair."

"And what else?" I asked.

"We have puffs, like the éclairs, but with fruit in the *slagroom.*"

"What fruit?"

"I do not know the name. It's like a tube and yellow." She curved her hand in the air as her face grew pink beneath her short, blonde hair.

"Banana," I said. " I'll take one. And one of the chocolate."

"Let's share *one*," Marguerite said. "We've had lots of desserts lately."

"But they're both very good, aren't they?" I gave the waitress a hopeful look.

"Vunderful."

Marguerite waited until the waitress was out of earshot and said, "I can't keep eating all of these."

"Sure you can."

"My grandmother was a size 18, and I have her genes."

We shared the treats, which were great. I did my best, short of licking the dishes, to clean both of our plates. The waitress asked, "Have you seen the witches museum? It's right there." She pointed to the antique building next door.

I shook my head.

"Well, you must to go." So we did.

The bottom floor of the old, brick weigh house consisted of one large room with a pair of square, wooden platforms hanging by ropes from a balance beam. Along the wall, witches and demons were pictured with tales of their burnings, hangings, or drownings. Wrought-iron lamps cast light along the sides of the room. A display of swords fanned out on the rear wall above antique tapestries.

A gray-haired, pink-cheeked man in a jacket and tie approached. "You come to be weighed?"

"I don't know."

"Everyone wishes to stand on the scales—to show they are not a witch."

"How do you tell by weight if someone's a witch?" Marguerite asked. "I thought they threw the poor woman in the water with her hands and feet tied."

"Ah. Weighing was a better test. In the water, if a woman were not a witch she would sink and drown sometimes before she was saved. If she was a witch, she floated, and then they burned her to death. Too many innocent dead. So here we tested by the scales. If a body were very light, so the people of that time believed, it would be able to fly. If heavy, one was set free."

"I don't have to worry," Marguerite said.

"Pardon?"

"We just had pastries next door. I'm not going to levitate."

"Good," he said. "An excellent time to test."

"Why did all the accused witches come to Oudewater?" As I asked the question, I began leading Marguerite closer to the scales.

"If a man in Polsbroek was feuding with his neighbor, he might accuse the man's wife of witchery and pay a sum to the weighman. Next you know, the poor woman would weigh out very low and be burned at the stake. But not here in Oudewater. In 1545, King Charles V proclaimed our scales honest. People came after that from Germany, even Poland, to have our certificate. And these are the same scales—500 years old."

"Here, Marguerite. Step up. Careful to keep your balance." I helped her onto the wooden base as the platform swayed.

"Wait. I haven't decided . . . " But her feet were following my directions, and it was too late. Our host added metal weights to the other platform until the pointer rested straight up.

The deed was done, and the man scribbled something on a parchment. "I give your weight in Dutch pounds, better than English pounds. You get a little help because I divide the kilograms by two." He grinned and winked.

Now that my wife had withstood the test and been proved mortal, how could I be less courageous? I helped her off the contraption and stepped on. Soon, I, too, was exonerated for all time.

Outside in the crisp, poststorm air, we walked across the wet bricks toward our bicycle. "How much did I weigh?" she asked.

"They have lots of gimmicks going for them here," I said. "Certificates of nonwitchhood, pancake restaurants in the old weigh houses, witch ornaments for sale . . ."

"How much?"

"And how about these Dutch pounds? Do you think they're really any better than good old U.S. pounds?"

"How much?"

I answered her, but diplomacy dictates that the results not become public, even though Marguerite has always been a trim size 9/10.

"I can't weigh that much," she said. "And that's giving me a break?"

"I'm not sure. Let's think about this. There are 454 grams in a pound, I think. Let me see. . . ."

"That does it. From now on, no more desserts. . . . Maybe on the weekend."

It took me a few minutes to figure out that the weighman had cheated us with his division by two, but the damage had already been done. For several weeks, her resolve held. When I wanted desserts during the week, I had to eat them without an accomplice.

Days and Evenings of Bliss

May 23, 6:30 AM

I haven't been writing in this diary. I feel a little guilty, but why write when you're in a state of bliss?

It's not at all like Paris here. We don't feel compelled to visit notable sights every day. Instead, we bicycle to nearby towns. Bicycling in Holland is a joy. (There's not much coasting, but the lack of hills more than makes up for it.) So we stopped in Gouda and paid a second week's rent for the tandem.

We cook at home in the evenings, nothing impressive but good. Then we sit by our canal or walk leisurely by the farms. Marguerite's energy has improved; either that, or she's coasting on our bicycling trips, leaving the pedaling to me. At any rate, she's available to be my companion.

Felicia seems to have gotten friskier, too. She's been up on the kitchen counter a few times to nibble the tulips. And she's adopted new ways to wake me. She pats my face with her soft, little paw or pushes her forehead against my hand. A couple of times she licked my chin, just a few caresses of the tongue to gently wake me. If I don't pet her, she climbs on my chest and settles, purring close by my face. Marguerite, of course, is jealous of this extra attention, but I love it.

Maybe we're all feeling a bit younger here in our happiness.

Late one afternoon, I put Effie in the baby sling across my chest and struck off down the drive that ran beside our canal. It passed our landlord's place and turned into a dirt path. Thickets of trees appeared along the canal, with a couple of travel-trailers nestled among them. On the other side was a field of vegetable gardens. The word *polders* came to mind: land reclaimed from the marshes where people can farm. In the field, a man and a woman worked new topsoil with hoes. As I waved at them, I raised the cloth to cover Felicia. Maybe they'd think I was carrying a baby. They stayed at a distance, and I wondered if the word was out about the strange Americans with their California cat.

Ducks launched from shore into the canal and quacked their complaints at me, but my kitty was unfazed. I reached the end of the path and retraced my steps, covering Felicia's face again as a cat appeared and rubbed against my legs. Ducks were one thing, but our girl wouldn't tolerate competition.

Back home, I found Marguerite in the kitchen, filling a pot with water.

"I found out what our landlord's dirt is for. They use it in the polders."

I took the Indonesian leftovers from the refrigerator and the box of elbow macaroni from a cabinet. I struck a match, lit a burner, and slowly turned it down. All of a sudden, I was in the kitchen of our Connecticut home. Mom was teaching me how to lower the flame so it wouldn't burn the food—do it carefully, so it won't go out. She wore a flowered apron and was much taller than I was. In a few minutes, we would put the elbow macaroni into the pot and get ready to make a ham, cheese, and macaroni casserole with sliced eggs on top—my favorite.

Marguerite rattled around in the cabinets, extracted a cutting board, and began cutting the ends off string beans. "You're quiet. What are you thinking of?"

"I'll give you a hint: elbow macaroni."

"Ah. Your mom . . . I think of her, too. When I wash the dishes in the big, plastic tub in the sink, it's like being in her kitchen. Are you feeling sad?"

"No. This time it feels warm inside. I'm grateful for her lessons." We hugged until I had to go back and adjust the flame.

We ate at the table on our patio. Then I carried two chairs to the side of the canal. Marguerite washed the rest of our cherries, and I opened some wine.

With Effie back in her baby sling—this time on Marguerite's chest—we assumed our evening canalside positions. I admired, as I did every night, the weeping willow by our landlord's pretty, yellow and green house and the row of dwellings across the waterway, modest and well kept. Ducks paddled over to us one at a time. First came our faithful ones, the white and the mallard/white mix. We broke up bread and tossed the pieces into the water.

From down the canal I heard flapping and honking. Two more waves flew in—one of ducks and one of coots. They splashed down in the water and paddled close. We ate cherries and sipped white wine. I held out some bread and enticed a few ducks onto shore. They quacked and pecked by our feet until they made Marguerite (but not Felicia) nervous, and I had to shoo them away. They plopped back into the canal and swam off.

Above the retreating fowl, I saw a train, miles away, skimming across the horizon. A cow bellowed, and the faint rumbling sound of the train arrived a few seconds later. I moved my chair next to Marguerite's and wrapped my arm around her shoulder.

One of our neighbors strolled along the drive. He grinned, nodded at us, mustered his best English, and said, "Good, it is life."

That's the way it went those days in Holland.

Looking Back, Looking Ahead

It would be our last evening in Holland, and I had a mission to complete. It was 7 PM as I walked north along the narrow road from Hekendorp to Driebruggen looking for photo ops. I knew I would find some shots to take, because I had driven the road several times and been impressed by the pastoral beauty.

The ideal shot would be a row of bridges over the small canal that hugged the roadside, with cute houses, a weeping willow, and flowering bushes. As I walked, I found quaint houses but not two that I could frame together. Trees would obscure one of the houses, or the light wouldn't penetrate. One whole side of the road was off-limits because of the slant of the sun at that hour. The streams that I admired, leading off into farmland, were on the wrong side.

I would kneel or lean over a fence to optimize an angle or catch the play of light on the shimmering, crystal-silver water, with lustrous black shadows setting off the tree limbs bowing low, leaves fluttering in and out of the sunlight. An artist would have been able to capture it, but with a camera it wouldn't work. The sun being where it was made these scenes unique and beautiful . . . and unphotographable.

As I had whizzed by in the car those other days, I had seen the elements and put them together in my head. I had thought, All I have to do is go back and find those things—or at least three of them—in one place. But here I was, and the cow wasn't by the windmill—the sun was instead, preventing a shot; and there was a fence to keep me from moving to the other side of the cow or herding the beast into place.

That was van Gogh's advantage. With a brush and canvas, he could pull in all the things he saw, not just the ones that lined up neatly. And with his special brand of lunacy, his mind created pinwheels from the type of luminescence I saw before me, which he was able to put to canvas.

As I neared home, Mr. Nederend ambled toward me. "You here zsventy day."

I stared for a moment, taking in the fact that I had understood him. Had the man suddenly discovered English? "Yes, we have been here twenty days. We go tomorrow." I gestured vaguely toward the autoroute, miles away over the horizon.

"No." He pointed at me. "You stay." He indicated our house. "Utter people not come. You here nutter week."

I was dumbfounded. Where had this fluency been during the ant crisis? What were the terms of his proposal?

"Tomorrow, no guilders," he said. "That zsventy-one day. Then anutter week, yes guilders. Okay?"

"I'll tell you to-morr-ow." I pointed at the house and hoped he got the idea.

Inside, I found Marguerite and Felicia on the couch. "Our landlord is a ringer." I filled her in on the conversation, and we decided to take advantage of the free additional day. But we were excited about moving on to Brittany and didn't want to delay longer—even though the price had been right.

May 30

Our May calendar is filling with little notes on what we've done, and soon we'll be pushing off. This place feels enough like home that we'll miss it, but moving on to new things will be a joy—and happily we have ten more months to go!

The big debate of the morning is whether to wake Marguerite for the Today *show. We've only seen* Today *twice since we arrived, and this is our last opportunity. It could be ten months before we see Katie and Matt's cheery faces again. So far, though, writing on the computer is winning out.*

Somehow here in Hekendorp I have learned to turn off the sadness like a switch. All of the bicycling and Marguerite's good cheer have sustained me. The only thing that still bothers me is my lack of creativity. Now that things are going so well, it's easy to put off writing, until it comes up into my soul and gnaws at me from the back. (Now there's an interesting image.)

Maybe now that I'm more at peace, I can get on with writing and just enjoy this great adventure.

Good, it is life.

The Fine Art of Packing

Our house by the canal had been home for these three weeks, but we were abandoning it, extracting the remnants of our presence and setting them down in the gravel driveway. One or two at a time, I lugged suitcases, satchels, and assorted containers to the Peugeot.

I swung our humungous, green, Boston Celtics bag into the trunk, added the backpack with the computer, shoved them deep, and added the other big suitcase. There was still space for smaller things, of which there were plenty. I met Marguerite in the entryway as she set down a shopping bag of kitchen supplies. "Are you sure you want all of this bagged separately?" she asked.

"It's a new strategy. I fill the nooks between the luggage with all the little things."

"But this is so . . . sloppy." Her cheeks pouched in disapproval.

"Maybe . . . but no one will see it in the trunk, and it will be lots safer than having things exposed in the car."

I tugged and tweaked, repositioned, and crammed the last shopping bags in. Next I added the sack of cat litter, Felicia's traveling bag of wet and dry food, and our satchel with three days of clothing. I stood back to admire the chaos. The lid caught on the third slam.

Ambling into our little Dutch house, I called, "Good news, Felicia. You get the back seat to yourself."

"You're kidding," responded Marguerite. "It all fit?"

"I'm just one packing kind of a guy."

She hugged me. "Great job . . . but you worry too much about being robbed."

Marguerite was wrong. I had to make the car less attractive to burglars to protect my family, and it felt like a major accomplishment.

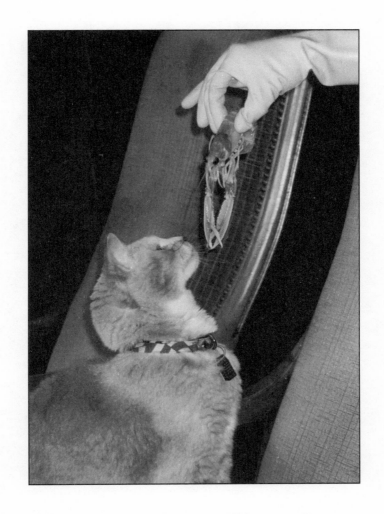

Brittany—Fish Brains and Bats in the Belfry

France—Home of the Gourmet

They say you can't find a bad meal in France. We knew from experience that mediocre meals do happen in the land of Dijon and crème brulée. The night we returned from Holland to the outskirts of Paris, though, we delved into the subdepths of French cuisine.

This evening found us at a very basic, motel-type room in Villiers-le-Bel, a place that fit our budget but did nothing to uplift our spirits.

By 6:30 P.M. Felicia was settled in and contentedly bribed with cat treats. It was early for dinner in France, but we were starving. We headed downstairs.

"The dining room is bright and fairly modern," I reported. "Pink cloth napkins are peaked on each table." I walked Marguerite past the salad bar. "There's your basic lettuce and veggie stuff, a couple of types of ham, mussels, even snails. Looks acceptable."

The hotel receptionist, a tall, long-haired redhead, seated us. In English interspersed with mystery syllables that I ignored, she said, "My husband is the chef, but he has another job in the day. He'll arrive soon, and you will be happy because he speaks very good English. If you want a salad, you may start."

Marguerite shot me a funny look, but I didn't get it. The receptionist departed, walking through the swinging doors into the kitchen. "Yes?" I said.

"If the chef isn't here, who prepared the salad bar?"

"I bet some great deli delivered it."

We should have thought long and hard about Marguerite's question. I have a failing—perhaps many failings—but one in particular pertained at that moment. Once I settle in a restaurant, I tend to stay. I don't want to embarrass myself or insult the staff. It takes quite a bit to get me to leave.

I began translating the menu, but Marguerite cut me short. "I think I'll go for the salads and escargot."

"I thought you . . ."

"You're right. This is France. These people know how to prepare food."

A mustached, plump, young man flung open the kitchen doors. Buttoning his white smock, he approached. "Good evening, Madame and Monsieur. I am Paul, the chef. I would like to tell you about our specials." He had spoken in French, but I got the drift. "Tonight we have . . . "

At this point, he lost me, so I said, "Your wife tells me you speak English."

"Ah, yes, the English. This food, I think it is called *blah, blah, blah.*"

"Let's try this—is it fish, chicken, or beef?"

It turned out that he had a fish special—maybe red snapper— and a sausage special.

"Is the sausage very good?"

"Ah, yes, *monsieur*. It is a special *andouille* sausage from the mountains. You will like it. And it comes with our marvelous salads." He swept a white-clad arm toward the salad bar.

I had heard something about those sausages. What was it? A regional specialty? "Yes, I'll have the *andouille.*"

At the salad bar, Marguerite and I followed our usual system. She held one plate and my arm. I asked what she wanted and scooped food as we traded dishes back and forth. I served us both a variety of salads, adding ham for myself, before we got to the seafood. "What would you like? We have mussels and snails—big snails and some really tiny guys. Actually, these may not be your garden variety. . . ." I bent closer and thought I got a whiff of the sea.

"Are they in some kind of sauce?"

"No, they're on ice, with mayonnaisey stuff and a red sauce on the side."

"You mean they're cold?"

"Good point. I'll just get a couple so we can try them."

Back at the table, I nibbled carrot salad and green beans and kept an eye on Marguerite's progress. "Hmmm. Nothing to write home about." I said. "Don't forget, your escargot are at the bottom right."

"Have you tried them?"

"I'm waiting for you. There's another customer over there—looks like a local—and he's *wolfing* them down."

"I'll eat a snail if you'll take the first shot at a mussel." Marguerite gripped a snail and stuck her fork inside. She twisted it out.

"Try some of this red stuff on it," I said.

I watched her dip it in the sauce and place the dangling morsel on her tongue. She chewed tentatively. Her nose wrinkled, and her chin seemed to grow longer. She put her napkin to her lips. The snail wasn't bound for her stomach.

"That was disgusting. Now it's your turn," she said.

Paul emerged from the kitchen, bearing a fat, purplish sausage on a white plate. He set it down. "It is beautiful, don't you think?"

"Very nice." Paul retreated to the kitchen, and I sliced into the meat. "Interesting . . . hard to cut. The skin is thick. There are chunks of . . . fatty stuff and little . . . macaroni-shaped pieces." I was afraid to name them. I paused to scrutinize, decided that wasn't a good idea, and plunged it into my mouth. Once I began chewing, there was no doubt in my mind. The sausage was made of genuine intestines and other gross parts of the beast, like the sausages of the good old days before they knew about meat grinders, before they decided to put actual meat into sausages. Maybe that was what I'd heard about *andouille*.

"What's it like?"

"To say 'chewy' is to call the Eiffel Tower a needle."

"And the macaroni shapes?"

I swallowed as much as I could before answering. "I'd say we're talking vessels and sinew, maybe part of a pig nostril." It was loathsome stuff, but I managed to choke down the rest of that first bite.

Paul dashed from the kitchen, carrying an identical sausage to the Frenchman. I tried to smile as he whisked past. Stealing glances at the other diner, I whispered, "Let's see what happens. . . . He's cutting a slice off the sausage. He doesn't seem surprised by the texture. . . . He must have a sharper knife."

"Sure," Marguerite said, "they give the reject-utensils to the tourists."

"He's raising the fork. It's entering. The eagle has landed. He's chewing . . . cutting off another piece . . . smiling. This is incredible. I think he likes it."

"Maybe you're being picky."

"Right. Have a taste."

She shook her head and grinned impishly.

I managed to choke down a couple more bites of the *andouille* and two mussels dipped in red sauce, which weren't too bad once I got past the fact that they were cold. I carved the sausage into pieces, pushed them around to make it look like I'd considered eating some, and then buried as much as I could under the mussel shells.

More salads were out of the question, the sausage having ended my desire for solid food. From the dessert bar I retrieved a bowl of Jell-O and two cups of chocolate mousse. "Well, at least this is good," Marguerite said, as she tested the mousse. We finished the desserts, and I got four more. It would be a long time until breakfast.

First Encounters with the Bretons

The next morning, I was coming out of the hotel to go to the car with our overnight bag when a frightening sight confronted me—a gap between the back seat and the window ledge. The seat had apparently unhooked the day before while I was packing in Holland and tilted forward a couple of inches, revealing the Celtics bag and computer case. My trunk-packing tour de force had not been a feat but a disaster, advertising to would-be thieves that our "goods" were ripe for the taking. I pulled everything out, reloaded, and returned to Marguerite.

"Felicia's not going to be alone in the back seat anymore. . . . The trunk was never big enough for everything." I explained what had happened.

She hugged me. "It made you happy for a day."

"Happy like a guy who wallpapered a room with the pattern upside down. We could have been robbed."

"It's all right."

"I was stupid."

"It's not just your responsibility. I could have checked."

"That doesn't make sense. You couldn't have seen it, so I needed to do it right."

❖

After a six-hour drive that afternoon, with our satchels heaped in the back seat, two much less confident Americans and a carefree cat turned off the highway and into the village of Bree, near the Normandy-Brittany border. A two-story home, faced in shingles and slate, displayed a *Chambre d'Hôte* (B&B) sign with a price equating to $35.

A ruddy-faced man sat in a folding chair by the garage.

"Do you have a room for tonight?" I asked in French "Two people and *une chatte.*"

The man's smile vanished, and he headed into the house. "I will get my wife."

Marguerite said, "Tell him she doesn't have any claws."

I called after him, *"Elle n'a pas de griffes."*

This was the first time we had experienced this phenomenon. It turns out in France that if a small hotel or B&B doesn't have a policy about cats, it is always the wife who decides. Is it because wives are better business people or because they clean the rooms perhaps? Or maybe Madame is *plus difficile* and Monsieur knows what it's like to get into trouble with her.

Madame returned. "You want a room?"

"Yes, for one night."

"But you have a cat?"

"Yes. She has no claws. . . ." I pretended to pull out the fingernails on my left hand, in case I had the wrong word for *claws*.

121

Marguerite was curling her fingers into paws beside her face to help Madame also. "She's a very good cat."

"La chatte est très bonne," I translated.

"Come along." Madame showed us two cozy, wood-paneled chambers on the top floor, and we chose one.

Back in the driveway I took Felicia from the car and turned to see Madame, her eyes lasering in on our kitty. She squinted, pointed to the claws on Felicia's hind foot, and shot a disgusted look, intended to pierce me to the heart. "What is this?"

I held Felicia's front paw out to her. "See—no claws," I said in French. Lacking the words at that moment, I added in English, "Cats scratch from the front." I made scratching movements with the paw.

Our kitty pierced me with a do-I-have-to-put-up-with-this? look.

"Madame," I said, "she is a wonderful cat. She cannot hurt your furniture. But, if you prefer, we can go across the street." I pointed to another *chambre d'hôte* across the road.

"Non. My husband will help you with the luggage."

Satisfaction swept over me. I had brought us to this place, negotiated a price, and defended my cat and my family—all in French. After settling in our room, we sipped wine on the patio beside Monsieur's rose garden and waited for the 7:30 PM opening of the nearby restaurant, where we would face our next culinary encounter.

A middle-aged woman in a navy cardigan, her black hair streaked with gray, showed us to a table. She set down our menus and observed as I pulled back a chair and put Marguerite's hand on the edge of the table at her place.

Marguerite sat and folded her cane. "Going for the sausage tonight?"

"I'll ignore that remark. . . . Let me tell you about this room.

The curtains are velvet with embroidered edges, once very red, now faded. On the walls are old-time pictures of mansions and of Mont-Saint-Michel. The chairs are antique and have a spindle-spooled design."

The waitress returned, and we ordered rosé wine, one salad, and two *plats du jour*—beef burgundy. All of this would cost about $30, which, when added to the cost of our picnic lunch this afternoon, would fit well within our budget. But would it be palatable?

The woman set down a carafe of wine, still watching Marguerite. As she placed the salad before me, she looked into my eyes. There was some sort of question there. What was it? Was she deranged or merely curious?

Marguerite and I shared the salad and sipped wine. Twice I caught the woman watching from the edge of the next dining room and then slipping away. It reminded me of my crazy Aunt M., who used to serve us food in her messy kitchen and then sit in the corner and cackle while we ate. I kept an eye out for the woman but said nothing to Marguerite.

After setting down the plates of beef, our waitress lurked as I described the beef and vegetables on the plate to Marguerite. The meat was succulent, the sauce rich with garlic and herbs.

Soon the woman returned. "Monsieur, the food is all right?"

"It's delicious."

"And Madame enjoys it?"

I translated, and Marguerite conveyed appreciation.

"Pardon me, *monsieur*, but would you tell your wife for me . . . ? My son is blind from an accident."

"I'm sorry."

The woman nodded and took a deep breath. "It has been very difficult for our family. But I have watched how you help Madame and how she seems to enjoy dinner." I continued to translate for Marguerite.

"Of course," Marguerite answered. "The meal is wonderful."

"But food, it is about life, is it not? I think, perhaps, you enjoy living."

"Yes. I'm very lucky. It's not always easy. . . ."

"How long ago was the accident?" I asked.

"Six months."

"That's very recent. Marguerite has an eye disease. She lost vision slowly, over a long time, and it's taken years to adjust. Now she helps other people in the United States, people who are losing their sight."

She spoke directly to Marguerite. "You give me hope, Madame."

Marguerite reached out a hand, and the woman clasped it. "Eddie, tell her to be patient. Tell her it's very painful for the whole family."

"God bless you," said the woman, and hurried off to the kitchen.

After dinner, I left Marguerite with Effie in our room and hiked up a hill in the early dusk. I crossed railroad tracks and walked by farms that sold honey and vegetables. At the top of the rise, I turned and saw the silhouette of Mont-Saint-Michel in the distance, as salmon-colored clouds feathered the sky above. I turned again and spotted a pair of cows, with dark chocolate splotches around their eyes. They observed from just beyond a barbed-wire fence. "I'm awfully lucky to be here with this sight before me," I said.

At Night We Hear the *Puisse*

We searched for a new home for three days, along the northern and then southern coasts of Brittany, rejecting several good prospects and hanging tough for a location by the sea and a duration of a month. Brittany might be the only place on the trip we'd be able to hear the surf. Finally, with the help of two bed-and-breakfast proprietors and the local tourist agent, we found it.

As we began the task of moving into our new home, I locked the furry girl in the corner bedroom with her litter and food. Marguerite and I divvied up closet space in the three bedrooms, and I set her suitcase on the bed near her closet. The next time I came through, she was unpacking and "organizing." Back to the car and into the house, I rounded the bend in the hall and almost smashed into her. "Yow!" She jumped at my exclamation. "I almost killed you—I thought you were working in the bedroom."

"I'm trying to figure this place out. Where'd you say the kitchen is?"

I led her there and showed her the cabinets, coffee maker, sink, and drawers.

From then on I kept my eye on Marguerite's whereabouts as I retrieved loads from the car. She felt her way around the kitchen, opening cabinets, touching their contents, calling out to me, "We have lots of cooking utensils. . . . Oh, good, a big soup pot. . . . There aren't any ice-cube trays in the freezer." She slipped back along the hall to the bedrooms and then out again. Next she crossed the living room, bending low, feeling for obstacles. I brought her over to one of the chairs, helped her touch the coffee table; the glassed-in fireplace; the sliding, glass doors to the patio that overlooked the Atlantic.

"Why don't you use your cane?"

"I left it somewhere."

"You know, you're just like Felicia."

She looked at me expectantly.

"You both poke in all the corners and crawl into the cabinets if they're open."

"I don't *crawl into cabinets.*" Her eyes narrowed, somewhere between wariness and hurt feelings. "I felt for the dishes, that's all."

"Then you went back to the bedroom to get your bearings and then out again. That's what Effie did at the last *chambre d'hôte.* Of course, she's lower to the ground."

"I'm *not* a cat. I'm a blind person, and I *have* to feel my way."

I hugged her. "I was teasing. That's okay, isn't it?"

She pressed her face into my chest and seemed to be crying. No, she was giggling. "She *is* my daughter. Of course, we're alike."

June 8

This is our second morning in our house by the sea in a settlement known as Kermeruzac'h, which is part of the town of Moëlan. Yesterday, we took Felicia in her baby carrier across the back lawn to a private nook at the end of the property. Three seats filled the spot, surrounded by heathery bushes at the clifftop. We sat on this perch and watched fishing boats come and go from the harbor of Brigneau just across the way, past the jetty with its miniature light tower. We sipped wine and ate slices from the six-inch round of cheese we'd bought at a farm in Holland. Marguerite asked if we'd had a car accident, died, and gone to heaven.

At night we hear the puisse—*that's what our landlady, Madame Jegouzo, calls it—the sounds of the surf beating on rocks, the wind whooshing through trees, the moan of a buoy at sea, a fog horn. We can hear this even though we keep the windows closed for Felicia. If they had window screens, we could let the sounds embrace us.*

It's early morning now. I look out to our driveway and see tall pines swaying to the rhythm of the winds—faster, slower, stronger— like the hand of an orchestra conductor. Little oaks bob, their individual leaves performing Lilliputian jigs. Down toward the sea, other pines are present. Some are broken off on top, by what force I'm not sure. Across the inlet, I gaze out at a beautiful, simple house— white with a black, slate roof and purple shutters . . . the roofless, broken-walled hulk of an old factory building . . . white surf bursting on black-brown rocks the color of the moules *(mussels) they take from the sea. Of course, the whole of this scene is more than the sum of its elements, because it's a feeling and a picture woven together. This is something Marguerite "sees" better than many sighted people. I'm not sure how, but she does.*

The Great Supermarket Expedition

I felt jittery as I pulled the Peugeot into the parking lot of the Intermarché in Moëlan. "She'll be okay, won't she?" I asked Marguerite.

"Sure." Marguerite's answer didn't sound as positive as I had hoped.

Felicia didn't seem a bit nervous. Reclining in the back seat, she calmly licked a champagne-colored paw. The three of us were about to attempt something in rural France that we would not even consider back in California. If Felicia messed up, it would become one of those big-time, ugly American incidents.

Then again, this was a matter of pride—pride and justice.

I spoke the words that had sparked this nation to revolution, *"Liberté, Egalité, Fraternité!"*

Marguerite added, "And equal rights for cats." Felicia stopped licking and looked up at Marguerite quizzically.

Two days earlier, Marguerite and I had visited this supermarket. I had reported what was going on around us while French shoppers glanced askance at Marguerite and her white cane. "Down this aisle, two women are shopping with dogs in their carts. . . . Wait, the women are greeting each other. . . . They're chatting, and their dogs—a white poodle in a red-knit jacket and a long-haired, brown, little guy—are sniffing the air in each other's directions, but staying put." The other French shoppers continued their covert observations of Marguerite, but they barely seemed to notice the pooches.

"Felicia could do that," Marguerite had said.

And so here we were on this most important of missions, to demonstrate the goodwill of American felines and to test the mood of the French. I gathered Felicia from the back seat and set her in Marguerite's lap. "Today you become an ambassador."

"A cat crusader," said Marguerite.

A light rain had misted my glasses by the time we got Felicia into her soft bed, perched in the baby-carrying area of the shopping cart. I clipped on her leash. Marguerite snapped the front of her denim jacket and hung onto my arm as I pushed the cart into the store.

The first indication of the French temperament came from a lanky teenager by the meat counter. He spotted Felicia and grinned.

"*Bonjour,*" I said.

"*J'aime bien les chats* (I like cats)." The boy saluted Felicia.

We rolled our way past trays of seafood on ice. The woman behind the counter waved a red snapper in our direction. Felicia turned this way and that, tested the air, and looked more curious than nervous. She stayed in place. "The perfect lady," I commented. "Good as any *d-o-g.*"

"You fret too much about offending the locals."

We entered the cat-food aisle. I picked out a box of Whiskas, handed it to Marguerite to hold, and then backed away to snap a picture as Marguerite bent close to Felicia. "See, honey," she explained to our kitty, "this is where cat food comes from."

I tossed a couple more boxes into the cart and wheeled toward the exit. By the checkout counter, a toddler in a shopping cart wiggled a finger toward Felicia and cooed. The clerk spoke to the child and then to Felicia in baby talk.

In the parking lot, we encountered a white-haired man with craggy Breton features and a black beret. He approached and reached toward Felicia. I nodded, and he patted her head.

Through French and pantomime, we spoke.

MONSIEUR: "Ah, but she is a pretty cat—very soft. A boy or a girl?"
PROUD CAT PARENT (PCP): "A lady."
MONSIEUR: "Yes, I see. And she comes from where?"
PCP: "California."
MONSIEUR: "And she is all right in the airplane?"
PCP: "Perfect. She slept all the way."

Felicia rubbed her cheek against Monsieur's fingers.

MONSIEUR: "What a grand cat."
PCP, BURSTING WITH PRIDE: "*Merci bien, monsieur.*"

We returned to the Peugeot, knowing that on this day Felicia had taken one giant step for catkind.

Progress, Success, and Lack Thereof

June 9

As the tide comes in, I mark its progress by the foam drifting upstream and the rising boats. As it goes out, I watch the seaweed floating past the dock and the boats settling back onto their stilts.

We mark our day's successes by whether we have found unique sites to explore, like the fortified city of Concarneau and the artists' enclave in Pont-Aven, whether we have dined on delicious seafood, whether we have accomplished household chores.

A few notes—

1. I calculated our expenses for May in Holland, and I'm encouraged. We spent about $93 per day on rent and living expenses for two adults and one frugal cat, including miscellaneous items, like the circus in Gouda, though not transportation. We stayed in unique and memorable places, ate great food, and were well entertained.

2. My goal is to stay under $100. In Paris we spent almost $59 a day on living expenses alone, plus our rent of $63 per night, which is remarkably low for Paris. But it made me worry about meeting my goal.

3. On the communications front, we have begun our quest for a cybercafe.

4. Marguerite is having trouble sleeping again.

5. Laundry is becoming an irritation.

In the morning, I hauled two pillowcases of dirty clothes to the cellar, popped them into the machine, added soap and softener, read the French directions as best I could, and messed with the dial until I heard gushing water.

Marguerite made coffee, and I drove to a bakery for croissants. We ate them with peach *confitures*.

After breakfast, Marguerite said, "I'll check the laundry."

"That doesn't make sense. You'd have to feel your way down those narrow steps along the dirty wall. You wouldn't be able to see the dial on the machine."

"I want to help."

I checked the laundry, which had made little progress. I came back upstairs to vacuum the bedrooms and hallway, while Marguerite cleaned the dishes. Later I found her lying on the bed in a fetal position, a pile of clothing by her feet. "Anything wrong?"

"I'm tired of being weary and mopey. I cleaned the cat litter so you wouldn't have to. Then I came here to sort my tops but ran out of energy."

"How did you . . ."

"I wrapped my fingers in toilet paper and felt for lumps."

"I could have done it."

"You'll want to get rid of me if I don't do my share."

"Save your energy for exploring."

"I'll still go out with you. I'll *make* myself. . . . Eddie . . . let me know if you're getting tired of so many chores, and I'll find a way to do more."

I bagged trash and checked the wash again, but the dial on the machine had barely budged. "What do you think about cooking up a creation tonight? I'll check through the 10,000 recipes CD on the computer, and . . . "

"Sounds complicated. Let's make dinner with that jar of Uncle Ben's curry sauce we bought. On the way home, we can pick up some turkey meat. . . . "

"*Dinde,*" I said.

"*Dinde?*"

"Yes, that's what our landlords, the Jegouzos, called it. They raise *dindons* on their farm an hour from here. You know, the big, ugly things with feathers that gobble, gobble around. They call the meat *dinde.*"

"Okay. We'll stick some *dinde* in a casserole with potatoes, toss on the curry sauce, and bake it for dinner. That way we'll have time for more important shopping—my pills from Dr. Wong run out tomorrow. We need to find remedies."

What would happen without the Chinese herbs? She needed to be sensible. . . .

She read my mind. "No hormones. I'll find natural things that are better than this crummy Chinese stuff."

I gathered paper and pencil and the book we'd brought with us from California, Susan Weed's *Menopausal Years, The Wise Woman Way*. "Let's try the chapter 'Herbal Allies for Women in the Midst of Menopause.' How about Black Cohosh or Vitex Agnus-Castii? Do you like the sound of those?"

"Yuck. Forget stuff we've never heard of before."

I recorded garden sage, ginseng, and Dang Gui on my paper— okay, we hadn't heard of Dang Gui, but the book called it the "finest woman's tonic in the world."

"Now I'll look up *fatigue*. Gee, there's lots of stuff in here . . . ginseng again and vitamin E. Those sound normal. Oh, and you should eat carrots and low-fat cheese. How about for headaches? Lavender sounds pleasant."

"Do I eat it or sniff it?"

I scribbled *lavender*, stuffed the list in my pocket, and retrieved our laundry. We hung it on the clotheslines in the front yard and then jumped into the Peugeot. "You wanted to look for e-mail, right? Let's try Quimper. It's the largest city in the area."

We drove an hour west to the city. At the tourist office we learned everything about the famous Quimper faience—dinnerware with rustic figures painted on—but no information about cyber-anything. It took us two more hours to track down a cybercafe. The café part of it was still there, but the cyber part had succumbed to minuscule profits and computer malfunctions.

"We spent half the day doing wash and half looking for something that isn't here." Marguerite brooded as we walked toward the car.

I wanted to cheer her up, but, naturally, I said the wrong thing. "The day won't be a complete failure. We'll buy some potions to help you calm down."

"I want my e-mail. Is that unreasonable?"

"We'll find it."

"I want it *now*."

"As soon as we can . . ."

We stopped in a supermarket and bought a great-looking salmon steak, lavender bubble bath, lavender air freshener, and megadoses of vitamin E and ginseng.

By the time we arrived home, a storm had come and gone. We knew because the laundry was soaked. We unpinned it, wrung it out, and rehung it on clotheslines in the musty cellar.

A Minority View of Effie

June 10, 6:00 AM

She is a joy and a delight and a demanding girl. She is as sweet as can be as she rubs against me or cuddles up into my armpit at night. She is everything a cat—or any creature—should or would aspire to be. She is Felicia.

I am sleep-deprived this morning. Felicia lies curled on an armchair ten feet away. She wants to be near me—no, not just in case I should open a can of cat food. She wants love, and she's willing to nag and withhold affection to get it. Right now she's withholding because I'm paying too much attention to the computer.

Well before dawn this morning, a furry cheek rubbed my hand. I woke but didn't stir—to stroke her face would encourage bad behavior. Her forehead butted my shoulder, but I held still. She licked my fingers and then my chin. I couldn't avoid grinning, but still I refused to pet her. She meowed softly . . . then a little louder . . . so I pulled her against my chest and held her to keep her from waking Marguerite. Just as I was drifting back to sleep, my furry companion leapt to the floor and began yelping.

What had gotten into our perfect cat? I wanted to yell at her, but that would catapult Marguerite wide awake. She needed sleep so badly after all the night sweats she'd been having.

I trudged into the kitchen and filled the coffee maker as Felicia mewed and rubbed against my legs. "No, I'm not giving you canned food. It will encourage this offensive conduct." I lifted her and turned her face to mine. "You're being a *bad cat*. Your mother can't sleep as it is because of the menopause. If you keep waking her, she'll be even more exhausted, and . . ." And what? And Marguerite would become miserable . . . and we'd have to give up and go home?

Her soft features melted my heart. I wanted to give her all the cat food in the world, but instead I took a blanket and settled in an armchair with her on my lap. She purred, and I petted her. After a while I bundled her up, carried her to the table, and put her back on my lap. I fired up the computer.

Effie jumped off with a little cry and stalked away. She settled in a ball on the rug by the fireplace, her back to me.

I wrote until light entered the sky, and I figured she'd been good for a half-hour. Sneaking into the kitchen, I forked canned food into a bowl. "Felicia . . ." I called to her. She didn't look at me from her spot by the fireplace. "Felicia, don't be mad." I approached, and she jumped when I touched her. "Effie, I have a treat for you."

I brought coffee to Marguerite in the bedroom. As she sipped, I said, "Don't be mad at Felicia."

"Why not? She's been terrible."

"I think our baby is going deaf."

Marguerite's face crumpled with concern.

A Boy and a Grieving Man

June 11, 8:40 PM

I am a boy. I am a young man. I am a grieving man, approaching old age and/or senility at an alarming pace.

Marguerite and I followed the dirt trail along the side of the bay, with forest above and fishing boats standing on cradles in the harbor below. It was low tide, and the cadavers of shipwrecks sat on mud flats. We reached the hamlet of Brigneau, where we bought a fish at the stand on the boat dock and half a loaf of bread at the restaurant. By the time we got home Marguerite was exhausted and went for a nap. Her interest in life seemed to be ebbing. Of course, she didn't have to do things, but I missed her being with me.

I headed out on a second walk. This time I followed a twisting track amid golden gorse, pink-purple thistles, and honeysuckle and berry vines—all manner of wild flowers, hugging close to the ground. To one side, rock cliffs dropped straight down to the sea. Clouds scudded overhead, a reminder of a morning storm that had left the ocean perturbed. Like water in a jar that had been shaken, the sea was rippling its way back to normal. It seemed to wash away the tension at my core in some primeval way and allowed me to drift back to thoughts of childhood.

I spotted a seventeenth-century fortress—very small, with a cavelike interior. Had I been a little boy, which was what I felt like after seeing the shipwrecks, the fortress would have been huge and menacing. But my six-foot-two frame rebelled at the tight quarters.

Back outside, the sun flashed on the ocean and cast it in brilliant shades of blue and green. I called out to the ghost of the artist Matisse, *"The colors! Isn't it grand?"* My words were ripped off my lips by the wind, swallowed by the roar of surf.

Breakers pounded, jagged rocks reached far into the sea. I clambered down the rocks and watched crabs scurrying in a tide pool. . . . Suddenly, my thoughts flashed to a family vacation we'd taken when I was young. I hollered to my long-dead father, *"Dad, look! It's like Bar Harbor."* He didn't answer. Emptiness overtook me. I crouched and let the feelings come. I wanted him there, wanted him to respond. I repeated over and over, finally sobbing the words, *"Will I ever find you again?"*

My mother had been on that vacation with us all those years ago. Why did I miss Dad so much more? Maybe because I was able to be good to her and know her as an adult. Damn it, he had died so young . . . just a few years older than I was now.

I watched as the sun slipped out from behind a cloud. Mounds of shimmering waves flashed from gray to green as they rode the wind into the sunlight. In the distance, white vacation houses sparkled atop a pine-studded headland. The effervescent sea, alive and moving, spoke to me.

June 12

I feel the deep churning of the ocean. I stop and sit to admire and savor it. My father is here in some elusive way. I talk to him. I thank him—for his patience with me, for his kindness, for the joy of nature he felt and passed on. Above all, I miss him—I miss his presence these twenty-nine years since his death.

Lobstrosities and Phantoms of the Past

Off on another lone exploration, I parked the Peugeot near the harbor of Bélon and followed a trail by the bay. Signs in French and Breton (the ancient language imported from the British Isles) told me I was going in the direction of an *allée couverte* (covered alley). The trail took me past little bays and more shipwrecks, then inland to the middle of a farmer's field. There it stood—a long, double row of standing, gray boulders, capped by flat slabs to form the covered alley. This megalith, set here at some unknown time in antiquity for some unremembered purpose, now had a tree growing, bushy and tall, straight from its heart. I sat atop a weathered stone nearby, ran my fingers over the lichens, and pondered.

I strolled back along the trail and visited a sixteenth-century chapel. Its crude Christ on the cross—made from the same rock as the megalith—had lost all of its features to water, wind, and time, yet it expressed a deep humanity. I felt kinship for the builders of all of these crumbling monuments, their connection to the earth, the sea, their gods. I thanked them for the wonder they had bestowed through their craft.

Back in the town of Bélon I headed straight for the fish market, a roof suspended on four timbers with tables below. Examining plastic tubs of silver-bellied mackerel and buggy-eyed red fish, I came to the little, brown crustaceans I was hoping for—langoustines (kind of a cross between shrimp and lobsters)—resting quietly on a mound of ice, occasionally twitching a feeler or a claw.

A thickset woman pulled gloves from the pocket of her white apron and stepped opposite me behind the table.

"Bonjour. I would like some of these," I told her in French, pointing.

She raised an eyebrow.

"Half a kilo?" I ventured.

"How many langoustines?"

"Ten, maybe? Enough for two people and a little for our cat."

For a moment I wondered if she had understood my French. Then the hint of a smile slipped by her lips. She put her lips back in order. Her gloved hand flopped four little lobsters onto a paper, then four more. She tossed it on the scale. "It is 120 grams," she said.

"Is that enough?"

She gave me a look that said, If you restrain your cat. . . .

"Twenty francs ($3.50), *monsieur.*"

I carried the plastic sack of squirming crustaceans to the car and set them carefully on the floor behind my seat. As I drove away, I spoke to my father. "I think we can have some fun with these, don't you?" I'm sure he would have agreed.

I wheeled between the pine trees along the white stone drive and pulled up short next to the blue-and-lavender hydrangeas by the front of the house. With sack in hand, I burst through the door. "Marguerite, Felicia, you're going to like this!" My curious females approached. "Here, Marguerite, put your hand in this bag."

She reached toward me, and I guided the sack closer. "Be gentle," I said.

Her hand froze.

"I don't think they're feeling well," I added.

Her hand recoiled like a screen door on a spring. "What's in there?"

"Here's a hint: they have tiny claws, and they're related to Stephen King's 'lobstrosities'."

"You want me to stick my fingers into a den of lobsters?"

"They're small, and they're not moving. . . . They *may* even be dead by now."

"*Eddie!*"

I explained how very small the little guys' claws were, and she took a tentative sniff near the bag—no foul odor, just a saltwater scent. Soon I convinced her to put on a rubber glove (actually, that was her condition for touching them) and pose with the langoustines and Felicia for some photos.

We cooked the lobstrosities and some rice, and chomped them down with butter, herbs, and white wine. After feeding a few morsels to our kitty, we took the last of our wine to the living room.

I opened the glass doors of the fireplace, crumpled in some newspaper, and added kindling.

"Have a nice hike?"

"A great hike, but . . ."

"Still feeling sad over your father?"

"More than that. . . ." I stuffed a split log on top of the pile and lit the paper. "It gnaws at me every time I go near the water. But I have to go there; that's the essential part of this lovely place."

"Must be something you have to go through now."

"But he died twenty-nine years ago."

"We were about to get married then. We were deciding where to live and looking for teaching jobs. You had lots going on."

"And I was a rotten twenty-one-year-old. . . . "

"No, Eddie. When people are so busy, they don't give themselves time to grieve." She wrapped her arms around me from behind.

"When Martin Luther King Jr. was killed, I felt awful. When Bobby Kennedy was assassinated, it hurt, too. But when my dad died, I just let it pass by." I felt tears running down my cheeks and watched the fire flare bright-orange through blurred vision and the smoke-stained glass of the fireplace. "And another thing . . ."

She came around to face me, and she was crying, too.

"I've been thinking about how he always wanted me to study and work hard for things." I grabbed a tissue from the coffee table and blew. "I know it's silly, but I've been wondering how he would like me taking this year off to goof around. I've tried to ask him. He seems to communicate about the tides and the shipwrecks, but he won't take a position on this one key point."

American Improvements

June 14, 5:30 AM

Light is creeping back into the sky, and the trees' silhouettes appear against dim gray clouds. The trees have taken the path of least resistance over the years: they bend away from the sea and its harsh winds.

Earlier, as we lay in bed, gentling sounds came to me—rain beating on the roof and windows; the soft, insistent rhythm of the sea; and the moaning of a buoy, warning fishermen away from the shoals.

The weather in Brittany so far is gorgeous—and not. Most days, there is at least one shower, but by about 9:00 or 9:30 each evening, the sun comes out, no matter what the day has been like. (Yes, it's light that late here.) That gives us an hour to savor. It's time that could be well spent reading, but it would be obscene not to sit and take it in. I light a fire, leash Felicia, and set her on one of our laps. We open the double doors, listen to the surf and wind, savor the sunset, and let peace come over us.

P.S. Despite all of this tranquility, the laundry still won't dry. . . .

Several times we hung our clothes outside, but this required constant attention and feverish activity when the rain came. We tried hanging things on the clotheslines in the dank cellar, where mold threatened to grow in minutes. Now, shirts and pants hung from the windowsills and the overhead lamp in the living room. Underwear and socks were draped over a chair near the fire.

"It's hard to enjoy the view, looking through undershirts,"
I said.

"Close your eyes and listen to the crackling, like I do."

☙

We began our search for a Laundromat that Thursday in Pont-Aven, a quaint town, full of art galleries, set in a gorge by a gushing stream. I asked at the tourist office where we might find a cybercafe and a Laundromat. The young (and very pretty) woman had no resources for either query.

Back in the car, Marguerite shot me a knowing look. "If the French don't have Laundromats, they must have dryers at home."

"When I asked Madame Jegouzo, she said they use the sun and the wind."

"There's plenty of wind—it comes up in the middle of the rain storms."

"Using clotheslines conserves energy. Europeans are good at that. Their cars get forty miles to the gallon."

"I want dry clothes like I have in America."

"The French are smarter than we are. We send billions of dollars out of the U.S. every week for foreign oil because we waste so much. And there's global warming. . . ."

"You think they're conserving energy? The washing machine runs for three hours." She had me there.

June 15
Marguerite is developing an "AI" list. The letters stand for "American Improvements." First on the list is a clothes dryer in every tourist apartment. She's also unhappy about the square, deflated pillows that want to ooze out of their cases. Then there's the fact that lunch is served only from 12:00 PM to 2:30 PM and dinner from 7:00 PM on—and other businesses close when the restaurants are open. At

first this seemed like a civilizing influence, but sometimes you really want a meal at 4 PM or a drugstore at 1 PM.

Marguerite suspects—and I'm starting to agree with her—that maybe, just maybe, the French possess secret dryers they're keeping for themselves. She poses questions like, "How else does Madame Jegouzo have all those sheets for us?"

Are we getting paranoid?

Among Marguerite's other issues: plastic storage bags with adhesive closures instead of compression seals—they stick together before you get a chance to fill them. And screens for windows—do Americans hold the patent?

P.S. I have found a way to keep the bedroom windows open at night so I can hear the surf. I stick a towel between the ledge and the window and then wedge a chair up against it. That leaves space for air and sound to enter, but our kitty can't escape.

Marguerite's AIs (American Improvements):
   Clothes dryer in every tourist apartment
   Screens for windows
   Normal pillows
   Firm mattresses
   Plastic bags with compression seals
   Stores and restaurants open all the time

Ed's FIs (French Improvements):
   Conserving energy (a foreign concept)
   Closing stores at lunchtime (a civilizing and relaxing influence)
   Including the tax in the price, so that the price on the tag is really
      what you pay (though the tax is a whopper)
   The most delicious tomatoes and onions
   Meals (and life) at a leisurely pace

When My Cat's Not Happy, I'm Blue

June 15, continued

When everything's going well, I still find things to worry about. Right now, it's Felicia's hearing. She doesn't respond to our voices at all. Now that I've noticed, I think it should have been obvious. If she's deaf, she's missing a big part of our love. Does she not understand what's happening? Does she think we've stopped talking to her, that we don't love her as much? Marguerite and I vow to touch her more.

All this worrying could be a sign of mental instability. Are we codependent-with-cat? . . . That could be the title for the book I'm writing about our trip.

"Before we go looking for our e-mail, there's something I'd like to discuss." I carried Felicia's soft bed into the room where Marguerite was dressing. "We have way too many things to lug around. Let's ship some home before we head toward Austria."

"Any suggestions?" She sounded wary, indicating an appropriate time for diplomacy.

"For one thing, Felicia packed too much." I let Effie's bed touch Marguerite's hand.

She felt it, grabbed it, clutched it to her chest. "You never wanted to bring this in the first place! She loves her little den. You wouldn't send it away?" I thought back to that last day in California when I had told her we couldn't fit Effie's sleeper in the luggage, and she had broken into tears.

"It's just that she has a bed *and* a baby carrier, and we've been getting a lot more use out of the carrier. She can sleep anywhere— and usually does."

"She doesn't have that much. She used it yesterday, remember? Or the day before. . . . You have lots more stuff than she does."

"All right, Felicia's off the hook. There must be things *you* don't need. How about sending home one of your *two* boar's-hair brushes?"

"I told you, I need them both. I use one to fluff and the other to curl. I'll think about things to send home if *you* will."

It took a while, but I finally accepted part of the finger of guilt. There were things I hadn't used yet, but it was hard letting them go. Eventually, we put together a box for shipment—our Holland guide book, a couple of Marguerite's blouses, one of my jackets, lots of books-on-cassette tapes that had been listened to—but no hair brushes and no kitty bed.

Cyberspace, Here We Are

We stopped to see Madame Audren at the tourist office in Moëlan. Within five minutes she directed me to a Laundromat in the nearby town of Quimperlé. Next she dished out brochures for several travel destinations and used her Internet connection to locate a cybercafe an hour east in Queven.

"She's a wizard and a godsend," I said, walking out.

"I only understood about every third word, but I can tell she really likes us."

I drove our silver car along the highway toward Queven, seeking the cybercafe. My ears felt like they were buzzing off my head. "Too much static from the radio."

"Can you hang on? I still hear voices between the crackling."

"What are they talking about?"

"Scores to cricket matches."

"We already heard the scores, and who cares?"

"It's in English. I *love* English."

I pushed the button for the other English-language station— a BBC broadcast from the Channel Islands off the north coast of Brittany—dead as a doornail. "Can we go on like this for a year? We need more than a radio, like live people to talk with."

"We could find a university with an English class," suggested

Marguerite, "or drive to Mont-Saint-Michel and eavesdrop on tourists."

At the cybercafe we picked up our e-mail and responded to some of the correspondence. The most important message we sent out was to Lester and Ester. "You told us how wonderful it was spending a year in Europe, and it sounded ideal. But were there times when you were lonely? Did you experience English-deprivation shock? Get depressed?"

From then on we stopped in Queven every chance we got, and each time we received new ideas from Les and Es.

E-mail from Les:

> In response to your questions, yes, of course, we had language-deprivation shock. It's a compound of unfamiliar customs and homesickness. The good news is it will pass. The bad news is it's recurrent. Find a store that sells American peanut butter. It'll remind you of home. The fact that we stayed at campgrounds kept us in touch with Americans. You might look into that yourselves. A stay of a day or two will allow you to swap books with the English speakers. Chin up! What you're doing will be something to look back on for the rest of your lives. The temporary inconvenience you'll forget, as I had, until you reminded me.

I finished reading the note aloud and said, "Thanks a lot, Les. You *forgot* to tell us we'd be lonely and depressed."

"But look at the good news. We'll have all these happy memories, and the sadness will pass out of us," Marguerite said. "If you had known about the sad part, would you still have come on the trip?" she asked.

"I can't answer that right now."

Good, Old-Fashioned Dentistry

I tossed the plump, dark cherry into my mouth, anticipating its sweet lusciousness. I bit around the edge, separating fruit from stone, but one bite missed the mark. My molar cracked full force into the pit. My hand flew to my jaw as pain zinged through. A hunk of dense, jagged material landed inside my cheek.

I probed the void with my tongue as we waited at the counter of the tourist office for Madame Audren to finish a phone call.

She approached, a smile shimmering in her brown eyes. "So, how are you doing? Did you find the cybercafe I told you about?"

"Yes, thank you. We got our e-mail, but we came for another reason. I've broken my tooth, and I need a dentist who speaks English." As I said the word *dentist*, I didn't know whether it should be masculine or feminine, which is a constant problem with these crazy romance languages. I said *une dentiste* because it sounded better to my ear.

"Yes, yes. I know *une dentiste* who speaks English. Certainly." She gave me the address and office hours.

It didn't occur to me that by using the feminine form of the word *dentist* I might be specifying a female dentist. If I had, I would have explained that the gender of the practitioner didn't matter. It was the ability to communicate in English that was vital.

Arriving at the address, I left Marguerite in the car, listening to the BBC. In the run-down waiting room, furnished with only three empty, wooden chairs and a coffee table, I perused a French magazine something like *People*. The inner door opened. A white jacketed, forty-year-old woman ushered a patient out and beckoned me in.

Sitting in the swivel chair with an old medical light hanging over it, I couldn't help but notice the plainness of the surroundings and the vintage of the equipment. The office conjured up memories of the kindly Dr. Hefferan, who tortured me once a year through childhood. *La dentiste* hovered over me, her expression seeming somehow amused.

"*Bonjour,*" I said. "Madame Audren at the tourist office said you speak English."

The dentist shrugged, and her face reddened. "Little." (In my experience, that meant "little to *none*.") "I try."

A wave of panic set my stomach boiling. Obviously, I would have to proceed in French. How would I explain? How did one say, "I don't want a root canal," if it came to that? How did one know if *la dentiste* was about to commence oral surgery? If she picked up a scalpel, I'd run like hell. "I have lost some tooth." I opened wide and pointed at the offending molar.

She dangled a mirror in my mouth. With two or three words of English and flurries of French she told me, "Your filling came out."

I tried to think of something intelligent to say and came up with, "Ah."

She crammed wads of cotton between lip and gum, and within seconds the ear-piercing sound of drill gouging tooth vibrated my cranium.

My stomach went on full alert, but I tried to comfort myself with the idea that she only had to clear out an old filling. Apparently, I was wrong. Several times during the interminable drilling, she struck a nerve, and I made the customary "Ohhh" and "Arrrg" to let her know.

"Good," she said. "You should tell me if it hurts." Without removing the instrument from my mouth, she resumed grinding, and I continued moaning when the need arose. Finally, she withdrew her weapon and wiped the spittle off my chin. "Would you like some anesthesia?" Apparently, *anesthesia* was comparable in both languages.

Yikes! Did that mean she had only begun a longer process? "Is there much more?" I didn't know how to say *drilling*, so I pointed at the implement.

"No more. Now I fill it."

Was this some new dental theory? Cause maximal pain and then soothe it after the fact? Like you have to eat the spinach before you've earned the desserte? I declined the offer, and soon the filling was finished. The good news—it only cost $30. I would have been happier, though, to have paid more and suffered less.

Ed's AIs:
  Novocaine before the pain

We Need Drugs to Fight the Laundry-Day Blues

June 22

Yesterday we spent six hours washing two loads of laundry in our cellar. Then we packed it in the car and spent two hours in the Laundromat drying it. I'm tired of doing laundry and tired of looking at clothes hanging in our living room. I'm tired of wearing damp, mildew-smelling undershirts and tired of writing about it. So I'll leave it at this—the stupid clothes are dry.

Of course, this isn't about washing garments. I don't want to admit this, don't even want the thought to enter my mind, but I'm becoming discouraged. Speaking French all the time, trying to keep everything afloat—from finding the right shampoo to getting change for the dryers to shopping for food—this was an adventure at first, but no longer.

I led Marguerite past a few half-timbered houses, down the shopping street, toward a set of green and blue neon crosses that gleamed in the window of the pharmacy. We waited by the counter in the tiny establishment as the clerk in white smock held a heated discussion with an old woman in black sweater, leaning on her cane.

Finally it was our turn. "We seek something for fatigue," I said, gesturing toward Marguerite. "And, for me, medication for anxiety."

I used the English word *anxiety* and tried to frenchify it. It should have worked, but the woman frowned and asked a question I didn't understand. I tried again. *"Tristesse* (Sadness)."

"Tell her we want natural remedies."

I told the clerk *fatigue* and *tristesse* and *anxiété* and *naturel,* and still, she asked unintelligible questions. Whatever the question, it couldn't be important. I answered with a definite, *"Oui."*

She handed me a box that said Stabilium on the front and a brochure full of complex words. I flipped it over in case there was English on the back, but no luck. "This looks good. . . . And for Madame's fatigue?" I nodded again to Marguerite.

The clerk offered a bottle of B-complex vitamins and something she called *homéopathique*—I guessed that meant homeopathic medicine—in a little vial with more indecipherable words on it.

"You do not touch these pills with your hands," she said, waving the vial at me. "You rotate the end of the container, so it releases a pill, and you let the pill fall under Madame's tongue." She made sure I understood by opening her mouth, elevating her tongue, and holding the cylinder in position.

Back home, I tried to read the information sheets for each of the remedies. The fine print about Stabilium brought me up short. "This is bizarre. The word *poisson* appears here right by a word that's about two letters off from cerebellum. This stuff must be made from fish brains."

"Does that mean you're not going to take it?"

"Hell no. I just hope they were well-adjusted fish."

Booking a 300-Year-Old Farmhouse

June 17

We're weighing the alternatives—lengthening our stay in Brittany or moving on. Although we both feel melancholy at times, it's lovely by the sea. We enjoy the down-to-earth people, the peacefulness, and the sense of antiquity.

On the one hand, we're mostly having fun. Each day we venture to new delights—the medieval towns of Vannes and Concarneau and the quaint ports like Brigneau, just across our inlet.

On the other hand, we miss friends and English. I mourn my father more deeply every day, and though I keep asking him to bless this trip, he won't respond. Marguerite's losing energy, so I spend more and more time on solitary walks. In August we'll see Tricia and Claire in Austria, then Bette for October in Nice, then Tricia for Christmas in Italy, if we actually spend December in Italy. . . . It could be a long haul just getting to August.

We had wanted to stay here a month, but this house was only available for three weeks. Our landlords are offering another place on their farm an hour inland—a different view of this charming land. If we like it, we might rent it for a while.

At the Jegouzo farm, Madame J. showed us into the *gîte* (lodging) and left us to look around. The house was huge, with three sleeping areas upstairs and the spacious living room and kitchen below.

"It's charming, especially the walk-in fireplace." I took Marguerite's hand and traced the dimensions of the hearth, capped by a flat, granite slab.

"Think we can get a good a deal?"

"It's worth more, but let's try for less than $50 a night. We'll use the savings to splurge on food or entertainment."

"I'll take my share in champagne."

The four of us met in the driveway surrounded by five stone structures. Madame Jegouzo, in a blue-and-white striped, crew-neck shirt and with short, rusty-blonde hair, pointed in turn at the three houses and two outbuildings. Both of the two-story *gîtes* were constructed from slices of gray stone and had roof lines that arched over the windows, giving them the look of thatched cottages. "Our farm, it is called Le Breguero. Besides the *gîte* where you would stay, we have this other—both 300 years old. And over there, our home, it's only 30 years. And you see the toolshed and the barn for the *ânes.*"

I understood most of what she told me except . . . *"Que veut dire* ânes?"

Monsieur Jegouzo chuckled and raked his light-brown hair across his tanned forehead. He placed his hands beside his ears and gave a "hee haw."

"So, it's the donkey barn." I nodded toward Marguerite. "Will she be able to touch the *ânes?*"

"Oui. Certainement."

Madame and I watched as Marguerite's face lit up. "She loves animals," I said.

Madame Jegouzo got down to brass tacks. "I propose to you this house—three bedrooms, fireplace, kitchen, living room, patio— for 2000 francs ($345) a week."

I tried my best to sulk. Of course, we had spent over 2100 francs ($360) a week for the house by the sea. It was a great price for this huge home, and 2000 francs *was* within our budget, but a better bargain would put us back on track or buy the champagne Marguerite wanted. "Oh, man," I said to Marguerite. "They want *2000* a week."

She shook her head. "Too much."

I was tempted to snicker at Marguerite's somber look but refrained. "We paid so much for your house by the sea because it is very special there, but now we must spend less."

"The house brings more than that," said Madame. "The high season is beginning. It is worth much more."

"We don't need so many rooms. We are only two people and a cat."

Marguerite said softly to me, "It really is worth it. Do you think they're going to budge?" Her face showed only worry, but I was willing to bet she was enjoying this a lot. Marguerite was a born negotiator. Normally, she'd do the haggling, but because of the language, I was stuck with the dirty work.

"And the *ânes*," I whispered back. "They've got to be worth something."

"We're going to take it even for 2000, aren't we?"

"Shhh. Don't let them hear you."

"Come inside, and we'll talk," Madame J. offered. She said some other things I didn't understand.

"Looking good," I murmured.

They led us into their house and took off their shoes, but they insisted we keep ours on. Monsieur showed us to armchairs in the living room, asked if we liked sherry, and poured four glasses. The Jegouzos sat opposite us on a couch and conferred quietly as we sipped.

Madame J. produced a sheet of paper with a picture of the *gîte*. "You see, this is the house we offer you." She flipped the paper over. "Here is the information. For July and August, the price is 2550— 2000 is an excellent offer. If it was June, it would be less, but it will be July when you come." She looked at me to see if I might agree.

"Now I think she wants to raise the price," I whispered. "Keep looking sad. Maybe you could moan or whimper."

Marguerite frowned on cue, but she flunked in the moaning department. I shrugged and nodded toward Marguerite as if to say, She's the miserly one.

"We would like to help," Madame went on. "We will give you the off-season price if you come for two weeks—1500 francs a week."

Marguerite grinned.

"I thought you didn't understand French," I said.

"I don't. But I heard her tone, and I know she's talking francs."

"She's offering 1500. Okay with you?"

We shook hands and toasted with sherry. The deal was done, and it was clear that they were as happy to have us as we were to have a charming, three-bedroom house in France in high season for $260 a week—with *ânes*.

We chatted. For each sentence in French, I provided my version to Marguerite in English. Then I would respond. Or

Marguerite would suggest something, and I would try to get the idea across. I began to feel like Grand Central Station, every sentence like an arriving train that I had to fill with new life and send on its way.

Monsieur Jegouzo added sherry to our glasses as he told us that he had been a cartographer. They had lived in Africa for several years. Madame had been a teacher and retired with a pension at fifty. French teachers can retire early with fewer years' service if they've had at least two kids.

Monsieur told us he grew *haricots verts, maïs,* and *petits pois* (green beans, corn, and peas) on the farm, and he sold them to a company for canning. (To get that idea across, he detoured to the pantry for a can.) They had two turkey barns crammed with birds. Their daughter, Marianne, lived with them, and they had an older son in Paris.

I struggled to explain our history of careers. Marguerite had been a speech therapist and then a special education teacher, and now she was a psychotherapist. I had been a math teacher and then an environmental engineer for an oil company, and I currently worked as an assistant to a county supervisor. We had also spent two years teaching Navajo Indians in New Mexico. The explanation wasn't easy. In fact, it was damned difficult. I found that *psychology, pollution, mathematics, Indians,* and *therapy* all worked when I threw in a little French inflection. *County supervisor* took a little doing (*politician* with a French accent got me close). It felt good to be able to communicate so much, good to hold a true conversation here in their home. I appreciated the Jegouzos' efforts to speak simply and to really try for understanding.

"You have children?" Madame asked.

"Only the cat. That's all we wanted." I waited for her to ask why.

Monsieur gave us a knowing look. "Yes, it is not easy, especially with a teenage daughter."

"But Marianne is a good girl," his wife added quickly, flashing one of those looks that husbands understand. "She studies English in school, so you can talk with her when she is home."

Madame J. asked if we had been to Pontivy, a town farther up the road. Then she wondered if we liked crèpes, and we nodded.

"I think she's going to recommend a restaurant nearby."

Madame spoke quickly, and I didn't quite get it. "You have a restaurant to recommend?" I asked.

"Yes. Today *we* are your café."

Monsieur and Madame ushered us to the table. Madame wiped it clean as she took our crèpe orders. Monsieur pulled out a bottle of Bordeaux from a cabinet. Madame slipped into the kitchen. Monsieur produced wine glasses, napkins, and silverware. He opened the wine, poured carefully, and then paused, looking at Marguerite.

"Slide your right hand to the right," I said. She slipped her hand over and grasped the glass. Monsieur's shoulders eased, and I thought I detected a warm glow in his eyes when they flashed over at me. Madame brought salads and plates covered with golden crèpes— cheese for Monsieur and Marguerite, ham and cheese for Madame and me.

During the meal, Madame spoke to Marguerite as I translated. "You are in France, Marguerite. Why do you not learn to speak the language?"

"Tell her I would like to learn. Tell her I'm lousy at languages."

"But you must try. It is very important." Madame wagged a finger as she spoke. "You see the little children. Everyone can learn."

"That's right, Marguerite." I joined the finger-wagging. "Even the little children do it."

"Thanks for your support, dear."

Monsieur Jegouzo came to Marguerite's rescue. "I think you could learn with three hours a day for two or three months. And you will be here, you say, for almost a year. Marguerite has plenty of time, and you, too, Monsieur." His firm look said, Stop picking on her. *You* still have lots to learn.

"But we will be in France and Spain and Italy and Greece and . . . everywhere" I said. "Too many languages."

Monsieur poured wine for Marguerite and turned to my glass.

I held up my hand. "No, I must drive. In America, we try to be careful, and we have limits on alcohol in the blood."

"Ah, in France, too, but I must be a good host and offer it."

Then Madame was taking another order. "In the crêpes we have two kinds, crêpe *blé* and crêpe *noir.* You have had the lunch crêpes, and there are also the sweet crêpes. What kind will you have?" Marguerite declined, and I chose a strawberry crêpe. Madame swept off to the kitchen.

To keep the conversation going, I said, "I see you have McDonald's restaurants in France."

"Yes, it is sad. The young people flock to them. I do not understand. Why would a person not want to eat a civilized meal?"

We had eaten at one the day before, a happy reminder of home and actually pretty tasty. I felt myself redden.

"Americans do not seem to care as much about their meals as we."

"That's true," I said, looking down at the table. "In the United States, our stores stay open at lunchtime. People grab a sandwich and go back to work."

"Tell him I think it's much more refined to take a two-hour lunch," Marguerite said. The day before, she'd been complaining about all the stores closing from 12:00 PM to 2:30 PM, but I passed Marguerite's comment on, and Monsieur smiled fondly at her.

Madame returned with crêpes and a bowl of cherries. "Tell me, Marguerite. Why do you like to travel? What do you get from it?"

"It's an adventure. I enjoy the exotic feel, the sounds and smells, the food—I love the food."

As I interpreted, I found myself feeling pressured and claustrophobic, walled in by my lack of vocabulary, mentally dashing in all directions, searching for ways to say things while circumnavigating expressions I didn't know. But at the same time, I felt exhilarated. It was intense and exhausting, but we were making a sort of intimate contact with two gentle people, seemingly in another world.

I asked Marguerite, "What else should I tell them about

blindness? Keep it simple. I'm running out of words."

"The best thing," she said, "is the people and how kind they are. We make a contact that's universal."

"Thanks, Marguerite, now how do I say *universal?*" I tried *universal* with a French accent, and it worked.

Finally, we all stood, and Madame J. said, "Now, Marguerite, you will learn the traditional greeting and farewell of our region." She took Marguerite by the shoulders and kissed her cheeks—left, right, left. "You see? It is three kisses, not two."

Menopausal Woman

I steered the Peugeot along a winding road through thick, oak forests. Now and then a patch of rocky shoreline jutted into view and then disappeared behind the trees. We scooted into La Forêt-Fouesnant, a village tucked along the edge of a bay, passed a few shops, a couple of cafés, and an old church hewn of stone. I pulled to a stop by the post office.

"I'm getting out to catch a picture of this chapel. Do you want anything?"

Lying back in her reclined seat, she rolled her head toward me. "I'm fine. Stay as long as you want."

When I returned, I found her asleep—understandable. There was nothing she could see, no reason to stay awake. If she had stirred, I would have told her how attached I felt to the crude, granite crucifix, weathered almost faceless by wind and rain. I would have described the planters of pink and white petunias along the sidewalk that led to the bay, and the fishing boats that were tied up to the dock, ready to have their baskets of shimmering mackerel unloaded.

I consulted the frazzled map that Monsieur and Madame Jegouzo had loaned me and continued on to Bénodet. As our landlords had promised, the town was set on a beautiful harbor, with a commanding lighthouse and stately, old, sea captains' homes.

Marguerite consented to walk with me, but within minutes, she asked to head back to the car. We drove to the other side of the inlet and found a restaurant.

I ordered an omelette, and she went for a chocolate crêpe.

Halfway through my meal, I noticed her dragging the wrong side of her knife across her crêpe, cutting here and there but mostly mooshing it around the plate. "What's going on?"

"This knife is like my eyes . . . useless." Her voice came out in a sob, and tears glistened.

"Turn it over and try. . . ."

She looked at me as if I'd spoken Martian.

"I'll cut some for you."

"You eat it, too. I'm not hungry."

"Are you taking the little homeopathic pills?"

She nodded.

"Maybe Dr. Wong's herbs *were* doing you some good. You didn't seem this drained before. Please think about trying the hormones."

"If I had sight, eating wouldn't be such a big deal. If I had energy, I could cope . . . but this *sucks*. I'm really pissed and sad about my vision. It's like I'm thrown back to losing it all over again."

I wasn't sure if she'd heard my comment about the hormones. I would have to repeat it later. We returned to the car, and she fell asleep. As I drove home, thoughts came to me of the moments we had spent by our canal in Holland, moments when she'd been alive and lively.

I remembered she had asked what kinds of birds she heard squawking in the canal. "They're like brown ducks with hairdos," I'd said. "No, that's not good enough . . . with swept-back hairdos."

"Like Elvis?"

"Elvis is close . . . or those women in the 1890s with their hair pushed up and back. Or picture this—they have no hair, only tremendous eyebrows that grow long and stick out behind."

"Works for me," she'd laughed.

After that we had talked about our day of bicycling and then moved on to planning our next destination. I remembered a grand smile that spread all the way from her eyes to my heart, transmitting joy and love right along with it as we spoke about how great it would be to live by the sea in Brittany.

But now there was no smile, no conversation, no joy.

Surviving the Great Storm

June 21, 6:30 AM

There's been a full moon the last two nights, which has been delightful. (It's also good for crones, according to Marguerite's book on menopause. We're calling her a "mini-crone," since she's only fifty.)

At midnight the moon rests in a pocket of deep blue sky, and the pines sway in that light, casting silhouettes between the squares of the French windows. Early this morning, the sky clouded over, and a storm blew in. A relentless, drenching rain commenced. A great day for staying in by the fire.

It was afternoon but nearly dark. Outside, the storm was tearing the world apart. Gushers of rain darted across the landscape, obscuring the ocean. Tree limbs jiggled and hopped. Inside, the fire ebbed to a hot, orange glow, warming us and finally making blankets unnecessary. Felicia snoozed blissfully on my lap, keeping me from throwing off the covers or stoking the fire.

I read aloud from our current book, one of those prehistory novels by William Sarabande. The main characters were the mighty Torka; his doe-eyed, fawnskin-clad mate, Lonit; and the first domesticated dog in the world, the faithful Aar. These stalwarts braved the ravages of the Stone Age winter and fended off menacing beasts, both human and animal. In the mountains outside their camp lurked a half-human creature called the wanawut, who howled eerily in the night and longed to slay the people.

When Marguerite and I read these books, we always got to calling each other Torka and Lonit, and Felicia became Aar, our stalwart protector. During these readings, and for a few days after, I might say over dinner, "Woman give leftover bison meat to faithful dog Aar"—that kind of thing.

But these days, with Felicia yowling at 4:00 AM to wake us, I had commenced another tack. "Lonit, I hear call of wanawut close to camp. Not be afraid. I keep spear hurler ready." At first, Marguerite resisted calling our lovely cat a wanawut, but, as Effie woke us more and more often, she had to accept our kitty's beastly side.

At this moment, the wanawut was peaceful. The rain poured outside, and we'd been sitting for hours, long enough to make me restless. "Torka read much time. Now must go out to hunt by ocean. Want to come?"

"Just a minute, great tracker of mammoth. I'll put on my Patagonia shirt and raingear."

We covered up and pulled drawstrings tight until only our eyes and noses showed from inside our hoods—mine royal blue, hers forest green.

We hiked for twenty minutes beside the thunderous sea. Then I stopped, looked at her wet face, felt her trembling fingers, and hugged her. "You're shivering. We'd better go back."

"I don't want to ruin your walk."

"Torka take Lonit back. Then come out and call to spirit of Torka's father, great hunter of our people, Willard. During roaring storm winds, perhaps father will take up Torka's question."

"This is hard for you, Eddie. If you need me, I'll stay."

A gust of wind almost lifted us off our feet, and I felt her quake in my arms. "Better Torka do alone."

Trying Not to Hit Bottom

I lay awake that night and felt grief form a solid mass in my gut. I kept asking my dad if I would ever meet him again, but there was no response. Apparently that *was* the response.

When I had walked out into the storm, with water dripping

from my face, I had asked if he thought this year's journey was frivolous or wrong—but again, no answer. I had to reach my own conclusion. That made sense. Dad had always let me choose my own path as a boy . . . almost always.

❦

Early in the morning I walked out to that rocky area where Dad's spirit seemed most present in the troubled waters. "I'm alone," I told him, "feeling completely abandoned for the first time. You and Mom have been gone so long that I'm kind of used to it. But I want Marguerite to wake up and talk with me." No comfort came from the crashing surf on the rocks below.

I drove to town and bought a cherry coffeecake. Soon, I was bringing Marguerite coffee and a piece of the pastry in bed.

"Thanks, but I don't deserve this." She sulked and sipped.

"I want to tell you that it's all right," I said, "but the truth is that I feel like I've been abandoned in a strange country."

"I can't help it. I'm lonely for my family and my friends and English. My body aches. I sweat at night and wake up feeling sticky and yucky and useless, because I can't do anything myself. So I lie here and listen to my books. Felicia snuggles with me and makes me feel happy—I couldn't make it without her. . . . There's nothing else I want to do."

"We can find things to hear and touch. We could get some clay and sculpt animal figures like we did that time in Taos, or we could buy a secondhand xylophone and make music."

"I don't feel like it."

"Shopping usually cheers you up. We'll find a store that sells seafaring clothes. I could use a captain's hat, and we'll get you a black-and-white-striped sailor's shirt."

She sipped coffee. "We can try that, but I want you to think about this, too: we don't have to stay in Europe. We could go home and just hang out for the rest of the year."

"If you'd said that a month ago, I'd have come unglued."

"Don't feel sorry for me, Eddie. Even though I'm miserable half the time, I love the ocean sounds." A crooked half-grin spread across her lips. "Part of me doesn't want to leave . . . I'm weird . . . and I have a confession . . . I'm glad you're feeling down." She peered at me and waited.

"I'm *not* sure I like this."

"I've spent time in my life feeling bad. When I was going blind, we cried together sometimes, but mostly I closed it up inside. I hid my pain, because it would make you sad and serve no purpose. And it wasn't just the blindness. Women *feel* things. We get depressed, and men don't. You're always so damned happy and well adjusted. It's good to see you vulnerable."

"You should be ecstatic then. I feel like crap."

"Now you'll understand me better." She looked sheepish and triumphant and miserable all at the same time.

"You think this will make us closer?"

"It already has."

"Great! . . . Now how do you feel about this? I think there's information about an animal park in one of those brochures from the tourist office." I walked to the kitchen table and rummaged through the collected papers.

"Are there monkeys?" Her voice picked up.

"The picture shows some."

A glint of happiness showed in her eyes.

June 24

We spent our early afternoon at the Parc animalier du Quinquis—a farm turned wildlife park. A teenage boy at the office in an old stone house sold us bags of grain. We were chased by geese and nudged by goats wanting a share of the feed. The monkeys were caged and unavailable, but spotted-brown deer stood on hind legs and pushed their velvety faces into Marguerite's cupped hands to eat. Seeing her gleeful look and hearing her laughter sent my heart soaring.

Next we called my brother John in Rhode Island. It was a great call. He was impressed when I told him how I had carried on conversations in French. It's comforting to know that John and his gentle form of cynicism (which was dormant during this conversation) are alive and well in R.I. He reciprocated when I said, "I love you."

Dark Humor

June 27

I keep reminding myself that I'm the luckiest man in the world, but I've begun taking something called Stabilium to ease my anxiety. As best as I can tell from the French-only information sheet, it's composed of the better parts of fish brains. Come on, little trout cerebrums, do your thing.

I am sitting in a house by the sea in Brittany, France. I have a year off from work and enough money to spend it in Europe with my lovely and loving wife and my similarly inclined cat. And yet, at this moment, I hover between depression and ecstasy.

I mention my blessings to remind myself . . . because I'm feeling paranoid about everything—from our laundry that won't dry to Felicia's deafness to the fact that my computer swallowed this document and made me write it a second time.

Sure, these things are minor, but here's the important part: I feel that I'm pulling a heavy sled, and they're sitting on it—Marguerite, Felicia, and my dad. They'll pull me all the way down if I don't take control.

I'm writing a poem to Dad to help me grieve. Then I'll try to throw him off the sled.

Reading over what I've written, I recognize the absurdity. And when there's absurdity, there's comedy. It's sitting in the lines I've written on this page. So far, it's pretty dark humor, but any levity is a plus.

A good sign—I brushed my teeth. I must plan to live for a few more hours.

Sending Willard's Spirit to the Winds

Marguerite stood by the front door as I buttoned my jacket. "I could go with you."

"No. I have to do this with just my dad." I gathered a copy of my poem, a notepad and pen, and headed for the shore. I sat on the rocks where sad thoughts of him had tormented me, and I wrote.

June 27

I have a poem for you, Dad, but before I read it to you, I want to set my feelings for this moment on paper.

Your spirit (I think) and the sea are tranquil this morning. I sit at the spot that most reminds me of you. When the waves are crashing, I know you would have loved it here. But you'd love it now, too, when it's quiet, and I know you love me.

I must leave you here—not all of you, not the peaceful healing, not the boyhood reverence. But I leave the grief and the longing behind.

I worry that you may disapprove of this year of freedom. I understand that when I was a teenager, you had to keep after me for things. I never got to be with you as an adult, so it's hard for me to get past this. I have to make my own decisions, and I know that this year—however it turns out—is right for me.

Here, by the nurturing sea, I leave any part of you that might have judged me for not working hard enough. I leave these parts and take the best ones on my journey. I cannot do otherwise, for you placed them in me through your patient, persistent, and caring example.

You must stay here. It's my turn.

I have a wonderful, loving companion, and I couldn't be luckier. I'll be well in her hands!

Sit on these rocks, Dad. Enjoy the sights and feelings and peace, the sea's pounding and its ebbing. Rest free.

Then I unfolded the poem and read it.

> You put so few chains on me
> When I was young.
> I ran a little wild
> But watched you still.
>
> Honest, quiet, studious,
> You set a tone.
> I watched you love the woods,
> The sea, my mother.
>
> And when you came to die,
> Distant years ago,
> I was so tied up in me,
> I pretended not to feel.
>
> Now,
> Thirty years gone by,
> I sit and sob
> For your lost guidance.
>
> When Momma went, twenty years after you,
> I wrote a poem mourning her,
> My final note
> To the concert of her spirit.
>
> And now I seek to patch this hole, this void,
> This uplifted, torn heart,
> As I did well and truly
> When Momma left to be with you.
>
> I soon will pass beyond your years
> And forge this path alone.
> No more trails ahead
> Of your making.
>
> I leave you here with the sea
> While I explore beyond,

In this place you would love,
A place where I leave a loving part of me.

I wadded up the paper and threw it into the ocean, to anchor my grief and leave it behind. I walked inland, away from the sea, away from the sorrow, talking to him, talking happily as an equal.

The trail to Brigneau had always been peaceful for me. I followed it around the bay and passed a Trail Closed sign. I climbed over the wire barrier and came to a crumbling old factory, parts of which seemed ready to fall at any moment. So that was the reason for the trail closure. I edged past the ruin and down to the inlet below.

I didn't disobey the sign in rebellion, I did so because I was an adult, autonomous, a man who could decide what risks to take.

Moving In with the *Anes*

Sunday, June 29

It's just after dawn. I am privileged to sit at a table in a 300-year-old farmhouse, a couple of miles from the village of Remungol, Brittany. We moved in yesterday, and it's a treasure—made of rock, with heavy beams to support the hardwood floors upstairs—the real thing. The fireplace is massive—five feet square with a metal plate in back showing a stag and some Breton symbols, like upside down fleur-de-lys. We had a great roaring fire last night, but we were pushing it with the balmy weather. We wanted to experience everything, though, that this ancient building has to offer.

This is our first "creeper-covered stone cottage," as they say in the guidebooks. Ivy adorns the outside walls. Little birds live in nooks between the slivers of stone. I watch them flit in and out.

Our cozy farmstead is surrounded by acres and acres of corn, wheat, beans, and peas. Fields roll downhill to a brook in the distance, and there are two barns full of turkeys, we are told. We shall see.

My biggest problems are (1) I have to wait for the coffee to finish brewing before I can plug in the computer, which I hope won't run out of juice too soon; (2) I can't find anyone who will speak English with Marguerite and me; (3) my cat's going deaf; and (4) it's ludicrous, but I never thought I'd miss television this much. Not a bad life, you say. I'm seeing it that way right now, too.

That's right, my father is no longer on the list. By some miracle, my grief is in remission.

The coffee finished perking, and I savored that first taste of anticipation for the day. I pulled on a jacket and carried my mug outside. I called out to the donkeys as I strolled past their enclosure and turned down the driveway to the narrow, blacktop road. Fog drifted in the valley. Its dampness seemed to cleanse the landscape and me with it. Sipping the rapidly cooling brew, I spoke, "I can't believe it worked. My sorrow really stayed there by the ocean, didn't it, Dad?" As before, there was no answer, but I knew I was right. I knew this was right. I felt confident in my ability to continue the journey.

The Big Decision

It was June 30, and we were wandering in the town of Pontivy, twenty minutes from the farm. I led Marguerite through a flea market, set up on tables under folding awnings. "Nothing interesting . . . blouses on this side, some toolkits, more T-shirts."

"Are any of the T-shirts in French? I want to find a gift for my nephew Michael's birthday."

"Only English, like all the others. Oh, wait. This one says, *'Grand Voilier.'*"

"What does it mean?"

"Damned if I know—"Large Something." Sounds a little dirty, doesn't it? It has pictures of old-time sailing ships."

"Let me feel it. . . . I guess it's okay."

I talked the fellow behind the table down to $5, received

Marguerite's approval, and paid.

We strolled for a while, and she said, "Would you hand me the bag?"

I passed it to her, and she reached inside. "This is *lousy*." Tears streamed down her cheeks. "I never should have accepted this. What's wrong with me?"

"You wanted something in French. It was this or a picture of a poodle in a hula skirt that said, 'Dog Days in Hawaii.'" Seeing no improvement in her expression, I put an arm around her shoulder.

"How can we give him junk like this?"

"He'll be happy we were thinking of him. I don't know if they'll take it back—this isn't Nordstrom's."

I led her into a dark, stone church and showed her to a pew, where she knelt. Roaming, I found a statue of Mary with an intricate silver halo, and rows of ornately carved choir stalls. Marguerite was still praying when I returned. Usually she didn't go on for so long.

Back outside, she said, "I prayed about my depression. If I'm going to take hormones, I have to start the first of the month. That's tomorrow. I told God I was desperate or I wouldn't consider it. I asked if it was okay for me to take them."

"Did God venture an opinion?"

"This is *serious* for me. I'm afraid of getting breast cancer from hormones, but I've done everything I can naturally. I know I'm being crazy. I know I'm ruining your trip, and I hate it. It's in God's hands. If He doesn't give me a sign by tomorrow, I'll start Prempro."

"You shouldn't be so scared of it. Prempro has estrogen *and* progesterone. Progesterone cuts the risk of cancer way down, remember?"

"I don't think anyone knows if that's true, but I can't keep on this way."

Had I had been religious, I would have prayed that a thunderstorm did not pass through in the next twenty-four hours.

July 1

Today Marguerite takes her first hormone pill, and the fate of our journey rests with these little, oval tablets. If they don't help, she'll continue feeling miserable. Whatever I do to keep my spirits up won't change that. Salzburg in August could be the end of our adventure or the springboard to new escapades.

Stalking the English Tongue

July 2

I totaled our June expenses, and we made it. The dollar has risen to 5.9 francs, which lowered our rent to $47 a night. Other expenses ran $50. Ninety-seven dollars a day means success.

Now our strategy is to seek the English language aggressively, and we are prepared to do just that.

It was day two of Marguerite on hormones, and the difference was obvious. She walked with me for a half-hour, exploring the old town of Josselin, and still wanted to go on. It had come to that—appreciating half an hour of sustained energy.

We stood outside the tourist office, surrounded by half-timbered buildings. Just down the hill stood the entrance gate to the Château Rohan, the majestic castle that has dominated the Oust River since the thirteenth century. The chateau's striking, cone-hatted turrets and massive stone walls filled the covers of the brochures about the canals of France.

We bought tickets for the 2:30 PM English-language tour of the chateau and passed through the gate to find a formal garden with sections of lush lawn, geometric walkways, and exotic trees. My eyes registered the ornate Gothic dormers on the substantial building, but I diverted to my more immediate purpose—the search for likely targets, tourists who might join us for dinner that evening.

I sidled up to a man who stood apart from the others, reading a guidebook. "Pretty impressive."

He nodded.

"Are you staying in Josselin?"

"No. I take the train for Nantes after the tour and then back to Paris tomorrow." Rats.

The young, brunette tour guide gathered together our group of fifteen and began relating the building's history. With my arm around Marguerite, I let the melody of the woman's voice settle over me. She explained the symbolism in the building's design and pointed out that Cardinal Richelieu had ordered the chateau sacked because of the Rohan's Calvinist sympathies in sixteen-hundred-something. I glanced at Marguerite, who is usually pretty quickly bored by history, but her gaze was intent. The content of this lecture wasn't important, but the language—a language in which we understood every word—was ambrosia.

The woman led us toward the building.

"Talk to someone, Marguerite. You're better at social stuff."

"I have to find them first. If you break the ice, I can home in on one and take over. You didn't do much with that last guy."

"He was a lost cause."

In a wood-walled banquet room, our guide explained the origins of the Italian ceramicware, the Chinese porcelain, and the equestrian statue on the side wall. As the group began shuffling toward the next hall, I tracked a middle-aged husband and wife. "Are you in Brittany for long?"

"A few days," the man answered. "Our daughter goes to college in Paris, and she's coming to meet us tonight."

It seemed like a losing proposition, but I asked, "I guess you'll want to be cherishing the reunion by yourselves then?"

The fellow questioned my motives with a scowl and backed off. Should I explain that I was just seeking conversation?

Marguerite gripped my elbow hard and smiled at them. "Have a great reunion with your daughter."

In the next hall, I glanced at the ancient tapestries and scrutinized our fellow tourists. The guide explained the decorative motif featuring the letter *A*, but did it represent the Duchess Anne de Bretagne, whom the guide mentioned, or some obscure motto of the Rohan family? There were lots of salamanders, too, but I lost track of their explanation. I brought Marguerite close to a pair of women in their mid-sixties. The guide paused, and we eavesdropped a moment, waiting for a lull in the women's conversation. Our leader resumed, the crowd shifted, and the opportunity vanished. Soon, our guide was saying, "I apologize again that we can see only these two rooms because of the public-television channel filming in the others."

In no time we were strolling out of the building, through the stone gate, and toward town. All of those English-speaking assets were dispersing to the far corners of France.

"This way, after this gray-haired woman." I pulled Marguerite in pursuit, but she resisted.

"You'll scare her. We can ask at the tourist office."

I watched the woman turn a corner, noting which direction she took. "Ask what? If they rent companions?"

"Ask if there's a B&B where they speak English."

"We *have* a place to stay."

"Some of them serve meals. Think of dining with a table full of comprehensible people."

"Great idea!"

A Spot of English with Our Tea, Please

At the tourist office, we found a well-tanned woman of thirty, in a lacy, cream-colored dress that could have come from the chateau's collection. She directed us to the one *chambre d'hôte* in town that had British proprietors. I led Marguerite toward it at full tilt. "What should I say to them?"

"This time, I will do the talking."

"But I'll be the first one to make eye contact. It would be sort of funny to say, 'Hi, I'm Ed. My wife wants to ask you something.'"

"Tell them we're looking for someone to talk to."

"Oh, God. How desperate that sounds!"

I knocked on the front door of the *chambre d'hôte*. A sandy-haired man opened it and peered out through his thick glasses. "Hi. We're the Websters. My name is Ed. The tourist office said you speak English." I held out a hand, and he shook it.

"Yes. Quite. Do you need a room?"

"We already have a place for the week, but . . ."

Marguerite nudged her way beside me. "I'm Marguerite. I know this sounds dopey, but we're looking for a little conversation we can understand." She cast a hopeful smile.

"We were wondering if you served a table d'hôte," I said. "I guess that would be too much to hope for. . . . If you did, it would give us a chance for companionship." Rats again. No way he was going to let us in.

He smiled cautiously. "I'm David. We don't serve dinners, but please come in for a chat."

We followed him down a narrow hall that revealed peeling paint in the stairwell ahead and a cluttered bookcase crammed with newspapers and bric-a-brac against the wall. David turned a corner and ushered us into a small room in which were squeezed a worn couch and two armchairs. A beagle padded into the room. "This is Tadd."

We shook hands/paws with the dog, and he settled on the floor.

"We've been in Europe three months," I said.

"Ah, yes. Missing the home folks," he nodded knowingly. "I can relate. Would you like some tea? You know how we British are about tea time."

"That would be great." Marguerite beamed, and our host bustled off.

"How old is David?" Marguerite asked.

"Could be fifty."

"A contemporary."

"Want to form a club?"

"No, but I have the urge to kiss him every time he speaks."

Our host returned with tea and cookies. "How long are you in Europe?"

"A year, give or take," Marguerite said. "But we may not stay that long."

"Not doing so well? Phillip and I sometimes feel that. He and I have been running the B&B for three years. This little town is quaint and all, but it's death to live in. Nothing going on. Back in London, we were big time. I set up computer systems, and Phillip was in banking. Always go, go, go, you know. After a while, we had to get out. I guess you two are doing the same, at least for a year."

"You're just a short hop from home, across the Channel," I said. "Go back much?"

"Once in a while. You could do that, too—immerse yourselves in English for a few weeks over there."

"No, we can't!" Marguerite caught herself and lowered her voice. "We have Felicia, our cat."

"Oh, yes. The dreadful pet quarantine. They're going to change that one of these days. . . ."

"So, we're feeling isolated and going a little crazy," I said.

"I never would have let you in if you were crazy. All that drooling would have been awful on the carpet. . . . You know, I'm rather glad you came by. I had a jag of the old homesickness coming on me, and I can't impose on our guests about it. They're all happy, just starting holiday. I'd drive them straight away."

"We're having a hard time finding people to talk with." Marguerite set her empty teacup on the table.

"Then let's get you a few resources. First there's Phillip and I. As long as you're nearby, come visit again if you'd like. I'll jot down the names of a couple of restaurants where they speak some English."

Tadd rolled over and flopped his back against Marguerite's ankles. She reached to scratch his head as she spoke, "My sister is going to visit us in Salzburg a month from now. I've vowed I'm not going home before that."

"That's the spirit. After that, you'll be fine for the whole year," David said.

When we got up to leave, David hugged Marguerite and said, "You know, I'm really glad you came. It feels good to be of genuine help to someone."

Striding downhill toward our car, Marguerite was more bouncy than she had been in weeks. "What did he put in that tea, an infusion of happiness?"

The words and the kindness did wonders for our morale. We weren't crazy, just lonely. We had unburdened ourselves and achieved our objective, spending time in quality conversation with another sympathetic soul.

Life Begins with Hormones

July 6

Good news—the ghost of my father hasn't bothered me since we left Moëlan. I've talked with him a few times on my walks, but they've been congenial monologues.

Marguerite grows stronger by leaps and bounds. With her renewed interest in life, we can be more active—visiting quaint villages, dining out, taking a cruise on the Golfe de Morbihan. The activities will affect our budget, but it seems worth it. Yesterday it was Carnac, where thousands of stones were arrayed by prehistoric man (not to mention woman and cat). When we got home we cooked Greek meatballs together. Then she wanted to go out and visit the ânes. *I bow in thanks to the gods of estrogen.*

The citadel of Mont-Saint-Michel was awesome on the approach, its hard stone spire looming higher and higher—a picture seen hundreds of times now real. We walked its one street, spiraling to the top, passing perfect medieval shops and restaurants. But it wasn't these things that caught my attention as much as the way Marguerite kept pace, seeing her eagerness to explore. Advancing up to the abbey, with a couple of stops along the way, my companion hung in there. Waiting to tour the building, we met Gloria from San Diego by way of Arkansas. She spoke our native tongue and effervesced about her own solo adventure—touring Normandy and

Brittany in a rented car, going to a wedding in Burgundy, and then heading to Spain.

The bare, stone halls in the monastery were cold and gloomy but astoundingly built on this rock removed from shore. An eleventh-century achievement beyond measure, where Gregorian chants would echo through empty corridors, and monks would surely fulfill vows of asceticism.

Marguerite and I ate lunch on the sunny patio of a restaurant, which had a commanding view over the vast sand flats that stretch from the Mont to the Normandy shore. The seafood was good and the setting grand, but it was Marguerite's interest in my descriptions and the way she chatted happily about the day's adventure that made the lunch unforgettable.

After lunch, Marguerite practically skipped down the street. "If Gloria can go it on her own, we can, too. We have three to her one. Felicia's our secret weapon."

The setting and that brief encounter with Gloria were like bubbles rising to the surface, helping us to become buoyant, healing our souls.

That Sunday, we headed for a *fête artisanale* (craft fair) in a little place called Caro. We arrived just before noon as bells rang out and townsfolk trooped from the village chapel.

The crowd led us to a field where long rows of tables sat under makeshift awnings. A line was forming. We bought lunch tickets and headed to the beverage tent for a bottle of red wine. Tables were filling with townsfolk. I picked a nice-looking group—two men in patterned polo shirts and a well-dressed woman about our age—and asked to join them. The woman, in white blouse and rich-blue scarf, laughed and answered, *"Avec plaisir* (With pleasure)." The men stood, and one pulled out a chair for Marguerite. Marguerite practiced her *Bonjour* and *Comment allez-vous?* The woman introduced herself and her husband, Madame and Monsieur Guyot.

We were soon sharing our wine as I told them about our trip, our cat, our lives. I tried to keep Marguerite up on the conversation, but the general commotion made it difficult.

They passed us plates with tomato slices, pâté, roasted chicken, vegetables, and parsley potatoes. Madame said she taught French in the local high school. From time to time, she corrected my language. "No, *monsieur,* the past participle of *comprendre* is *compris*"—that sort of thing. She did it gently and constructively. I welcomed the corrections but still felt challenged. If I made the same mistake a second time, would she drop my grade?

Marguerite tugged at my arm. "I want to have a conversation with Monsieur. How do you say, 'The chicken is delicious'?"

She repeated my words to Monsieur, who rattled off something that stumped me. "He's talking fast, and he has an accent that's hard for me. Just tell him his wife seems very nice." I gave her the words, and she passed them on. Monsieur Guyot said something else I didn't comprehend, but then the *curé* (priest) arrived and Madame introduced us, so I was rescued.

We ate to the limits of human capacity. Monsieur Guyot bought more wine, and we toasted. Yet another plate of meat arrived. One of the servers prepared to fork some onto my plate, and I held up my hand. "I cannot."

"But it is the best part of the feast," Madame G. said, naming a dish I didn't recognize—some kind of stewed beef from the look.

I gave in. "Can you eat a little more? It's their specialty."

Marguerite puffed her cheeks in the international symbol for "I'm full."

"Only a little," she said. It was savory and tender but way too much.

"How did you know about our luncheon today?" Madame asked.

"From a brochure about the *fête artisanale.*"

"The *fête* doesn't begin until two o'clock. You must be the only ones at the lunch who don't live here."

I translated, and Marguerite asked, "Is it all right?"

"Far more than all right." Madame beamed. "It is wonderful. In fact, I invite you to stay with me. My teaching job ends for the summer, and I would love company. I could take Madame Webster to an Yves Rocher store, where they have excellent prices."

Plates of Camembert cheese and salads were passed along the table. We abstained, but I couldn't resist the Breton cake (a flan with raisins).

Madame G. passed me a slip of notepaper. "Call me when you leave the farm where you are staying. You will lodge at my home. But I am not a *chambre d'hôte*," she winked, "you will be my guests."

Madame went off to attend her duties at the event. Marguerite and I joined the crowd that drifted to the road for the parade. Soon we heard clanking and rattling and the thrum of a diesel engine.

"What's that?"

"An antique tractor, and the guy in overalls driving it is an antique, too. And there are two funky fellows herding a flock of geese. Wait . . . one is keeping them in line with a baton. He has a few days' growth of beard and is wearing an Ozark Mountains hat with a floppy brim. The other guy is bending down by a goose and puckering his lips. The goose is pecking the side of his mouth. Ouch. He's grinning at the crowd, and his cheek is bleeding."

"Yuck. Why did he do that?"

"Now we have a schoolteacher in black sweater and black beret carrying his slate. Six little girls in matching berets and uniforms are carrying chairs. They're stopping. The girls are sitting in their chairs, and he's pointing at the slate and lecturing. He's shaking his ruler at one girl. She's bending over his knee, and he's pretending to spank her."

"The goose and now this—what's wrong with these people?"

"Here's a guy with fly-away hair leading an ox and cart—a big brown ox—and the man looks a little goofy, in a Peter Sellers kind of way."

Soon it ended, brief and simple, lacking the glamour of a Disney show of lights, but it fit the rural village, which was hosting us to a down-to-earth, pleasurable day.

The ox man agreed to pose for a picture with Marguerite and the ox as long as she stayed well away from the beast. There would be no touching or riding.

We visited the fair booths, full of local pottery and leatherwork, and an art sale in the town meeting hall. Back on the main street the same parade repeated itself, complete with sadistic schoolteacher and masochistic goose merchant.

In the car heading home, I said, "Maybe we should accept Madame Guyot's invitation when we finish up on the farm."

"I'm not sure that's what I want. Let's see how we feel then."

Visiting the Guyots would provide an adventure and human companionship, but it would also mean lots of translating. We would wait and talk about it later.

E-mail from Les:

Dear Ones,

Thanks for your letter and all the inserts. I'm saving that stuff, along with your e-mails, for your return. Someday you'll thank me.

After reading your letter, the mama and I are a little concerned about you. We'll arrange for a support system with our friends Sophia and Rick when you're in Athens, but the upcoming winter will be hard for you. Es thinks that if you aren't happy there, you should come home this winter, but I'm opposed. You're still piling up memories that'll stand you in marvelous stead in coming years. We still say to one another, "Remember when . . ."

I'll be talking with you in a few weeks when you reach your Austrian home. Until then,

Love,
L & E

Another e-mail from L & E:

>   I just spoke to Sophia in Athens, so she's expecting a call. Sophia says that right now all they have is a room and a bathroom, but things will have changed by September. These are warm, loving, friendly people, and you'll find them great landlords. Love to you both."

"Aren't Lester and Esther sweet?" Marguerite cooed.

My voice broke just a little as I replied. "I know how to pick 'em, don't I?"

Speaking Simply

July 7

It's day seven after Marguerite's release from menopausal captivity—hormone replacement is wonderful.

Monsieur and Madame Jegouzo are a wealth of information. They loan us maps (in the middle of repairing our washer), list places to see and eat, offer a vacation guide with dates of events, and provide other miscellaneous items.

Marguerite practices new phrases in French every day to please our gracious hosts.

I spotted Madame Jegouzo getting out of her brown station wagon. "I have something for you," she called. She pulled two plastic sacks of groceries from the car and a cluster of flowers. She nudged the car door closed with her hip. "For you and Marguerite." She handed me the blooms.

They looked familiar—big, blue and lavender clumps of hydrangeas. "Are they from the house in Moëlan? Marguerite and I loved living by the ocean."

"Yes. I went to mow the lawn and to see my father in the rest home near there."

I noticed melancholy in her eyes and said, "It's hard when people get old."

"Hard for me *and* for him. I visit twice a week, and he never seems happy."

"When they don't get old, it's difficult, too. I'm still missing my father, who died thirty years ago. I thought of him when we stayed in the house by the sea, and it made me sad."

"My mother, also." Madame Jegouzo looked toward the pavement and back at me. "I lost her many years ago. We had issues not complete, you understand? I wish we had more time together."

"It's sad either way. When I was a boy, we vacationed by the ocean in places like that. . . ."

"They are here for a short time. Then we miss them. It is life."

"I wrote a poem for my father, and it helped me. You might try that."

"Perhaps."

I trudged home, marveling at the depth of that unexpected conversation, at the speed with which we had each driven to the heart of our need. But most of all I was surprised by my willingness to raise this personal issue. It wasn't like me, and I doubted it was normally in her nature. Apparently, we both had needed to say something about our dead parent. Carrying it off in French was rather amazing—or had the language difficulty helped by forcing us to speak simply? Things that come from the heart are best said that way.

Winged Demons of the Farm

July 6

This morning I found a bat inside by the front door. It seemed in a bad way—sick, maybe rabid. Yikes! I pushed it out with a fly swatter, and it lay there after I slammed the door. Later, it disappeared. Don't tell Marguerite.

July 7

Now there have been two bats, and this time, Marguerite was the one who found it. I'm still not admitting anything.

I was aware of early morning light creeping in through the window—that and Marguerite fidgeting in the bed beside me. "What's that?" she asked.

"Try to sleep. It's probably Felicia."

"Up by the ceiling. I hear wings. Unless Effie's learned to fly, there's a bat in here."

"You always think the worst." Her comment got my attention, though, after my encounter the day before. I peered toward the dark recesses under the peaked roof, flipped on a light, and spotted it.

"What is it?"

"I think it's a moth." I had seen this guy's brother the day before and knew he was no moth. "Wait here."

"I'm scared."

"Duck under the covers. I'll be back in a minute."

I clambered downstairs and returned with my fly swatter and a big cooking pot. I leaped as high as I could and smacked the beast with the swatter, pursued him to the floor, and jammed the pot bottom-down on top of him. I applied maximum pressure and twisted, felt and heard the crunch.

"It was a bat, wasn't it?"

"No. It think it was a big moth."

"What do you mean *think?*"

I stuck with that story for a full day until she questioned me again. "You can tell me the truth, Eddie. It was a bat, wasn't it?"

"Okay. It was. Are you glad you wormed it out of me?"

"Damn . . . I didn't want to hear that."

July 8

This morning at dawn, two semitrailers roared up the driveway toward the turkey barns. Naturally, I followed.

From inside the corrugated barn, I heard the cackling and warbling of thousands of birds, complaining at the top of their gobblers. Beside the barn sat a semi, its flatbed trailer stacked ten feet high with metal cages. A man in blue jeans and a dirty T-shirt stood on top of a wooden crate, straddling the space between it and the truck. Another fellow—one of three who fetched the turkeys—hurried into the barn and returned carrying a fluffy, white bird in each hand. He swung one up to the man on the crate, who grabbed the big fowl by its legs, jammed it into a cage, and bent to accept the other. Two more birds arrived in the hands of another man, and the truck slowly filled. I pitied the birds and felt very glad not to be one of the men.

Later that day, I came upon Madame Jegouzo in the driveway. "So, they're taking the turkeys to market."

"Yes, they must go right away. The weather is getting hot, and it's not good for them."

I didn't mention that taking them to market wasn't good for them, either. "It looks like hard work for the men."

"Especially my husband—he spends all morning inside the barn, catching birds. He's not so young anymore. He comes home exhausted, and I worry. They will load two thousand turkeys today and again tomorrow. That will empty the shed. Then they load from the second building two times. Four days, and each day, he'll be more tired. If you and Marguerite are going to visit the birds, we must do it soon. You would like to go this evening, when it's more cool?"

I was far more aware of the stench outside the barn than I had been that morning because Marguerite was there with me, following reluctantly and wrinkling her nose. Madame Jegouzo beckoned as she slid the door open. "Come right in. See our turkeys."

Marguerite said under her breath, "This is your fault. You could have told her I'm allergic."

"I don't know the word for *allergic*, and she wants to show you. Stop screwing up your face and pretend you like them."

The putrid odor of turkey excrement and the intense humidity of a hothouse enveloped us. I led Marguerite over damp straw, trying to pick spaces that weren't saturated with goop. The gobbling grew frenzied as the birds waddled away from us.

"I get one for you," Madame J. offered.

"No," Marguerite said. "You don't need to. . . ."

Too late. Madame Jegouzo crouched and advanced on the turkeys. They scrambled to get away, bumped into each other. "Ah, ha!" She caught one and dragged it over. I dragged Marguerite closer. Who was more reluctant, she or the bird?

I chose a spot on the turkey that was not caked in dung and placed Marguerite's hand on it. "Say, 'Nice *dindon*,'" I suggested.

"Okay. 'Nice *dindon*.' Now let's get out of here. . . . And maybe we'll skip Thanksgiving this year . . . just have potatoes or something."

Au Revoir, Nos Amis

The turkeys had all been loaded, and it was our last night at the farm. Monsieur and Madame knocked on our door, and Madame handed me a container of pastries. "You can use these for breakfast, or take them in the car for a snack."

I thanked her and eyed Monsieur, who looked thinner, depleted—but satisfied, I thought, with a job well completed. "Maybe you worked too hard with the turkeys," I said.

Madame nodded at me, and Monsieur smirked, taking in his wife with a glance. "No, no. It was the other men who worked."

"Tell him it's worth all the work," Marguerite said. "We've been eating lots of turkey meat—I mean *dinde*—and it's very good."

After the couple departed, I asked, "Where to next? We could call Madame Guyot and accept her invitation to stay in Caro."

"I'd rather move on."

"It's a chance for warm, human contact. That's something we've been needing."

"They're lovely people, but it's not English."

"It's hard doing all the translating, but exciting, too."

"It's not so exciting for me. I listen to you and them speaking a foreign language, and from time to time, you tell me what's going on. I wait for my food to arrive and for you to tell me what it is. It might be an adventure, it might be fun under the right circumstances, but it's not what I want right now."

We decided to move on and seek English-speaking companionship.

In the morning I loaded the car, keeping out a bottle of my favorite wine. (At $4, I spared no expense.) We knocked on the Jegouzo's door, and I presented the wine to Monsieur.

"Ah," he said. "Côtes de Bourg. You know your wines well."

Inside, Madame showed us to the sofa and poured steaming coffee into porcelain cups. "So, where do you go now?"

"We may stay a few nights by the Loire. Then maybe to Germany before moving on to Salzburg in August."

"You'll fit in there," Madame J. advised. "You have the blue eyes and the strong features."

"Thank you."

"This is not a compliment. We are not happy with the Germans."

"Because of the war?"

"That, yes, and also because of the tourists from Germany. They demand things. In the restaurants, they push to the head of the line."

Monsieur fidgeted and then interjected, "Marguerite, I am watching you. I think you are comprehending French better."

"Did you understand?" I asked.

"Something about me and French."

"He said you're understanding better."

She thanked him.

"And you, Monsieur," he said. "You are speaking faster. You

should stay in France two more months and talk with the people to get better. I am proud of you, and I give you a prize. This picture I showed when you first visited our house . . ." He pointed toward the side wall to a colored-pencil drawing of the two 300-year-old *gîtes* and the Jegouzo's home, clustered around the drive. "I have made a copy of this for you. It's the first one we have given away. Ever." He handed me the color copy on oversized paper.

And people say the French are not friendly.

A lump formed in my throat as we thanked Monsieur and Madame. We kissed them good-bye three times on the cheeks—left, right, left—in the local way.

On the Road (to Better Sanity)

Breaking Away

We departed from the farmhouse, headed eastward and bound for hope. With fish medicine and hormones flowing through our veins, we were healing. Movement and contact with the outside world would surely dispel any lurking melancholy.

The Peugeot carried us over the rolling hills and past clustered dairy farms, protected by sheltering trees. "I feel the way I did that first day we left Paris," I said, "on the open road, free of burdens."

"Me, too," said Marguerite. She turned toward the backseat. "How about you, Effie?"

Our cinnamon-colored girl ambled to the front, settled in Marguerite's lap, and commenced washing her stomach.

"She's ready, too," Marguerite reported. "Taking a bath to prepare for chateau country."

We aimed for somewhere in the Loire Valley that day. After that, plans were sketchy until August with our rental near Salzburg.

By late afternoon we were following the Loire River, which was peeking in and out at us from behind stands of willowy trees to our right. Fields of sunflowers rippled in the breeze to our left. The chateau of Amboise appeared on a bluff above the opposite shore, dominating the landscape. It was ornate and spectacular, just like its pictures.

We followed signs down a country road to the Moulin de Pasnel, an inn housed in an old water mill, with canals on the grounds and geese and ducks paddling about—a perfect place to stay.

Inside the breakfast room the next morning, the works of the old mill—shafts, gears, sprockets—seemed oiled, polished, and ready to work. We shared our table with a couple from Frankfurt, who spoke rather good English. They were en route to a nudist camp to join like-minded (and bare-bodied) individuals. (If you were a nudist from Frankfurt, would you tell casual acquaintances over breakfast?)

As he finished a piece of nut cake, the fellow said, "We prefer France for vacations. It's reasonable here, and it's friendly. In Germany, innkeepers add extra costs to the account." His words forewarned of possible things to come.

In the afternoon, we joined a tour of the chateau in Blois, with its gold salamander designs, ornate rooms, and gruesome history. Henri III had the Duke of Guise murdered there and his body parts roasted in the fireplace to dispose of the evidence. We stood on the spot where the dirty deed was done, eyeing the roasting spit on the granite hearth—pretty cool. I offered Marguerite a chance to sneak into the fireplace and get a feel for it, but she declined.

That evening, July 13, the city of Blois held its Bastille Day celebration. As we dined at a restaurant with tables set in the square, fire engines paraded past. Blue lights pulsed over the buildings, over Marguerite and her plate of roasted chicken and fries, over the passing procession of celebrants.

"Can you believe we're here for Bastille Day?" Marguerite exclaimed, her delight showing in her eyes as she sipped from a glass of Loire white wine. "What a great table on the square! We're so lucky."

After dinner, we followed the crowd toward the river, while a band beat out "La Marseillaise." Cymbal claps and drum rolls echoed. We stood by the riverbank at the center of the throng with our arms wrapped around one another. Fireworks rocketed from the opposite side, their scatter-shot reports punctuated with chest-pounding booms. Between explosions I spoke. "That one's an expanding flower of red. . . . This one's trailing down blue streamers. . . . Those booms are intense white bursts. . . . The reflections are dripping blue, white, and red into the rippling Loire River."

"You know I don't like fireworks, but this is romantic and lovely," Marguerite said, tugging at my shirt and pulling me in for a kiss. I savored it and the message it sent—my bride and our journey were on the mend.

Partygoers strolled to three of the city squares where two orchestras and a band, whose name translated into something like "The Flea Breathes at the Ear of the World," beat out rhythms into the night, from booming ultramodern to soft rock. We danced and kissed and wandered from square to square, hearing not a word of English. It felt like it was 1789, well past midnight on a historic eve.

The next day we would join the masses in Paris to storm the Bastille, but tonight we partied.

After two nights by the Loire, we headed east toward Alsace, seeking the wine country of the Rhine River Valley, the last territory of France before the German border.

Scattering Our Blues

July 18, Riquewihr, Alsace, France

We are renting a room in a modern, two-story home just outside the walled town of Riquewihr. For $47 we have a large room with a balcony, its view filled with row upon row of vivid green grapevines advancing up the hills to a dense forest. When we wake, there's a cart outside our door with fresh bread and croissants, jam, cheese, pâté, and coffee. We roll it in and eat on the balcony.

Felicia loves the pâté breakfasts. The little tin is labeled foie gras, *which makes her feel very much the gastronome.*

There are pink and red geraniums everywhere outside, especially hanging from our balcony rail. I haven't told Marguerite, but tiny, very quiet bees flit between the blossoms in the afternoon.

Speaking to people here is disconcerting. Although we're in France, the residents speak German, or some related dialect, to one another. French is spoken with gruff intonations—such a shame to treat the melodious language harshly. At first I didn't appreciate our landlady, but when I asked if we could stay for two more nights, she flashed a warm smile and said it would be fine if we settled here until Christmas. The smile obliterated her thick-tongued French and endeared her. The complimentary bottle of Gewürztraminer didn't hurt, either.

I should note that cat discipline is still an issue. Felicia makes a racket with her meowing early in the mornings, and I'm afraid she'll disturb the other guests. I tried zapping water into her face, with limited success. I have another idea but don't know if Marguerite will go along.

"You want to let her out on the balcony? She'll wander off and get lost." Marguerite eyed me like I was an axe murderer.

"Come with me." I led her onto the balcony. "Bend down." She reluctantly complied. I ran her hand along the bottom of the railing. "There's only an inch from the railing to the floor—not enough space for a cat to wiggle through."

"She could jump off the top." Marguerite's expression had gone from revulsion to skepticism. I was making progress.

"It's at least a twelve-foot drop to the garden, plus the three-foot railing. She'd have to leap onto the railing and then plunge like an Olympic diver. How long has it been since Felicia jumped off even a kitchen table?"

"Not long."

"Yesterday? Last month?

"A little longer . . ."

"It was years ago. She was probably eleven or twelve." One thing I had learned on this journey was that it wasn't easy to convince a menopausal woman, but Marguerite reluctantly accepted, with the caveat that Felicia's safety was my sole responsibility.

After Effie's first cry the next morning, I opened the doors. She ambled out, inspected the balcony from end to end, and flopped down onto the tile floor. Her eyes gazed peacefully across the hills, her voice silent.

July 19

In Riquewihr, we can stop in wine-tasting rooms to sample local vintages. Our favorite place is a sixteenth-century Weinstube, *a cool, damp, earthy cellar, permeated with centuries of spilled wine, where we have a glass of* crémant *(sparkling wine) while we stand at a round table that must have been in the cellar since opening day. We have found other tourists to talk with, like the three middle-aged professors from Amherst, Massachusetts. The room they are staying in has CNN—and are we jealous! Visiting with them for ten minutes did wonders, and we are contemplating a stay in a chain hotel to earn a television treat of our own.*

Each day in Riquewihr we explore a castle or the quaint, German-style, wine towns nearby. Yesterday we took a boat ride in the section of Colmar known as Little Venice. Our boatmates, a newlywed couple from Sweden, seemed very sweet and young, and they spoke great English. Today we'll walk the vineyard footpaths. There are nineteen of these trails in the area, and they sound very appealing.

Being on the move, experiencing new places, and talking with new souls feels comforting and adventuresome. It is scattering our blues to the four winds that blow over the hills and down the valley of the Rhine.

I scanned the map from the tourist office as we headed in search of the trail from Riquewihr to the nearby town of Hunawihr.

"What a great day for a walk. How far to that other town?" she asked.

"The map doesn't say."

"Give me an estimate."

"Three kilometers to Hunawihr and three back."

"In miles that would be what, 1.8?"

"Yes, my metric wizard. We're passing into Riquewihr now through a gate with wooden spikes pointing down at our heads. Careful on these cobblestones. . . ."

"We're passing that bakery where they gave us free macaroons last night, aren't we? They smell great."

"Maybe we'll stop by on the way back. Here on the main street, houses show stout timbers between triangles of color—cream, burnt orange, gold, green. . . ." We passed out of town through another gate, climbed a stairway leading up into the vines, and then followed a vineyard road that wound uphill. "Doing okay?"

She mock-panted like a dog. "Giving it my best."

We paused, and I took in the landscape. "What a quaint and beautiful town, with the clock towers and city walls . . . a stork in its nest on a chimney. I wonder if maybe they'll have forgotten what we look like and give us another free macaroon tonight at the bakery."

"You're *trying* to take my mind off this hike. How much higher is it?"

Looking upward I saw not a summit but a road curving out of sight. "It's pleasant walking here between the vines. Did you know there's a stork park and a butterfly garden in Hunawihr?"

"It's getting hot, and you're not distracting me from my question."

"Feel these." I placed her hands around a clump of bright-green grapes, smaller than peas.

"Take my picture with them. You can use it for a newspaper article."

After three more rest stops, some cajoling, pleading, and flat-out lies about how close we were to our goal, we reached the crest. "Nice job! We made it."

"Phew. That was some 'stroll' through the vineyards."

"It was worth it. From here I can see the contoured hills, the mountains behind, and not only Riquewihr but also other sweet villages, with orange roofs and church steeples."

"You're going to have to bribe me with a really nice lunch if you expect me to walk to Hunawihr and back."

"Isn't it reward enough to see me happy?"

She tried to frown, but I caught the upward tilt at the corners of her lips.

We paced along a blacktop road across level ground. "We're entering the woods. On the left are dark, angular evergreens. Over there," I pointed her hand to the right, "are lighter and fluffier deciduous trees."

"And the birds are making music in the woods. This is much better." She hung onto my hand and swung it forward and back.

We listened to distant church bells, shared the warmth of the sun, and sniffed the scents of pine, herbs, and blossoms while descending past meadows of purple, lavender, and yellow wild flowers. In Hunawihr, another half-timbered, fairy-tale town, we stopped for lunch under a grape arbor at a place called the Wistub Suzel. On our empty stomachs, the wine we ordered bathed us in warmth. I gazed through an archway that sat squarely behind Marguerite. "You, my *Fraulein*, are as pretty as can be."

Her eyes lit. "I'm all sweaty. Besides, this is my French hairdo. I can't be your *Fraulein.*"

"Ah, *mademoiselle*, you look perfect. You are framed by a gateway behind you, and your background is a street lined with storybook houses. Those children I see, I happen to know, are named Hansel and Gretel."

"What could be better than a year in Europe with you?"

Cruising the Bodensee and Being Taken for a Ride

July 20

We are on the move, and each day we seem stronger. Our new residence is a modern, little hotel in Hagnau, a cute-but-not-historic village near Meersburg, Germany. We're a block from Lake Constance, which the locals call the Bodensee. Our landlord is very genial, speaks good English, and provides a nice breakfast of cereals, cold cuts, and yogurt. (The latter is doled out like gold.) There's no balcony, but Felicia, so far, is not complaining.

On our first afternoon, the sounds of an oompah band drew us to the village green where a fair was underway with food booths all around—a good, inexpensive meal in the offing. We partook of the wine, the wursts *(sausages), the fish-and-kraut casseroles cooked in huge iron pots, not to mention the oompah music. It started to rain, and the audience scurried away with the band right behind. When the shower passed, everyone emerged to resume the party.*

We continue to experience the idyllic life we had dreamed of for this trip. Tuesday we took the ferry west to Konstanz. Yesterday we went east to Lindau. A wonderful way to while away the days.

I look back on the sad days I spent searching for insight. It seems that there's something boiling inside me. My spirit swims in it, occasionally slipping under, as in those days in Brittany, but always trying to keep above the surface. When I'm happy, I look up at the sky, never down to see how exposed I am to turmoil. Is this why alcoholics and drug addicts imbibe? To avoid feeling melancholy? The rest of us work and achieve and keep moving to hold it at bay. Now that we're on the road experiencing new things and meeting other English-speaking tourists, I can restrain it below my consciousness. I've been a strong swimmer up until now, but this year may be changing that.

I descended to the hotel office for checkout. Our landlord gestured to a chair and pushed a bill across the desk. "Did you enjoy your visit?"

"Very much." I glanced at the paper and froze. "This says 120 marks ($72) a night. We agreed to 100 ($60)."

"No, you are mistaken."

"When we came, you said 100."

"That is not possible."

"And what's this other charge?"

"Ten marks a night for the animal. That's right."

I stared open-mouthed. "I'm very unhappy. I wanted to be able to recommend your hotel. We liked it here, but you said 100, and now this charge for the cat." I stood and paced.

The innkeeper studied me, waited, cleared his throat. "I don't think so, but perhaps . . . I call my wife."

He spent a couple of minutes on the phone as I glowered at him. Should I pay if he demanded it? I thought back to the nudist couple and what they had told us about hotels in Germany and the charges they added to the bills.

The man smiled half-heartedly. "Yes, okay. My wife explained. It was she who quoted the incorrect rate."

We had never spoken to anyone but this man about the room. I wanted to chastise him for blaming his wife, but I felt more relieved than angry. Two-thirds of the problem was solved.

"And the charge for the cat?"

"You must pay. It is posted in the room."

"There's lots of writing on the door, all in German. When we checked in, you never mentioned a charge for the cat." I remembered exactly what he had said, which was, "You can keep an elephant if you want. We don't care." I wondered now if they charged by the pound.

"It is posted. You must pay."

I gave him the Visa card, feeling pretty good about standing my ground for the 20 marks but a little wimpy for accepting the pet fee. Back in the room, I reported to Marguerite. "What should I have done?"

"You did great," she said.

"Sometimes I worry because you're tougher about these things than I am."

"Not this time. You're the king of the hagglers today. And we had a grand time in Hagnau. You can't let a petty thief ruin your memories."

Marguerite's absolution went miles toward soothing me, that and her naming the scoundrel for what he was.

Edging into the Alps

We were establishing a valuable German vocabulary. Early on we learned the amenities—*please, thank you, good-bye, good morning.* Marguerite stalled at that point, but I continued on to the days of the week, numbers, and dining terms—*fish, pork, potato, cake, strawberries.* The menus still seemed like so much oompah, but I was able to say, "Chicken?" and let the waiter point at items on the list. Then I would say, *"Nicht Huhn Leber* (Not chicken liver)," to make sure.

Voyaging with no guidebook, we followed our noses, our memories of our 1970 trip, and our Michelin map book to the northern fringes of the Alps. After a long day of searching for a room, we came to Benediktbeuern, just north of the mountains, and found a hotel outside of town and away from the highway.

At the reception desk, a white-haired, stoop-shouldered woman came from behind a curtain to greet me. She didn't offer any

English, and the rate she quoted sounded very good. I was pretty sure of the numbers, but I gestured for her to write it down. She jotted 53 marks ($32) on a magazine. It sounded almost too good. I'd heard about places that quoted prices per person, so how could I make sure? *"Zwei* person? (Two people?)" I asked. *"Für Zimmer?* (For room?)" She nodded to both questions. *"Und Katze?* (And cat?)"

"Ja, ja," she answered. That seemed pretty definite.

The Frau took us to see a couple of rooms. As we climbed the stairs, she watched Marguerite closely, noticed how I led her, and pointed at a floor mat so I would be cautious. I liked that. We booked a second-floor room with a balcony, a view of the foothills, and the faint sound of rushing mountain streams.

In the morning, we loaded up at the breakfast buffet and carried everything to the covered patio with a view of the Alps.

"This spread seems elaborate for a $32 place," I said, as I spooned down fruits and cereals.

"You always worry," commented Marguerite, slicing her ham and cheese and forking a bite into her mouth.

"This is such a good deal compared to the other places we checked," I pointed out, as I enjoyed some yogurt with fresh berries.

The Frau stopped by our table to pour coffee and asked if we wanted more fruit. *"Danke,"* Marguerite said. The Frau left, and Marguerite looked back to me. "Stop worrying, and enjoy it. Oh, and pull out that little phrase book. I want to look something up."

When the woman returned with some strawberries, Marguerite employed her new phrase: *"Sehr freundlich.* (You're kind.)"

July 27

Our hotel has soda and beer machines in the hallways, a good innovation, don't you think? Maybe even a GI (German Improvement). At night we hear sheep baaing and the brooks burbling. Our room is grand, large with a nice balcony. Overall the place is clean, but I avoid mentioning that the carpets are stained. Full disclosure would serve no purpose.

At dinner they save a table for us and bring our napkins in folders with Herr Webster *and* Frau Webster *on them. That made me feel a little guilty when we dined elsewhere for our anniversary dinner, at a chalet restaurant up the hill last night. We were the only diners, and it was a glorious anniversary—number twenty-eight—with a striking sunset to honor the occasion.*

I'm happy they've been so nice to us here. It makes up for our last landlord, and . . . what I've been trying not to think about or write about is the stereotype I carry about the Germans. The pushy German who shoves his or her way into the buffet line; we saw them in Morocco several years ago. And Madame Jegouzo spoke about them the same way. It's the reason we gave no thought to staying for any length of time in Germany while planning the trip. Okay, there's Hitler and the concentration camps, too, but I don't want to think about those. I want to be fair. The Frau is a great hostess, so I'll choose her as my stereotypical German.

From our base in Benediktbeuern, Marguerite and I traveled by train to Munich, where we boarded a double-decker bus for the English-language city tour. Another day, we walked the attractive streets of the spa town of Bad Tolz and the resort enclave of Mittenwald, where peaks soared like a granite cathedral and buildings showed off alpine murals. From Garmisch-Partenkirchen, a cable car carried us up the mountain. We rambled down woodland trails with German families out for a stroll and lunched halfway down at a country lodge on a patio surrounded by lush meadows, pine forests, and towering Alps.

That final morning, I entered the lobby and rang the bell. A clerk I'd never seen before appeared. She spoke fairly good English, but the bill she produced charged us 106 marks—not 53 marks—a night.

"This isn't right. It should be half this much," I said. "The older woman wrote it down. Look, the magazine's still here beside the counter."

She peered at the number 53 scrawled on the cover. "That's for each person."

"But I asked for the price for the room, the *Zimmer*."

"Mister, you did not understand," she said with elaborate patience. "Some places, they charge by the room. Like when I go to Italy, I know they give the price each person."

"Go and ask the Frau. She's been very nice to us."

She took off to the back and returned. "That is the price. It is reasonable. She will not change it."

"If I had known and had agreed to it, then it would be reasonable. I don't have that much currency. Do you take credit cards?"

"No."

"Better not to use credit anyway. You might cheat me more if I gave you a card."

Her eyes narrowed. Perhaps I had hurt her. I felt a pang of guilt, but so be it. "I don't mean *you*. I mean the *Frau*." I stalked away from the desk.

After hearing the news, Marguerite cried out, "The fascists!"

"What happened to *sehr freundlich?*"

"*Sehr* fascist."

I pulled all the francs from my money belt and combined them with my marks. It was enough. As I paid, I looked the woman in the eye and said, "It isn't fair." I caught a shamefaced look that let me think she sympathized.

An hour later I was maneuvering the Peugeot through some switchbacks above a mountain lake. I should have been relishing the view, but I wasn't. We were headed for Seefeld, Austria, where we had booked a suite in a castle for three nights, based on a review in our Austria guidebook. It would be expensive ($69 a night) but sounded worth the splurge.

"You're awfully quiet," Marguerite said.

"I'm sulking."

"Maybe it really was a misunderstanding with the Frau."

"I suppose it's possible. . . . We had some great moments these last days in Germany—the lake and the mountains were grand. But when it counted, the people let us down."

"Do you want to cancel our suite at the castle to make up some of the money? I know sticking to $100 a day is important to you."

"I won't let that cheat spoil our plans. But, damn, it was what all the travel articles warned about. When it happened, I just handed over the money."

"We both decided. . . . It's only money."

"No, it's faith. I feel gullible and ashamed. All of my traveler's confidence is shot."

"You don't have to pressure yourself this way."

But I couldn't help it. Later, in Italy and elsewhere, I always worried. Yet it turned out that the hotels seldom charged by the person, and when they did, they always made the exact charges clear, all except the Frau.

Summer Is the Best Time at a Ski Resort

We arrived in Seefeld and checked out our castle. It was compact and pretty—a three-story, cream-colored structure, with one round turret and carved, wooden balconies outside; armor and hunting gear ornamenting the halls; and a bar and lobby inside. The cheerful brunette at the desk spoke English, and I questioned her thoroughly. She swore that the price covered the cost for all three of us—Marguerite, Felicia, and me. She commiserated about our misfortune at the Frau's place and assured me that they wouldn't think of adding any surprises to the bill. Then she led us to our suite, which was a knockout.

July 30
Our hotel, the Wildsee-Schlossl, is paradise. It's an old castle, or manor, from 1662, with a paneled bar and prosperous-looking guests.

I'm glad we came in the summer; we couldn't afford this place in ski season. And it's great that this highbrow resort hotel allows us to bring our kitty. That's a European Improvement, as far as we're concerned.

Our suite includes a living room; a kitchen; a huge, modern, marbled bath; and a round dining area, round because it's built into the castle's tower. Our front rooms and the narrow balcony overlook a mineral-green lake and ragged mountains. Brass lamps sparkle on every wall and dangle over the dining nook.

For breakfasts, which are included and delivered to our room, we order bacon and eggs or an omelet, plus ham, cheese, fruit, yogurt, and breads. Bacon and eggs—my first such meal since leaving the U.S. four months ago—is a longed-for treat. We save the ham, cheese, and bread for lunch, which makes the hotel a pretty good deal despite the fact that it's a bit of a splurge.

That first afternoon, we explored Seefeld's expensive clothing shops and hotels, with mountain views all around us. We entered the glassed-in patio of a restaurant, took a table surrounded by tropical plants, and questioned a bow-tied waiter about prices and specials. "Don't worry," he said, "the dollar has gone to 13 shillings."

From the Austrian specialties, we ordered one plate of kraut with meat dumplings and one of goulash and noodles. The sky steadily darkened outside, and rain began to pour.

"What's that, some kind of music?" Marguerite asked.

For a moment I was confused. Had they put on a CD just as the rain started? "It's like hundreds of little drums. It doesn't sound right, but it has to be the rain on the corrugated, plastic roof. Now there's hail, too." The sound intensified, thrummed inside my ears.

"It's like having 120 tap dancers overhead," she said.

Not to be outdone, I ventured, "Like living inside a rain stick."

"A hail stick," she corrected.

"It's driving thoughts of the evil Frau from my head."

Once we were back at the Schlossl, we took turns luxuriating in the deep tub. We wrapped ourselves in the thick terry robes from the bathroom. Felicia was sunk into the folds of the down comforter on the bed and not about to budge. Using cat treats, we lured her into the living room. I flipped on the television and discovered another wonder—English. They had CNN. We rejoiced at the prospect of our first TV in two months.

After catching the second half of *Larry King Live*, we watched the news until the same stories appeared the third time. I had Marguerite pose for pictures with our "castle cat" out on the balcony, but we retreated inside under the comforter when frigid winds brought more rain and lightning over the Alps.

In the morning, Marguerite asked, "What time is *Larry King?*"

"Three o'clock."

"He's the closest thing to intelligible entertainment I've seen since Holland. No matter what, we'll be on this couch by 2:45 this afternoon."

I didn't argue. I even brought my watch when we went out for the day.

We took a cable car up the mountain for the grand view of the Alps and the town nestled in its valley. As we walked along rocky paths, Marguerite said, "This brisk air feels good, but have you checked the time?" Having a cup of coffee in the snack bar, she asked again, and then once more as we rode the tram to the valley floor. We returned to the village with plenty of time and bought salads, fruit, cookies, and wine in the basement market of the town's upscale department store.

After another quick bath, we donned our robes. Marguerite kidnapped our kitty as I went to the kitchenette to retrieve the leftover ham and cheese from breakfast. I spooned salads onto plates, added cold cuts and bread, and set everything out on the coffee table. I flipped on the TV and popped the cork from the wine to punctuate the *Larry King Live* theme. The sight of Marguerite in her fluffy robe, sitting upright, anticipating happily, filled me with delight. It was a glorious moment in the history of television.

People who have never been in this situation may scoff, but I must report that Larry is a witty guy, and his shows have moments that are very interesting and stuffed with bits of Americana for the dispossessed traveler. Aside from a touch of home, it was a confirmation that the world was still out there. Wars, violence, and politics notwithstanding, it was somehow comforting.

July 31

Looking over our July expenses, I was upset to see the total. After deducting transportation costs and gifts, it came to $3,600. That's $116 per day in living and lodging expenses. Costs in Germany and here at the castle were high, and $150 was because of the two swindlers in Germany. The rest I attribute to our depression and our need for entertainment. We ate out, took tours, and went on boat trips as diversions.

Marguerite adds another American Improvement—shower curtains. Even here in the castle, they are absent. It's hard not to spray the whole bathroom.

Now for the bad news. We suffered a potentially serious failure with the Internet.

In Seefeld, we passed a hotel with a sign that said, "Internet Access, Weekdays 9:00–5:00." With the sign in English, it was easy to tell for whom this service was provided.

Marguerite tried to pass me as we marched through the hotel's lobby. I stopped and hung onto her hand to keep her from crashing into a doorframe. Back in the pilot position, I led her to the conference room, where four tables held computers. A fellow at one of the tables acknowledged us, and we quickly discovered that we had no language skills in common. No French, no English, but by now I had the e-mail thing pretty well figured out. He pointed us to an English-speaking clerk at the hotel desk, and we paid her for an hour on the computer.

Soon I was set up at a computer . . . set up at a Netscape screen all in German. I messed with it for a couple of minutes, but there was no way. Retrieving e-mail in Germany from your home account in the United States wasn't just a matter of clicking a little picture of an envelope.

I tried to explain to the guy what I wanted to accomplish. I used terms such as "e-mail in United States" and "e-post, America," but he didn't get it.

"The woman can translate," Marguerite suggested.

With translator in place, the cyberguy and I took turns hacking at the keys. Marguerite hung on every word. But the fellow shrugged his shoulders, rolled his eyes, and gave up.

The desk clerk said, "Fritz doesn't know how to do what you ask."

Did Fritz even give a damn? "What we have to do is change the address in the program to our e-mail address." I pointed to the words at the top of the screen. "Where does it say *Edit?*" The woman helped me find *Preferences*, and I entered my home e-mail address. I clicked *Retrieve Mail.*

"We're close," I said. "It wants my password." Marguerite was looking excited. I felt mostly relieved; I wasn't going to fail at e-mail in German. The computer ruminated and the stop-sign logo flashed. The stop sign disappeared, but no mail came up. *"Crap."*

"What's going on, Eddie?"

"Not a damned thing."

"Can't we get our mail?" Her distress motivated me to try again, but without any luck.

The clerk refunded our money, and we headed toward the castle. "Maybe I retrieved the mail, but somehow we didn't see it."

"What would happen then?"

"We could pick it up in Salzburg, *I hope.*" She looked at me with alarm in her eyes, but she didn't ask, and I didn't volunteer the alternative. The words *lost in cyberspace* were set in the hard drive of my mind.

The Land of Mozart

The New Digs

August 5

We have moved into the upstairs of a three-story farmhouse in Oberesch, 4 km from Salzburg. We had booked this neat place last January from the U.S. through a company called Pego to make sure that we had a home for the Mozart festival and a place where Patricia (with her friend Shirley) and Claire could visit. At $58 a night plus electricity, it's steep for us, but it's reasonable for a place this large, booked from overseas for the high season.

We have half of the third floor. There's a cozy-but-dark bedroom; a roomy living room with couches and a skylight; and an efficient, little kitchen. There's also a balcony for Effie from which I see farmhouses, meadows, and hills. The outskirts of Salzburg are in the distance with a backdrop of hazy mountains. The weather is perfect for sitting out on the balcony for breakfast and dinner.

The information book from Pego said we would have a washing machine available and a phone for incoming calls—but where?

On Sunday, our second morning, I approached the landlord, Herr E.—a short chunk of a red-faced man, perhaps seventy years old—with my bag of laundry in hand. *"Vo ist Wasche?"*—my attempt at "Where is washing?" He glanced at the sack and led me outside into an open garage that housed a half-pint tractor. He pointed to a trash can by the wall and said, *"Das Plastik."* I looked at the scraps of plastic and back at him. The man was taking me on the wrong mission, but I was intrigued to see where it would lead. Perhaps I would learn everything I needed to know about trash disposal—a useful piece of information.

He peered at me, and I frowned. *"Verstehen Plastik?"* he asked. I nodded. I did understand *plastic*. He led me around back to a covered bin, which he opened to exhibit the garbage.

"I'm glad to know where the trash goes," I said in English. Then I hit him with my best German. *"Nein Garbage."* I indicated the shirt I wore and a shirt in the bag. *"Die Wasche."*

Herr E. grinned foolishly and said a few words I took for an apology. He had insulted our clothing, but it didn't bother me. Back inside we climbed a flight of stairs, and he knocked on the door to his home. When Frau E. opened it, he rattled off a couple of sentences and chuckled. Frau E.—whose physique and complexion closely resembled her husband's—scowled and led me inside to the washing machine. She gestured to a spot on the floor, and I set the laundry down.

I pointed at myself. *"Ich wasche."* Then in English, "I can do the wash."

"Nein, nein." She said something I took for, "I will do it," although I'm not sure why I got that understanding. More words flowed, including one I knew—*Sonntag* (Sunday)—all the while shaking her head. She ushered me out and whacked the door closed behind me.

Back home with Marguerite, I reported. "Either she doesn't work on Sunday or she's telling me we'll get the laundry *next* Sunday. I don't know which, but she sure doesn't want me touching her machine."

"That's ten days' laundry. We can't wait a week."

"There's hope we'll see it sooner. I just can't guarantee it."

"Is she going to charge us?"

"I don't have a clue. Maybe *you* should ask."

Monday afternoon as we returned from exploring, two baskets of wet wash sat in the hallway. As we draped underwear on a laundry rack on the balcony, Marguerite renewed her French refrain, "You know she has a secret dryer that she won't share." We stretched shirts, pants, socks, and everything else over our outside table, the molded-plastic chairs on the balcony, more chairs under the open skylight in the living room, and along the edge of the bathtub. The drying time proved acceptable, and it actually turned out pretty well having the Frau do the work. We went on this way for the four weeks of our stay, and the only disagreeable part was enduring her grimaces and scowls each time I brought a new batch for cleaning.

That afternoon we also discovered the promised telephone. Frau E. appeared at our door, glared when I answered her knock, and said, *"Telefon."* We rushed downstairs to her apartment, and the Frau showed us a phone in the hallway. I picked up the receiver, and a cheery Esther greeted me. "How are you kids doing? We've been worried."

"How are the new digs in Austria?" Lester asked from their other line.

"It's great to hear your voices, and *complete sentences* in English."

"I speak English a lot," Esther said. "It's a fad here in California."

Marguerite tugged at my sleeve. "Stop hoarding them. I want to talk."

"Just a minute," I told her, "I have to tell them we're going to stay with their friends in Athens."

"Let me. I'm the one who spoke with Sophia and made the reservations."

There was no controlling Marguerite. I handed over the phone. "Make sure to ask how Lester is doing and about their trip to Australia."

We passed the phone back and forth for half an hour, during which it became clear that Les was feeling chipper, their trip to Australia was a go, and they would not relent about their intention to consume kangaroo meat. After hanging up, we basked in the glow of their friendship for hours.

Little Annoyances

I knocked on their door, and Frau E. appeared, with a pout on her face. Did I tear her away from something important? Did she find me repulsive? Were her dentures chafing?

I mustered my willpower and my new vocabulary from the dictionary. The German word for *pillow* was *Kissen*. It was a little embarrassing, and she frowned in her familiar way as I said, *"Haben Sie mehr Kissen, bitte?"* If she asked how many I wanted, I would go for two.

She said, "You already have three." At least that's what I guessed she said from recognizing the word *drei* (three). She frowned harder, expecting, no doubt, for me to slink away in shame.

"I told you the first day that we will have company," I said in English. "Marguerite's *Schwester und Freund kommen* (sister and friend come). *Vier persons, drei Kissen.* (Four people, three pillows.)"

She turned away resignedly with a look that I read as, You're a spoiled, wasteful American and I'm only doing this because I promised Pego to make the lodgers happy. I mentally practiced apologizing to Marguerite's sister for having gotten her only one pillow. I knew she would prefer at least two.

August 6

Language, washing, shopping where you don't understand . . . all the little things seem to mount up. Communications are so much easier when both sides want to communicate. Being a tenant is so much more pleasant when the landlord wishes to please.

But the biggest little problem is bugs. With hot weather and no screens on the windows, we're talking possible catastrophe.

We left all the windows and the skylights in the kitchen and living room open until dusk that first night to cool the place off. Then we closed the kitchen window and the sliding glass door to the balcony. It was still warm in the house and a little sticky, so we left the two skylights and our bedroom window open. Why did they have no screens? Were European insects less bold in aviation than the American kind, not daring to soar the three tall stories to our windows?

The answer found me around midnight, when that terrible mosquito-buzzing tormented my ears. The beastie swooped and soared as I swatted, batted my own forehead, ducked under the sheet, tried to sleep, and pretended to sleep. And still, I heard the evil droning, felt an itch on my neck. I cursed and climbed out of bed.

"What are you doing?" Marguerite murmured.

"Damned mosquitoes. I'm going to get them."

"Crawl under the covers and hide."

"Doesn't work." I found the light switch, latched the window closed, and began searching. There. I smacked it, impressed a red-and-black emblem on the wall . . . then another. But a third one got away and spent the night attacking.

In the morning, I found Herr E. I swooshed my hand around in front of my face and buzzed at him, saying, *"Mosquite."* I figured the final *o* wouldn't help the translation.

"Ah," he said, triumphant recognition in his eyes. He entered a room on the ground floor and produced a plastic container, which looked like an air freshener you stick on the wall, and blurted an enthusiastic sentence.

That evening, we sat on the balcony in our three molded-plastic chairs. Marguerite and I sipped wine as I watched the sun sink into the mountains behind Salzburg. Our companion rested in her soft kitty bed on the chair between us and accepted pats from both sides. Hundreds of sheep baas drifted up from a distant meadow—what an absurd yet pleasing sound. Cows moaned occasionally. Then a new noise, a loud swooshing, descended from somewhere behind us. We both jumped. "What's that?" Marguerite asked.

"I don't know. Maybe they're drying apples with some kind of a burner." A giant, blue and red, hot-air balloon appeared, its wicker basket not more than thirty feet overhead. It passed rapidly and disappeared with a blast of its burner behind the other side of the roof. "Monster mosquito."

She laughed. "It was a hot-air balloon, wasn't it? But we better not have any monster mosquitoes in our room tonight."

And we didn't. Herr E.'s gizmo worked. The bad news was that it worked for only one night. On day four, with lots of little, pink hillocks on our skin, we headed to the store for a better solution.

In one of our guidebooks, we had read about plug-in mosquito repellents. We found a lawn-and-garden store, threw out the word *mosquite*, and buzzed a couple of times. The clerk showed us what we wanted. It was shaped like a palm-sized, green flying saucer with a three-pronged plug coming out the back. It came in a box labeled *Gelsenstecker*, with rectangular wafers called *stücks* included inside. From the pictures on the box, I understood that each night we were to insert a new wafer and plug it in. We bought lots of wafers, and despite Marguerite's skepticism, it did the job!

Our Long-Lost E-Mail

As most visitors approach Salzburg for the first time, they keep an eye on that imposing white fortress perched atop the horizon, sheltered by distant peaks, growing larger and closer until it dominates the city. But I was enmeshed in a parking-lot tango, trying to drive and decipher signs at the same time.

Unlike France, there were no indicators for the center of town, no solitary church steeple marking my destination, no gridded road system that led inexorably in the right direction. The blue signs with the white P for parking kept guiding me the wrong way. What good was a parking lot two miles out of town, especially with a sometimes weary comrade? Finally, I was on the right track, literally. "I'm following a trolley that's leading me downtown." As I cruised behind the tram, the road narrowed, but the streetcar continued. *"Rats!"* I stomped on the brakes.

Marguerite waited a moment and said meekly, "What happened?"

"Damned trolley kept going straight, but there's one of those red and white, international Do Not Enter signs." I turned, recirculated, repeated the same mistakes, and eventually found a parking spot in a garage under the Sheraton.

"Now you can relax." Marguerite patted my knee. "Forget traffic and think of those Viennese pastries."

I did, and it helped, and so did the map I had ripped from our guidebook. It took us down streets lined in three-story, baroque, cream-colored buildings toward the Salzach River. The view opened up near the waterway. "Ah, there it is—the fortress. I've seen it in photographs and in *The Sound of Music*, but I didn't imagine the river or the park across the way, lush and green." We strolled to a railing by the riverbank. "The castle looks pure white, massive, indomitable. Can you hear the river rippling below us?" She smiled a yes. "Then at the base of the cliff is the enclosed city. I want to make it sound as special as it looks. It's like a rich stage for the castle, sparkling, golden, decked in gray-green domes."

Crossing a bridge to the city, she asked, "Where's the violin music coming from?"

"On the pedestal at the end of the bridge—you're going to love this—there's a guy dressed in a red cloak wearing a midnight-blue, feathered mask. He's fiddling away. And the best part—he's wearing red sneakers that match his robe."

"Think he's part of the music festival?"

"Looks like a free agent. He has a jar for donations."

She gave me a don't-you-think-we-should-give-him-something? look—you recognize these things after twenty-eight years together—and I dropped some coins into his tub. He pulled two hard candies from his pocket and tossed them my way. Every time we approached the city after that, "Mr. Feathers" threw candy to us.

Strolling through town, the citadel hid again and again. We walked down shopping streets lined with five- and six-story, seventeenth-century buildings. European craftsmen signs jutted out overhead—a silhouette of a pig; a workman with hammer; a fat, smiling baker with billowy, white hat; black signs with gold letters; gold ringlets lettered in black for coffee, leather goods, and books. Then we'd come to a square, and I would spot the citadel again— now sitting above a collection of green domes, now over an old palace built into the cliffside—always the invincible, white stronghold. Details grew more clear. I could make out the dark stone ramparts protecting the castle from below; the cable train that climbed the cliff; a restaurant, off to the right, with red-and-gold sun umbrellas; and the cylindrical tower of the casino.

The bluff where the castle looms is the Monchsberg, a precipice from which the prince-archbishops of Salzburg defended their fortune. For the tourist, it is a vantage point to observe close-up the sea of verdigris-copper domes atop many of the city's forty-five churches. The Monchsberg, together with the Salzach River, confines the old city to its elegant nucleus and maintains its intimate feel, making it walkable. It's a complete voyage unto itself to sift through the prosperous shops, museums, and churches decorated with art treasures. We dined on the second-floor balcony of the Café Glockenspiel. In the square below, water cascaded down the famous baroque fountain to the rearing, stone horses at the base.

At the tourist office we learned that an old palace under the bluff housed a temporary cybercafe. We tracked it down—a gravel-floored room with rows of high tables and perhaps twenty-four computers with twenty-three young adults before them, sitting on stainless-steel stools, absorbed in cyberendeavors.

A Norse god—tall, broad-featured, with long, golden hair—greeted me in German, but he switched easily to English. "I am Helmut." We shook hands—his immense, mine paltry. "We put the computer room together for the festival, to see if we can make a success."

"It's wonderful." Marguerite glowed with anticipation. "I can't wait to hear from my friends."

"You're doing a booming business," I observed.

"The Mozart festival is our big event. Sad, isn't it?" Helmut shook his head. "He is dead these 200 years, and everyone comes to see 'his city.' Salzburg shunned Mozart when he lived, and he was buried in a pauper's grave near Vienna."

Helmut collected $4 to cover half a day on the Internet—much more time than we needed, but what a deal. He set us up with a computer, and I felt a surge of relief. "Netscape in English! The last place we went to," I explained, "it was in German, and it was awful." That brought back the question—would there even be e-mail to see, or had it disappeared during the Seefeld fiasco? I had to come through for Marguerite and find it.

Helmut left, and I went through the steps to call up our mail, entered the password, and waited. The familiar pattern of icons across the top of the screen appeared, but the page was empty! A note flashed and disappeared, "You Have No New Mail."

"That's what I was afraid of."

"I don't want to hear this." Marguerite grimaced.

"It's not here. We must have retrieved it at that place in Seefeld but not been able to see it somehow." I tried looking in the Trash folder, but it was empty.

"You said we'd be able to pick it up."

"The end of that sentence had been, 'I hope.'"

"Don't touch anything. Find Helmut. *He'll* get it."

I skulked over and retrieved the computer man. He clicked the mouse and typed a few things, with no success. He tried again, but apparently not even a Norse god could vanquish the spirits of cyberspace. Our e-mail, like the Habsburg dynasty, was no more.

As we trudged away, I said, "It's all right. Patricia will be here in two days."

"It's *not* all right. I want to hear from Bette and Robyn."

"We'll telephone them," I said lamely.

Her response was a miserable look.

We walked silently. Then I stopped, took her hand, and placed it on a cardboard cutout standing about her height in the middle of the sidewalk. "This will cheer you up."

"It *won't*." She ran her hand along the edge. "What is it?"

"Not what, who."

"Okay, who?"

"He's wearing a white wig and a red waistcoat with gold spangles."

"I don't know. . . . Liberace."

"He has a piece of candy in one hand and a box in the other."

"Are they Mozart Balls?"

Despite herself, Marguerite cracked a smile. She wasn't clairvoyant. Every shop we'd passed in Salzburg seemed to sell Mozart Balls. Eventually we tried the chocolates wrapped in foil with the composer's fanciful likeness. They were extremely mediocre, but the picture and life-size cutout of the composer were very cute indeed.

A New, Long-Lost Friend

It was late afternoon on the farm as I bargained with Marguerite. "If you walk with me, I'll handle dinner."

"Can we take Felicia?"

I positioned the blue baby sling across my chest and settled Effie inside. "She's such a sweet girl."

"She's a wonderful, wonderful cat. But that's not what you say at five in the morning."

"No, then I'm tired and pissed, but right now I'm in love." Careful with my precious cargo, I led Marguerite down the steep stairs and rushed past the flies outside the front door. "Let's introduce Felicia to our animal neighbors."

A stream bubbled beside us as we followed the path along a meadow to a spot where forty or fifty sheep grazed. A chorus of baas greeted us. The sound obviously cheered Marguerite. Felicia gazed with mild curiosity. "Remember these guys?" I asked. "You met a couple in Holland."

"I'll take your picture with them if you let me carry Effie afterwards."

I set up the camera, handed it to Marguerite, backed off toward the herd, and gave directions. "A little higher. More to the left. Okay, let 'er rip." Gingerly lifting our kitty's carrier off my shoulders, I slipped it onto Marguerite. Felicia squirmed to get comfortable and then looked at me as if to say, Where to next?

As we headed downhill toward the cow barns, smells of earth and hay wafted out to greet us—and a bit of cow stuff, too, but not bad. "There must be thirty of them in here, all black and white. Stand over this way so I can get everyone in the shot." I began positioning Marguerite (and Effie).

"Can they get at us?" she asked.

"They're too busy swatting flies with their tails and gazing sleepy-eyed at the ground to attack." I eased her back a couple of inches. "And there are galvanized gates. I think you're safe."

"This is close enough. I hear them chewing whatever it is they chew."

"It's hay. You've still got a few feet until she starts munching your heels."

"Their necks are longer than you'd expect. Don't they say they can strike out to half their body length?"

"That's for snakes."

I took a couple of shots. Then one of the bovines let out a wail that sent Marguerite halfway to the ceiling, her rocket action hurling Felicia almost out of her arms. Too bad the camera missed it.

I took my ladies home and headed to the pizza parlor housed in the ground floor of an A-frame hotel at the bottom of our hill. I settled at the handsome wood bar with wineglasses and Chianti bottles hanging above.

"*Sprechen Sie English?*" I said to the curly-haired waiter.

"Oh, English? Yes, I *love* English. Are you by any chance from America?"

I nodded.

"I *love* America. My wife and I have visited many times. She has cousins in Illinois."

I ordered two pizzas to go. The fellow wrote up the order and then stuck out his hand. "I am Jamal. I come originally from Tunisia. Are you here with a tour? Staying at the hotel?"

"My wife and I are renting a place up the hill. We'll be here for four weeks with our cat."

"Welcome you to our village, sir." Walking out from behind the bar, he shook my hand a second time. "Here, sit in this booth. Make yourself comfortable. You like wine? What kind of wine do you like?" He poured a glass of red.

Feeling overwhelmed, welcomed, as if I had a newfound friend, I asked Jamal how a guy from Tunisia came to be running an Italian restaurant in Austria. "Ah, my wife is from Italy," he said, as though that explained it.

I spoke about our travels and our cat, then poured out how happy I was to meet him, how glad he spoke English.

My chum reciprocated with valuable information. "We are in a recession in this area. Many people with no work. To do my part, every Wednesday night many of our pizzas cost only 80 shillings ($6). It's a nice thing for the families."

I commended him on his beneficence and mentally scheduled our dinners for the next four Wednesdays. Not only was he helping the unemployed of Austria, but he was also aiding two travelers from America and their budget-minded cat to survive and entertain company on a shoestring.

The Forces of Felicia

We so badly wanted to get our kitty to behave before Patricia arrived with her friend Shirley. If she screamed at dawn, they would awaken. Their jet-lagged brains would remain sleep-deprived for the entire visit. I tried the water-in-the-face trick, but Effie managed to outmaneuver me. First she hid and screamed from undercover. Once I caught up with her, she would close her eyes and keep yelling as drops splattered across her face—a dripping totem to animal determination and human brutality. The next day she didn't bother to run. She stood her ground in the center of the kitchen floor and let the liquid zing her face as she yawped. Water had failed. The cat had my number.

Our third day at the farm, Robyn (our hometown friend who's a psychologist) called. We talked about our adventures, our progress dealing with loneliness, our trials and tribulations. I confided about Felicia. "She's going deaf, so I can't talk with her about how unhappy she's making me. I can't yell no. I pick her up and cradle her in my arms and try to reason with her, but she's stubborn. Everything I try makes me feel like a tyrant."

Robyn responded with a calm but concerned voice, "She's old. She's a joy in your life, and she doesn't understand. She can't hear herself to know how loud she is. Give her whatever she wants, and let go of it."

Despite Robyn's pleadings, Marguerite and I devised another tactic. The next morning at first meow, I locked her in the cat carrier. As if she'd been a step ahead of us, she hesitated not at all—she let out her worst wanawut scream, the loudest we'd heard in a month. Then she attacked the carrier from the inside. The sides of the bag shuddered with her fury. "I can't do this to her," I said.

"It's a mistake. If we use the carrier to punish her, she'll go crazy every time we put her in there."

I unzipped the bag and led our kitty to the kitchen for a nice, huge bowl of wet food.

August 7
  Felicia has won a complete and final victory. We have given in to her persistence, our consciences, and Robyn's pleadings. We throw ourselves on her mercy.

Effie knew the principles of reward and punishment, and I was finally responding to her training by giving her all the canned food she could eat. She acted in every way the good and loving cat again. At night she snuggled against my side, quiet and affectionate, my reward for good behavior. We felt at peace with our kitty and wondered why *we'd* been so stubborn. She was plumping up, looking glossy and content. Litter was in short supply, and I was scooping often. But what about the eleven-pound limit for pets to fly in the airplane cabin?

Reinforcements Arrive

August 7, continued
  Why do they rave over Austrian pastries and coffee? The pastries in the morning are good enough but nothing like France. The slagroom (whipped cream) is almost up to Holland's standards, but

217

shouldn't Vienna torte be great this close to the source? It isn't. And
the coffee should be out of this world. I bought a bag from the friendly
woman at our bakery—the one who speaks a touch of English and tries
to wait on me every morning. She swore the coffee is wunderbar.
What it is is nothing. I try to make it stronger, weaker—it doesn't
matter. Those Viennese coffee beverages sound great in the travel
articles, with whipped cream, chocolate shavings, cream, cinnamon—
obviously they have to doctor this stuff up to make it good.

We placed an emergency phone call to Patricia two days ago.
"Bring us Starbucks." She arrives today.

We waited in a stark, modern hallway at the Munich airport,
the only amenity a coffee cart. Passengers filed in, and I sighted
Patricia's red hair bobbing among them. "Get ready."

Marguerite stood on tiptoes, as if trying to spot her sister. I
held firm to prevent her charging the door. Soon Patricia broke
loose from the crowd and rushed to hug Marguerite. "I'm so glad
you're here to meet us!" The sisters clung to one another like vise-
grip pliers.

Tears streamed down Marguerite's cheeks. "I told you we'd be
waiting."

"It's been four months. I've missed you," Tricia sobbed.

I tapped them on the shoulders, and they allowed me into the
hug. "We don't see you this often at home."

"At home, you're five hours by Amtrak!" Patricia dabbed an
eye. "When you called in June, I thought you might give up, and
you wouldn't meet me in Salzburg at all."

"So we're just here to facilitate your seeing the Alps," I accused.

"I wanted you *and* the Alps, and I've never been in a country
where they don't speak English. That's why you had to be here to
meet us."

Tricia's friend Shirley stood just outside the huddle, a good six
inches shorter than either sister, with short black hair, a green carry-
on bag, and a look somewhere between bemused and abandoned. I
opened a gap in our circle and brought Shirley in.

❧

What a cool sister. She had flown economy class, but she had descended on the wings of an angel, with love and hugs, gifts from friends and family, books on tape to keep us entertained, more Prempro for Marguerite's sanity, and two pounds of Starbucks. She came to speak English with us and brought Shirley, who was happy to go wherever we wanted and narrate from travel guides as we toured the sights.

Back at the farmhouse, Patricia handed me a giant envelope with all the bills she'd paid for us and bank statements galore. After hours of gabbing, Marguerite and our guests fell asleep, and I pored over it all. The stock market was going gangbusters, thank you. Our credit-card charges were correct, and the exchange rate for purchases and ATM cash withdrawals was right on target. It reassured me to see everything well organized, all the bills paid, and the cash reserves in place to fund the rest of our trip.

Patricia and Shirley gave us a week. After that they would explore Europe by train. Together we took *The Sound of Music* bus tour, which led us to locations from the movie and to two gorgeous lakes, the Wolfgangsee and the Fuschlsee. Mitch, our guide, played music and joked with us, but he also cast out some of the popular myths. For example, the cable-car ride the von Trapps took out of the country with the Nazis in hot pursuit? It never happened. The real von Trapp family packed up and took the train past Innsbruck and on to Switzerland. Oh, well. We forgave Julie Andrews and still loved her at the end of the day. Mitch also introduced us to a sidewalk restaurant in Fuschl, where we ate the best apple strudel with hot custard in the world as we gazed across the square at the baroque, yellow and white church where Maria and Baron von Trapp were married in the movie.

Another day we took Tricia and Shirley to visit a salt mine in Halstatt. Salt mines made the region rich centuries ago. *Salzburg* (with a *u*) means "salt fortress," or a fortress city constructed to protect that wealth. *Salzberg* (with an *e*) is "salt mountain," which we would explore that day. We rode a tram railway up the mountain and hiked to the mine. In a dressing room, we donned red jumpsuits with leather patches covering the butts and backs of the thighs.

From behind them, I watched Tricia and Shirley tramp uphill toward the little train that would carry us into the mountain. "You should see their leatherized tushes," I told Marguerite. "They're a riot."

The train turned out to be only one person wide, with passengers perched on a central rail. The young woman who directed people on board took one look at Marguerite's cane and raised a palm, the international symbol for "Halt!"

"It is very dark down there," she said. Did she think darkness would bother Marguerite?

"And narrow, and cold, and you must climb steps, and . . ."

So *that* was it. "Can't be any worse than the Métro in Paris," I said.

"It's all right," Marguerite addressed the woman. "I do this stuff all the time."

"And we paid." I waved the tickets.

She escorted us to the train and made sure I showed Marguerite how to straddle the rail. "Keep your arms close," she said. "The tunnel is very narrow."

Soon we were rumbling our way deep into the mountain. Once we were down in the cool heart of the earth, we got to use our specialized garments. We skimmed our way down wooden slides to lower and lower levels of the mine, as the miners had done in its active days.

As we followed tight passageways into wide rooms with crystalline ceilings, we met two college girls from the United States. Trekking from vault to vault, the brunette asked, "Do you know about the chapel in Halstatt?" Answering our blank looks, she continued. "The town is wedged between the mountain and the lake, so there's not enough space for a large cemetery. They bury the bodies for several years, and then they dig them up again to make room for new ones."

I recognized Patricia and Marguerite's family resemblance by their expressions of disgust. Shirley seemed intrigued.

The blonde finished the story. "They save the skulls and give them to the families, who decorate them and place them in the chapel."

"We definitely want to go," I said. The others accepted with varying degrees of enthusiasm.

After the mine, with the college girls in the lead, we hiked downhill, rode the tram to the valley, and sought the little church. Inside, as promised, the candle-lit chapel was lined on all sides with shelves covered in skulls—skulls inscribed with the names of the deceased and adorned with ornate crosses, ivy leaves, or flowers.

Why was I so fascinated by old bones? The church sanctuary in Evora, Portugal, back in 1991, the catacombs in Paris, and now this. . . . Part of it was the fun of suggesting that Marguerite touch the bones and then watching her cringe—like those days as a kid when I put caterpillars in the girls' shoes—but there was something deeper that drew me.

We spent the week with Tricia and Shirley singing "Do-Re-Mi" from *The Sound of Music;* holding contests to see who could remember the most songs from the movie; teasing each other; and eating great sausages, cutlets, and trout at lakeside restaurants. We took them to the cybercafe to send out an All Points Bulletin for e-mail. They swooned over Helmut.

One night, in recognition of all the driving and arranging I'd been doing, the three women gave me the night off. They kicked me out of the kitchen. It did my heart good to watch the three of them lined up at the counter slicing and dicing, giggling, and sipping wine as they prepared salad and pasta primavera

That Wednesday evening we took Patricia and Shirley to meet my personal pizza friend. It was my third visit and Marguerite's second. Jamal welcomed us and laid on the charm. "Ah, beautiful ladies, I am so happy to meet you. You come all the way from America to see your sister? How nice. How very nice. We will make for you our best pizzas tonight." He took our drink orders and headed to the kitchen.

"You've been here ten days," Tricia said, "and he acts like it's been ten years. He did everything but kiss you on the lips when you came in."

"I don't know, he seems a little distant tonight," I joked.

🐾

The crowning event of our week was our ascent in the cable train to the top of the Monchsberg. We enjoyed dinner outdoors on the mountaintop and then a Mozart violin and cello concert that followed in a baronial hall of the *Festung* (fortress). It was heaven.

For seven days Patricia and Shirley had shared their easygoing selves, their news of home, their bright and friendly spirits. Our family and our homeland had come to us and bestowed a huge gift. Would Marguerite be restored, or would she long miserably for California when they left?

She and Tricia sobbed, and I discretely wiped a tear when we dropped the two wayfarers at a train station outside Munich. They boarded the coach to other adventures, and we climbed back into the car.

As we accelerated onto the autobahn, Marguerite sighed. "I'm really going to miss them, but I'm glad we have a few days alone before Claire arrives."

That sounded pretty good, but I needed more information. "Did Tricia's visit help you feel better?"

"Absolutely. I'm glad we're in Europe, and I plan to stay." News most welcome!

Supermarkets Are Tough All Over

Notes from my diary on Austrian supermarkets—

At the checkout: *Marguerite and I still look like Lucy and Ethel in that I Love Lucy episode with all the chocolates flying down the conveyor belt. The checker rings things up, and we try to match her speed as we stuff our goods into whatever bags we brought with us (no free sacks in these markets). I stop to pay, Marguerite keeps stuffing, and pretty soon the checker begins whipping the next customer's purchases at us. I'm still juggling the last of our goods, while Marguerite tries to organize the cart.*

What there is and what there isn't: *Don't count on a variety of fruits and vegetables. Even now in midsummer, there's no corn on the cob. I think they use it for hogs over here. It's a disappointment, especially after Holland and France where the fruit and veggies were wonderful.*

Restaurants serve superb lake fish, and most have fowl in some form, at least a chicken schnitzel. Where are these items in the supermarkets? The bigger ones have a butcher/deli with pork, beef, sausages, and dozens of bologna-type things. There are knuckles and shoulders of beef and pork, browned to an inviting crisp. There are ribs and shanks, flanks and franks, but not a chicken to be seen, let alone vegetables. Okay, there's potato salad, a few appetizers, and side dishes that come mostly in cans or jars. The country is perfect for picnics and chop hounds. Do all these people hanker for clogged arteries?

A few days later: *Finally, after two weeks, our supermarket has some corn, but it's ugly, misshapen stuff and costs a dollar an ear. We pass it by, feeling disappointed.*

And for the hard-to-locate items: *We were at wit's end yesterday in the store, and the staff didn't speak English. A perky Scotswoman (a two-year resident of Salzburg) volunteered to help us find laundry detergent (for Frau E.), drain unclogger (which works wonders in our bathtub), salad dressing (paltry few choices), and paper plates (the entire variety had pictures of Pluto the dog at a birthday party).*

The most vital necessities: The only clumping cat litter available smells like a chemical toilet. Felicia has to hold her nose every time she steps into the box. We would buy her a surgical mask to wear, but how would we shop for it?

How Do You Say *Birthday* in German?

August 15

> It's a little before 9:00 AM, which makes it close to midnight in California. Marguerite is still asleep, so no one who is awake on this planet knows it's my birthday.
>
> I'm trying to think back to what my father was like at fifty years old. It was 1962, and I was going into tenth grade. In the fall he would be driving us to school in that really old (1947), embarrassing car we had inherited from my grandmother. He was working hard, exercising little . . . would die in five years. That has something to do with this morning's melancholy.

I sat on our balcony sipping coffee, listening to the hum of distant traffic and the moans of cows, and feeling the crisp morning air. Below me, Herr E. ambled into the field with a teenage boy pushing a wheelbarrow. The Herr sharpened his scythe for a few minutes and then cut the grass from around a fruit tree.

Felicia jumped onto the plastic chair next to mine, and I stroked her. Down on the ground floor, I heard Frau E. exit the house. I looked over the edge and saw her turn on a hose to water the plants on the patio. What had I heard as she came out? There was a sliding glass door opening, then another . . . a *screen* door had opened and closed! I leaned out and confirmed my suspicion. The dirty dogs had screens! I couldn't wait to tell Marguerite. It fit in nicely with her theory about the secret French clothes dryers.

The Herr sliced grass around a second tree and then quit—five minutes' work. The boy hauled the grass off in the wheelbarrow, a snack for the cows.

Marguerite made her way toward me. "Happy birthday, honey." Her words erased my melancholy. "What can we do to make your day special?"

I hugged her. "Remember good old Mitch on *The Sound of Music* tour? He told us about the boat that runs from town to town on the Wolfgangsee and about the White Horse Inn. Let's check it out."

A couple of hours later we were in St. Gilgen, climbing on board the 12:45 PM lake steamer and mounting to the top deck for seats in the sun. As the boat chugged away from the dock, Marguerite asked, "Is it pretty out? I want this to be your best birthday ever."

I looked at the picture-perfect, chalet-style hotels of town; an onion-domed church; and the classical, yellow, two-story buildings. "Like something from a fairy tale—or a model train set." Ahead, the lake stretched, dark and clear, toward an arc of hazy Alps. The vessel skimmed along the shore from one tiny resort to the next, ending, for us, in St. Wolfgang. "The town is just as neat as St. Gilgen. Near the dock there's a substantial, four-story, gold and white building, with a porch on the water and three tiers of wooden balconies. I'll bet that's the White Horse. The sign says, *Weisses Rossl.*"

"You're learning lots of German."

"No, it looks like the fanciest place in town, and everyone there looks happy."

"White Horse or not, I'm taking you."

My hunch proved correct, and soon we were seated on the terrace, feasting not only on trout and "salmon trout," which tasted and looked like salmon, but also on views of the lake and mountains. A thunderstorm came up and drummed on the plastic roof of the terrace, a repeat performance of our first lunch in Seefeld and a romantic birthday gift.

At a bakery back in St. Gilgen, we bought a chocolate tart for my birthday and a heart-shaped cake for Frau E. We presented it to her and received a skeptical look and a murmur that did not resemble *"danke."*

It was evening, and it was Wednesday. Naturally we would visit Jamal for his special pizza deal to finish off the day. Marguerite pulled a bottle of sparkling wine from the refrigerator and a pair of plastic glasses from the cupboard. "Before we go, let's have a toast." I popped the cork and poured. She raised her glass. "To my darling, the greatest companion and lover, who is fifty today. Happy birthday."

We toasted and carried the bottle and glasses to the phone booth at the base of our hill. I dialed the endless series of numbers—long-distance carrier, credit-card number, phone number in the States—to contact Marguerite's dad. Uncharacteristically, I insisted on spending my full share of time on the phone with him, savoring the English and the "Happy birthday, Ed" that he repeated at the beginning and the end of the call.

The late-day sun beat on the phone booth. The heat and the celebratory atmosphere made the wine go down nicely, and, after dialing up our friend Bette, I poured the last drops into our glasses.

When Marguerite passed me the receiver, I chatted with Bette about her job, our farmhouse apartment, and her planned October visit with us in Provence. I waited. Bette was usually the best at remembering my birthday. Often she made me a delicious cheesecake, but she wasn't saying the words, and we were winding down. In my mind I was deciding that I would tell her what day it was if I had to, but I prolonged the conversation another minute. Then she came out with it. "So it's fifty today, right?"

"Right."

"If I recollect, fifty is a bitch, but happy birthday." Bette was fifty-one. It was a bad sign if she had trouble remembering fifty.

"It's tough, but I'm bearing up. Thanks for remembering."

I felt pretty good after those two birthday greetings, but there could never be too many. We settled at a table in the pizza place and listened to the gentle melodies coming from the speakers overhead. "Would you mention to Jamal that it's my birthday?"

"Hoping for a free dessert?" Marguerite, as usual, was obsessed with bargains and freebies.

"That would be great, but a birthday wish would do fine."

Jamal finished chatting with a group at another table and came by. "Ah, my favorite couple. What can I get for you?"

I ordered and nudged Marguerite. "It's Ed's birthday today," she said.

"Oh, yes. That's nice." Jamal scooped up the menus and bustled toward the kitchen.

"I'm sure he heard you. . . ." I said.

"Don't worry. He'll bring you a prize later."

Jamal returned with our salads and wine. Later when he brought the pizzas, I mentioned casually, "It's my fiftieth today." Surely, that would bring an acknowledgment.

He set down the pies and smiled. "Have a nice dinner."

Had I offended him?

When he came for our used dishes, Jamal recommended grappa with coffee, whatever grappa was.

Marguerite agreed, "Yes, we should have it for Ed's birthday." He left, and she added, "And a nice piece of cake with a candle in it and a choir to sing for you—it's the least he could do for his 'favorite couple.'"

The grappa and coffee came without the cake or choral group. When the pizza entrepreneur brought the bill, I said, "I guess I'm over the hill now at fifty."

"Aw, that's not so old." He took my Visa card and ran it through his portable credit-card machine. It spit out the receipt, and I signed. "Have a wonderful evening and come back soon," he said.

So as we climbed the hill past the cows in their barns, Marguerite, her dad, and Bette had greeted my birthday. And I had received the gifts that Patricia brought from friends back home. I was glad of those, but I wished it were more. It was amazing how important it felt to have people remember me in this foreign spot, far from friends and family.

We sat on the balcony, watching the almost-full moon over the mountain and feeling the balmy breezes. Laughter rose from a nearby house. Incredibly, a pair of voices rose to sing Happy

Birthday—in English. Ah, sweet happenstance, my day now felt complete. I still shake my head in disbelief. Did that really happen? Marguerite swears it did, too.

More Reinforcements

August 22, 9:00 AM

I'm on the balcony looking out at Salzburg and the mountains. Wolfgang—that's the name we've given the German guy who's renting the place next door—and his wife are quietly shuffling dishes on their balcony, just beyond the wooden partition.

There's a tractor mowing in the field below me. The sheep have moved to a lower pasture. Hay that they mowed on Wednesday has been winnowed (is that the word?) into rows that snake across the meadow—a beautiful pastoral scene. But what do they do to the cows to make them holler?

This is Claire's third day, and the scheduling has worked out great. Having a week between guests has given us the time alone we needed so we can appreciate Claire's company.

Claire is a good friend, a member of my writers' group, and another mentor for this adventure. I've seen her in many lights, but these last two days, visiting this farm and the city of Salzburg, has brought on a metamorphosis. She's always been a butterfly, never a caterpillar, but her wings are more vivid in this alpine light, her lighthearted laughter more joyous and contagious. In the city, I watch her lead Marguerite through a shop, pick up a leather wallet, and place it in Marguerite's hand. I see the care she takes, the love she shows, her delight in helping and sharing this experience. I know how much it helps Marguerite to have another woman to escort her to the women's room, and the benefit is twofold.

Last night we attended another concert at the Festung, even better than the one with Tricia and Shirley. Claire and I had made reservations over the Internet way back in March, and we ended up in the front row center for glorious Mozart and Schubert concertos. We watched the expressive eyebrow movements of the lead violinist. He got to almost hopping when the tempo sped up. It added to the excitement of the very special evening.

A big part of the pleasure is watching Claire relive memories of the European trip she took in 1971. In our writers' group, she has dropped clues about that journey and shared passages that she wrote about it, but I still know surprisingly little. If I am right and correctly reading her broad smiles, the elevation of her eyebrows, and the bits of information she drops, she had a series of romantic adventures. She's frugal with details, but when we ask if she was ever lonely, she giggles and breezily answers, "Oh, no. There were always guys around."

The three of us were having breakfast on the balcony. Claire gazed toward the city and sighed, the silver streak in her hair shining in the morning light. "It's such a delightful morning, everything so fresh and green. The city, the farms, the mountains, it all reminds me of when Terri and I were here in Salzburg."

"Is there something you'd like to do, some special place you and she went that you'd like to see again?" Marguerite asked.

"I'd love to stroll along the shore of the Wolfgangsee again. It's got to be the loveliest lake in all of Austria, maybe the entire world, as far as I know. Can we do that? Can I take you to lunch at the White Horse Inn?"

So we were off for an encore, and I was ecstatic to relive my birthday lunch.

We sat by the terrace railing of the inn, lake water lapping at the pilings below us, half-empty salad plates on the table, forks in action. Claire looked from the inn to the lake to the distant mountains. "Except for some new coats of paint and a few more tourists, this age-old village hasn't changed much."

"So the White Horse is special to you," I said. "Is that because you had some golden-haired, Austrian baron to escort you?"

Claire's eyes sparkled as she shook her head. "No . . . Terri and I were taking a leisurely drive, just wandering around these mountains one day and found ourselves in St. Wolfgang." She swept her arm across the panorama. "I can't believe I'm actually here again. I remember leaning out the window of our *gästhaus*, geraniums spilling out of flowerpots, the strains of a zither coming from somewhere, feeling I had discovered this fairy-tale place. It was mine—lush hills, alpine peaks, gingerbread chalets. . . ."

"It sounds like you *loved* it here." Marguerite leaned forward over her salad, clearly caught up in Claire's fervor. I saw questions spinning in her mind like a roulette wheel and then settling on one. "How long did you stay in Europe?"

"Until our money ran out." Claire chuckled. "We started in London and ended in a little fishing village on the southern coast of Spain six months later. I'd been dreaming of this trip for years and saving every penny. Terri, too. I stored my furniture and sold my car. Terri took a leave from her job, but I quit mine cold turkey after ten years, and we took off."

"What a romantic and courageous thing to do," Marguerite said.

Claire dismissed the notion with a brush of her hand. "I figured everything would work out, and it did. We just wished we had more money, so it wouldn't have to end."

The waiter took our salad plates and poured wine. Claire's face glowed with the fresh air, the wine, her memories. Marguerite seemed fascinated with her chutzpah, but there were lots of other thoughts floating in my head. Our companion had experienced Europe so differently than we were experiencing it. What would it be like to be ten years younger, no job waiting back home, single, fancy free? "Last night you said there were always guys around. What about here in Austria?"

Claire laughed and considered a moment. "Well, of course, after we left Salzburg, we headed toward St. Moritz. I must have made a wrong turn in the mountains—I did that a lot—and we found ourselves on an impossible road without a spot wide enough to turn the car around. Terri, my navigator, assured me we were headed south, and there was nothing to do but keep going. We inched along in low gears, the earth swaying beneath us, my heart lodged like a tennis ball in my throat, when two men on bicycles whizzed by, waving victoriously. Gunter and Gehrhart, stockbrokers from Vienna, were training for the . . . oh, I forget what it was called . . . the Austrian version of the Tour de France. They pedaled seriously, heads down, like jockeys on a pair of thoroughbreds."

She swirled wine in her glass, sipped, and continued. "It became a game of tag. They overtook us on the downgrades, and we passed them as they pumped their way up steep rises. When dusk began to close in, we found them waiting on the side of the road, like knights in shining armor. Gunter asked in a thick Austrian accent, "Don't you know St. Moritz is very far away? Don't you realize you can get lost out there? Don't you understand it will be dark soon, and you won't be able to see the road?"

"They guided us through dense woods to a village *gästhaus* in the bowels of the Tyrolean Alps, a place so remote that Romansch is still spoken. For three nights we downed mugs of wonderful Austrian beer and danced to accordion music. Then Gunter said, "We will race you to Menaggio." And therein lies the tale of how we happened to end up in Italy."

I waited to see if she'd offer more details, but our main course arrived—steaming plates of schnitzel, salmon trout, and beef *rouladen* with parsley potatoes and red cabbage.

Between sharing tastes of our dishes and complimenting the meal, Marguerite said, "I love what you told us about Gunter and Gehrhart . . . getting carried away like that on the spur of the moment. Was Austria the most romantic place for you?"

"No, that would be Vence, in the hills behind the French Riviera. Fields of lavender and olives, the ancient walled city, charming cafés . . . Driving crooked roads on cliffs above the sea, swooping down to Cannes for the day . . . Balmy, star-lit nights. The men spoke rich, passionate French, and the language rolled around on my tongue so just the right words came out. And there was that 400-year-old stone farmhouse, and . . ."

Claire's rapturous words paused long enough for her to give me a mock reproving look. "Ed will ask, so I'll tell you. His name was Marc. His hair was sandy and his beard red. He was somewhat moody and intense, but it made me happy to know I could love a man who wasn't perfect. And the last thing he said to me the night before Terri and I were finally leaving after two months was, "I give you my love to take with you wherever you go." I took it, of course, and I still take it with me . . . wherever I go."

She set her fork on her plate and cast a faraway look toward the mountains across the lake. She was her younger self again, living the most amazing adventure of her life. In her mind, I knew it was the Mediterranean she was gazing over, and the mountains were somewhere near Monaco along the Côte d'Azur. I had more questions to ask, but that would break the spell. Her bliss was far more important than my curiosity.

After the meal, she led us out of the restaurant. "I can't tell you how glad I am we came today and how grateful I am to you. I never would have come to Salzburg again if you hadn't offered a home base." She hugged Marguerite, then me.

"So, you're not mad about my prying?"

"Are you kidding?" She smiled. "Do you mind if we stop in this gift shop? I want to buy postcards and a souvenir for Terri. I can't wait to get home and call her."

As I drove toward the farm, I felt myself beaming almost as wide as our guest. Her gratitude for being part of our trip was genuine, and it felt good. It had been months since we'd really had a chance do something for another person. With this trip and this day by the lake, we'd given Claire a unique and priceless gift.

August 26

While Claire was here, we attended yet another concert. This one was a pair of flutists—father and son—in a glittering chamber at the top of the famous staircase of marble angels in the Mirabel Palace. We

232

shopped in Salzburg and visited several lakes and Hitler's Eagle's Nest in nearby Germany. We were surprised and indignant (especially Claire) to find no trace of the maniacal Führer's stronghold, only a spectacular bus and elevator ride to the top of the Alps and a crowded, block restaurant serving sausages and Black Forest cake.

I guess we wore Claire out, poor thing, like she and Terri had done to those bicycle hotshots back in '71. When we dropped her off at the Munich airport, she seemed very happy for having come . . . and relieved to be heading home for a rest.

I'm feeling—dare I say it?—whole again. I realized at the concert in the fortress that I had no anxiety that night or the last few since. All the company from home, the exhilarating scenery, the music, and the sharing of such happy memories with Claire has contributed to my state of well-being.

And think of this: In twenty-five years, we'll be looking back on this journey with bright eyes, just the way Claire is now on her long-ago trip.

On the Move Again

August 26

At the American Express office in Salzburg, we booked ferry tickets from Italy to Greece, departing in a week and returning in early October. I've read that Greece is tough on importing pets, and I lie awake at night imagining customs agents impounding Felicia in some sort of quarantine. Then I picture Marguerite kicking and biting the immigration officials. My nighttime musings sometimes end with my two women behind bars, my role relegated to delivering chocolate bonbons and cat treats on visiting days. So we took Effie to a vet for up-to-date health and vaccination certificates.

August 29

As I type this, the computer screen is rubbing against the sunflowers on our kitchen table. Petals drop from the best-preserved flower. The flowers make me think of Claire, since we bought them

*with her. They also remind me that it's time to move on. It's a little
sad when flowers wilt, and the wilting of these flowers—like the roses
in Paris and the tulips in Holland—means leaving a cherished bit of
our lives behind.*

A month before, we had been like the Energizer Bunny's
defeated rival—sad-looking, mechanical, energy depleted. We had
been surviving on dribs and drabs, little jolts of power to keep us
moving. English-language tours, boat rides, cable-car treks,
fireworks on Bastille Day, Larry King, our big splurge on that grand,
five-course, French dinner with champagne . . . even the German
nudists had contributed.

In Salzburg, we received what is known in battery parlance as
"a complete, overnight charge"—lots of love (and English) to help us
on our way for the rest of the journey. Calls from Robyn, Lester and
Esther, Bette, John and Doree; gifts from Dave and Judy and
Marguerite's mom; visits and more gifts from Patricia, Shirley, and
Claire. . . .

As we loaded the Peugeot and pulled away from the farmhouse,
our spirits crackled and sent sparks into the universe. We headed
down the road, bound for Greek adventures.

Greece—Voyage to Cats and Chaos

Fleeing the Teutonic World—a Stop in Italy

We drove south from Salzburg, ascending through meadows and dense woods with the highway perched on the mountainsides above fast-flowing rivers and the car climbing easily. As we waited in line to pass through a tunnel, I turned to Marguerite. "How are you doing?"

"Great."

"You sure?"

Her smile ebbed. "What are you getting at?"

"Not thinking you want to go home?"

"You'd *better* be taking me to Greece."

"*That's* what I wanted to hear!"

Another tunnel and another line of stationary cars . . . we ate sandwiches made from the last of our Austrian olive loaf as we waited to pass through. I unscrewed the lid on the jar of potato salad and stuck a plastic fork into it. "The Austrians have the best cold cuts, don't they?"

"Personally, I'm glad we're headed for the land of taziki and mousaka."

"Me, too. I could live happily for a decade without another cold cut."

She pulled a sliver of meat from her sandwich and fed it to Felicia. "Why do we have to wait to go through the tunnels?" She looked at me expectantly, and I felt an obligation to think of an answer. It was a compulsion programmed into my brain in second grade and encouraged by Marguerite's trust in my responses.

"Do I look like the Austrian Auto Club?" At the front of the line of cars, the signal turned green. I wrapped the rest of my sandwich in a napkin and inched the car forward. "Maybe they have to let the tunnel air out, so we don't get gassed by exhaust fumes."

"Thanks. I knew you'd find the answer."

We descended in one swift run, from deep conifer forests and jagged peaks to lush, palm-studded hills; from oompah-pah to romantic melodies; from Teutonic formality to Latin warmth (and, as it turned out, from plumbing that performed flawlessly to some lesser standard).

At a roadside *albergo* (inn) outside of Udine and northeast of Venice, I reconnoitered, asked the price, agreed to it, and retrieved Marguerite from the car. "There's some kind of a party going on in here. A room full of people with waiters bustling."

We checked in, fed Felicia a snack, and headed down for something to eat. Settled at a sidewalk table outside the *albergo's* bar, we listened to some fast-paced music pouring out through the doors. Our feet started tapping. A waitress took our order for a bottle of Pinot Grigio and a mixed-seafood appetizer, and left us to relax in the late afternoon sun.

The snack arrived, and we became engrossed in eating delicious shrimp drizzled in a perfect vinaigrette and the most delectable, tiny octopi. From where we sat, I could look inside the bar. Old men—some in sport coats, others in polo shirts—sat at the counter watching the younger guys play pool. A few of the old ones strolled out onto the sidewalk and settled at a table, smoking and gabbing, swirling red wine in squat, stemless glasses. The sun descended behind distant mountains. Clouds turned orange and deepened. The men retreated inside, leaving the sidewalk to us. We emptied the wine and ordered another bottle, a tomato salad, and ravioli Bolognese. By the time we finished the food, stars had begun to appear.

"Is that the bunny hop I hear inside?" asked Marguerite. "It must be a wedding."

I scouted it out and returned with a report. "In the banquet room there are tables full of drunken Italians, all laughing and carrying on. And you were right—a bride and groom are circulating. There's one guy playing the accordion, one on the saxophone, and another one singing. The waiters are serving cake. Care to go try a bite?"

"Did they offer?"

"They would—if they knew us."

Marguerite sent me a shrewd look and said from the side of her mouth, "If you steal from Cousin Guido, you'll be *sleeping* with the octopi."

"I guess I'll settle for being a music thief, if I can have this rumba."

"You're silly. It's not a rumba."

"It's slow. That's all I care." I stood and took her hand, and we embraced on the sidewalk. As we swayed together to the music, I murmured in her ear. "I'm in love and mystified and a little bit drunk."

"Is it because of me or the Pinot Grigio, music, and balmy night?"

"I'm high on the wine and music, and mystified by the serendipity of this Italian evening. But the 'in love' part is all you."

"Mmmm."

As the wedding guests partied inside, we savored some of the most romantic dances of our lives on our own private dance floor outside.

Soon we departed to take a leisurely stroll down a back road in the moonlight, past fragrant fruit groves and a lit-up chapel on a hill, with the sensuous sounds of church bells and crickets accompanying us. Outside of a hole-in-the-wall bar, we sipped coffee as aromas of citrus and espresso drifted over us. The romance of Italy kissed us tenderly on our cheeks.

Voyage to Chaos

September 1, Cervia, Italy

We are biding our time until our ferry leaves tomorrow from Ancona. After our romantic night in northern Italy, we moved south to this resort town and the Hotel Haiti, set among pine trees and two blocks from the Adriatic. For breakfast we have great chocolate or custard-filled doughnuts for less than $1.00 and cappuccino for $1.40. We walk by the sea in the mornings and then hide under a canopy to sip drinks, while the blistering sun sears beach-loungers in rented chaises. For dinner, we eat tasty pasta or pizza—what else?

I have totaled the August expenses. We were over the target, but considering our social activities, we did okay. Our rent ran $58 per *night. Other living expenses totaled $62 a day, including more than $100 for concerts, $100 for a surprisingly high electric bill from the Frau, a $16 veterinarian bill, and tours that ran $100+. These costs represent good entertainment value and lots of fun.*

Felicia is being good. The wanawut has turned into "cappuccino cat."

September 2

We made it onto the ferry. While boarding the boat in Ancona and passing through Greek customs I was as tense as a drug smuggler, worrying about Felicia. The customs men in their white captains' uniforms checked our passports thoroughly but ignored our girl, her new health certificate, and her vaccination record.

September 4

I'm not a linguist, but I'm betting that chaos is a Greek word. When I get home, I'll look it up. Never mind—I'm living it.

The overnight voyage was uneventful. Our cabin was small and efficient; the Greek cafeteria food, a tasty introduction to the next adventure. As the ship approached Patras, I viewed the busy port and the fortifications atop bleak hills behind the city, which our guidebook called the *kastro*. Eons of history awaited us in this new land.

But the ferry crew sent us too soon into the hold with the vehicles. Trucks stood with idling engines and diesel fumes spewing. I left Marguerite and Felicia by an open area near the stern where fresh air was available and went to find our car. Slithering between tightly packed, soot-caked trucks, I became disoriented and found myself among the wrong group of cars. Filth rubbed off on my shirt, and smoke stung my throat and lungs.

It must have taken me twenty minutes to find the Peugeot and make it back to Marguerite and Effie. "They've poisoned my lungs," I wheezed.

"Did you find the car?"

"Diesel exhaust is a carcinogen. If I die, promise to sue the ANEK Ferry Lines."

"Did you?"

"I won't tell you unless you promise to sue."

"Okay. Okay."

"It's on the other side."

We stuck near the openings by the stern. Breezes blew in from the sea. I gulped air and tried to expel as much crud as possible from my lungs. We commiserated with other passengers about the inhumanity of the shipping line.

Finally, the trucks began to move off the boat. I led my entourage into the car, joined a line of trucks and cars, and broke out into clean air. A minute later I was complaining again. "I can't believe this traffic."

"It's probably not that bad. Your senses are dulled by carbon monoxide."

I glanced at Marguerite, cat on her lap, fingers stroking the white spot under Felicia's chin. Her smirk appeared only half-malicious.

"This street is supposed to be two lanes plus parking on both sides."

"So?"

"It's really one meandering lane with double-parked cars and motorbikes everywhere. . . . *Oh, my god!*" I spun the wheel left and tromped on the brake. A motorcycle buzzed by, inches from my right front fender.

"What happened? Never mind . . . drive."

We had entered a sea of swirling action—cars, buses, motorbikes, pedestrians, bicycles, all darting in and out. Taxis stopped dead in front of us to let out their fares. A motorcycle pulled up beside a parked car to chat, leaving just enough space—maybe—to get by.

We found a hotel for the night and set off the next morning for the City of the Gods.

From Hell on Wheels to Hell on a Rooftop

Driving had never before reduced me to a trembling mass of protoplasm, but here I was, struggling through the worst bedlam imaginable for a driver—Athens traffic—trying to find our next lodging. There were no street signs to guide me, at least none that I could read (Greek sigmas, deltas, and the like did me no good at all).

Armed with an address in Piraeus, the port of Athens, I sought our new landlady, Sophia—Lester and Esther's friend. Directions from people along the way conflicted with one another. Endless construction delays; darting, frenzied motorbikes; pedestrians; and cars that looked like fugitives from demolition derbies all served to make me crazy.

In a bookshop where I stopped to ask directions, employees pulled out a book of maps, and argued. I peered over a shoulder and saw neat pages of street diagrams, but no words—no street names. No wonder there was confusion. Finally, a friendly, bilingual Toyota dealer offered to call our new landlady to arrange a meeting between us on a bridge along a main boulevard that ran near the sea.

Keeping to the right lane, I drove slowly. There was no way I was going to miss this rendezvous. Mrs. Anagnos and I spotted each other simultaneously. She waved, and gold hoops glittered on her wrist, neck, and ears. Her bearing; her smooth, well-tanned skin; that bright smile; the simple elegance of her sleeveless, brown-and-gold jumpsuit helped ease my tension.

She beckoned me to the end of a row of vehicles, which were parked with front ends on the sidewalk, rear ends in a turnout lane. I pulled in where she indicated, easing forward until the bumper nudged a light pole. The Peugeot straddled part of the sidewalk and the turnout, and the rear end hung into the boulevard.

Mrs. Anagnos peered in through Marguerite's window. "You must be the Websters. Welcome. You may leave the car here." More relief, her English was comprehensible.

"It's sticking out."

"Only a little. It is no problem." A warning flashed in my mind.

Was her bright smile one of serenity or of madness?

A little, yellow pickup cut off a bus to avoid hitting our car. Horns blasted. Marguerite winced and protected her face with her hands. "Mrs. Anagnos, is this a bus stop we're parked in?" I asked.

"Please, call me Sophia."

"Thank you, Sophia. Please call me Ed."

"And I'm Marguerite." We all shook hands.

Our hostess surveyed Marguerite and her cane. "It's a pleasure, dear." She patted Marguerite's arm.

"So, Sophia, is this a bus stop?" I repeated.

"Yes. But the bus man knows this is off-limits, so he stops on the street."

"Maybe I should find a better spot, since we'll be here for two weeks."

"As you wish. Tonight the owners of the other cars will go home from work. You can pick a better place then."

"A better place in the bus stop?"

"Yes, yes. In the middle of the bus stop, not in the street at all. It's perfect."

Marguerite murmured. "Ed, don't forget Effie."

She was right. We could tolerate a car wreck but not a cat wreck. I rescued Effie in her cat carrier and held her up to Sophia. "This is Felicia." Our little girl looked out wide-eyed through the plastic mesh.

"Mrs. Webster told me on the phone there would be an . . . animal." Sophia gave a tight smile, turned, and led us down a flight of concrete stairs to the base of the bridge, past sheets of paper, discarded bottles, and old fragments of cloth and leather. We followed a side street to the entrance of a drab, concrete building. We entered and rode the elevator as high as it would go. Sophia. led us up a flight of stairs and gestured to the floor outside the apartment. "You will be able to leave the animal here."

"I don't understand," I said.

"Surely, you won't need her in the apartment. We have no mice."

"But, Sophia," Marguerite stammered. "She's our companion. She sleeps with us."

Bewilderment ran over Sophia's features, followed by a look that said, Oh, well—they're American.

Inside the apartment, several things struck me in quick succession—the stench of mothballs; the tight space; the hodgepodge of knickknacks; the papers, pots, and dishes covering the small table and shelves. My eyes pushed past these things and darted through the glass double doors to a patch of bright blue bay outside. I tried to focus on that and think of the positive as my olfactory senses throbbed.

What impressions were floating through Marguerite's mind? Beginning with the stink, she could conjure up something at least as bad as this reality. She would hear the echo of our voices and detect the smallness. She hated clutter and dirt, and somehow she would know. Would she turn and run screaming to the filthy street?

"This is the bathroom," Sophia said. She led us a few steps into a side room with a half-size tub wedged in one end; a pile of pails, stepladders, mops, and junk on the other; and the sink in the middle.

"Oh, it's one of those minitubs," I said. That would clue Marguerite in that we wouldn't be taking baths together.

Sophia led us back to the main room. "Over here, you can cook." She pointed to the hot plates and pots on the cluttered table.

"This pan is brand new. You didn't buy it for us?"

"Mrs. Webster said on the phone that you wanted to make breakfast here."

"You went to too much trouble," Marguerite said.

"No, no, dear. It is no trouble to do for friends. Over here is the bed. It is for one person, but you can open this chair and it makes a comfortable place to sleep." The tiny bed and drab armchair had seen better days.

Sophia swung the doors open. "Now, the best part. You are living on the top, with nothing but the view." She led us onto the roof and swept her arm toward the cobalt arc of the bay, a few hundred feet past the boulevard. "It is beautiful here at night with the breezes. My husband and I live in the building next door, and we love evenings on the balcony. And over there, the Parthenon."

"Oh, yeah." I looked around a cylindrical tank on the roof of another building to the landmark miles away near the city center. "That's cool." I chalked up the pluses—views of the Acropolis and the bay.

Marguerite whispered, "Do you hear all that traffic? We won't be sitting out here."

I hadn't noticed it that much, focusing as I was on the sea and the antiquities, but the noise was obnoxious. Heavy trucks, cabs, and rickety busses roared, rattled, and beeped below us. I peered down and flinched as vehicles whizzed by just inches from the Peugeot's bumper. "But the view," I said. "In the evening, there won't be as much traffic."

When Sophia headed to her apartment for supplies, I hustled into the bathroom and cranked open the window. "Oh, man. Give me air."

"Not so loud," Marguerite hissed. "You'll hurt her feelings. Just how bad is this place?"

"You know the little boxes on top of buildings, where janitors store their tools?"

"The place a kid named Willard might keep his pet rats?"

"Yes, that's our new home. But do you have to use my dad's name that way?"

"We have to stay, don't we?" Her voice pleaded for contradiction.

"She *is* Les and Es's friend. And look at this." I walked two steps to the table. "It's not just the pot, the hot plate's brand new, too. She bought all this stuff for us."

"When you said the bathtub was small—I could tell by your voice—it's dirty, isn't it?"

"Your hearing is very keen, little Mousaka."

In ten minutes, Sophia returned with a couple of bags.

"Here are more pillows and extra sheets," she said. "They're still in the package from the store. They may be bigger than you need."

245

Marguerite held our kitty in her arms. "Here, Sophia, you can pet her. Felicia's really soft." The landlady glanced at me, but I offered no escape. She tentatively tapped Effie's head. "Very nice. Thank you, dear." She held that hand away from her body, as if it had been defiled.

"I thought you would be thirsty from your trip, so I brought beer." Sophia opened the second sack, pulled out a can, and set it in my hand. I popped the tab and offered it to Marguerite. She declined, and I gulped. Cool relief swept down my throat.

"And now I leave you to settle in." She whisked out the door, still treating her hand like a wounded paw.

After giving Sophia a minute to clear out of the elevator, I hustled down and moved the car from the boulevard to the side street. I retrieved our sack of kitchen stuff and found the plastic bags. Marguerite pulled mothballs from the cabinet and crammed them into the bags. I put Effie in her cat carrier, opened the doors wide, and turned on the fan to air out the place. The result was a partial success, which, if you translate it into plain talk, means mostly a failure.

That afternoon I hauled our belongings up to the apartment as Marguerite explored, cleaned, and did her best to keep from crying. "I'm proud of you," I said, "considering the enormity of this mess."

"Thank the Prempro. Without it, I'd have thrown myself off the roof."

We stowed our belongings, took showers, and went out to buy a few essentials like instant coffee and ouzo.

Late in the afternoon, the phone rang. "You should answer," I said.

"Why me?"

"I did the talking in France. It's your turn." I handed her the receiver.

"Hello? . . . Hi, Sophia. Yes, this is Marguerite. . . . Everything is fine. . . . Oh, I don't know. Can I tell you tomorrow? . . . Thank you very much."

"Liar," I said.

She looked indignant.

"You told her things were okay."

"She called to invite me shopping tomorrow. Should I have told her to shove it?"

"She's really nice, isn't she?"

"Yes, damn it."

"It would break her heart for us to leave."

"Yes, damn it."

That night at our first Greek taverna, we sat out on the sidewalk under a trellis covered with plastic vines, sipping white wine from Crete, and sampling an array of salads, stuffed pastries, and roasted meats (total cost—$16). We savored the scents of unidentified blossoms and the recorded music of bouzouki and tambourines. We shared scraps of roast lamb with stray cats that waited patiently for our hospitality.

Heading home, we had to use all of our senses and mobility tools to traverse the sidewalks, which were torn up in places from some forgotten project. Our normal hand signals didn't accommodate bricks lying haphazardly on the pavement. We shuffled along—Marguerite feeling with her feet and cane, hanging onto me and supporting me as I supported her. We detoured into the street to pass parked autos on the walkway and the biggest piles of debris. I watched emaciated cats pick at garbage overflowing from refuse bins. At one point we came across a mattress that had been laid on the sidewalk beside a Dumpster. Two cats, unaccustomed to such luxury, lay atop it, licking their paws.

"So that's why the Greeks don't understand Felicia," Marguerite said. "To them, cats are just beggars and rat disposal units."

Back in the apartment, we sought to make ourselves comfortable. Assuming mosquitoes didn't fly up to the sixth floor, we left the bathroom window open. The doors stayed closed for cat security.

We decided to share the bed, doing our best to get cozy but wedged in so tight that I had to ask permission to roll over, my feet hanging off the bottom. Sweat formed on my back, chest, and forehead. I removed my T-shirt. My back stuck to Marguerite where our bodies touched, and my side clung to the sheet. The fan swung back and forth, providing a tickle of relief from time to time. I told myself it wasn't so bad—I would get used to the fragrance of camphor. I lay still, trying not to wake Marguerite, for what seemed like everlasting hell.

A whisper from Marguerite in the dark—"You awake?"

"You're kidding, right? Look, I'm going to open the doors."

"I'm afraid for Effie."

I flipped on a light and stood. "It's okay. There are louvered, inner panels. I'll keep those across. Come feel it. There's a hook. And I'll put a chair against them."

"You're responsible if anything happens."

I opened the doors and wedged the panels closed. Was there a bit of coolness in the air that whispered across my bare chest? "This is going to work, and I'm going to try to make this thing into a second bed."

A truck groaned by outside. "What about the noise?" she asked.

"Don't complain about everything."

"This is okay with you?"

"No, but it makes it worse to call out every problem. I can't do anything about it."

"It's not your responsibility, Eddie. You're not the cruise director."

I took Effie off the chair. She shot me a dark look and slinked under the bed. Now both my women were mad at me. "I'm sorry, Effie, okay? It must be worse with fur."

With a little prying, the chair flopped open. "Well, the three pieces lie kind of flat on the floor, but not really. I'll try using the highest piece as a pillow." I pulled the sheets from their package. They felt grainy, but I spread them out and climbed on top.

On my back, I clearly felt the three distinct parts of the bed, three hard lumps that didn't mesh with each other. If I stayed in that position, my back would be destroyed by daybreak. I rolled to one side, then to the other. Whichever way I turned, I felt hotter, sweatier, and itchy—very itchy. "This is terrible." I jumped up and stood by the fan.

"Now who's complaining?"

"You want to try it?"

Marguerite moved to the foldout, but within seconds she was up, dusting herself off with frantic strokes of her hands. "These aren't sheets. They must be curtains. It's like fiberglass. It's ripping my skin."

Two in the bed, we suffered, we sweated, we sniffed acrid air, we cursed Sophia, and finally, I guess, we fell asleep. At six o'clock the traffic began in earnest—heavy, chugging diesels with air brakes and those damned motorbikes—and propelled me upward. Marguerite still lay in an exhausted daze as I closed the doors, dressed, and went outside to explore our neighborhood.

A half hour later I returned with doughnuts and made two cups of instant coffee. Tasting mine, I yearned for the Austrian ground coffee I'd shunned a few weeks before.

Marguerite sat up in bed and sipped hers. "Oooo, that's bad. We can't stay here, Eddie. I'm going to be sick in this place."

"But what about Sophia? We can't just leave today. Can you make it for a week?"

"I guess. . . .What will we tell her?"

"A death in the family?"

"I bet she's heard that one lots of times," said Marguerite.

"We'll blame it on Felicia."

"Sure, the cat decided she wants to see the mountains."

"Okay, we'll tell her the truth, sort of. The place is just too smell . . . I mean small."

"Very funny. Who gets to tell her?"

"I did all the talking in France."

Living Within View of the Acropolis

Before Marguerite got up each morning, I toured our neighborhood, taking in an array of alien and poignant scenes—an elderly man with only one hand, sweeping the sidewalk with a broom made of twigs; a fish peddler, selling his goods to housewives from the tailgate of a camper/pickup; a mother leading her tots aboard a mini yellow school bus, kissing the driver on both cheeks, climbing off, and waving good-bye.

Shapely young women strolled to market. Stooped old men sold lottery tickets on street corners. Bells on red-domed churches clanged a multitoned cacophony as old women in black dresses and shawls hobbled up the church steps for morning devotions.

Apartment buildings everywhere, made from slabs of concrete, seemed picturesque but dingy. Wild cats and loose dogs browsed through ripe garbage on sidewalks blocked by rubble, a burned-up oven, and the cab of a semitruck. Trucks spewed caustic exhaust that threatened to lacerate my lung tissue like locusts on a wheat field.

One afternoon I came upon a crowd of people—some with noses pressed to a window, others gathered in clusters—talking excitedly. I looked past the poster signs taped to the window to see a modern little market with employees in crisp brown aprons moving about. I tested the door and found it locked. A man sidled over. "It is new store," he said, correctly assessing my nationality and going straight to English. "Will open tomorrow, first time. We come watch. Good thing for our quarter." This minor event was the day's entertainment, and it seemed quaint, naïve, sad, and happy all at once.

I pulled two molded-plastic chairs to the corner of the roof where I could see the Acropolis and brought Marguerite out to enjoy the evening. I leaned toward the edge of the roof to get a better view around the solar panel and tanks on the other rooftop. "There it is, the Parthenon."

Marguerite turned her chair away from the city and ducked her chin against her chest to protect herself against the dusty wind. "Pretty view?"

"It's little more than a speck on the horizon, but it's such a grand speck, the heart of Western Civilization."

"What about the lungs?"

"The lungs have gone to hell, and there's an orange-brown haze moving this way from downtown." I glanced over the edge to the street. "Poor Jean de Florette (the name we'd given the Peugeot). He's accumulating a coat of grime on his pretty silver paint job. . . . So I guess this isn't an ideal picnic spot."

"The whole of Athens is less than ideal. The subway is clanky and dirty, the traffic deafening, and the sidewalks piled with trash. Everything I touch or breathe is full of grit."

"Want to go inside?"

"No. You brought me out to see the Parthenon, and you wanted to share it with me. I'll hold your hand and defend myself from the wind."

I gazed at the Parthenon and sighed. "I wanted to get a feel for what's special here, but I'm finished. Let's go lounge in our opulent apartment."

September 6

Although Marguerite is singularly unimpressed with Athens, I love the Plaka district, with its little shops and restaurants tucked under trees beside old ruins.

We took a city bus tour (with a guide not the least bit interested in her patrons), which concluded at the Acropolis (acro meaning "top," e.g., top of the hill; polis having to do with "politics" or "people" or "city"). It was awesome and solemn to visit the famous site, but perhaps more grand was the view of simply looking up at it from the city.

The Parthenon and most of the other buildings were hemmed in by scaffolding for restoration. Close up, I felt partly in awe and partly annoyed by the pipes and planks, frustrated not to be able to stroll inside one of the temples. But from a distance, I could see the whole impressive picture. The city must be viewed that way, too. If you can overlook the refuse in the foreground, it's one amazing array of antiquity.

We finished our tour at the Acropolis and strode down a sidewalk toward the city. I looked at the ground, down to our right. "This is amazing. Between the scattered pine trees, there are slices of Doric columns. Marble blocks, pieces of old temples, markets, homes . . ." We continued downhill. "Thousands upon thousands of stones, probably a square mile of open-air museum. Back up behind us is the Parthenon and all the other temples, and farther ahead, there's another one . . . must be the Temple of Hephaestus. Do you want me to help you down into the field to feel some of these old chunks of stone?"

"After all those pillars on the tour, I've had enough stones for today."

"A hundred feet from where we're standing is a fragment of floor—Roman tiles depicting part of a hunting scene. In any other part of Europe, it would be the focal point of a museum, but here it lies neglected."

As we continued toward the heart of the city, I alternated between gawking at scraps of early Athens and focusing on the ground ahead to avoid tripping over rubble or losing Marguerite in a ditch. Ahead, an archaeological dig, surrounded by chain-link fencing, was set up next to a construction site for a new subway stop. How casual the Greeks were about their antiquities.

We stopped for a bite to eat and then sought out Stavros Melissinos's famous sandal store in the Plaka district. From outside, I described the store to Marguerite. "It's just another stall in the marketplace, wedged between a trinket store and a store peddling CDs. There are leather goods hanging from every square inch. Here . . ." I put Marguerite's hands on a cluster of pocketbooks hanging beside the entryway. "And here . . ." This was a rack of belts, inscribed with scenes of Athens. "And these . . ." She fingered about thirty pairs of children's sandals in chocolate tones and light-sand colors.

"Mmmm. Smell," she urged, turning her head slowly and taking in the rich scent of leather. She reached for a pocketbook and sniffed it.

"That must be the owner inside. He looks like Einstein, with frizzly, white hair sticking out all around and a rumpled shirt. He's cute as hell."

We entered the shop, which was probably fifteen feet wide and somehow accommodated two rooms. Permeated by the essence of rawhide, every square inch was stocked with leather goods. The white-haired man and a woman of about seventy were busy with customers at an old cash drawer on a table nestled toward the back.

We came to an area where maybe twenty designs of sandals were nailed across the wall, with hundreds of pairs tucked into the cubbyholes below. "These might be nice for you," I said, pulling one from a bin and handing it to Marguerite to examine.

"Ah, ha. Very fine choice," said a gentle, male voice from close behind. Einstein stood by my shoulder. "And you also might consider these." He took in Marguerite's cane, slid another pair from a shelf, and placed it in her hands.

She fingered the offering and smiled. "I like them."

"Take off your shoes and get comfortable. Let me see what size you are. People shouldn't wear shoes anyway. They confine the foot. We are in Greece, where the foot and the spirit should be free."

She uncovered her feet, and he said, "Yes, I think the one I gave you will be fine."

She slipped it on, and he bent to help her adjust it. "Yes. That's good, is it not?" He half-cackled the words. "Oh, I am such a good judge of feet."

"We read about you in our guidebook. Is it true?" I asked.

"You mean about the Beatles coming here? Yes. True. First it was John Lennon, and then he brought the others. Funny boys . . . very nice."

"I guess you have it made. The travel books advertise for you."

Mr. Melissinos rolled his head back and laughed, and then he turned to his coworker. "Do you hear that? This man thinks it's easy for us. So why are we still working? I tell you what I think. If Madame buys these sandals, and you purchase some, too, *then* I will have it made." He cackled again. "So, sir, what size are you?"

"At home it's about a 12."

"Ah, a big one. Why are you wearing those shoes in Athens when my sandals would be so much more comfortable? Take them off."

I strapped on some new footwear. "I understand you're a poet, too."

"Ah, yes. Let me get you copies. Try these." He set a second pair on a pile beside me, bustled to his desk, and brought back copies of a couple of poems and a newspaper article about him. "Before you start thinking I'm getting rich with the poetry, let me tell you. . . ."

"Don't worry. I'm an author, too, but I still have my day job."

We bought two pairs of sandals and a belt for 11,000 drachmae (about $40). Before we left, I shook his hand. "I'm Ed, and this is Marguerite."

"Good to meet you. I'm Stavros, like on the American television show—what is it?—*Kojak.*"

Marguerite and I left, feeling very happy indeed.

We returned to the sandal shop the next day to buy a belt for Marguerite's brother, John, a hard-core Beatles fan. A television I hadn't noticed the day before was propped on a shelf over the desk, and I was startled by voices speaking English. When I realized the reason, a shiver darted through me—it was Princess Diana's funeral. Speeches were being delivered and aired live around the world from her service.

That evening, Sophia came by to offer a new box of cookies.

"We were saddened today about Princess Di," Marguerite told her.

Our hostess stiffened. "The woman embarrassed her husband in public with other men."

I could see that Marguerite caught Sophia's tone, but she

forged ahead. "It's just that she seems like someone we all knew, someone who worked for good causes. . . ."

"You don't do those things; that's all I'm saying. When you're in public service, you must do everything for the good appearance. I know. My husband was an officer."

"But what about Charles? Didn't he . . ."

"That doesn't matter. Diana took on a public trust, a responsibility, when she became princess. You never criticize the prince. And you are *faithful*."

I took Marguerite's hand and stuck a cookie in it. She took a bite and the hint.

September 9

Yesterday Marguerite informed Sophia about our departure, and today we sprang into action, making plans to get out of here. At a travel agency (Zeus Diplomatic), we booked lodging for two islands. This Thursday we go by ferry to Syros, where we'll stay for a week. Then after a few days on the mainland, we're off to the island of Poros. The first place will run slightly over budget, and the second a bit under, so they average out just right. Here in Athens we've spent $179 for the whole week, but I'd hardly call it a deal.

September 10

This week we've eaten more feta cheese and eggplant than we've had in fifty years of life, perhaps more than we ever would have wanted in a lifetime. We hate this apartment, and we're more than ready to go.

I set the alarm *very* early that last morning, to make sure we weren't late for the ferry. We stuffed our camphor-saturated clothes into our luggage, wrote a thank-you note to Sophia, and set the note on the table with a bottle of wine. As dawn approached, I hauled our suitcases and bags downstairs, onto the elevator, and, eventually, to the car. Marguerite swept, sponged, mopped, and arranged, while I crammed. The apartment would be infinitely cleaner than when we had arrived. Felicia was locked in her cat carrier and no doubt praying that we were really leaving (to the extent that cats humble themselves to pray).

Returning for the last bags, I saw Marguerite kneeling near the table, but I didn't focus on her as I reached for the sacks. "I'll be back for you and Felicia in a few minutes." Something crunched underfoot. And why were my shoes sticking to the floor? "Yuck. What *is* that?" Then I really looked at Marguerite.

She was bent down and sopping at some liquid with paper towels. "Careful, Eddie. There's glass." She turned and slammed the soggy towels into the garbage can as tears came down her cheeks.

"It's okay. We can't let this slow us down."

"I was sweeping, and the broom handle hit the bottle of wine. It went everywhere."

I helped her up and hugged her, my mind forming a determined path. I would not be diverted from our goal, the ferry to Syros, which was probably only a little more than a mile away. But how long would it take? I had to drive us through the horror of Athens traffic and get us onto the ferry. Not until then could I relax. "I'll look for glass and throw these paper towels out. After that, I'll take the last bags to the car, while you mop up the rest. We have to leave." I scanned for glass, swept it into a wet pile, and picked it up with paper towels. "I'll be back in a couple of minutes."

Five minutes later we left the sticky-floored apartment-from-hell behind. As I carried Effie and led Marguerite, her last refrain echoed in the hallway. "Sophia was so nice. I wanted to leave it clean for her."

"We'll send her an apology from Syros. She'll understand."

Kini—Harbor of Dreams on the Island of Syros

As the ferry rounded the headland, I spotted the city. "Ermoupolis. It's like a collage of white and cream structures rising from the dock. The hilltops are garnished with church domes in shades of pure blue."

An announcement rang out in Greek, and the other passengers pushed toward the stairs. I picked up the green-with-leather-trim carrier containing our faithful, traveling kitty, and we headed down to the car. On this ferry, there was no giant hold stuffed with cargo trucks and exhaust fumes, just a couple dozen cars, a few rickety trucks, and a throng of pedestrians waiting to file off. The three-hour trip from Athens had gone fine. Even Felicia, tucked in her luggage and draped with our jackets, had scarcely offered a mew of protest. Like a bird in a covered cage she was.

I drove us off the ship, passing storefront businesses and the docks. Ahead, black cranes towered over mammoth ships in dry dock. Stores gave way to homes, and we emerged into the country. "That wasn't bad. Now we just drive to Kini on the back side of the island and find our cozy little inn." It felt so free to be out of Athens, so safe. I accelerated up the crooked road. "The hills are covered in dry grass, like a Bakersfield summer; and there are lots of falling-down stone walls. Imagine a thriving commune on this hill centuries ago, with churches built by hand and donkey power, one stone at a time . . . long since tumbled down. There are goats, too. Want me to stop so you can hear them?"

"Goats are a dime a dozen. Keep driving, unless you find monkeys."

Approaching a curve, I slowed down. My eye caught sight of a vehicle hurtling toward us in our lane. I stomped on the brake pedal and slid the car to the shoulder. Gray paint and rust zipped past my side of the car, the vehicle swerving vaguely toward its own side of the road.

Marguerite grabbed the armrest and Felicia simultaneously. "If you're stopping for a goat . . ."

"A dirty, old, pickup truck tried to run us off the road." So much for security.

I drove to the top of the mountain and stopped to gaze across the drab hills to the cobalt expanse of sea. My eyes felt the coolness, took in a far-off island, and lingered, before drifting in to port. "That must be Kini."

"Big or small?" Marguerite never thinks in terms of medium.

"We're talking small. Could be talking Greek paradise—crisp white buildings and an azure keyhole harbor."

Felicia looked up from Marguerite's lap. I felt sure she was engrossed in my report.

We descended past a red-roofed monastery complex, then houses, a little store, and a taverna. I turned right just before the beach and took a quick glance at the ten or twenty sun worshippers on the sand and the handful of swimmers in the water. We passed two more little restaurants—both simple, white, block buildings with reed-covered patios—and located our destination, the Harbor Inn.

The two-story inn, also white, with bright blue accents, looked more modern and substantial than the rest of the town. Bougainvillea issued from a pot by the main doorway and climbed in a bright red stream to a trellis on a second-floor balcony.

We left Felicia in the Peugeot and entered the inn's courtyard, where shade from vine-draped slats provided a cozy living space.

A small woman with wire-rimmed glasses, short-cut black bangs, and a raspberry jumpsuit descended the outside stairs with quick steps. "Hello," she called from halfway down. "I'm Trudy Boukas. Welcome to Harbor Inn."

We shook hands as Trudy glanced at Marguerite's white cane, but she didn't ask about her blindness. "I hear you brought your cat all the way from California."

"Want to see her?"

"I always want to meet cats."

We introduced the cat lover to our kitty, and she said, "She's one lucky girl. I hope you don't plan to let her outside. There are so many strays."

Felicia flashed her I-don't-mingle-with-other-cats look and burrowed her cinnamon-colored face into my armpit.

"Do you know about Greek cats?" Trudy asked. "We try our best to help them, but their lives are horrible." She showed us to our room, charming and bright—sort of a Greek, Southwestern-U.S. style, with pine doors, colorful mats on the beds and floor, and some unique touches like a built-in bed with storage below. I turned on the ceiling fan, opened the window over the kitchen sink, and leaned out. I spotted some delicate trees a ways down the little road and, just beyond, the beach and harbor, where fishing boats bobbed at anchor.

Once our clothes were hung and our kitty settled in, we joined other guests on the patio for afternoon tea. Trudy arrived with a medium height, fair-featured man in a "Desert Storm" T-shirt and swim trunks. "This is my husband, Kiriakos, aka Kirk," she said. "He designed the Inn."

Trudy scanned the top of the wall, spotted something, and grabbed a water pistol. "Get out of here," she yelled, and began squirting and then chasing a fleeing feline.

"I thought she liked cats," I said.

Kirk gave a crooked smile. "He's not one of *ours*. We have eight with collars. They're allowed on the patio and in the house."

"But you feed lots more?"

"Twenty or thirty now. When the tavernas close for winter, we have a crowd. We fill the car with fifty pound bags of food. They eat it all, and we buy more."

Trudy returned while Kirk was filling us in on day ferries to Delos and Mykonos. "Wait a minute," Trudy interrupted. "Before you go running off to other islands, check out Ermoupolis, our capital. You'll find a neat, old city hall and lots of sea captains' mansions from the last century. Take a look at the port and the shipyards. They've been building ships here since 3000 BC."

"The most important thing to see is Ano Syros," Kirk said. "It's up the mountain above Ermoupolis."

"There's a fabulous monastery, and a settlement that dates back to the thirteenth century, with narrow, winding alleyways," she added.

Kirk put in, "Ano Syros is the Catholic side of the hill. The Greek Orthodox side is called Vrodado. The Orthodox arrived in the 1820s while Greece was fighting the Ottomans for independence. Syros was the soul of Greece for the next fifty years."

"Take your camera," Trudy said. "There are lots of elegant buildings, and you'll love the alleyways in Ano Syros."

That evening Marguerite and I strolled to a taverna and sat on the patio as orange clouds turned deep red across the little bay and above the mountains. White block houses and a tiny chapel transformed to amber in the light of the porch lamps, and a string of white lights flicked on along the shore. Water lapped at the base of the patio. We ate Greek salad, mousaka, and little deep-fried fish—which Marguerite dubbed "French fries with eyeballs"—complete in all respects, including scaly tails that scratched our throats as we swallowed.

Four or five felines roamed between the tables, casting hungry, expectant stares our way. At the far end of the patio, several ducks accepted treats from other diners. (This was our only encounter with duck panhandlers during our Greek sojourn.) "Had enough of these fish?" I asked. "I want to give some to the cats." The felines jockeyed for the best morsels and gobbled happily.

Back in our room, our own inquisitive cat homed in on the scent and began sniffing my fingers. She looked up at me with a guilt-provoking question in her eyes. "Yes, Felicia," I confessed. "There *were* leftovers, but we gave them to the less fortunate cats of Kini." Her soft cat features turned to a scowl, and she stalked off to a corner to sulk.

The next day, we explored Ermoupolis, starting with its sparkling harbor, past the neoclassical city hall, and along narrow streets and sidewalks that ascended the hills. In the heart of the city, fashionable jewelry shops and markets laden with vegetables and dried fruits called out for us to browse. We finished with a dockside meal at an outdoor restaurant, watching a man at a charcoal grill barbecue octopus to a blackened-red color.

As we entered the patio of the inn, afternoon tea was ending, and our hostess was heading toward the back gate. "Sorry to run," she said, "but the cats need their supper."

"The wild ones?"

"The strays. There's nothing wild about them."

Marguerite and I followed out the back gate to a paved area. Healthy-looking kitties swarmed from behind buildings, under a rowboat, and down a little alley. Two black-and-whites and a tiger rubbed Trudy's ankles as she produced a bag of food from a storage room and scooped it into piles on the pavement. Cats gathered in little clusters to eat. "It's a disgrace," she said. "All over Greece, cats beg at tavernas during the summer. In winter the tourists go home, tavernas close, and they starve."

I heard the gate bang, and Kirk approached. He bent to stroke a calico. "Did you tell them about the vets?"

"I was about to. Next month, when all of you tourists go home, we'll have free guests. Veterinarians will fly in, and we'll put them up. Hotels on the other islands do it, too."

"Every day they operate on cats," Kirk said. "Twenty on a good day." He bent near a cat's posterior, flashed a boyish grin, and swished his hand with an imaginary scalpel back and forth.

"A group called Friends of the Cat organizes it from Athens," Trudy explained. "They raise money, and the vets come from England. British Air helped get the program started by providing free flights those first years. It's a wonderful thing they all do."

"Trudy knocks herself out. She captures cats, schedules everything, and cares for them while they're under anesthesia. She even makes supper for the doctors."

"Why don't you use Greek vets?" Marguerite wondered.

"Kiriakos should tell you. He's the native Greek." Trudy shot him a sly glance.

Kirk raised his palms to decline.

"Male Greek vets won't neuter male cats," Trudy said, still looking at Kirk.

"Well," Kirk said. "You have to understand."

"One time we adopted a big male named Mad Max. What about Max, Kiriakos?"

"He was a fighter," Kirk said, puffing with pride. "A great cat."

"And . . ." Trudy tapped her foot, and a couple of the cats jumped before settling back to their suppers.

"He was a lover, too. . . ." We waited, and Kirk finally finished. "When the vets came, I hid him." Kirk looked at his feet but grinned. "They couldn't do old Max."

More Tea, More English, No More Feta Cheese, Please

September 15

This week we are learning the meaning of relaxation. I swim every day at the beach in the cove, but I've only managed to coax Marguerite in once. Usually one or two topless beauties sun themselves among their more fully covered sisters. At first I didn't mention them to Marguerite, but now I've decided to report fully. It's one of my duties, after all, to observe discreetly but conscientiously and to fill her in on all aspects of these exotic lands.

We've found that Stavros, the spiritual guide of leather, knows his stuff. The sandals we bought from him in Athens are wonderful for walking in town and along the beach. His claims about liberating the feet and the soul are justified, but we stick to standard footwear for explorations along rocky coves, which rim the seashore.

From the tiniest village in one of those coves to the island's capital, Ermoupolis, we dine in Greek style with splendid views of the sea and islands. Marguerite takes in the clean sea air, the fun of hiking narrow trails through the scrub vegetation, and the balmy breezes as we dine on patios by the water. The romance and foreign feel of the island content her, and her happiness is enhanced by my enjoyment of these crystalline vistas.

Instead of rushing home for Larry King, we hurry back for tea time to savor the company of our fellow guests.

In the courtyard, we joined couples from the U.S., Canada, and Britain, and compared notes about Greece and our travels. "Let's see. This is September." Marguerite counted on her fingers in response to a question. "It's our sixth month in Europe. We have four or five more after this. We haven't decided yet just when we'll go back."

"How could you leave home for so long?" Julie from Denver asked.

"It's okay," I said. "We brought our cat along."

"Well, you fit in here." Julie laughed and nodded toward a tiger cat lounging on a cushion in a recess in the wall.

"Not just because of your cat," her husband, George, added. "Trudy and Kirk have wanderlust, like you. They took off in a camper one time for almost two years and explored India and Sri Lanka."

Julie poured her husband a glass of iced tea. "Didn't they get kicked out of Iran when the Iatollah came in?"

Trudy breezed in to drop off a bowl of pretzels. "Talking about us?"

"Sounds like you've had a wild life," Marguerite observed.

"Every day is wild," exclaimed Trudy. "Oh, I almost forgot the cookies." She headed back inside. "When I come back, maybe I'll tell you about my time in the Peace Corps. . . ."

What was the story on our hosts? We kept getting dribs and drabs.

One early evening, Trudy waylaid us. "You have to see my girls."

"You mean your cats?"

"No, the high-school girls I'm working with for the fair. This way."

"What fair?" Marguerite's question came too late, as Trudy disappeared into the courtyard.

Inside, we found five teenage girls in saris and veils, looking exotic, lovely, and embarrassed. "These are my beauties," Trudy said, rattling off their names. "This red-and-black costume with all the coins is from India, and the purple from Iran. The cream color came from Sri Lanka, the other two from Saudi. I bought them on my travels."

"They're exquisite," I said.

263

"So, it's a costume fair?" Marguerite persisted.

"Let's say a geography fair. I have hundreds of pictures I've taken around the world—temples in India, underground cities in Turkey, the U.S. Capitol in Washington. The men of the village will set them up on metal frames out in the street, and my girls have written up posters to explain the pictures."

"What an education for the girls," Marguerite said. "Isn't it a lot of work to organize?"

"I don't think much about that. You know what? We need a picture." She took me by the arm and propelled me forward. "That's it, right in the middle." I found myself posing with the girls as she snapped a photo. I felt very regal indeed with these giggling, mysterious beauties at my elbows. And I, too, was a little embarrassed.

That night we followed one of Trudy's recommendations, hiking up the road to the restaurant at the top of the mountain as the sun sank below the horizon and explosions boomed off in the distance.

"It's the fishing," I guessed.

Trudy had told us that Greeks still fish using dynamite, thinking to improve the catch. Because this area of the Mediterranean is so overfished, though, and because the dynamite kills everything nearby, the catch is small. We found very little seafood on menus. What there was consisted of those "French fries with eyeballs," octopus, and some choicer fish that came very dear.

"It seems so foolish," Marguerite said.

"You were thinking humans are rational? This sort of thing happens all over the world. Men try desperately to support their families, work harder to get less, deplete their livelihoods, and threaten their communities' survival." I thought I might mention global warming and all the fossil fuels we waste in the United States, but the evening held romantic promise, so I refrained.

Near the top of the mountain we found the spacious restaurant. It would have been indistinguishable from dozens of other places, with its linoleum floors and white-paper tablecloths, but for the wall of large windows looking down toward Kini. It was eight o'clock, and we were the first patrons. A middle-aged, dark-haired woman in a denim pinafore showed us to a table. Her husband sat on the other side of the L-shaped room in his white T-shirt, gulping wine from a squat glass. He poured from a carafe and took another swallow. We ordered white wine from Macedonia, *taziki* (cucumber dip), *dolmas* (stuffed grape leaves), roast pork with potatoes, and green beans in olive oil.

With the wine and taziki, the woman delivered a warm smile and a plate of little turnovers. "Here," she said. "Something for you to try." She saw the question in my eyes and added, "A gift."

At the far side of the room, her husband finished his glass and ambled toward the back. We nibbled the savory pastries stuffed with spinach and feta cheese, called *spanakopita*, and the woman returned with the dolmas and green beans. We had abstained from feta since Athens—because the huge slabs of the stuff they put on salads had overwhelmed our taste buds—but these little pastries were tasty, with just the right amount of cheese to complement the spinach.

"Where you are staying?" she asked.

"Down at the Harbor Inn."

"Miss Trudy's place. But how you come? I not hear a car."

"We hiked."

"You cannot walk down hill in dark. Trudy not tell you how bad the road at night?"

"She said to bring a flashlight." I pulled the light from my pocket and showed her.

"No. My husband will take you in truck. Hill is very dangerous."

Our proposed chauffeur appeared from the kitchen with grease now smeared on the front of his T-shirt. He wobbled across the room, poured another glass, and carried it, with the empty carafe, to the back.

"You're very kind, but we'll be fine." I displayed the light again and stuck it back in my pocket.

Our server shrugged and headed to the kitchen.

Marguerite frowned. "If the road is dangerous . . ."

"It would be worse with Zorba there driving on it. He's been drinking like a camel all night. It's got to be *retsina* (a Greek wine made with pine tar that tastes like lighter fluid)."

Marguerite flattened her brows skeptically. "But she said the road . . ."

"Trudy thinks it's a nice walk and not a problem."

"Trudy may be nuts. She was in Iran when the Iatollah came in. She told us to take that hike along the coast the other day and only mentioned the snakes once we got back."

"It was a great walk, and she was right about this restaurant. Trudy's just adventuresome—like us—a world traveler."

"Greek drivers are crazy. Maybe we should take a cab."

I vaguely remembered that Marguerite had been more fearless before the onset of menopause. "We'll be fine. And what makes you think the cab driver will have drunk less retsina than this guy?"

The walk home was uneventful. Few cars passed, and the night was beautiful. But how do you keep the romance in a moonlit stroll when your partner insists on rushing downhill at top speed? Whenever a car approached, we scurried to the opposite side of the road, aimed the flashlight at the driver, and waited for the car to pass.

September 17

Syros has sustained us in every way, from the bright sunshine to the English conversation that buoys our spirits to the tender nature of life. We have loved being away from Athens in a room that's clean, uncluttered, and fresh smelling. We even picked up our e-mail, thanks to a friendly guy in a computer store in Ermoupolis. (Note: We had searched Athens for a cybercafe but to no avail. The tourist office and bookstores had never heard of such a thing.)

Even take-out food in this Greek paradise can be a moment-

most-romantic. Last night we strolled at sunset to a taverna and bought skewered roast lamb, bread, water, and a small bottle of ouzo. We carried it all to a bench under wispy trees by the beach, listened to the waves lapping on the sand, and dined as the orange ran out of the sky.

Of course, our most lasting memories will be of Trudy and Kirk and what we learned about them and their mission to save the cats. We never did figure out the whole chronology of their wild and crazy lives. Let's see. There was the Peace Corps, the trip to the Far East, the Iatollah, the fact that Kirk was a diver for the allies in Operation Desert Storm. . . .

Detour to Autumn—the Pelion Peninsula

We bid farewell to Trudy and Kirk and the fair isle of Syros, drove aboard a ferry to the mainland, and embarked north along the sea to the Pelion Peninsula.

September 20

We've come up into the mountains, and suddenly it's fall. Huge chestnut trees shade the squares of little towns named Kissos, Millies, Vizitsa, and Makrinitsa. Dry leaves, as big as both my hands, and horse chestnuts fall to the ground around us. Pocket-sized churches are decorated in gilt-wrapped portraits of saints, who stare eerily from the walls. Hundreds of candles choke the rooms with their wax scent.

Gregarious restaurateurs, who speak not a word of English, summon us to their kitchens, where we peek into steel pots of bubbling, aromatic stews and guess at the contents.

We are living in Vizitsa in a traditional mansion of the Pelion Peninsula. Entering each afternoon feels like coming home to our own personal museum. It's a splurge at 15,000 drachmae ($54) a night, but it's a mansion and one of the most elegant lodgings in these parts. On the top floor, besides our room, there's a grand living room. Spindled wood railings set off the stairway. We sit there on cushioned *banquettes like potentates. I look out windows set forty feet above the ground at hills rolling downward forever into the mist. Feeling regal, with Effie on a leash so she can explore only a little, I spend evenings reading to Marguerite from* The Agony and the Ecstasy. *We learn about Michelangelo and look forward to Italy.*

This is also the land where shower curtains don't exist and every toilet leaks each time you flush. We've also encountered the first centipede of our trip. That is, Felicia encountered it. She sniffed at it and then backed off, leaving it for me to handle. I decided to dispose of the beast and leave Marguerite blissfully ignorant.

On the Crazy Road Again

From the Pelion, we headed down the mountain, along the sea, and inland through Athens on a road the map depicted as a main highway. Yikes, more Greek drivers.

September 23

I'm fighting to restrain the judgmental part of me as well as my inbred seriousness. After witnessing Greek drivers, it's clear that we Americans are too concerned with etiquette. Obviously, people in Greece can break all the rules of traffic law, not to mention civility, and live to drive another day. Why bother with regulations?

Letting go of standards, I begin to feel the Greek temperament— the rhythm of meandering through life between randomly spaced hazards, the ability to blot out fear and outrage, to soar. I sometimes park like the locals—blocking the sidewalk, hanging off into a ditch or a traffic lane or whatever—it's the only way. But I swear on my oath as a cat father that I will never stoop to double parking. Rats, there I go getting rigid again.

A few notes on highways—if the map shows a main highway or freeway, don't believe it. The Greek National Road . . . yes, okay, it is a road. Sometimes it's a conventional, two-lane road, with a lane in each direction and shoulders. Sometimes it's a divided highway. Often it's under construction, and anything goes then. Through Athens, the Greek National Road picks up and loses lanes, then merges into surface streets. It may unexpectedly take a right turn at a signal, the only warning being a sign hidden behind a truck. The sign might be in Roman letters or Greek, capitals or lowercase. It's good to know the name of your destination in all of these forms. I comb my brain from my fraternity days for remnants of the Greek alphabet.

Past Athens we turned south, down the east side of the Peloponnesian Peninsula, and toward the island of Poros.

September 23, continued
    On two-lane roads of sufficient width, it's customary to drive half on the shoulder and half in your lane. That way, passing cars fit nicely between you and the opposing traffic, as long as the cars coming the other way pull halfway off the road, too, and provided no one is passing on the other side, and provided you don't come to a bridge or other impediment. I manage a good rate of speed doing as the locals do. Some drivers are so accustomed to this technique that they continue to drive with the painted stripe centered under the car on multilane highways.
    Is it a machismo thing to hold supremacy over two lanes of concrete? Could they be half blind, squinting at the lines intently like the cartoon character Mr. Magoo? Whatever the reason, it feels damned dangerous watching in the rearview mirror as a car zooms close. I decided early on that half of my lane is not an unreasonable demand here. I yield it willingly so each maniac can continue his chosen path.
    P.S. Marguerite seems happier with my new driving attitude. I'm not so tense and irritable.

Maintaining the English Connection on the Island of Poros

September 24

> *Heaven . . . I sit on a marble-floored balcony much larger than many of the apartments we've occupied. Overhead, bamboo slats keep the sun off. Purple bougainvillea drapes down from the roof, filling the corner. Pine trees take up the center of my view. I glance left to watch a hydrofoil cruise toward the port. On the other side, I savor a view of villas and hotels stepping down to the sea and to the smaller part of our island, where the city of Poros lies. Behind everything loom the majestic mountains of the mainland Peloponnese.*
>
> *We live on the second floor of this idyllic villa, which sits along a country road a hundred yards uphill from the Aegean. The front yard is small and steep, so we park in the street and enter through a gate. The sidewalk meanders upward, crosses the corner of a patio (which belongs to the downstairs apartment), up a flight of stairs to our entryway. We have a bedroom with a sliding door to the balcony and an ample living room with a double-sized sliding door to the same balcony. It's like living outside. The kitchen is well equipped but for two essentials—a coffee maker and a washing machine. To compensate, we have something amazing—all of the windows, except the huge sliding door, have* screens! *Even more exciting, though less practical, is the wooden-winged, Hindu goddess that hangs over the living-room coffee table. Marguerite isn't enamored with this artifact—she hit her head on it—but she'll come to love it as I do.*
>
> *One more piece of good news: we have yet to meet our neighbors who rent downstairs, but they left us a welcome note, and they're from the United States!*

A knock on the door pulled me from the computer. Outside stood a sixty-plus-year-old woman, tanned in a way that indicated a life of sun worship. She had wet platinum hair and wore a gold terry robe over her flowered swimsuit. "Hello, hello. I'm Rita, your neighbor downstairs." Her mellow voice cut out any of the sharpness of her New York accent, and it pleased my ears.

"I'm Ed, and . . ." I turned to see Marguerite feeling her way past the coffee table and ducking to avoid the flying Hindu goddess. "Here comes Marguerite. The furry one on the couch is Felicia."

"You brought your cat from America? There are plenty here."

Marguerite arrived, carrying Effie. "But Felicia's special."

"I can see that now. Yes. . . . Special. Anyway, I'm making chicken marengo tonight. Would you come for dinner?"

I caught the excitement in Marguerite's eyes, so I answered, "Great. We'll bring the wine."

"Not retsina! That stuff is gasoline. Now, before I go, the landlords are in Athens, so I agreed to show you the ropes. First, you never flush toilet paper. I guess you know that, since you've been in Greece a while."

Marguerite wore a guilty smile. "What do you do with it?"

"Put it in the garbage can, of course. Otherwise, it clogs the cesspools, or whatever they have here. You see all these little tank-trucks that drive by? They're called honey pots. When a cesspool clogs, they summon the trucks to pump it out."

"Those trucks fly by our car and almost hit it every time they pass."

"Get used to it, honey. This is Greece. Pull the car off as far as you can and pray. Oh, and here's the on-off switch for the water heater. Turn it on a half hour before you wash dishes or take a bath. If you leave it on, you'll use lots of electricity, maybe burn the place down, for all I know. Anyway, cocktails are at seven. You'll meet Tim then."

🐾

We arrived at seven, with bottles of Cretan white wine. Rita greeted us at the door and introduced Tim.

A debonair-looking fellow with a mustache and a full head of white hair stood by a counter. "I'm fixing up gin and tonics. Care for one?" His speech, in a cool British accent, completed the sense of sophistication.

Seated in the comfy living room, sipping Tim's drinks, we shared tales of our trip. "We have something in common," Rita said. "I retired eight months ago from the garment industry in the city. Been traveling ever since. First, I took a round-the-world trip on a freighter. Then I moved here two months ago. Tim's been with me the last three weeks."

"You know what they say about dead fish and houseguests." Tim flashed a toothy smile. "I'm way past stinking."

We paused to see if Rita would contradict him, but it was Marguerite who ended the silence. "Well, Tim, what line of work are you in?" Changing the subject had always been one of her talents.

Tim was a former commodities man in both England and the States, now retired and sharing his time between Connecticut and Florida. We were at the table, enjoying Rita's excellent chicken-vegetable dish, when Tim turned to a familiar subject. "I guess you noticed the bowls of food and water down on our landing." He flicked a glance toward Rita and continued, "I've been feeding a mother cat and her kittens."

"Not to mention some others across the road." His housemate pursed her lips but then reset her face to neutral.

"Rita and I will leave in ten days, and I'm afraid they'll starve." All traces of British coolness disappeared, and his voice cracked. I thought back to Trudy and Kiriakos feeding scores of cats after the tavernas closed each year and wondered how we gravitated to so many cat lovers. Tim was right to fear for his foundlings.

Rita watched her guest the way a mother watches a child just before she sends him to his room. She wasn't keen about hosting the felines, but she held her tongue.

As the evening ended, Tim handed me a precious bundle, the previous two days' worth of London *Telegraphs* and *International Herald Tribunes*. "Here you go, old boy. We've read these. Thought you might enjoy them." I not only enjoyed them, but I devoured them over breakfast the next day, commenting to Marguerite and reading some of the articles aloud.

From that night on, we had a steady stream of English company and news. Arriving home each late afternoon, we found our downstairs neighbors lounging on their veranda. We shared greetings and gained valuable information—like the laundry where they washed, dried, and folded a machine-full for $6. Often we received the newspapers and a glimpse of the cats that were becoming tame with Tim's care. We took turns treating each other to dinner at an upscale restaurant they favored, named for the god of wine, Bacchus.

We grew accustomed to our downstairs neighbors and their steady, unobtrusive company.

Felicia Is My Greek Word for "Love"

October 2

Effie has come into her own, or is it just that I'm appreciating her more? She can't accompany me for walks in her baby sling like she did in Holland because there are cats all over the place, and she despises the beasts. But she's the perfect balcony or living-room leash cat. The three of us spend hours out there with me reading to them aloud. I clip the leash (a feminine lavender) to her collar (a red, white, and blue U.S. flag design) and hook it around a chair leg. Felicia stays put wherever she is. Last night, Tim and Rita came for drinks before dinner, and we set five chairs out on the balcony. Effie joined us while we talked, and our guests admired her sterling behavior.

For the record, I now admit: Whatever flaws I imagined in Felicia earlier in the trip derived solely from my own dementia.

Life is grand and serene. There's even television in English—not exactly Larry King Live, *but it's something.*

Our black-and-white TV in the bedroom brought in three UHF stations, all fuzzy. At night I clicked from one to the other, seeking comprehension. For hours each night, one channel broadcast scenes from the subway construction in Athens—

273

sometimes there would be a talking head in front of heavy equipment or vacant holes in the ground, sometimes just a nighttime picture of a torn-up section of town with no action at all. Fascinating to think anyone would watch. I flipped it off and tried again later . . . construction scenes, quiz shows, news reports in Greek.

In the morning, my scanning bore fruit. Each day, it turned out, there was a half-hour long, informational show from the U.S.— about Florida, Colorado, Alaska, visa requirements for traveling from the U.S. to Russia, the history of golf.

One morning, as usual, we piled pillows at the head of the bed and leaned back to watch a show—Alaska was the day's feature. Marguerite was finishing off her yogurt as I ate cereal and sipped instant coffee. Our kitty yelped and hopped up.

"You're being very meowski this morning," Marguerite said.

"She wants your yogurt."

Marguerite offered the plastic container, and Effie began licking her way in. Soon she was so deep inside it looked like a yogurt cup with fur ears. She pushed to get a little more, and Marguerite giggled, an indicator that all was right—happiness, health, and contentment—in our lives.

When our kitty got everything her tongue could reach, she abandoned Marguerite and curled up beside me. Scenes of Kodiak bears ran across the TV, and an announcer talked about life in the Alaskan tundra. Effie started licking my hand. I didn't know whether it was the satisfied look on Felicia's fur face or her steadfastness, but somehow I knew there would be more than just a few licks. I began counting. "She's given me fifty licks so far," I reported.

"Aren't you interested in this stuff about Mount McKinley?"

"Seventy-eight, seventy-nine . . . I'm watching the program and counting." Felicia kept on. At 173 licks, the show ended.

"Do you want me to turn off the TV?" Marguerite asked.

"Don't disturb her."

"You're taking advantage of my blindness. She's not really licking you. She's washing herself, isn't she? If she'd given you that many licks, your skin would come off." Marguerite reached toward our kitty.

I headed her off with my free hand. "Hold it. She's going for the record, and she's licking very gently."

The record turned out to be 524 licks—maybe not enough to get into *Guinness*, but I considered it her personal best.

Poros was another easy-going, quaint island. On the back side we found a remote little cove, surrounded by palm and olive trees. A charming, white house with red doors and window frames sat on a knoll nearby, and a man rested in a stand under palm fronds, selling drinks and renting lounge chairs—the only signs of civilization. I left Marguerite resting on our blanket and took a swim. When I came back, she was listening to the tinkling and clanking of bells as a herd of goats came down from the hill, followed in a few minutes by the herdsman. At the sound of his whistle, the goats climbed a rock-studded hill beside the cove and disappeared over the top. "Great sound effects," was all Marguerite said.

Circling the island by car, we passed hills cloaked in pine and olive groves, and white houses with vine-covered patios. We came to the site of the temple of Poseidon and what little was left of its ruins—a bit of foundation, a few chunks of pillar on a pine-needle carpet, and a view of the blue sea and the Peloponnese, which would please any god. I learned from our guidebook that all the good parts of the temple had been hauled off to Hydra to build a monastery.

I stopped often along the road to examine shrines to dead drivers—some just metal boxes with glass doors; others more elaborate, like the white, multilevel monument with gold trim and a bench to sit on nearby. All contained candles and pictures, mostly of young men, who must have soared off these hillsides on their motorbikes or in their cars. So much for abandoning safety rules.

Another day, we walked to the monastery at the end of our

road, a lone, white structure with an orange-tiled roof; a central courtyard with arcades below; and a long, narrow, wooden balcony above, like the hacienda in an old Zorro movie. In the center of the courtyard sat a Byzantine chapel with candles aglow, casting shadows, filling the air with their scent, and crackling quietly. Pilgrims entered, crossed themselves, kissed the picture of a saint, crossed again, and moved on to the next picture, repeating the process.

Marguerite and I followed a trail from the monastery to another waterside taverna. What else could we do but order wine, stuffed peppers, and mousaka? Every corner of Greece seemed filled with tavernas, good food, and beautiful beach scenes—the easy life. . . .

Closing Greece

Seeking drinking water, I walked the road from our front steps down toward the beach. I entered a mini-mart about the size of an office, with Greek magazines, candy, sodas, canned foods, beer, doughnuts, cigarette lighters, and knickknacks. The thirty-five-year-old owner with dark stubble on his face greeted me.

I set a few liters of bottled water on the counter. "Our friends said you'll be closing for the season." Rita and Tim had the inside track on everything.

"Depends on the weather." He rang up my water on an adding machine. "My wife will come from Athens Friday. If it is warm, she will stay to swim, and my store will be open all week. If it is cold, we go home to the city."

It must have been too cold. When I ambled by on Saturday, the windows were covered with white paper.

A few days later, Marguerite and I strolled past the Oasis Restaurant, where we had eaten our first lunch on Poros. "It's a funny feeling. The patio was full of tables and chairs yesterday. Now—poof—they're gone. Just vine-covered pillars, a slatted roof, and a vacant building."

That Saturday we drove Tim and Rita to the docks to catch the *Flying Dolphin*, a blue and gold hydrofoil that would take them to Athens. Their stay was over. We unloaded their bags from the trunk, and Tim led us to a table at one of the cafés by the quay. "This is my breakfast place. I walked here almost every day this past month." He introduced the owner and asked us, "What will you have? It's on me. I have drachmae to burn."

We ordered cappuccinos and doughnuts, and watched fishing boats unload. Men in yellow rubber overalls weighed buckets of fish on scales that hung from a pole on the dock, totaled the sale, and exchanged cash. Nearby, cats eyed their doings expectantly. Sunlight sparkled across the water of the strait. The town of Galatas sat just across it, overshadowed by the mountains, looking like a postcard from Greece, quaint, innocent.

"So where are you off to next?" Marguerite asked Rita.

"Manhattan for a few weeks. Then I'll board a tramp steamer or something. I haven't decided."

"Look here." Tim stood. "This money's burning a hole in my pocket. I'll be right back." He headed to a store and returned with newspapers. "These are for you." He handed me a *Herald Tribune* and a *Telegraph*. Before I could protest, he showed me another *Telegraph* he'd bought for himself.

I thanked him and directed a question to both of them. "What will you miss about Poros?"

"That little beach down below the monastery. Sunbathing every day without a care," Rita answered.

"Eating at Bacchus with you," Tim said. "But more seriously . . ." His voice became trembly.

"He's worried about his cats." Rita frowned, but besides disapproval, her expression held concern.

"I left two boxes of cat food. If it wouldn't be too much trouble . . ."

"Not a problem at all." Marguerite looked at me guiltily. "Oops, I guess I've volunteered you again." She turned back to Tim. "Eddie says I'm more trouble than any three people in Europe."

"I guess here in Greece I'd say, 'more trouble than a horse full of Trojans,'" I said. Rita turned her frown on me, and I added, "I'm teasing, of course."

"Yes, old boy, you must have your hands full," Tim said, "but would you add to your travails and feed the poor cats?"

"Sure, but we're here for only four more days."

"It's something, anyway. There was a kitten the other day— white and orange—did you see him? A friendly tyke. I thought he'd join us for our last few days, but he was sick." Tim swallowed and looked at the table.

Rita thumped her coffee cup down and looked as if she'd startled herself. "The cat had diarrhea on one of our cushions."

Tim continued. "I wrapped him in a towel and carried him down the road to a place with some other cats. I've brought them food every day since."

"Tim has this terrible soft spot," Rita said. "But your compassion goes too far, Tim. You let it ruin the way you feel about Poros."

"You're right," he said. "I couldn't ever come back here. All I think about now that we're leaving is what will happen to them." He looked miserable and perplexed, and I pitied him.

The hydrofoil pulled to the pier. I helped them set their luggage aboard, and then we bid them adieu.

Poof. Rita and Tim were gone.

October 4

We miss our neighbors. When we come home, there's no one sitting on the downstairs patio sipping gin and tonics. There's no swimming report, no leftover copies of the Herald Tribune *and the* Telegraph. *There's no Rita, with her New York accent and helpful hints about the island; no Tim, so British, stroking a cat's head while giving us the latest on the new ones he's feeding down by the beach. That's part of the closing-down feeling.*

The floating docks disappeared on Monday. We canvassed the remaining grocery stores for cat litter and found only one bag available on the island, not the preferred clumping kind, but it would do. Poof—no more cat litter—we had bought the last.

Tuesday, our last evening, we sat with Effie on the balcony as the sun disappeared and its glow brushed scarlet halos among the clouds. I poured wine into Marguerite's glass. "This will be our last Macedonia white wine. Will you miss it?"

"They'll have great wines in Italy . . . but that's not what you're thinking of missing."

"They're practically rolling the streets up around us and kicking us out of here. It's time to leave, but . . ."

"It's not the same with Rita and Tim gone, is it?" Marguerite said.

"And Tim's cats will have no one to feed them. But mostly I'm thinking about our villa and this carefree life."

October 7

We are happy and looking forward to steaming back to Italy, but there's a minor melancholy floating in the background. Will we ever again occupy such a perfect paradise as this?

On Wednesday we loaded up and drove to the ferry, bound for Italy. Need I say it? Poof, we were gone.

Cinque Terre, Italy—Desperately Seeking Hot Water

Bal-con-y or Spumoni

We survived the voyage, including another encounter in the hold with all the pollution-puffing trucks. Six hours of driving from Ancona put us clear across Italy in the Cinque Terre, a group of five small cities perched in canyons leading down to the Mediterranean.

Hanging tightly to the steering wheel, I guided the Peugeot along winding, narrow roads in a dense fog, slowing to a crawl around the curves. Without fog lines on the right, there was no telling where the road ended and the cliff dropped off. On the left, ghostly pines and ferns appeared from out of the mist; downward, another turn. "It's getting easier," I said hopefully.

Descending . . . more bends in the road . . . "Ah, yes. We're coming out below the fog. I see the Mediterranean way down there, a little, dull-green spot wedged under a cloud." Tropical-looking plants projected from the cliff side, their stalks piercing the air; their succulent, pointed leaves jutting out over the roadway. "Wow, a real highway, complete with a line down the middle. And a sign— Riomaggiore to the right."

After we had piloted through the fog for over an hour, the first village we found had no accommodations. But the town of Riomaggiore would have lodgings. I came to the outskirts and swung into a parking space at the edge of a steep bank. "I'll leave you here with Felicia and hike down to find a place for the night."

"Why not drive into town?"

"There's a barrier, and a guy in a little booth. It looks like cars don't go down. Guess I'll have to pay to park."

"Whatever it costs, you'll get a room, right?"

"I'll try for under $50."

I left my women and paid the parking attendant for an hour. With my receipt, he handed me a business card. "*Signore*, you look for a room? Best place. Clean. Nice. Bathtub. TV. They got everything." The card said, "*Edi Appartamanti* (apartments and rooms, *appartamenti e camere, Privatzimmer und Wohnungen*)."

"Walk straight down," the attendant continued, "on the . . ." He held out his left hand, struggling for the word.

"Left," I said.

"*Sí, signore*, the left. You will like the apart-a-ments."

Gravity propelled me down a narrow street between four- and five-story buildings. Gold, pale green, light cranberry, the buildings blotted out the hills on either side. I spotted the railings of balconies on their top floors and laundry strung on lines beneath windows. Maybe I should have paid for two hours of parking.

I spotted the Edi Appartamenti sign and entered a pigeon-hole office. The dark-haired woman behind the desk and I greeted each other with *buon giornos* and nods. I tried English and she Italian. No luck. "*Parlez-vous français?*" she asked. So French became our best common denominator. I asked if she had a room with a balcony. She did, for about $50 a night. She led me across the street to a narrow gold building. We went up three long flights of impossibly steep stairs that had me gasping for air and my head ducking to avoid a rough-looking ceiling, which dipped low and threatened to brain me. She unlocked a door. Inside, I inspected an entryway, with more stairs leading upward, a spacious bedroom, a half bath, and a living room. "The balcony?" I asked.

She pointed up. At the top of the stairs was a second bathroom, a kitchen, and a dining nook, plus the balcony with a view into the canyon of buildings on the main street. At the far end, a slate-gray sea peeked out from between the structures. Other pastel, four-story homes ascended the sides of the canyon to a ruined fortress and a church steeple. Nice, acceptable price, but was it the best . . . at the lowest rate?

"You have nothing for less?" I asked.

"Not with a balcony."

"My cat likes balconies. If we stay for four days, can we pay less?" She pursed her lips and shook her head.

With forty minutes left on my parking tab, I rushed on and spotted a sign for an *immobiliare*—similar to the French *immobilier*, a real-estate agent. Within a few words, the agent and I established English as the language of least resistance. "Do you have any apartments with balconies? *Balcone?*"

His eyes sparked understanding. "No." The young man shook his head and his curly black hair bounced. "Wait. Yes, yes. I find," he said. "Come." He beckoned. I was hot on the trail of a second prospect with thirty-six minutes left on my parking clock.

The fellow led me to an ice-cream parlor. Was he thinking spumoni instead of bal-con-y? He summoned the middle-aged, balding proprietor, who was wiping his fingers on an apron streaked with strawberry, pistachio, lemon, and chocolate. We quickly established Italian as our best common language, which was the worst outcome for me but the only option. The aproned man said something indecipherable, then led me next door and up another flight of near-perpendicular stairs. Inside the cramped apartment, I registered the decor, a hot plate on a shelf next to a sink, and a swaybacked bed with a cheap bedspread. I pressed the bed with my hand, and it slumped deeper—bad for the back and bad for the marriage. And no balcony that I could see.

Losing faith in the ice-cream man, I opened the window, unlatched the shutters, and looked through. "No *balcone*," I said. He shook his head. To show a little interest, I asked, *"Quantos lire?"* Okay, so *quantos* was Spanish, but it was the best I could do on short notice. It worked.

He held up fingers and spoke numbers. I frowned. He pulled a pad from his apron and wrote it down. The room cost about $30.

"Camera con balcone?" I said. *"Capisce?"* The first apartment was growing on me more and more as I eyed the wreck of a bed.

Plus the clock was ticking. What did they do in Italy to a car whose time had expired? What did they do with the blind woman and cat inside when they tossed the Peugeot into the sea? Felicia liked her fish from cans, not swimming at eye level.

The man seemed to *capisce*. He led me down to the street, walked me three doors up the sidewalk, and pushed the buzzer to an apartment. A balding head poked out of a fourth-story window. The men conversed. Thirty-one minutes left. Gelato man held up a palm to me and then pointed down at the pavement, the international symbol telling me to wait there.

Minutes passed. Three little kids kicked a soccer ball in the street. A woman picked through melons in a crate outside a grocery store and haggled with the proprietor. Was the guy upstairs sprucing himself up . . . cleaning the apartment? Did he know my wife and cat were at risk?

The unshaven man emerged from the building in a tank-type undershirt, with black hair matting on his shoulders and twining from his armpits. So he hadn't been touching up his image. I said, *"Buon giorno. Camera con balcone?"*

He escorted me up several interminable flights. My legs ached, my lungs wheezed. My heart thrashed itself to smithereens inside my chest. My host unlocked the door to an apartment and swung it open, revealing a room smaller than the last with a bed more dirty and misshapen. And yes, there was a balcony, with one folding chair and barely enough space to get past it. I pressed the chair against the wall, contorted my way around it, and looked over the rail—soccer kids, ice-cream shop, soft colors of the city. It was the atmosphere of Italy outside, but when I turned back, there was still the same filthy room before me.

To be polite, I asked the price—$25. A bargain, but not a bargain for me. I pointed at my eyes then swung my hand around toward the town, my version of the international symbol for, I'm going to look at some other places. I bid the dazed man farewell, hurried down the stairs, and hustled to the Edi Apartment rentals. Back in the postage-stamp office, I found a man this time. I looked him over and assessed his likelihood of foreign-language skills— modern, not wrinkled attire; a discerning look. "Do you speak English?"

He grinned. "Yes. Good I speak." This, I thought, was a decent sign. I told him I would like to rent the apartment and asked if he would reduce the price for a four-day stay. "I am sad, I cannot do."

"Oh, and we have a cat. Is that okay?"

He squinted.

"A gatta." I meowed for him.

"Oh, yes. No problem. We love the *gattas.*"

I booked the place for three nights. Then, heart chugging and lungs gasping, I strode uphill to the parking lot to retrieve my sweet wife and our sweet cat and to deliver the Peugeot from the threat of a watery grave.

We hauled in our luggage, paid for three days' parking, and fed Felicia. I opened the windows and sat on the side of the bed. Sounds funneled up through the canyon of buildings, and the room was instantly filled with chiming church bells, children shouting as they played, women talking, and cats mewing. Soon, townspeople swarmed from their homes for their evening *passeggiata* (promenade) along the street. The murmur of hundreds of voices resonated. We were immersed in the real Italy.

October 10

We are happy again to be in a land that honors cats. Our landlord seems pleased that we brought Felicia, and a nearby trattoria has a cat, too. Unlike Greece, the cat has a name, and the name is spoken in a gentle voice. Not only that, our toilets don't drip, and we can flush toilet paper without guilt. We get CNN and BBC on the television. We have news from two continents and Larry King Live!

One problem—the water heater keeps going out. It's a catalytic type, without a tank of hot water. When the pilot is out, the water's cold. I keep relighting it while Marguerite jumps in and out of the shower. I don't get to shower; I have to take a bath.

Exploring Our New Universe

Passing crates of melons, grapes, and tomatoes sitting on blocks beside the street, we entered a grocery store not much larger than our kitchen back home. The shelves were packed with cans of sauces, jams, and spreads, and boxes containing pastas, crackers, and cookies. Sausages, legs of dried meat, and cheeses hung on ropes overhead. Wooden baskets on the floor displayed apples, pears, and more cheeses. Two thirds of the room was taken up with a large, glass case. Stooped Italian housewives in black sweaters and long skirts pressed up to the counter, peered inside, chattered, and demanded items from white-shirted clerks behind the case.

"This looks like a cutthroat crowd," I said. "We'll have to fight for a place at the counter."

Marguerite squared her shoulders. "I can take any three of them."

At a shelf in a back corner, with barely enough room to stand between the racks of food and the women shoppers, I examined some antipasti in glass jars. A clerk scurried from behind the counter, elbowed Marguerite aside, grabbed a box of biscotti, and returned to the cash register.

"I take it back. They're pretty tough," she said.

"Prepare to fight with your cane."

We selected a jar of chopped-olive antipasto and one of roasted red peppers, picked up a barbell of cheese tied in the middle on a rope, and some pears. Approaching the counter, one of the oldest women—clearly a veteran of guerilla shopping—eyed us and spoke to a companion. The two glanced at Marguerite's cane and then her face. What was that look in their eyes, a challenge? They stepped back, making room. One spoke to a clerk, who abandoned his current customer, a woman with a blue scarf around her neck, and asked for my order.

"They were first," I said. *"Primeri. Señoras primeri."* I didn't know if that meant "first" in Italian, but it sounded right.

The blue-scarfed woman said a few words, which I took to mean, "No, you are guests." I could argue, but how would I go about it? I thanked her and addressed the man behind the counter. I pointed and gestured while he packaged up some green ravioli, black and green olives, and a tub of pesto sauce. We paid and thanked the women, who rattled off colorful nonsense syllables and curtsied.

"Aren't you ashamed?" Marguerite asked. "They were very sweet, and you called them cutthroats."

"It's the cane. Without it, the shrews would have torn us to shreds."

We packed the cheese and antipasti into our picnic bag, along with utensils, a cold bottle of wine, and the fresh bread I had picked up that morning.

We'd been looking forward to this moment since reading an article about the Cinque Terre—idyllic walks on trails beside the sea, quaint villages, and comfortable rides home by train. This region of northwestern Italy had been isolated for centuries, with access only by boat. Times had changed, but the charm endured.

With the picnic bag slung over my shoulder, we strode down the main street. Following signs for the *Via dell'Amore* (Romantic Trail), we soon paced along a fine promenade cut into the hills above the sea. Waves crashed against the rocks below us. The sun flitted in and out from the cover of puffy clouds. Sea spray misted our faces as we leaned over the railing. We asked other hikers to take our picture on a bench whose back formed the silhouette of two lovers, a heart cut out between. Romance crept into the day.

The trail tapered to a dirt path wide enough for just one person. Uneven steps led uphill to a humble church with plaster crumbling from its walls, and an austere graveyard. Marguerite followed, one hand holding mine while the other held her cane to locate obstacles. I raised or lowered my hand to indicate steps, or I would tell her things like, "It's rough and rocky. You'll have to feel your way."

"Your next wife may not want to do this with you," she told me. Marguerite was still game, but she was getting tired from the climbing and the concentration it took. She stumbled and gripped my hand tighter.

Up ahead, I spotted a serious mound of rock. "Wait," I told her. I climbed ahead, reached back, and guided her cane to show her a level spot. "Put your foot there."

She dispatched a fatigued, little smile, hung onto my hand, and pulled herself up.

"Now this is interesting—loose sand and pebbles. Don't lose your footing. There's a slope and then a sheer drop to the rocks. But it's nothing you can't handle."

"I think we've done this before."

"Martinique in 1979?"

"The famous canal walk," she confirmed. "I scared the heck out of that guide."

We edged forward. A pair of hikers waited in a wide spot up ahead. I took a step, brought my other foot close, steadied my stance, and let Marguerite move forward. I watched the couple. By their expressions I could tell the moment they spotted Marguerite's cane. The pretty young woman, in a white top and sun hat, shifted her look from, Don't hurry—I'm glad to rest here a while, to Wow—look at what that blind woman is doing. Her companion, a well-tanned, thin man with classic Italian features and a diamond-studded ear, had a look of put-upon patience. At the moment of realization, his eyes shot to me. He was thinking, What kind of animal would take her here?

We came to a level stretch and a stairway leading down to the sea. Sitting in the shade of a wispy tree, I pulled food from the bag. Marguerite sliced a pear and handed me a chunk. I munched it and popped the cork on the wine. "Great place for a picnic."

"Delightful with the sea breeze."

"I see Vernaza up ahead."

"Is it close? There's a train station there."

"Not far. Looks like a flat walk from here."

"We're going to take the train back, right?"

I let the question linger as I poured wine.

"You didn't answer about the train."

"The hills are full of these cool, succulent plants. I'll take your picture with the sea, the plants, and Vernaza behind you."

"Only if the next shot is of me getting onto the train."

In Vernaza, we found a smaller version of Riomaggiore, with cranberry, gold, and pastel green, five-story buildings set in a canyon leading to the sea. A few of the houses sat atop a stone arch above the surf—a striking site for a villa. At the lower end of town, we found a tiny harbor with blue and white boats pulled up on a ramp and a view along the spectacular, undulating coastline to another pastel town. I left Marguerite on a bench to rest and walked the road above town. A brook cascaded beside me. Terraced vegetable gardens scaled the mountainside. Stone houses perched here and there, built to blend into the hillsides with vines flowing over their patios.

Back at the bench, two children and their big fluffy dog were visiting Marguerite, speaking Italian as she responded in English. She asked the name of their dog, and my best guess was they wanted her cane. Kids in foreign countries always did that. I approached, taking hold of the cord at the end, and let them touch it. I folded it up and showed them how it snapped back to full length. They jabbered at me, but no matter what they said, there was no way I would let them have the cane to themselves. They didn't look larcenous, but one never knows.

Of course, we took the train home. (For $3, you can go anywhere in the region.)

Water Heater Repair 101

October 11

English flows during the daytime in Riomaggiore from tourists and students who come on day trips. Though we crave our language, it's disappointing, too. It erases the feeling of Italian isolation. In the evening, the day-trippers go back to Naples or wherever, the locals take over the streets, and we're back to small-town bliss.

After our hike along the coast, a shower sounded great. I checked the water heater—pilot out again. At the rental office I asked the signora in French for help with the *chauffe-eau*. She accompanied me home. "You see, this is the way to make it work." She lit the pilot.

"Yes, but it goes out again." I didn't mention that I had already lit it several times just to wash dishes. That was too much to say in French.

"If you need, I come and light it again," she said, as if that would solve the problem.

"But it will snuff out during my shower."

Confusion wrinkled her brow. Maybe my French was better than hers, our versions of French didn't work well together, or she didn't want to understand.

"I am glad to help you anytime," she repeated with an innocent smile.

I tried to think of other explanations but gave up. *"Merci. Merci beaucoup."*

I messed with the pilot several times and ran enough hot water for a bath. I relit the flame, stood in the partially full tub, and tried the shower. It ran quickly to cold. A bath would do just fine.

Miraculous Vision in Riomaggiore

The day after our Romantic Trail adventure, Marguerite and I climbed a hill in Riomaggiore. Striding toward us from above came a thirty-five-ish couple—a woman with curly brown hair in a red vest and jeans; and her husband, sporting a Greek fisherman's hat and a white-and-red cane, the international symbol for . . .

"Look, another blind person," I said.

We approached, introduced ourselves, and chatted. Hans said he was completely blind and worked for an organization in The Hague that trained the visually impaired. Elsa was a travel writer. Not to waste this opportunity with English-speaking folks and an actual blind person, we arranged to meet later for dinner.

We met them that evening outside the railroad station and strode through the train tunnel toward the village. Marguerite held my hand, while Hans and Elsa walked separately. He stuck his cane straight out in front, the tip not even skimming the pavement.

When Marguerite was really using her cane (and not holding my hand while I guided), she swung it from side to side to feel the way. Our friend Keith in Santa Barbara can get by without swinging his cane. Keith has peripheral vision, which helps a lot. But Hans said he was totally blind. Was he navigating by the echo of footsteps on tunnel walls? Did he have bat radar? A train hissed and rumbled into the tunnel. Its brakes screeched as it slowed for the station. Surely the racket would interfere with bat radar, but Hans just kept rambling along, surging ahead of Elsa from time to time. Something didn't compute.

I suggested a restaurant, one that Marguerite and I hadn't tried yet. Within twenty seconds of entering, Hans said, "I don't know about this place. It might be expensive." I did my best to interpret the menu. The prices seemed about right.

"You know what it is?" Hans said. "It's too touristy."

"Why do you say that? Do you think it's noisy?" Elsa wondered.

"I feel it. You can sense it, too, Marguerite. Can't you?"

"Seems okay to me," she answered.

"No. It's too *touristy*."

Arriving at another restaurant, Hans tramped ahead of me and up the step to a roofed patio that held six tables—all full. At the owner's suggestion, we waited in the street. When we heard chairs scraping, we knew people were leaving, but a planter obscured their table. Hans rushed forward and beat me to the patio. He peeked around the planter and said, "That table's no good. It's only for two. This other party will be leaving soon."

Sure enough, four people pushed back their chairs. Was the "blind" man psychic?

Soon we were seated, telling life stories, swapping tales about our month in Holland and their trips to the U.S., and feeling the pleasure of a balmy night. Hans confided that he had been blinded in a motorcycle accident three years before. He told us about his use of the computer and e-mail.

"So, you're totally blind?" I asked casually. "No peripheral vision?"

"Right. To me, everything's black." He swirled the red wine in his glass and sipped.

"I can't believe it's only been three years," Marguerite said. "I lost mine over the course of twenty-five years, a little bit at a time.

Every time I lost more vision, I felt crazy, depressed, and pissed off."

"It doesn't do any good to make a big deal out of it." He put on a satisfied smile.

"And all that work with the computer must take special skill." Marguerite shook her head. "It's hard for me just to do a little word processing."

"It's easy. I could teach you."

Marguerite and I shared a tomato salad, tagliatelle with garlic and tomato, fettuccine Bolognese, and delicate sole sautéed in lemon. Fabulous! But throughout the meal I wondered about this man who shared our table. What was going on? Did Marguerite have a clue?

Dessert arrived with three cappuccinos. "I bring yours in a minute," the restaurant owner told me. Marguerite and I passed our chocolate cake back and forth, and I sipped her cappuccino.

"Elsa would never let me get away with that," Hans said.

"What?" Marguerite asked.

"He took some of your coffee."

That was when Marguerite got it. Her mouth opened, but she stopped short of speaking. We paid the bill, said good night, and strolled toward home. "Is he . . . ?" she asked.

"No way."

"But he said . . ."

"Not like any blind person I ever saw."

"He could be more skilled than I am. It's possible, don't you think?"

"So, you're a failure as a blind person because you can't run ahead of me into a restaurant? You didn't see the way he bounced onto the porch of that place. And how about when he knew that table had seating for only two?"

"He's more sensitive than I am," she said.

"He's more sensitive than Mother Teresa."

"But it made sense. He could tell that place was too touristy."

"Right."

She pondered. "He *might* be a ringer, but here's an interesting question: Does *he* believe he's completely blind? If he does, and he's not blind, we could be talking psychiatrically disturbed."

"What do you think, counselor. Is he dangerous?"

"I recommend serious testing."

"And what about Elsa? Does she believe? If she does, she probably thinks I spoil you.

"She would have a point, but I love it."

Hot Water—Yes, I Can Fix

The next morning, our third in Riomaggiore, it was time to come to grips with the water-heater problem. I found the signore in Edi's rental office. "We would like to stay a fourth night in the apartment."

"Ah, good, *signore.* You make me happy."

"But you must fix our water heater. It hasn't worked for three days."

"Must be pilot."

"I relit the pilot twenty times. The signora tried it, too. It probably needs a new thermocouple. . . ." I caught his blank look and elaborated. "You can put in a new part to make it work."

"Oh, I am so sorry that you live with this." His voice oozed compassion. Expressive black brows formed a thick line of concern. "It is all right now. I come and fix right away."

A few minutes later he arrived, toolbox in hand. We greeted him in the entry hall. "Ah, *signora,*" he said to Marguerite. "How are you this beautiful today?"

Marguerite chatted with him about the beautiful today, while I tracked down Effie and carried her back in my arms. "This is Felicia. She wanted to meet you."

"Ah, the little *gatta. Molta bella.*" He stroked Felicia's head, and she purred on cue.

Glancing at the toolbox and the landlord's confident smile, I felt better. The shower would be hot and comforting in no time.

We climbed the stairs to the kitchen, and he approached the water heater, set down the box, and extracted a small paint brush. "This the secret."

He opened the cover, brushed the gas jet several times with a flourish, closed the unit, and lit the pilot. "You see. Now is fine." The brush went back neatly into his toolbox, the box in his hand, a smile on his lips.

"But . . . let me try this." I opened the tap in the kitchen sink. The flame burst to full bloom inside the heater. Signore smiled. I opened the faucet wide, and water gushed. We focused on the heater. The flame continued. Signore nodded confidently. The flame fizzled, popped, and vanished, as did our landlord's smile.

"See what happens?" I said.

"It died again, right?" Marguerite asked.

"This all right. I light again."

"That won't help when I'm in the shower."

"I tell you the problem. The heater no good. I glad to light it anytime you want."

"You must have another heater you can put in." Marguerite stared at him, incredulous.

"No, no. Only this. We get new soon. This been no good long time." He hurriedly relit the pilot, smiled as if all was well, and escaped down the stairs.

I slung a pot of water onto the stove for another bath.

October 13

Tomorrow we leave for France. We hope to find a place in Vence or Saint-Paul de Vence, towns near Nice in the hills above the French Riviera. Claire spoke in glowing terms about these villages, about the artists who settled there, the flowers in the hills, and the romance of everyday life in the little hilltop hamlets.

And we are lucky. Signore may not know his water heaters, but he has arranged with the authorities for us to bring our car down the hill. That way, I won't have to endure a heart attack carrying our luggage and our kitty up to the parking area.

Perched in the Hills of Provence

The Côte d'Azur for Connoisseurs

I strolled onto our balcony and gazed over the ancient, walled town of Vence to the gleaming Mediterranean. The sea spanned the horizon. To the left, it blazed brilliant white beyond the city of Nice, where the sun had begun its ascent. On my right, the Cap d'Antibes protruded into the same sea, but on that side, pale sapphire glistened. How could we have found another perfect place so soon after leaving Poros?

October 16

We have moved to heaven on a hill in Vence, a few miles back from the French Riviera. Picture the mountains behind Santa Barbara, with their deeply carved foothills running down to the sea, but instead of one Mediterranean-style city, there are several exclusive cities along the coast and age-old hilltop hamlets dotted here and there among the wooded hills. The French call them villages perchés, *these towns perched perilously above ravines.*

Our third-floor apartment has two bedrooms, so our friend Bette will be lodged in style when she arrives. Her room is French Provincial, with inlaid wood roses on the headboard, dresser, and vanity table; gilt-framed pictures of lords and ladies in the Louis XIV style; and wallpaper with pink, embossed flowers. Our room is in a more masculine style and has a balcony that offers a view up the hills, past silver-green olive trees and a chateau, to sheer, rocky cliffs above.

The apartment is well stocked with cabinet space and includes a dining room, three antique clocks, and a kitchen with washing machine, dishwasher, and television, no less. There's another TV in the living room, but neither one is bilingual. The living room has a view of the town and the sea, and sliding glass doors on two sides for easy stepping out onto the balcony. Not including electricity and a final cleaning charge, all of this will cost us only about $40 a night—the advantage of off-season travel.

At the local tourist office, they provide us with an invaluable map called Côte d'Azur for Connaisseurs *(French spelling), which shows all the attractions for miles around, with pictographs denoting the special features of each town.*

Morning hunger gnawed at me. I saved my diary entry in the computer and went to our bedroom at the back of the apartment. I opened the drapes, and light illuminated Marguerite cozily curled up in the bed, and above her, the cheery pink roses of the chandelier. There could be no doubt—Marguerite would want to be awake on such a morning. I rattled dresser drawers, picked up my keys, and checked my still-dozing beauty. Felicia jumped on the bed and pushed her face against Marguerite's hand. What a helpful cat! Maybe it was mean to gang up on her, but we just wanted her company. She groaned, and I seized the opening. "If I run out for pastries, will you make coffee?"

Only her fingers moved, rubbing Effie's forehead. She mumbled something affirmative. I kissed her, grabbed my jacket, and ambled downhill to the bridge that led to the modern part of town (anything built since the 1500s). Below me, near the bottom of the gorge, a stream and yellow-leafed trees shimmered in the canyon.

At the far side of the bridge, I passed two bars and a fish market that weren't open yet. My favorite patisserie, the one with the most-buttery croissants, the most-custardy raisin wheels, and the most cholesterol per gram, was also closed for the second time in three days. The windows were covered with paper. What kind of schedule did they follow?

I continued another block to my second choice. Inside, the aroma of chocolate, almonds, and fresh-baked bread pried at my will power. I forced myself to order only three items: a croissant, a raisin pastry, and a pear tart. The woman counted out my change in musical, happy French; wrapped the items in a waxed-paper bag; and twisted the corners the way they do in patisseries. She wished me, *"Merci, au revoir, bonne journée* (Thank you, good-bye, have a nice day)," and turned to the next customer before I could muster so much as a *merci.*

Back at our apartment, Marguerite had resumed blissful sleep.

I crinkled the bag and held it beside her nose. She sniffed. A smile spread across her face, and she snatched the bag as fast as any trap-door spider. The day was coming to life.

Five minutes later I had the coffee perking and the pastries cut into quarters. I carried the coffee and goodies to the balcony table, with Felicia right behind. Marguerite followed us, with cups and paper towels.

We settled. Effie explored. Marguerite took a bite of pear tart. "Mmmm . . . How can they make so many delicious things when the bakery at home can't even make a decent bran muffin?"

"If I knew that, we could be rich. So, what'll we do today?" I unfolded the map. "On this special chart for the *connaisseurs*, I see icons for craftspeople, for baroque architecture. . . . Would you like to visit a belle époque city? An art museum? Perhaps you want to play golf? Ski? No, it's too early for snow in the mountains. But my map shows you where to find all these."

She laughed. "Let's just explore a 'village of character' and have a nice lunch."

"We can go to Grasse to check out a perfume factory and come back through Tourrettes sur Loup, where they make local crafts, according to this little pitcher icon on the map."

"Didn't we read about a good restaurant in Tourrettes?"

"We're still licking crumbs off our fingers, and you're already hungry?"

"I will be after we shop for a few hours."

"Okay, Tourrettes is first." We read our guidebook for a while, and then we kissed our kitty good-bye and went to free Jean de Florette from the basement garage.

After a ten-minute drive, I parked a quarter mile from the heart of Tourrettes sur Loup so we could get out and explore. We followed a stream that ran under the main road then dropped off into the valley below. "We're coming to an old water mill with rusted works." I stopped and took in the view. "The town stands out on a rocky finger above the gorge. Nothing modern is in sight, just granite ramparts, light brown buildings with chestnut shutters and tiled roofs, and a stone church with a tower and wrought-metal belfry. It's a timeless picture."

A walkway took us through an arch under one of the city's white stone defense towers. A footway wound past gray and beige, three-story houses, all made of rock, with workshops on the ground floor. I stopped to peer down the dead-end alleys, where rock stairways spiraled up and past planters full of geraniums to polished wood doors. We wandered through a shop's doorway and into a rudimentary room.

"Something's burning," said Marguerite, wrinkling her nose.

"That's the pottery kiln. There are two guys in denim aprons. One is sculpting; the other is painting clay." I handed her a ceramic tablet.

She traced the figure that was carved into it. "A cat," she said confidently.

"It's a plaque for outside a front door. There's space for them to inscribe your name and address."

"Our address is 'At Large in Europe.'"

"They could engrave that, but it might look funny hanging from Jean's bumper."

We strolled from shop to shop, watching the artisans and touching their products—carved wooden bowls; watercolor scenes of the village; dyed calico fabrics in 200-year-old, wood-block designs. We purchased decorated sacs of rosemary and thyme, and oak-and-glass herb grinders as gifts for friends back home. The white-haired woman who waited on us stayed close to the blazing stove in the corner as she protested about the chill of the old buildings. Her French was rhythmic, simple, and about seventy-five percent comprehensible. She longed for spring and the festival of violets they hold in the village. She complimented my French, all the while eyeing Marguerite and her white cane. "And Madame, how long is she . . ." She waved a hand toward her eyes.

"Since she was sixteen."

"Poor child." She took Marguerite's hand and placed a cloth pouch of lavender in it. *Bon courage, madame.*

I guided Marguerite out to the cobblestone street. "Do you know what she said?"

"It sounded like 'good courage.'"

"Right. I'd say it means 'take heart.'"

"When I was twenty-five, I might have thought she was pitying me. I might have been angry."

"And now?"

"I'm touched. She's acknowledging me. It's hard being blind. But I'm not hiding from my disability, I'm out here doing things. I can use the encouragement . . . not to mention the gift." She sniffed the sac and smiled.

October 18

In the shops today, we touched, sniffed, and described our way through items such as vivid linen goods; terra cotta Santon dolls, with expressive faces and distinctive clothing—a hunter, a shepherd, a priest, a gypsy dancer, and more; and scented soaps of passion fruit, lavender, and tea rose, . . . but we held off from buying.

Bette arrives in two days. She and Marguerite are shopping partners, and we must leave things unbought, so they can share in the delight. As much as Marguerite looks forward to Bette's usual visits back home or their overnight adventures at the South Coast Shopping Plaza, she's ten times more excited about this rendezvous in France.

For my part, I am loving France and the simple rural life. I love speaking the language and taking care of our needs with little difficulty. Unlike those days in Brittany, when I craved company as much as Marguerite did, I feel complete and satisfied as a twosome (make that a threesome, with Felicia on my lap).

Bette is a terrific guest when she visits us in California, and I know she'll help with the chores that Marguerite can't do. Funny . . . although it is work sometimes providing for our little band, I'm not sure I want to share the company or the work just now. Must I confess to a bit of jealousy?

A Shipment of Happiness from Home

October 20

Marguerite seems to be losing her concentration. An example: she started to press her denim top with the embroidered cats but then set the iron down flat and burned a hole in the ironing board's plastic cover. A moment after I had scraped the melted plastic off the iron, another shout brought me running. The iron lay on the carpet with water spilling out.

At first I thought it was due to menopause, which affects her even when Prempro is doing its best. But now I've decided it's caused by back pain, which is a new development. My guess is that she was injured as I drove through the switchbacks on those back-mountain roads between the perched villages, the car tossing her from side to side. Not being able to see the curves ahead, she couldn't brace properly. I'm worried and told her she needs to rest for a few days, but Bette arrives today and Marguerite is intent on showing her a great time during her ten-day stay.

That evening, we met Bette at the Nice airport. She rolled through the gate in what I assumed was the latest Liz Claiborne black pantsuit, with a matching suitcase in hand and a broad smile dimpling her cheeks. Marguerite hugged her and sobbed, as I explained, "It's the 'pause."

"Hormones, hormones, hormones. Get a grip, girlfriend. I thought you were taking Prempro." But Bette, cheek to cheek with her playmate, shed a few tears of her own, too.

It felt good to see Marguerite so joyous, and it was great to see our friend, but did Marguerite's joy point out some flaw in our relationship? How lonely had she been traveling with just me?

Within minutes of getting home and entering her French Provincial nest, Bette burst into the living room carrying a bag of treasures. First there were the essentials—more hormone pills and cassette books from the Braille Institute that Marguerite's mom had sent. Then came the delectables—homemade cookies, one pound of

See's candies, and two pounds of Starbucks coffee. We talked until exhaustion overcame our guest.

In the morning, Felicia nuzzled me awake at eight o'clock. Bette was already brewing Starbucks in the kitchen. "It's about time, lazy bones." She handed me a steaming mug.

Felicia yelped a few times.

"What's her problem?" Bette asked.

I savored a sip of coffee and then pulled a can of cat food from the refrigerator. "Shhh. You'll wake Marguerite. Aren't you supposed to have jet lag or something?"

"I'm *supposed* to be high on adrenaline. I want to see Vence."

I fed Effie, finished my coffee, and took off with Bette. I conducted her along my favorite lanes where structures with cream or earthen hues nestled in well-manicured plots, some topped with distinctive little towers, others with odd chimney ornaments. We stopped to admire my favorite villa—an umber-colored, square, two-story building, high above the road, with a Greek-columned porch and a broad blue band decorated with white swans running beneath the roofline.

How strange it seemed after all this time to be walking with a sighted person. My reflexes told me to reach for her arm each time we came to a step. When she exclaimed, "Look at how those palms frame the view," it caught me off guard. It was really neat to have someone else spot those things, someone with whom to share the visual pleasures.

Hunger led us across the bridge to that great patisserie, which was open! I held the door wide, but Bette lingered outside, gazing at the window display—croissants, golden with butter; rolled-up *pain au chocolat* (croissant dough filled with chocolate and baked to brown perfection); glazed custard-and-apricot rolls; pastry cups, heaped with chocolate, pears, or strawberries.

"If we go in, we can buy some," I urged.

"That would spoil the window's symmetry. See how they're arranged just so on the doilies?"

Eventually, we entered and selected our morsels. On the way out, I gestured at the window. "Still looks good."

"But it lacks a certain *je ne sais quoi.*"

"Yeah. It's missing three croissants, two apricot pastries, and a chocolate cup. Want to give them back?"

❦

The three of us sat on the balcony in the morning sunshine, finishing the last of the baked goods. Bette kept her eyes on the view over the Mediterranean, but her mind was clearly focused on the splendor of the patisserie, which she described in detail to Marguerite.

Marguerite finished her croissant and wiped her lips. "I tell you, Bette. Pastries are one of the joys of France."

"All the more so since you send Ed out for them while you get your beauty sleep. You put up with a lot, Ed."

"I keep saying she's more trouble than any three people in the Mediterranean world, but no one listens."

"I'm listening," Bette consoled.

"I'm worth it," Marguerite chimed in, but Bette and I were on to other things.

"Should it be to a museum today?" wondered Bette. "Or to Nice or to Saint-Tropez or . . . ?" I nodded and raised a finger for each option.

"You two may be going somewhere, but I'm calling my mother to come take me home." You had to give Marguerite credit; her voice sounded just the right plaintive notes.

"None of your whining," Bette said. "We're going to a museum, and you're coming."

After having shared in the scenery with her, and now sharing in the teasing, Bette's visit was looking pretty good.

❦

That day we visited the Maeght Foundation, just beyond the town of Saint-Paul de Vence. Paintings, stained glass, and mobiles by Picasso, Miró, Léger, Chagall, and others lit the walls with color and imagination. Gardens outside were sprinkled with their playful, unconventional sculptures and mosaics.

As we strolled outside the gallery, Bette took pictures while I narrated. "Over here there's a sculpture like Casper the Friendly Ghost." We appreciated the piece, but then I spotted something else and changed course. "Wait, here's a ghostly creature, sort of a spirit-cow with horns, but. . . . Hmmm, now I don't know what it is. It has a third horn in front like a rhino, and buggy eyes; and its front legs are out to the side like arms." I put Marguerite's hands on one of its limbs.

She felt her way down its shoulders, up its neck and cheek to one of the bulbous eyes, and then across to the misplaced horn. "Pretty weird . . . kind of a combo-creature."

"You've got the idea," said Bette, snapping a picture. "We'll call this shot *Marguerite and Her Friend Combi.*"

"Over here," I called. "You're finally going to feel one of Picasso's goats."

"I remember. There was one at the Picasso Museum in Paris," she told Bette. "Eddie told me it was made of sticks and old rags, but there was a sign not to touch it."

"This one is bronze, and touching is definitely allowed." I put her hand on its forehead. "Start here and follow down."

"Be gentle," Bette said. "I think it's pregnant."

Marguerite began with the horns and moved to the bearded chin, across the back, around the belly, and down to the hooves. When she was finished, she wore a satisfied grin. "Feels like a real goat to me."

"Real and not real," I said. "With a few deformities and an attitude."

"You mean the extra-skinny neck and the huge belly?"

"Yeah . . . its face is really expressive, too. And its back is kind of flat. But you're right, it's more real than almost anything else we've seen here." I helped Marguerite straighten up and noticed her wince. Her back obviously still hurt, but she re-ignited her cheery look.

As we explored, I shot pictures of Bette—snooping among the abstract and the weird, leaning close like a meticulous sleuth. Meanwhile, Bette took photos of Marguerite and me, feeling our way over statuary, displaying delight at the unique and diverse collection. Aside from her assistance in brewing coffee, Bette became something else we had lacked, our photographer—a very handy guest indeed.

That afternoon, after a rest, we walked into Vence. We passed through the more modern part of town near the bridge, where we encountered patisseries, a stationery store, restaurants, a supermarket, a movie theatre, and a chapel with a multicolor tiled roof.

Rounding a bend in the road, we saw the walls of the old town come into view. "This is the best thing about Vence," I said. "It's so real. The modern-day life of a French town is here around us—with everything that the 15,000 people living here and the folks in the little towns nearby need—but up ahead, we enter the middle ages."

We walked under a stone arch and came to a carved granite fountain pouring water from four spigots spaced evenly around. "Here's a sign." I read from the top, translating as I went, "This is the square of Peyra. The gate dates back to 1810, but the original was built during the middle ages. . . ."

Bette politely cut in. "The first fountain was constructed in 1578." I took my eyes off the sign and let her do the work. "It was one of only two sources of water for the city until 1886. . . ."

I was amazed. Bette understood way more than I had thought. Her French accent was not, in my view, *très élégant*, but her interpreting skills seemed *magnifique*.

With her narration complete, Bette exclaimed, "I can see what

I'm going to like about Vence." She pointed at the shops lining the square, with green awnings shading their wares. "Did Ed tell you about the gorgeous fabrics?"

"He put me off," Marguerite answered. "Made me wait until you came."

"Of course," I said, "you two don't have to *buy* anything. . . ." But it was too late. Bette swiped Marguerite's hand from me and placed it on her elbow.

"Come on," said Bette. "Look at the vases! They match the bright colors of the tablecloths."

I tracked their progress—Bette in her denim jacket and skirt, Marguerite in her red jogging suit—through Provençal spices and soaps, fabrics, and perfumes. Sometimes I wandered off on my own. Other times I spied from close at hand.

They followed alleys between cobblestone squares, where shops showered bright fabrics out into the air. Bette took on the duty of describing, and I got to relax a little. There was no need to strain my color vocabulary to pick the right descriptions. Bette selected *sunflower yellow* and *royal blue* for picturing the predominant colors, and she chose the items to describe and for Marguerite to touch.

But, aside from the relief, that touch of jealousy stayed close to me. When Marguerite expressed interest in a sequined blouse and Bette called her a "hooker honey," the two of them dissolved into giggles. Misgivings lurked in the corners of my smiling eyes. Did Marguerite and I act as carefree as the two of them?

The two shopping pros added more color to the scene. From their wallets they extracted credit cards of silver and blue and others with red-and-gold circles to brighten the day for obliging shopkeepers.

The afternoon progressed, and grocers set out their wares to attract predinner shoppers. With the promise of food, I lured my companions down the narrowest of alleys to my favorite place in Vence, the *Impasse du Grand Four* (Dead End of the Large Oven). Between opposing rows of stone buildings, we first stopped at a flower shop to sniff; moved on to the produce stands, selecting tomatoes and pears by touch and scent; and crossed the alley to a *traiteur* to contemplate the delicacies from squid salad to *aubergine farcie* (stuffed eggplant). With purchases in hand, we came to a seafood market.

"Looks like really fresh fish," Bette said. "Their eyes are bright."

"Don't make friends," responded Marguerite. "We have all the pets we need."

I guided Marguerite's hand toward an ice-lined carton. "Want to touch an octopus?"

She yanked it back. But after a minute, she said, "Don't you love this little street?"

Coming into a square, we came upon another sign, and I read, "Clemençeau Square was probably once a Roman forum. There are two stones with Latin inscriptions on either side of the cathedral entrance. . . ." Again, Bette took over the translation, while my eyes drifted up the narrow, buttermilk-colored face of the cathedral to the niche where a golden Madonna and Child looked down on the square.

Bette concluded, "The cathedral contains the remains of Saint Véran and Saint Lambert and a mosaic donated by Marc Chagall."

"Bette, you're doing great with the French."

"What French? I'm reading the bottom of the sign."

For the first time, I let my eyes pass all the way down. Sure enough, there was English. "I didn't notice it."

"Sure you didn't, honey," Marguerite said. "And all this time I thought you were so smart."

"He's a cad. He'll stop at nothing to take advantage of a blind person." Bette wore the smirk of one who had just trampled her rival into the dirt.

"But I . . . I really . . . *Oh, man.* They screwed up the whole atmosphere of our town by adding English."

"Give it up, Ed. I've exposed your trick."

Did you ever have one of those days when no one will believe you?

Despite the newly revealed English on its signs, Vence was full of character and history, a perfect abode. And despite my apprehension, Bette was a great addition to our days. Her presence liberated us. Marguerite could indulge her shopping urge without restraint and have "girl fun," which she had been missing since our time in Salzburg with Patricia, Shirley, and Claire. Knowing that she was well entertained freed me to spend more time roaming.

Another pair of eyes was also a dandy help while looking for poorly marked streets. But what amazed me most was the pleasure I received from sharing the views—gazing from the ruined castle above the village of Gillette into the canyon of the Esteron River or taking in the coastline of the Riviera with the toes of the Alps plunging into the Mediterranean from the fortress walls of Antibes—not necessarily talking about the sights but just enjoying them together.

I confess, though, that I reverted to jealousy once in a while, and after we said good-bye at the Nice Airport, it hurt just a little to see how Marguerite missed her friend.

The Big Question Is When?

After leaving the airport, we headed for the office of Nouvelles Frontières in Nice, the travel agency that would arrange our flight home on some yet-to-be-determined date. But first, we entered a bar a block from the travel agency, where we settled on stools at the counter. (No point in spending double for sitting at a table.) I ordered two *cafés crèmes*.

"I wish Bette could have stayed longer," said Marguerite.

"It will be nice getting back to just the three of us."

"She reminds me of home; and now that she's gone, I miss it more. I miss Mom and John."

I watched the barman steam milk and pour it into the coffee. "You still want to go to Italy?"

"Sure, but . . ."

"And Spain? We planned to . . ."

"Don't worry. I want to stay through Christmas so Tricia can come see us again. But California is so nice in the winter. Aren't you longing for home at all?"

The coffee arrived, and I set her hand by the saucer. "Of course, I miss the ease of dealing in English. Even the French that I love can make life a pain, and I'd love to see our friends and home. How about this: we'll spend most of November in Italy, do Venice and Tuscany at a minimum, and head to southern Spain. Then Tricia comes for Christmas in Seville. After that, we spend a few days driving north, stop in Paris for a week, and fly back to California."

"We'd have a couple of months at home before we go back to work. . . . *Voilà*. I like it."

"You're also very fond of the word *voilà*."

October 28

In Nice, we stopped at Nouvelle Frontières to make our return reservation—Paris to L.A. on January 20. Then we called PSR in Paris and arranged an apartment for our last eight days in the city.

Lessons on the French Language, Customs, and an Ugly American

Random Entries

Ooo-la-la: *We walk uphill toward our apartment. A dog dashes from a driveway to chase a van on the road. A sixty-five-year-old woman with copper-dyed hair trots after him, her high-heeled feet pumping in hard, eensey-beensey steps. I approach, and she stops, hoping, I guess, for commiseration. "Ooo-la-la. Ooo-la-la," she cries. She rattles off the whole story in French. In the meantime, a neighbor has retrieved the dog, and she repeats everything for him, complete with the ooo-la-la expletives.*

I enter a bookstore to purchase an International Herald Tribune. *The woman at the counter asks where I come from. "California," I answer. "Ooo-la-la" is her response.*

We leave Felicia in our apartment and drive two-and-a-half hours north to the Alps and spend a night at a hotel in an isolated town. I mention to our hostess that we're staying in Vence for three weeks. "Vence, near the sea? Ooo-la-la."

So now whenever Marguerite misplaces her comb, she calls out, "Ooo-la-la." Whenever she can't find Felicia, she calls, "Ooo-la-la, Effie." If it works for a lost dog, why not?

❧

Toilette: *In America, we scrupulously avoid this word. We say we're going to the restroom, the lounge, or the bathroom (even if there's no tub in it). In France, you must ask for the toilette. They're quite bold, these French.*

❧

Protégé: *It's the French word for "protected," and they take it seriously over here.*

It was the end of the maximum six months allotted for our purchase-buyback program, so we drove to the Nice Airport to turn in Jean de Florette and pick up our next car, a leased Citroën. At the leasing counter, we found a young, pretty blonde, who smiled right into my eyes. I felt myself beaming back at her, not only because she was attractive, which she absolutely was, but because I was looking forward to the new vehicle that represented our continuing adventure. The car was ready! (though we *had* ordered it ten months before). Everything was going without a hitch, which made me unreasonably jovial. Best of all, the woman spoke English, so Marguerite could share the responsibility of remembering instructions.

The blonde placed a piece of paper on the counter and became serious. "If you have an accident, you must file this form by mail in five days. But if the car is stolen, you must mail it within two."

Still smiling, I was thinking that if the car were stolen, the thief would have the form with him.

Her coworker, a woman in her thirties, hung so close by that her chin practically touched the blonde's shoulder. At a pause, she cut in. "You understand that you must put in the paper within five days, but it is two if the car is stolen. This is very important."

I nodded. "She's doing an excellent job." I indicated the younger woman, who beamed her pretty smile my way.

"But she is new, and I must make it certain."

Clearly, she was intent upon protecting her protégé. If we messed up and didn't mail the forms in on time, she could tell her superiors, "It was not Jeannette's fault. I explained it to the stupid Americans myself."

The older woman cloaked an arm around her new employee's shoulder and murmured ardently by her ear as they led us to the parking lot. The arm seemed to shelter the younger woman like a mother bird's wing preparing her offspring to fly. The trainee got into our new green car with me and explained about the horn, headlights, gearshift, radio. . . . She climbed out, and Mother Bird replaced her to explain it all again.

This was the meaning of *protégé*—"protected, assisted, and taught." I doubted it would be possible to find as full an understanding of the word back in the States.

Customs: Why is it that bakeries are closed on seemingly random days each week, and on those days, the windows are covered with paper as if the buildings were vacant? Why is it that some supermarkets provide plastic bags and some do not?

Marguerite and I stopped at a strip mall to pick up a chicken at a place called Poulet à Go Go. We knew what to expect from previous visits: the best roast chickens in the world with an herb-infused broth. After the *poulet*, we visited the baker next door for a warm baguette and chocolate éclairs. Back in the car, I handed Marguerite the baguette.

"Where's the bag for this?" She looked and sounded indignant.

"This is France. There is no bag, only the little piece of paper around the center."

"When I get out of the car I could bang it on the garage wall, and *voilà*, dirt. This isn't sanitary." I pictured her using the baguette as a cane to feel her way along the street. "This is another American Improvement," she said. "If I lived here, I'd make a fortune. How much could it take to make a long, skinny, paper bag like this?" She measured off the baguette between her hands, length and width, and held them up for me to see.

"They may have this one covered. I'll show you when we get home."

Back in our kitchen, I unhooked the cloth bag stenciled with *Sac à Pain* from the wall, and handed it to her. "Before you empty our bank account to invest in long, skinny bags, check this out. With this, there's nothing left for the landfill."

"Why didn't we take this great invention with us?"

I had no answer.

Traiteurs: These little, gourmet delicatessens dispense lots of different salads and a few hot dishes—stuffed tomatoes or eggplants, a pasta dish or two, ratatouille, snails baked in pastry, for example. On Thursday, a sign appeared at one: Couscous Saturday. We placed an order and picked up our tasty meal two days later—a huge portion of couscous, chicken, vegetables, and lamb, complete with a casserole dish to use and return—for about $12. It's excellent, and more than that, it makes us feel like we're trusted members of the community.

❧

October 29

Why are there no standards? Why does the American State Department issue passports to anyone with $65 and a mug shot? Ugly Americans enter France without restriction. It reflects poorly on us all.

In front of the tourist office, we heard two couples speaking English. I set a course in their direction. Marguerite, like the second stage of a Saturn rocket, pushed me forward. I called out, "We're from California. How about you?"

They turned to us, broad smiles blazing. A heavy-set man in a plaid polo shirt reached to shake hands. "I'm Bert from Chicago. We've just been complaining at the tourist place. They recommended a restaurant. We went there, and no one spoke English. They didn't even have an English menu. Can you believe it?"

I was thinking these folks might not be the compatible souls we were seeking. "Lots of places are like that," I said. "Was the food good?"

"They sure had a nerve, and I let them know about it."

I was trying to find diplomatic words, when Marguerite put in, "That's what makes it an adventure. We're never sure what we're going to eat."

"I didn't come here for no adventure. I could end up with those snail things or goose gizzards. In Chicago we treat people better than this. In Chicago the waiters speak other languages. You can bet on it."

Right. I could buy that. We shifted the subject, and we shifted ourselves away ASAP.

October 29, continued

Vence transforms itself each time we walk to town. In the common, outside the walled center, a market usually blooms with assorted flowers, fruits, and vegetables, but sometimes groups of vendors come to town—antique sellers, a home show, displays of garden decorations. . . .

Inside the walls, we find an exhibition called "The Garden in the Town." Under the trees by our favorite restaurant, a bonsai garden flourishes. Beside the cathedral, a gazebo full of flowers and a temporary cactus garden have sprung to life from mounds of imported sand.

One day, a flea market occupied the main common. Browsing from table to table, we came to an artisan and his wife selling carved stone plaques. I took Marguerite's hand and traced her fingers over a tablet with a cat carved on its face. The artist's wife eyed Marguerite's white cane and took the cue. She retrieved another tablet and another. They were crests of cities in the area—Vence with a tower etched in stone, Tourrettes with a bear, Nice with a proud eagle. Marguerite touched each one as I described them. "You are *très gentille* (very kind)," she told the woman.

The carver—a stubby, middle-aged man wearing a dusty leather apron—pulled another plaque from beneath the counter and put his finger to his lips, so I wouldn't spoil his secret. "Tell me what this is," he asked in French.

Marguerite ran her fingers across it and said, "A horse."

"*Un cheval,*" I translated, and the artisan offered me a knowing smile. "You're close," I told her. "Feel around the head."

The fellow frowned, his look accusing me of giving away his game.

Her fingers were more careful this time. "A unicorn," she grinned.

The man asked quietly, "How did she become blind?"

"It was a disease called retinitis pigmentosa. It took her sight a little at a time."

He shook his head sadly. "*Dommage,*" he muttered.

We purchased a small cat carved on slate, and then we all shook hands. But the artist clung to Marguerite an extra moment and said with an emotion-choked voice, "*Bon courage!*"

So Marguerite had scored her second *"Bon courage!"* In America, people who didn't know her well never spoke of her blindness, but in Europe, it seemed common to just jump right in, one way or another. And the more she got used to it, the more she seemed to welcome the good wishes.

At Harmony with the Rhythms of Rural France

October 29

With Bette gone and our airline reservations made, our responsibilities are finis, complets, accomplis. *Now we'll stay away from the more frantic, glitzy coast, and spend our time in the little towns.*

During our last days in Provence, we settled into an easy rhythm that matched the local lifestyle. After my morning walk and breakfast on the balcony, I would read aloud from the novel we had bought at the secondhand English bookstore in nearby Antibes. After a while I would pull out the *Côte d'Azur for Connaisseurs*, and we'd choose a town of character or maybe just a dot on the map not listed for character, crafts, or any other feature.

In the countryside of Provence, life had its own tempo. Restaurants served lunch only at prescribed times. Stores closed during lunchtime, presumably so their clerks could eat a civilized meal. It would do no good to fight this schedule, nor did we want to. Was this rhythm part of some European genetic code, which American customs, happily, had not displaced? In Brittany, we had been off-balance (hormonally *and* mentally). Though we dined when other people did, though we had to abstain from shopping when stores were closed, the serenity had not taken us. Rural French life was the epitome of harmony. Now in the perched towns around Vence, it had caught up with us, and we with it.

The tiny, stone towns—the ones in the low mountains behind Vence, which had no special designation on the map—had charming names, such as Gréolières and Coursegoules. I drove into the towns cautiously and proceeded along ever narrower streets between slate buildings until my sideview mirrors were threatened. Then it was time to park.

Dining at a table in a rock-walled chamber beneath beamed ceilings or on a patio watching the passers-by, we selected offerings from the three-course, fixed-price lunches. These delicious meals, including an appetizer, main course, dessert, and sometimes a glass of wine, were set out at a relaxed pace, which allowed our palates and our souls to be satisfied for about $10 each.

After lunch we wandered the town, taking photos of clustered buildings framed beneath limbs of fluttering yellow leaves. Back in the car, I complained, "Why not call *these* towns 'towns of character'? Okay, they don't have fortifications, but they're perfect, simple communities from a past age."

"They don't have shops with pottery and tablecloths."

"What does that have to do with character?"

"Bette's only gone a couple of days, and already you forget what the tourists want."

"But Coursegoules is delightful."

"It has a chance of staying that way if they leave it off the maps."

We drove home by circuitous routes over ancient-looking bridges that spanned percolating streams, through forests with trails that ran from hilltop town to hilltop town.

To rest Marguerite's back, we came home early each afternoon. Effie knew instantly when we arrived by the percussion of the closing door. She stalked toward us, meowing a complaint. "Hello. Where have you been? Feed me a treat. Have you been home long? I'm deaf, you know, and I can't be sure if you're hiding somewhere in the apartment." Once Her Highness had dined, she settled onto one of our laps for the afternoon reading of our novel.

November 1

So what's to say about paradise? Life is sublime and peaceful. When we have visitors like Bette, we are wrapped up in that relationship. We exchange exuberant ideas but experience less intimacy with the local people and the area. Now we're back to real contact.

The draw of Provence was the ancient atmosphere, the people, the rhythm of life. Each restaurant was charming and tranquil, the service friendly. Each shopkeeper took time to chat. Much of the time I understood what people were saying and could translate for Marguerite. Oftentimes when we made a purchase, or sometimes when we didn't, there was a small gift for Marguerite—a tiny bottle of perfume; a greeting card designed by an artist we met; or profuse wishes for a good day, a delightful journey, and support for Marguerite's fortitude. A gentle mingling of our souls and theirs.

Late in the afternoon on our last day in Vence, I pulled out the *Côte d'Azur for Connaisseurs*. "Look here," I said. "Just beyond Carros, the village where we had lunch the other day, there's another town of character we never visited called Le Broc, and there must be ten more not far away from there."

"And we never did take that train that goes to the mountains," added Marguerite.

"We ate *pot-au-feu de la mer*, but what about *bouillabaisse?*"

"And I'm really longing for another chocolate cup filled with chocolate ganache, but there's no time."

"One good thing, there's still dinner tonight."

To See or Not to See

Marguerite and I sat by an upstairs window in the Pigeonnier restaurant on that special square in Vence. It was our final night in town and our third visit to the Pigeonnier. A couple of tables away, two well-dressed women in their late sixties sat at a table, with their cocker spaniel occupying a third chair. Old, splintered beams spanned the ceiling at more or less regular intervals. A fireplace with a built-in compartment above held a ceramic pigeon. Outside, lamps illuminated the square, with its huge fig tree in the center, and cast the fabric stores in ghostly shadows. The fountain spurted water in four directions as it had for centuries.

Marguerite was savoring her baked dish of mussels au gratin as I took the last bite of my goat-cheese salad. I refilled our glasses of local rosé wine. "How's your food?" I asked.

"Delicious. Want a bite?"

I took advantage of the offer, and her obvious pleasure with the meal sparked a mischievous thought in my mind. "Do you remember the book I read to you . . . the one where a character is talking with a blind guy and asking if he'd want his sight back for a few minutes if he had the chance?"

"The blind man turned it down because he didn't want to know what he'd been missing all those years."

"Right. Well, I have a proposition for you. If you could choose between having sight or taste buds, which would you take? Hold on. Move your hands."

Our server, Alain, strode over to take our appetizer plates. "And how was everything?" He spoke good English, and like our pizza host in Austria, he had won us over completely with his warmth.

"Wonderful," Marguerite said.

"I am glad, and I know you will be pleased with the next course, too." Alain hurried off toward the kitchen.

"I'll be back in a minute," I told her. Slipping the camera from my pocket, I approached the women with the dog. "May I take your photo?" I asked in French.

"But, *monsieur*, we are not anything special," said the redhead, half-giggling the words as she straightened her chestnut-colored scarf.

"Oh, yes, you are. And with your puppy, you make a perfect trio."

They consented. I completed my task and returned to the table. "So, have you decided?"

"You mean the taste buds? I'll answer after I've had a bit of salmon."

Her fish and my herb-crusted chicken arrived. I showed her where to find the salmon, vegetables, and potatoes on her plate, and she tasted each. "You ask a question most difficult, *monsieur*. You mean I wouldn't be able to taste this salmon?"

"Certainly not."

"And champagne?"

"Never again. But you'd have the joy of seeing me."

"I wouldn't know the difference between champagne and urine?"

"Well, the champagne would be cold, you'd still get a buzz, and you could probably feel the tiny bubbles dancing along your palate. I'm not sure, but I don't think urine has the same little bubbles."

She grimaced. "And when the chocolate mousse comes for dessert, I couldn't . . ."

"No taste buds, period."

She nibbled a forkful of string beans with tomato and onion. "I'll stay blind, thank you. I'm looking forward to my dessert. If I couldn't taste it, especially here in France, my trip would be ruined. And once I was miserable, I'd make sure to share the feeling."

Given that information, I was grateful the choice was hypothetical.

Cleaning Up Is Hard to Do

November 3

I have totaled the October expenses, and there's good news. We are precisely on budget at $100 per day. We dined like royalty, but we were saved from overspending by the $40-a-day rent and the $3 to $4 bottles of good French wine.

It was our last morning in the apartment, and things were not going well. When we had arrived, we had discussed the price of lodging with Madame, and she had offered us the choice of cleaning the apartment ourselves or paying for the maid at 80 francs ($13+)

per hour. We had opted for self-cleaning over possibly paying up to $60.

It took me an hour to drag our suitcases and assorted bags to our car and cram them into a now smaller trunk. We'd sent home what seemed like a lot of stuff, but half of it had been new acquisitions; and even though Bette had taken our largest suitcase home with her, nothing seemed to have changed—two bags would ride with Felicia in the back seat. I returned to find Marguerite on her hands and knees dusting under our bed. "Everything's in except Effie and her litter box," I said. "What should I do here?"

She straightened and grimaced. I helped her stand. "You can't do any more with your back. I'll finish."

"How long until Madame comes?"

"An hour."

"You'll never finish alone. If I can stand up for a while, I'll be all right. I'll do the kitchen counters while you take on the bathroom floor."

"We can still pay to have it cleaned."

She gritted her teeth and headed to the kitchen. I set her up with some cleaning fluid and a sponge and requested her solemn pledge that she would only scrub things above waist level. On the way to the bathroom, little specks on the living room floor drew me in to touch up Marguerite's work. Then I diverted to the bedroom to straighten a picture on the wall. In the bathroom, I cleaned the mirrors and mopped the floor. Out by the kitchen door, I found Marguerite kneeling, running her sponge along the base of the cabinets. "You're not supposed to bend."

"I can't quit now. You need me."

"I need you healthy. I need you to still be with me tomorrow in Italy and next month in Spain."

"Okay, okay. But I want to help."

"You could make more coffee."

She stopped suddenly and called out, *"Felicia. . . .* I hear her scratching in the litter."

I turned and looked. "Felicia, no! I just cleaned that floor." I yelled, but there was no point. Even if she hadn't been deaf, it was too late. Our kitty walked toward me, innocent as could be, but the bathroom floor was another story.

I carried Felicia and her litter down to the car and returned to the kitchen, hoping for a fresh cup of coffee. What I found was Marguerite sitting exhausted in a chair with a puddle of brown liquid spreading across the floor toward her foot. "Yikes! The coffee . . ."

"You wanted some, right?"

"Oh, man. There's a problem. Looks like the carafe is off-center. There's some on the floor . . . not very much." I opened the water reservoir on the coffee maker and found it empty. Where had it gone? I opened the drawer below. "Oh, yuck!"

"What is it?"

"Yuck. . . . I can't explain right now." I slid the garbage can over and pulled from the drawer a carton of plastic wrap, a pile of coffee filters, a box of spaghetti—all soaked. Marguerite tiptoed close. "Ruined," I told her. "Most of the coffee ran into this drawer." I plopped the soggy items into the trash.

"I'm sorry, Eddie. I was trying to help."

"It's not your fault." I wanted to slam something, but I could only hug her.

"We're beaten. We'll be lucky if we can clean up this mess before Madame Livadaris arrives."

"I'm going to try anyway," I said. "Can you clean the drawer?" I handed her a sponge and pulled the vacuum toward the bathroom.

After Athens and now this stay, I was thinking that maybe departures weren't our strong point. I heard a knock on the door, so I jammed the vacuum back in the closet, ran to the bathroom, wet some toilet paper, and dabbed the worst of the cat litter from the floor. I flushed it down the toilet and answered the door.

Madame greeted us cordially. She walked from room to room— slim and professional in her impeccably pressed brown pantsuit— eyeing every corner. She had been a most efficient manager, and she had rented us a spotless home. I should have told her right then we would pay for cleaning, but instead, I held Marguerite's hand and awaited the verdict.

She looked reluctant when she approached, then resolute. "I'm afraid I will have to charge you for some cleaning."

"It won't be very much, will it? We did most of it."

"It's the closets," she said. "They need a little more."

It took a moment to realize she meant water closets, the British term for the room where Felicia had just tracked litter across the floor. "You're right," I conceded. "The closets do need more."

"I think two hours."

I handed her 160 Francs ($27).

An hour later we were cruising in our green Citroën along the autoroute in the mountains above Monaco. Marguerite shifted in her seat and stretched her back.

"Doing okay?" I asked. "I wish you hadn't worked so hard at the cleaning."

"That's something that will be nice about going home in January—we won't have to worry so much about a budget."

"So you're missing the cleaning lady. . . ."

"Missing home."

I wanted to say something about how strong I felt these days, how Greece and Provence had been wonderful, how we could go on and on in Europe, how setbacks like the cleaning debacle hardly fazed me anymore. But Marguerite preempted me. "Won't it be great to get back in January, to see Mom, and to spend time reading by the fireplace?"

I pictured us on our swing in the back yard, Marguerite listening as I read from a novel. Felicia lay between us in her soft bed, lifting her head to sniff the fragrant air—rosemary from the herb garden and sage from the hills—then curling back into a sleepy ball. I saw myself setting the book aside to savor the scene, which was moving from winter into spring. Scents of orange blossoms filled the air. Roses dotted the slope with brushstrokes of color. The limbs of the plum tree drooped with their offerings. The hammock dangled from its branch on the sheltering oak, waiting, in case we wanted to stretch out for a nap.

"Yeah. That does sound good."

*Feeling Our Way into
the Italian Soul*

The Great Lake Maggiore Rescue of '97

We drove along the Mediterranean to the Italian border, turning north and then east—destination: Venice. By evening, exhausted, we skimmed the lake region in north central Italy. I accepted the first reasonable hotel, two blocks from Lake Maggiore, even though the bathroom was a few steps down the hall from our room.

We brought in our overnight bag, Effie, and her supplies. Marguerite settled on the lone chair in the room as I rolled up the shutters and watched the traffic on the street appear and disappear into an ever denser fog.

When I turned back to Marguerite, she looked contemplative, so I asked, "What's up?"

"I've been thinking about something since this morning when I made that mess with the coffee and then during the drive today. Remember our talk about taste buds and eyes? When you were driving on the highway with the map propped on the steering wheel trying to pick the right direction and keep from having an accident, I felt for you. And then you had to cruise around looking for a hotel, spot one, and go in to look it over. You have too many responsibilities."

I sat on the bed and stroked her arm, "That's just the way it is."

"You offered me an alternative the other night, and I turned it down, but I've changed my mind. If I could have my sight back, I *would* give up the flavor of chocolate and champagne and all of those tastes. If I could see, I could help you do everything."

Her acknowledgment of the pressures on me affirmed feelings I sometimes had. But the mischievous part of my mind carried me in another direction. "So what about sex? Not that it's in my best interest, but would you give up that feeling to be able to see?" After she answered that one, I would propose wiping out her hearing in trade for vision.

"I surrendered my taste buds for you. Isn't that enough?"

"Okay. I'll give you back taste buds *and* your vision, but you lose sexual pleasure. Would you go for it?"

"Before you deprive me of the ability to feel my bladder, I'm going to the bathroom."

She grabbed her cane, and I led her to the door. "It's that first one on the right. Be careful, there's a stairway just beyond."

I read the guidebook for several minutes and petted our kitty. No Marguerite, no sound. . . . Another minute . . . I opened the door to the hallway and called softly, "Are you there?"

"Eddie! Is that you? *Help me!*" Her muffled voice issued from the bathroom.

"Why didn't you call?"

"I did. Didn't you hear? *Get me out of here. I'm not kidding.*"

I grabbed the knob, twisted, and pushed—no luck. "The handle turns, but . . . Did you fasten a latch?"

"I think . . . maybe . . ."

"See if there's a knob or a lever above the door knob."

A bolt clunked, and Marguerite ripped the door open, eyes wide. She flung herself into my arms. "I got a little panicky," she moaned against my chest.

"It's okay."

"Okay for you. The toilet doesn't have a seat. I had to hover over it like a helicopter. Then I had to feel around the grungy walls for the roll of toilet paper and grope for the lock. Feeling for everything sucks! I know—when I complain about blindness, it makes you feel bad, but you had all day seeing the hills and the flowers. All I had was the stupid radio, and most of it was in Italian."

After she had calmed down, we labeled the adventure "the Great Lake Maggiore Rescue of '97." Perhaps after her tactile tour of the bathroom, I could have talked her out of her sense of touch, but I decided to give up that sort of bargaining for the moment.

Venice in the Murk

November 8

We are staying in Ruban, a tiny spot outside Padova (aka Padua), Italy. We have a really nice suite in an upscale hotel that cost us $70, which included a huge discount. All the hotels from Verona to Venice cost this much, even the crummy ones, so we took it. It comes with a balcony, covered in vines with leaves turned yellow, and a spare bedroom for Felicia—not that we want her to use it. Marguerite is loving the robes, plush towels, and plentiful hot water.

For the last two days, we have driven into Padova and taken the train to Venice. Coming back, we stop at a place called Lulu's for great Chinese take-out. We've been Chinese-deprived since Seefeld at the end of July, so Lulu's is a godsend.

Today was our second run to Venice, and it should have been routine. The weather was the same as the day before—misty with a dense overcast. I was familiar with the parking lot at the Padova station and with the train schedule. But in Italy, each day was unique.

At the parking lot, the machine that dispensed tickets was on the fritz. We sat in a line of cars for several minutes until the woman from the cashier's cubicle ran out to open the gate for us. That was the first sign.

The guy selling tickets at the station charged us 8,000 lira ($4.80) more than we had paid the day before. I asked why. The fellow understood some English, but his answer was unintelligible. I said, "Yesterday 10,000 lira, today 18,000 lira." He repeated his statement with an air of pained perseverance. I paid. On the schedule board was another change—fewer listings than the previous day. It was another weekday, so why was the schedule different? The trains to Munich and Lucerne were still running, but there was only one to Venice. How could they charge us more and then reduce the level of service?

We walked through the tunnel beneath the tracks and up to the designated platform. Time passed, and the crowd grew. Numbers on the board spun. The arrival time metamorphosed. "We *still* have a half hour to wait."

An announcement blasted over the speaker. People rushed from our platform, clambered down the stairs, and emerged on the other side of the tracks. "Maybe we better go over there," I said.

"What does it say on that board?"

I couldn't see it from our side and didn't want to drag Marguerite over for no purpose, so I hustled downstairs, under the tracks, and up to the platform. A train was rumbling into the station. I looked for a sympathetic face. "Venice?" I asked. *"Venezia?"* You would have thought I was selling insurance the way people passed me by. Finally, a woman with a brown scarf over her head made eye contact. "The train will go near to Venice, but you will have to get off and find second train."

"Will there be a second train?"

"God only knows."

I expected her to cross herself, but she didn't. I ran back and retrieved Marguerite, but by the time we arrived on the other side, the train had begun rolling. I considered jumping on and pulling her aboard, but better judgment prevailed. We waited another hour and a half before a train to Venice came through.

As we neared Venice, I waited for the view that had offered a magical impression the day before. A canal appeared to the left, and then the lagoon opened on the right. Little posts and dilapidated docks projected from the water here and there to no apparent purpose. The whole scene washed past our windows, misted in fog, like some eerily cast reflection from centuries past. We were lost in an endless waterscape, completely isolated from time and the city so near. Though it was our second passage, it still moved me.

"It's creepy out there," I said. "Reminds me of those books we read about Venice."

"You mean the Anne Rice novel about castrated opera singers? I've been thinking of that, too."

"Right. Foggy nights in Venice . . . perfect times to meet your rival in some dark alley and thrust a stiletto into his chest. There was that other book, too, about the Venice ghetto. A family of Jewish diamond merchants persecuted over the generations—first in the Spanish Inquisition, later in the ghetto of Venice, and finally in Germany as World War II approached." Outside the window, the city drew near. Then the walls of the train station slid beside us and cut off the view.

"What a sad book," said Marguerite. "I can't remember its name, but it left an impression on me, too. It showed such a contrast between the nobles in their palaces and the squalid ghetto."

We descended from the train into the tumult of the Venice station. At the entrance to the building, I approached a man at the information booth. "When will we find a train back to Padova this evening?"

The fellow considered me casually from under his blue visor. "The trains, you know, they are on strike."

"No one told us. So there are no trains?"

He shook his head as if addressing a slow child. "Only the local trains will not run, *signore*. National trains, they go okay. One for Bologna, stops at Padova, it leave at six and a half tonight—track 12. After ten in night, strike is over."

We left the station and plunged for the second time into the maze that is Venice—a maze of charming, crumbling alleyways with little stone bridges over picturesque yet murky canals. "Hurry up," Marguerite would say. "It smells here."

"Imagine when things heat up in summer," I said.

Unlike the rest of Italy, there were no motor vehicles, no loud Vespas to rattle our brains, no crazy drivers darting out from all sides. What a relief!

Still, a more insidious menace presented itself: umbrellas. Drizzle and fog brought out the exotic feeling of the city, but as we tramped along and the buildings drew closer together, the narrowing alleys compressed the flow of umbrella-carrying maniacs. The stature of Italians assured that their rain shields glided by at a lower level than mine. The tips of the umbrellas' ribs flitted past our faces like dull-pointed darts. On this rainy day in Venice, I could not lower my guard. I walked defensively, dodging and parrying each thrust of the umbrella-weapons with artful maneuvers and jabs of my own lance, protecting not only myself but also my faithful companion.

To her credit, Marguerite followed the directions of my hand adeptly, paying attention to my grousing at the inconsiderate passers-by and their reckless conduct. "But listen to their speech," she said. "It echoes off the water of the canals and between the buildings. Italian is so romantic."

"That's the trouble. They're too busy talking to watch out. Their hands jig and jag with every word. Don't they realize those hands are holding spears?"

She climbed each bridge with me and descended without complaint, except for the occasional comment about another "stinky canal," but I could tell by her narrowed eyes and compressed lips that her back troubled her. We both wanted to experience Venice, so there was nothing to do but stop and rest once in a while.

Truly, it was a thrill to be there, trekking those narrow byways and following the signs to San Marco. Along the way, we entered workshops whose walls and ceilings were covered in masks—eagles, cats, jesters, and kings—the air dense with turpentine and pigment, a worker in the back dabbing paint on the next creation. We climbed the Rialto Bridge lined with shops and saw windows full of bright crystal figures, glass bonbons, and gaudy masks. Counters were covered with gold jewelry. Beneath the bridge, motorboats and gondolas floated past seventeenth-century palaces and faded into the vapor that hung low over the Grand Canal.

I held Marguerite's hand and gazed at the waterway. "With all this glitter and fading elegance, it's hard to think of the dark side."

"You mean the ghetto?"

"And the countries the rulers plundered. Remember the Venetian forts in Turkey? They ran the crusades out of here, and the *Doges* (dukes) raked in the booty."

"It feels important to be here. It completes that piece of history."

Narrow alleys like tunnels led us to the edge of the grand piazza. "Now this is cool. Ahead of us is a huge, old pile of stone with pointed arches, domes, and statues of critters. It must be Saint Mark's, but it looks almost drab today, except for the gray slate domes up top that glisten in the rain."

"What kinds of critters?"

"Lions, gargoyles, and lots of teeny saints standing on steeples."

"Calling saints *critters* could get you in trouble."

"Anyway, it's one hell of a church." As we turned the corner, I sped up to take in the front of the edifice. "There's nothing drab about these arches, even in the rain—they're filled with golden, mosaic scenes. That has to be the picture of Saint Mark's body arriving in Venice. The corpse looks pretty good, considering it was hauled from Egypt in a pork barrel; and the outfits are so vivid, especially the dead saint in his rich blue robe. We have to make a wide circle around these puddles and funky wooden ramps that lead to the church."

"What for?"

"The place is sinking, remember? The lagoon is reclaiming its share of the square."

We walked around the huge piazza, its multistory arcades lined with posh shops, restaurants, and coffeehouses. Music from a brass band drifted from the far side. Pigeons flocked to tourists who braved the drizzle to hand out seeds in the square.

"There's the brick campanile, soaring into the fog, and the columns, too—one topped with a winged lion, the other with a dude in a robe."

"The *dude* is Saint Theodore."

"I know. I'm the one who read you the guidebook. Over here the square opens to the lagoon, all foggy and mysterious." I lowered my voice and spoke from the side of my mouth. "Tonight there will be a heinous crime, a murder, along one of the canals. The body will drift to the lagoon with the morning tide, a banquet for the fishes."

"You're not only blasphemous, you're creepy."

"I can see some gondolas waiting at the quay—black with prows that curve into the air—but the gondoliers must be hiding from the weather."

"With the water lapping at the dock, it *sounds* like Venice."

We continued around the square and entered the Doges' Palace through its flamboyant, Gothic entrance. As we strolled through, I gazed up at the ceilings and along the walls of ambassadorial waiting rooms and council chambers. "There's some really good stuff here," I told Marguerite. "Scenes of battles, weddings, coronations, heaven, and hell, but they don't identify the pieces. Some were painted by Tintoretto and Veronese, but which ones?"

Marguerite waited on a bench while I explored. I returned to find her chatting happily with a middle-aged couple. The man was wearing a white golf hat with *Paris* lettered in red and the Eiffel Tower stitched in blue. "Oh, hi, Eddie. Meet Doris and Jeff from Des Moines. I heard them speaking English, and I reeled them in," she explained, looking impish as she wound a make-believe fishing reel.

"She's getting *awfully* bold lately," I said.

Jeff shook my hand. "Your wife is charming. She's telling us about your adventure."

"It sounds wonderful," said Doris. "I'd love to have so much time here. We're giving ourselves five hours in Venice, and then we drive to Bologna for the night. Tomorrow we do Florence. Right, Jeffrey?"

He nodded.

"You're certainly brave to take your cat along," she added.

"Not brave," I said. "Felicia's perfect."

We talked for a few minutes more about cats and paintings and things we missed from the U.S., but our new acquaintances had to move on, which they did.

"So what else have you been up to," I asked Marguerite, "besides grabbing passing tourists and pumping them for Americana?"

"I liked Jeff and Doris. Aren't you glad I captured them?"

"Well, yes . . . but I'm still taking you to the dungeon."

◈

We walked from cell to cell between huge blocks of glacial stone. "Want me to tell you about this place?"

"No. It's musty here, and it gives me the creeps."

"Just think—upstairs the duke was being pampered by servants and fawned over by kings, while his ships in the lagoon off-loaded spoils from their crusades. And down here, his enemies were imprisoned."

"They probably froze to death. But don't forget the other prisoners—in the ghetto."

We stood for a few moments, imagining, until Marguerite's shivers reminded me to keep moving.

We left the palace and crossed a series of ramps into Saint Mark's. I paused to take it in. "The floor is extraordinary. It rolls in gentle waves, and it's covered in geometric tile designs. Here, pretend you're skating." We skimmed over a low hump and down into a trough.

"Wow. I like that."

"Enjoy *this* visit, because this baby's descending into oblivion." Noticing her edgy look, I added, "Of course, it's held up for nine centuries since the last time it burned down."

Marguerite sat to rest while I perused the treasury. Once I'd seen my fill, I plunked down beside her on the bench. "All those domes and spires outside; the gold-encrusted mosaics, the Byzantine incense burners, and do-dads in here . . . the treasury is full of chalices, gem-encrusted swords, skulls, and silver tubes holding the bones of martyrs. All that plunder from the crusades—it's too much stuff." I'd been making light of it, but something about Venice and this basilica was really disturbing me.

"So you went in there to see skulls? Isn't that a little weird?"

"What about the priests who collected these things? They were the spooky ones."

She gave me a look that said, And you're not?

"I look at these things, and I see beauty, but I *think* plunder. The Doges gave the commands to steal and kill, but they expected to go to heaven because they hoarded gold in God's name and worshipped the bones of saints. The sanctimonious bishops conspired with them and created kingdoms built on the fear of God, death, and superstitious hoodoo rather than on the love they preach today. I have to admit that this beguiling church fascinates me, even though it was built on the bones and blood of its victims. In the ghetto, we'll see more of this piety."

Back outside in the fog, we caught a water taxi headed along the Grand Canal to the north side of the city and the ghetto. The boat was crowded, and we stayed inside near the entrance, ready to hop off when and if I spotted our destination. Marguerite seemed to delight in the crush of humanity and the buzz of conversations. I kept one hand on my wallet while fighting to keep the two of us together, as throngs poured on and off at each stop. A tableau of palaces and boats bobbed by outside, but I saw little through the clouded windows. We extricated ourselves near the railway station and found a small bar with a fine minestrone and great, fresh bread.

As we ate, I said, "It would be good to see the ghetto, but you need a rest. Let's go back to the hotel."

"There's no train until 6:30 PM."

"We can rest in a bar or a hotel lobby."

"The way you feel about the bones, that's how the ghetto is for me. I'll rest tomorrow."

After lunch we plodded to the heart of the Jewish quarter. There we found not a thriving commercial endeavor but a plain square where tiny shops sold prayer shawls and menorahs, and storefront kitchens dispensed kosher meals. The buildings, four- and five-stories high, were decidedly plain, and the plaza was paved in asphalt rather than marble.

The dreariness of the place seemed to enter our moods. I thought of books I had read to Marguerite—like *Mila 18* about the Jews in the Warsaw ghetto as the Nazis closed their murderous noose around the trapped inhabitants. And that other book about the diamond merchants, whose title we couldn't recall—fiction based on fact about the extermination of human respect and human lives, about the gallantry of spirit among those who suffered.

At the Jewish Museum we joined a guided tour through three of the beautiful, sixteenth-century synagogues. Our guide, a young Jewish woman with long, black, wavy hair, discussed the history in matter-of-fact tones. "The island here where the ghetto formed was built around the old foundries of Venice. The word *ghetto* is now used in many lands, but it derives from the Italian for "foundry," *geto*. In these few city blocks, no buildings over four stories were allowed, but all Jews from the region were confined from 1516 until the nineteenth century. As the population grew, they rebuilt the interiors to make each level shorter."

I looked at the dark, wood ceiling of the synagogue we were in and imagined it squeezing down toward us.

"Of course, they could go out in the day to work in the city." Her brightness seemed to imply that permitting Jews outside made everything all right.

The diamond merchants from our book had left each morning to enter the opulent, glorious city to visit princes and to buy and sell gems and fine silver. By night, they returned here. The story of the Warsaw ghetto came to me again, and the words *all the better to exterminate you* rode through my brain.

She continued, "The gates were locked at night, and there were guards. The residents paid the guards' salaries. But Venice was more tolerant than most places. The population in the ghetto grew to 4,000 as Jews fled from the Spanish Inquisition."

"What happened to them during the Holocaust?" Marguerite asked.

Our guide seemed reluctant to respond. "It wasn't so bad for the Jews *here* in the war. Most of them dispersed to the country, where people sheltered them before the Nazis entered the city. Only about a quarter of the original inhabitants were taken to camps and killed."

Only a quarter—how could she even utter the words? How could her voice be level and dispassionate?

When we left the museum, Marguerite and I couldn't speak for several minutes.

November 8, continued

Why am I so affected by the centuries of atrocities against the Jews, and the bones and plunder of the crusades? When I read about them, hear a story, or even when it's told objectively as it was today, I feel sick—and guilty.

Searching for a Home, Searching for Health

November 9

I'm trying to keep the cat food as un-exotic as I can to protect Felicia's delicate tummy. In three local stores, I have found no Whiskas, which has become her standard on the trip. So I got a box of Friskies. At least the packaging is written in a familiar language. The last time I tried a different brand was back in Austria, and she puked. I'm crossing my fingers.

We are headed to Siena, Tuscany. Guidebooks say Siena is charming and not as frenetic as Florence. We're hoping for less expensive, too.

As we drove into Tuscany, the scenery became more artistic. Olive groves climbed hills to beige and brown farmsteads and hamlets, surrounded by bushy-topped pines. Rows of cypress sheltered contoured fields, shaded from umber to russet in the barrenness of fall. In spring, the plots would be swathed in new green, and the near-leafless orchards would be in blossom.

Along with the scenery, I watched Marguerite as she shifted uncomfortably in the passenger seat trying to find a good position. It was time to find medical help.

We stayed in a hotel near San Gimignano, a half hour from Siena. In the morning, we got to visit the famous hilltop town with its thirteen towers that made it look like a miniature city of high-rise buildings. We entered town through a stone gate and tramped up the cobblestone walks. Stuffed wild boar stood as sentinels outside butcher shops. Ham legs and cheeses hung like war clubs from their ceilings. Restaurants presented menus, and shops showed off pottery and postcard racks—all in historic, three-story, stone buildings. We found the tourist office in the upper square and obtained a list of apartment rentals. Then I tried a question. "Is there a doctor in town who speaks English?"

"We can do that later." Marguerite sounded peeved.

The woman glanced back and forth between us and then pulled out a directory. "I think this only one *doctore* does English . . . in office beyond fountain." She wrote an address and waved a hand toward the downhill side of the square.

Leaving, Marguerite blurted, "You should have asked me. We need an apartment first."

Okay, I had sandbagged her, but I had good intentions. "*After* the doctor."

"You're wasting time. We need a place to live for Felicia."

"Effie will be fine. It's cool, and the car is in the shade. If *I* were hurting, you wouldn't let me put it off." So was it anxiety for our kitty that made her cranky, or was it menopausal angst or the pain in her back? I scanned the old cobblestone square, surrounded by three- and four-story stone buildings and a tower here and there, like square-ended spaghetti boxes turned on end. These had been the fortresses of rich families back in the Middle Ages, constructed to demonstrate power and protect fortunes, and all hewn from that same brownish rock that I thought of as Siena-tone. Past the fountain, we entered the doctor's building, finding inside not a receptionist but a hallway with chairs. Two men and a woman waited. *"Doctore?"* I asked. They nodded. "Does anyone speak English?" They shook their heads no.

We sat. *"Doctore aquí?"* I pointed at the floor, the international symbol for "here," hoping it would supplement the Spanish word *aquí.* I got back one nod, one shake, and a shrug—a toss-up.

The woman volunteered, *"Dieci."* She pointed at her watch. My watch read a few minutes before ten, so we could expect him soon.

Another man entered and sat. I wondered if we needed to reserve ahead. *"Appointamente?"* I asked. I received only blank looks. I scanned the office but didn't spot a place to write our names.

A prosperous-looking fellow in a brown leather jacket entered, hustled past us, and went through the door at the other end of the hall. The woman bolted from her chair and followed.

"We could wait here all day," Marguerite said. "Let's get a place to live, and try for a doctor later."

"You're not getting off so easy. When the door opens, I'm going to communicate with this sucker, even if I have to tackle him."

The door opened, and the woman zoomed out of the office. Then the doctor appeared. One of the men stood and headed toward him.

I stood, too, and all activity stopped. Everyone eyed me. Was the foreigner trying to go out of turn? No, I wasn't, but I needed information. *"Scusi,"* I said to the doctor. "Do you speak English?"

The man stammered something, clearly not in the Queen's language. I shrugged and thanked him. The other patient passed into his office. The door closed.

There was no use. If we stayed and tried to communicate with this fellow, we'd never know for sure what he said. Marguerite always questioned her physician closely. She wouldn't take medicine prescribed by a doctor who could not pass her test of credibility, and I couldn't disagree. Her health was not something to risk on less-than-complete information. Reluctantly, we retreated.

The Real Don Corleone

After a day of seeing rooms and apartments, all too grubby or too expensive, we returned at sunset to Siena to pursue an offer by the owner of one of the city's hotels—a small house in the country at $65 a night. The owner, Signore R., was a white-haired, ruddy-cheeked, refined gentleman in a navy cardigan, who bowed courteously to Marguerite and to me. In order to get to the house, the owner led us in his white compact car while we followed in our Citroën. We flew along winding roads, out of the city, through a tiny village, and down a two-way road not quite wide enough to accommodate two cars. He pulled down a gravel drive, past darkened buildings, and slid to a stop by a little stone cottage.

Black clouds against the graying sky highlighted the surrounding hills. The cottage sat alone among olive trees, above a vineyard that stretched downward toward the base of the hills—a romantic hideaway! Inside, we found two immaculate bedrooms and a modern, efficiently appointed kitchen/living area. Modern colors surrounded us, with cabinets and beams washed in sea-foam green. "It's very nice," I offered, "and the countryside is beautiful." It would also give us a home from which to pursue a physician for Marguerite.

"Yes." Pride shone in Signore R.'s smile. "My family is very old in this land. Our home was in the city near San Domenico church. My ancestors . . . contribute . . . much money, so our name is on the wall in the church. That is how you say, is it not, 'contribute'?"

"You speak very well," Marguerite assured.

"I have an associate in New York, and we discuss many things. I study his talking. If I say something not right, please correct me. It would be a favor to me. . . . What was I saying?"

"About your family."

"Yes, yes. Some generations ago, my family had many square kilometers of land, but then my great, great, great-grandfather, he fathered thirteen children . . . many boys, far too many. All lived to be men. In those days, it wasn't common to live so long." He sighed.

"The estate was broken up. The family no longer all lived by San Domenico. That part of Siena, it is the Goose Contrade. You know what I mean, *contrade*? Each part of town have an animal to represent? We are goose, and there's porcupine, turtle, wolf. . . ."

Marguerite nodded. "They're like neighborhoods, and they compete in that horse race."

"The Palio. We compete very hard with each other. Two times a year is this special pageant. Riders and squires, they wear medieval costumes and typical colors of their contrade, very bright and . . ." Signore R. continued talking about his loyalty to the goose clan and about the Palio. Finally, we agreed to rent the place for two weeks.

I followed our new landlord out of the house and strolled with him toward the driveway. "*Signore*, you have been very kind, and I wonder if you'd help me with one more thing. We need a doctor who speaks English."

His eyes narrowed. "Nothing serious, I hope. Don't answer. I have no place asking this. Go to the hotel tomorrow and, at the desk, ask Carlo to find a *doctore*. Now I will help you with your bags."

"Thanks, but I'll handle it. It's late. You should go home to your wife."

"I like your American expression—*handle it.*" He chuckled. In the privacy of the darkening night, he lowered his voice. "How long you are married, Mr. Webster?"

"Twenty-eight years, *signore.*"

"Ah. That is a long amount of time. I have been married since 1956. Too long, I'm afraid. My wife, she was only fifteen when we married. That is the way we did in those times, but now I think it was not always for the best."

What could I say? Get a divorce? Try harder? Hire a sex therapist?

Signore R. climbed into his car and peeled off into the night. I hauled Felicia into the cottage, locked her in the spare bedroom, and headed out for another load. The sound of a vehicle disturbed the silence. Signore R.'s little white car rushed toward me. He climbed out and approached. "There is something else I must tell you. Here, I help you with that." We each carried a bag into the house.

"I forgot, so my wife sends me," our landlord said. "If you want a *ristorante*, there's a very good one up the road and right at the stop sign. If you wish to cook, the little store in the village—you know, Costafabbri—it is only open until 19:00 at night. Seven o'clock."

We thanked him and ushered him out.

Five minutes later, he reappeared. "I must also tell you, last people who stay say dishwasher doesn't work. I don't know about these things, because I am a man."

I stepped back to give Marguerite room and waited.

"Excuse me?" She eyed him with a look that might have contained a touch of admiration for his audacity.

"In Italy, the older men don't clean dishes or do housework. My daughter and her husband they share these works, but in my day, no." Signore was watching Marguerite warily. "I'm not saying this is the right thing. . . ."

"I see. So what is this about the dishwasher?" she asked.

"It may not work, but I do not know how to test it. Perhaps you and maybe your husband know how. But if dishwasher it doesn't work, you tell the clerk at my hotel, and someone will fix."

❧

By the time Signore R. returned the fourth time, I had unloaded everything, Marguerite had hung some of our clothes in the closets, and we had gone to the market and brought back dinner supplies. En route to and from the store we discussed our landlord, the apartments he owned, his hotel, his associates in New York, and his quiet demeanor. We dubbed him Don Corleone, the Godfather, and we decided to christen our Citroën with the same name.

"The Don" arrived, looking apologetic. "My wife, she reminded me. We do not know if you are Catholic, but . . ." He watched as Marguerite nodded and I didn't. "The church up the hill, it has mass on Sunday morning at ten o'clock. And there's something else I thought to tell you about the history of Siena. In the city you will see many statues of the infants Romulus and Remus, suckling from a wolf. The statues like this are also in Rome because the men, who were twin brothers, you know, they founded that city."

I wondered what this had to do with anything and if this visit was really necessary, but I noticed Marguerite listening with rapt attention.

"Most people, they do not know that when Romulus killed Remus, the departed man's son fled to the hills and founded Siena; so we, too, have that lineage. Very important information about my city."

I found myself shifting from vague impatience to feeling touched that he wanted to share so much with us.

That was the Don's last visit of the evening, but a couple of nights later, he returned to tell us the schedule for fixing the dishwasher and cleaning the place. We introduced him to Felicia and emphasized the necessity for the maids to protect her.

A few nights after that, Signore R. checked in on us to make sure that the cleaning had been accomplished. He reported what a good girl Felicia had been. While the maids had cleaned, our kitty slept. We were proud of Effie, and our host seemed impressed and happy with us and our cat. Before leaving that night, seeming both astonished and pleased, he commented, "I think you two are fond of one other. That's very nice."

To Puncture or Not to Puncture

The morning after we settled in the cottage, we arranged through Don Corleone's hotel for a doctor's appointment at a Siena hospital.

As we passed through the hospital halls later in the day, Marguerite seemed impressed that it was a real medical center with antiseptic smells, patients' rooms, a gift shop, and an elevator.

In the appointed room, a white-coated, chestnut-haired doctor greeted us. "I yam Doctore X. Do you speak *italiano?* My Eenglish iz not . . . *buono."*

Oh, crap. The hotel had promised an English-speaking doctor. Before my eyes, Marguerite's confidence faded to wariness.

The fellow made another offer. "How about *français?* My *français,* it okay."

Experience told me it was important to maximize Marguerite's direct comprehension. If the doctor spoke French, and I explained, she would believe my translation only if she liked the diagnosis. If not, she'd accuse the doctor of malpractice or me of maltranslation, probably both.

We agreed to use as much English as possible and fill in the gaps with French. Soon we were in the middle of a pretty professional-type exam. Marguerite explained the pain in her left back. I threw in words like, *"Mal ici* (Pain here)."

"It's pretty deep in there," she said.

I looked for understanding in the doctor's eyes. Not finding it, I switched to French. "It is not near the skin . . . more distance inside." Then I asked her, "How deep are we talking? You sound worried."

"It's not a big deal. I just want to make sure he knows all about it."

The doctor probed, pressed until she winced, and verified he'd found the spot. He felt her stomach, asked about her digestion, and questioned if there had been pains in her arms. Next he took out a flashlight, examined her eyes, and inquired about her eye disease. Doctors tend to do that with Marguerite. This bit of curiosity is okay if they don't get hung up on the novelty of her retinas and forget the symptoms at hand.

I let it go on for about a minute before asking, "So, what do you think about her back?"

He took the cue and laid a palm against the offending area. "It is just . . . the muscles are. . . ." Clasping his two hands together and flexing, he gave the international symbol for knotted muscles.

"It's only my back then?" Marguerite sounded surprised.

"Yes. That is all."

"It seems like it's near my kidneys. It doesn't have anything to do with them?"

So that was why she'd put this off.

"I don't know everything about the back, because I am doctor of cardiology. But I study all internal . . . parts. Is not involving the kidneys, the heart, none of those, because I am able to touch the muscle that is problem. Now I find something to help." He thumbed through a thick volume on the desk.

I caught skepticism in Marguerite's eyes. "I hear him. He's looking through some sort of book, isn't he?"

"That way he'll find the best medicine. You should have talked with me about your fears. You tweaked your back while I was driving those crooked roads in Provence, that's all."

"I *was* a little scared." Relief was plain in her eyes. "I didn't want you to worry."

Il doctore looked up from his book. "Today we give you . . . I do not know word in English . . . puncture."

"Wait a minute." Marguerite stiffened.

"You mean an injection?" I asked.

"Like I say, I do not know the word. A . . . what is the word?"

"Needle?" I pretended to push a syringe into her arm.

"We're not doing a puncture," Marguerite said. "I don't trust needles in other countries."

"But, Marguerite, if it will help. We can make sure. . . ."

"We do five punctures," *il doctore* said. "Today one, tomorrow one, each day, puncture. Five times."

Each time he said that word, Marguerite sank lower into her chair. Was she preparing for the prick of the needle or getting ready to spring for the exit?

"So we come to the hospital five times?" I asked.

"No, *monsieur*. I give *you* medicine. *You* give her punctures."

"Wait a minute." Now *I* was seeking escape. "There has to be another way."

"Finally, you're on my side." Marguerite sent me a quick, fierce look.

In the end, the doctor prescribed two sets of pills. The first was for the pain in her back. The second would protect her stomach from the pills for her back.

We both felt very relieved indeed.

If Siena Won't Hold the Palio in November, We'll Have Our Own

November 12, dawn

Sunlight has just found an old bell tower and the brown stone castle named Belcaro at the top of the hill opposite us. Fog drifts around our valley. At the bottom of the valley, beyond the rows of grapevines—their thinning leaves turned yellow by the fall—five men and a woman harvest olives from silver-green trees. They spread burlap on the ground, climb ladders, pick the fruits by hand, and toss them down. Later, they gather the burlap, shake the olives into boxes, and load them into their pickup truck.

Marguerite spent the next day, her birthday, curled in a fetal position on the sea-foam green, living room couch, totally out of it from the drugs. Felicia tucked herself into the nook between her mother's torso and thighs, and barely moved. I explored the sparsely populated hills around our home, the little castle at the crest of one, the vineyards with their villas, and the village of Costafabbri—consisting of a bar, a produce store, a grocery on one side of the main road, and a large brick convent on the opposite knoll.

Marguerite awoke long enough to nibble some of the tortellini and salad I whipped up for dinner but dozed before I could serve the special (and expensive) birthday tiramisu I had bought at a bakery. I saved most of the dessert for my snoozing comrade and shared a few dabs of whipped cream with Felicia. For our kitty, it was the perfect day.

The next morning, with back pain abated, Marguerite recovered consciousness. "Are you still willing to take me out for my birthday?"

"That was yesterday. It's over," I told her, testing her spunkiness index. She ignored the comment and suggested we seek one of the restaurants our guidebook recommended in Siena. Naturally, I agreed.

I parked as close as possible to Siena, and we strolled into the medieval town. Along the cobblestone streets of the pedestrian-only center, autumn shadows chilled the centuries-old, urban canyons. Walking toward the main square, our pace picked up, and I saw no indication of pain on Marguerite's face.

I felt like a gladiator striding to the arena or a bull running to the ring, pacing downhill, surrounded by history, and flanked by our fellow pedestrians. A few of them stopped to gaze in shop windows at music CDs, stationery, and clothing. We continued with the mass, advancing, hemmed in by the four-story stone buildings. Veering left we followed a chute, much narrower than the main thoroughfare. A slot of sky appeared and then the campanile—majestic, lean, and lofty. It was constructed of red brick with a white crenellated balcony and a bell chamber. As we continued downward, the patch of sky broadened. The square fanned out ahead, immense and arenalike. Finally, we paused. Before us was the famous seashell-shaped square, the Campo ("field," in Italian), known for its spacious elegance and for the horse race called the Palio. The race is run once every July and once every August.

Brown stone walls shaded much of the Campo, but we chose a restaurant on the sunny, uphill side with a grand view of the Palazzo Publico (town hall) and campanile. "We'll splurge for your birthday. How about a 'classic Siena feast'? We each get to choose an appetizer, a main course, and a dessert."

She unbuttoned her coat, slipped it onto her chair, and leaned back, facing the sun. *This* feels great."

As we sipped Chianti and awaited the first course, I spotted a stand selling dazzling banners with turtles, wolves, snails . . . the symbols and colors for each contrade of the city. I formulated a yarn and shared it with Marguerite. "Think of this. It's July 2 and nearly sunset on the day of the Palio. Throngs of people pack the center of the square, and we are among them. The space in front of us will soon fill with racing horseflesh. Across the way, hundreds sit on bleachers set up by the buildings. Others hang from windows all around us. Can you hear them?"

She held her wineglass in two hands before her face, the ruby liquid dancing in the sunlight. "Yes," she said. "They're buzzing with anticipation—and you won't believe this—I understand every word!" A smile spread from her lips up to her eyes, a comfortable smile that showed how much the medicine and a day of sleep had accomplished.

I continued the tale. "We stand at the front of the crowd near the sharp turn where many horses lose their jockeys. Padded walls wait to cushion their fall. Horses will gallop by, three times in a minute and a half. For you, I have chosen this spot with many sounds to hear—pummeling hooves, screams of the men, thuds as they hit the wall, perhaps the bawling of a dying horse if we're lucky. . . . It'll be a great day."

"But even if our jockey flies off, our horse may finish first and win."

"Exactly. And the steed that represents our borough, the Goose Contrade, is a valiant beast. If only our rivals, the porcupines, hadn't raised 150,000 American dollars to hire that jockey from Sardinia. Yesterday afternoon we geese gathered in San Domenico. They led our horse into the church, and the priest blessed him by the Altar of Saint Catherine."

"The sacred altar that holds only the head of the saint. The rest of her is interred in Rome." Marguerite looked smug for knowing this trivia from the guidebook.

"Very good. Now listen as the voices rise to delirium. Old women wring their hands. Drums beat. Jockeys atop their mounts clatter down the ramp to the square. Each horse is padded to protect it from the grinding fury of the race and festooned in the colors of his contrade. The turtle's jockey is in blue and yellow, the wolf's in black and white. *Here comes our man*, wearing green and gold, waving the banner high, carrying our pride on his shoulders."

Marguerite raised a hand like a traffic cop. "Wait! There's a commotion in the crowd. The jockey for the porcupines is missing."

"Excellent! There were rumors of a kidnapping, and someone's pulled it off."

She gave her version of a wink (more like a narrowing of both eyes). "Now our day will be a success!"

It looked that way indeed.

Our appetizers arrived, and we abandoned the whimsy. For my first course (the one the waiter recommended as most typical), six meats faced me in a circle on the plate. There was a deep-red ham, which I had seen hanging in the markets (and which I didn't especially like) and five various salami-like things. I sampled each. "This is more meat than I usually eat in a week. Want a taste?"

Marguerite wrinkled her nose as she spooned Tuscan vegetable soup into her mouth.

"But it's important to experience the local fare."

The nose shook with the rest of her head. "I'm already trying the local soup, and it's very good."

I did my best to nibble away at the sausage. After a while, the waiter presented my white bean and ham casserole and Marguerite's chicken piccata. He poured more wine. The sun warmed our faces. We savored the delicious food, our good health, and the day's contentment. For dessert I again tried the local specialty, *panforte*, which turned out to be a wedge of dense fruitcake. Marguerite made out better with a chocolate sundae.

Back home among the olive trees and vines, Marguerite yawned, smiled, and said, "This has been the most delightful birthday. Don't you think a nice nap together would round it out?" My satisfied stomach and happy heart accepted, and the three of us curled up to snooze away the afternoon.

Frozen in the Middle Ages

On the succeeding days, we visited Siena often. Its twelfth-century Duomo (cathedral) was built and ornamented while Siena was among the mightiest of Italian cities, fighting regular wars with Florence for regional supremacy. Had it not been for a turn of bad luck, the cathedral would have become the largest in the world. We walked beside the walls of the huge addition, which never became fully enclosed and remained roofless. The grandiose plans were abandoned after the plague struck and decimated the population, ending the city's dominance and preventing Siena from fully entering the Renaissance. But how much more enchanting it seemed today, still frozen in the Middle Ages.

Inside the Duomo, we crossed over mats that protected the floors. "It's amazing in here," I said. "The pillars are immense, made of horizontal slabs of black and white, striped like a zebra."

"Is it too glitzy, like Saint Mark's in Venice?"

"Not at all. Here's a roped-off area on the floor. There's a white marble picture inlaid in black—brilliant and full of character. It's an old hag, a Sybil, with a stalk of leaves in her hand. Her features and the folds of her dress are etched in the marble. I've never seen a floor like this. You know, with the black-and-white pillars and the blue ceiling with gold stars . . . it's magical."

Around us, organ music resounded, the notes cascading among the pillars. We sat together in a pew as sopranos joined. "This is delightful," said Marguerite. "If you want to explore, just leave me here." She leaned back, looking serene, as male voices blended in.

I strolled from alcove to alcove, peering into dark corners and sampling the transforming melodies from different positions in the church. Coming to a timer with a slot and a note that said 1,000 lira (50 cents), I popped in my only coin. A floodlight filled the nearest chapel. Its painting of Madonna and Child suddenly became vivid, its radiance harmonizing with the music. But I had only a minute before the light switched off.

Roaming, peering into more dark places, and feeling the music, I came to the white marble pulpit carved by Nicola Pisano—a raised, octagonal platform on nine pillars. It was brighter here near the center of the church but not bright enough. Should I run out for more change? But I'd miss the music.

Other visitors arrived, and one inserted a coin. I shot pictures of the sad-faced, marble lion supporting one of the pulpit's pillars, and a carved panel on the side of the platform depicting a mournful, restless crowd surrounding the crucified Christ.

Darkness, another tourist with a coin, another burst of light . . . I studied the next carving—anxious, intricately carved heads with curly hair and pious faces awaiting God's judgment. Again, the pulpit was bathed in light for just a minute. To photograph or to savor? Oops, the light went out again.

Country Life

November 18

Today we visited Volterra, a stone city at the top of a cliff with vistas overlooking vast plains. Frigid winds cut across the bluff, but the warmth of a restaurant cured the chill in our bones. Later, the cathedral we entered rewarded me with flawless wooden statues. In one scene, four sculpted figures were taking Christ from the cross. They were highly polished, unique, and attractive, if crucifixions can be considered so. With such a profusion of marvelous art, all the churches we've visited have become a blur. And when I'm inside them, I'm confused. Am I seeing masterpieces or just plain great stuff? Does it matter? Is art more pleasing or meaningful if it has been recognized by an authority?

On the way home from our daily excursions, we stopped at the little grocery in Costafabbri for provisions. We had come to know the women who worked there. One even spoke a few words of English. The narrow room was packed with pastas, canned goods, cold cuts, meats, premade hot dishes that varied by night of the week, and the best herb-marinated olives ever, which were delicious with the fresh, local bread and cheese. How would we ever enjoy an olive or a slice of cheese in the U.S. again?

One evening, a large man stood behind the counter. He was round and balding and wore a black polo shirt under a white apron. "The owner is here," I said to Marguerite.

"How do you know?"

"His picture is on the liter-and-a-half bottles of red wine we've been drinking. He's big enough to need a four-liter jug, though." I plucked a wine bottle from a basket beneath the counter, got his attention, and pointed at his picture, then at him. *"Famoso!"* I roared.

He grinned as wide as his likeness on the label and nodded, *"Sí, sí."* A torrent of words boomed out in a deep, mellow voice. His swinging arms almost took down a cluster of sausages hanging from the ceiling.

"Tell him we like the wine," Marguerite suggested.

"Vino molto buono."

The big man lowered his head shyly, thanked us, and added something I took for, "It's only simple wine of the country."

Marguerite and I conferred and agreed on a menu. I pointed at the deli case and said, "Lasagna, *per favore."*

He opened the glass door from his side of the counter. *"Quanto?"* he asked. Now we were communicating.

I held my hands a few inches apart to indicate an amount. *"Para due persona."* I didn't know if *para* resembled the Italian word, but Spanish mixed with Italian seemed a good bet.

He hacked at the lasagna with a spatula, slipped a chunk into a plastic container, and tossed it on a scale. He spoke another question, which I reckoned as, "Is this all right?"

I nodded, pointed at some cheese in the case, and made a slicing motion. *"Un poco, per piacere."* (More blended Spanish-Italian lingo.) We did a similar dance for olives and bread.

The fellow rang up a sum for the groceries, accepted my payment, and then gestured to the little bar at the end of the counter. On other nights, I'd seen men standing there for a quick drink and some banter while their orders were being filled.

Our new friend lumbered down, rattling out indecipherable words of Italian hospitality. With one giant hand, he set two stubby glasses on the bar. With the other, he pulled a bottle from underneath—not the mammoth type with his likeness, but a shorter, rounder one I took for sherry or something similarly genteel. He poured the drinks and then sliced some bread, cheese, and dry sausage, offering them to us on a plate. We sipped the sweet liquid. "*Delicioso!*" I exclaimed.

Marguerite agreed. She forced herself to eat a piece of sausage wedged between some cheese and a round of bread. Our host ambled back to the counter to help another customer. "The rest is up to you," she whispered.

"I ate all that stuff at the restaurant the other day. There are five more pieces. I'll handle three."

"I'm sorry, but I just ate my last salami of the trip."

"One more piece won't kill you."

"He's *your* friend. Be polite."

I would have sneaked the rest into my pocket, but the greasy, vile stuff would have stained my clothes. I forced myself to finish it. We thanked our stout friend profusely and headed home, where we would feast on lasagna and cherish our cat.

After that, every time I saw the entrepreneur, I pointed to him and said, "*Famoso!*" and he grinned back like a big, shy bear.

The Agony and the Ecstasy of Florence

November 20

We'll fly home in just less than two months. How easy everything will be when we're speaking our native tongue. We muse about our morning walks to the nearby breakfast restaurant. Marguerite longs for iced, blended mochas, and I picture the three of us sitting in our backyard swing—Felicia curled between us, rose bushes blooming.

Switching now to more mundane matters, the variety of lavatories here is amazing. Yesterday at a restaurant inside the fortified walls of Monteriggioni, we found toilets shaped like giant porcelain moths. You step up onto the wings, squat, and do your thing. I had to give Marguerite detailed instructions before letting her loose in the women's room.

Marguerite is adding to her list of American Improvements. "Toilets with seats" is the latest, although I'm pretty sure it was on the list before. The biggest Italian Improvement far overshadows plumbing—it's the long, leisurely, delicious meals we eat every day in the medieval villages.

More of the mundane—I finally found Italian clumping litter, which made Felicia catstatic, but when she pees, it turns to mud. How do I scoop cat mud?

Now that Marguerite is feeling so well, we're planning a couple of day-trips to Florence by bus.

Since we had read *The Agony and the Ecstasy* the month before, our two visits to the Renaissance city of Florence became pilgrimages to Michelangelo.

First, we made a beeline to the Galleria dell'Accademia, where I ignored all the other statues and focused on Michelangelo's *David*. This was the artist's depiction of the city in her prime, accepting her role in the world, as David had accepted the sling and stone to vanquish Goliath. As we stepped closer, I felt the strength growing. A few more steps . . . pacing forward . . . statue dominating. At last we stood beneath the monument. "It's amazing. The marble is so white it seems blue. He seems so strong, but his power has somehow been made fragile and human by the veins in his arm and side. He's going to face the giant, and he's determined, but he knows he could lose everything."

"So, it was worth coming?" The glow in Marguerite's eyes told me she knew the answer, and she was happy to be sharing the experience with me.

"This is worth the trip to Florence from anywhere on Earth."

Gray skies and a cold November wind greeted our exit from the Accademia. We passed leather merchants' stalls and T-shirt stands on the street, and I spotted the imposing red dome of the Duomo between the buildings. As we approached, my view expanded to the cathedral, its tower, and the baptistery. It was incredible—more ornate than Siena's. Everything was pastel, including the campanile, as if it all were made of taffy blocks— strawberry, green mint, and vanilla. And there were taffy arcs— vanilla and strawberry—twisted like ribbons over the entrance and hundreds of statues. Even the pink ribbon had a face in the center, as though someone had squeezed the taffy while it was pliable to pull out a nose and chin, and poke in the eyes.

I told all of this to Marguerite. "Don't the pastels clash with the dome?" She clutched her khaki collar tight to ward off the cold.

"But the dome is wonderful. It dominates everything. How did Brunelleschi build such a thing way back in the 1400s?" I looked from the façade to the dome and back. "Maybe you're right. Lavender would have gone nicely, but it would be hell to clean."

I pulled out my map from the tourist office. "Okay, we've done all this visual stuff for me. Do you want to go to the cybercafe?" That idea really lit her up.

Three blocks from the Duomo, we found it—not remotely a café, just your basic office with four computers. The college-age attendant asked in fluent English, "Shall I print the e-mail for you?"

Marguerite almost levitated. "You can do that?" she asked. "Then we can read again and again what Bette and Robyn wrote!"

It was so simple. Why hadn't I considered it before? The fellow printed it, and we took the pages to a nearby bar. I ordered cappuccinos and carried them to a table.

"I can hardly wait. Who's first?" Marguerite was already sipping.

"Easy now, they're not printed with vanishing ink." I sat, tasted my own coffee, and began reading the messages. We commented on each and reminisced for a while, and I promised a second reading that evening.

"What a great day," she chirped. "I was getting tired, but now . . ."

❧

Diesel trucks and motor scooters vroomed by as we entered the courtyard of the Medici Palace, where Michelangelo had served as an apprentice during the 1490s. The clatter reverberated all the way back to the garden, robbing us of any chance for peaceful contemplation. We found no reason to linger.

We fled across the city to Santa Croce, a church in the neighborhood of Michelangelo's youth. Instead of my usual mode of finding a place for Marguerite to sit and then going off to explore, I needed to feel the artist's presence. We shared a pew in the hushed church. "Remember the book?" I whispered. "Michelangelo came here sometimes as an adult and knelt on this floor." I pictured him just across the aisle—a small man, his face disfigured by a rival's fist. "He prayed for guidance when the popes and nobles ordered him to paint the ceiling of the Sistine Chapel against his will, cheated him out of his fees, and forced him to renege on contracts."

"All he wanted," added Marguerite, "was to take his chisel and carve marble into brilliance."

"Yes. That's just what he did."

We spent half an hour there reflecting, and then we stopped by the artist's tomb and the memorials to Galileo and Dante before leaving.

Outside, the wind had subsided, and the sun was breaking through. I surveyed the buildings of Florence. "Michelangelo's boyhood home was that way." I directed Marguerite's hand back to one side. "Imagine him sneaking along these streets on gloomy nights, taking *that* alley." I swung her hand to follow his imaginary route. "Crossing the river to the monastery of Santo Spirito to do autopsies."

359

"He must have been scared *and* cold. They would have executed him if they knew."

I lowered my voice for effect. "In a dingy room, he found a corpse in white cloth awaiting burial. Gagging from the smell of rotting flesh and the sensation of squiggly intestines in his hands, he tried to understand how the body worked." I eyed my companion and knew by the curl of her upper lip that I was hitting the mark. "Later, our man cleaned up the mess and fled into a square before dawn to wash in a public fountain . . . *this* fountain, below us in the square." I waited to see if she would call me a ghoul or a fiend, but she surprised me.

"Thank you. You're really making his spirit come alive for me."

On that first visit to Florence we had been thrilled by some of its treasures. We had overlooked what moles and wrinkles we encountered, but by the second journey, they were beginning to stand out. Sure, there was the lovely skyline; the River Arno, with the Ponte Vecchio lined with gold merchants' shops; the Signoria (city hall), with its square full of bold statuary, but the buildings seemed modern after Siena and its hilltop villages, even though they were old and European. After searching the city for a reasonably priced restaurant, we settled for a cafeteria—without atmosphere.

The city was full of expensive restaurants as well as shops with trendy, exorbitant goods and aloof shopkeepers. When we took an English-language tour of the city, the tour leader, too, was disinterested. Florence seemed too full of itself.

All the hubbub began to chafe us—not only when we were at the Medici Palace that first day but all over the city. There was no point trying to take a peaceful stroll along the romantic River Arno, because the clattering, blasting, blaring traffic prevented it. It was difficult to navigate with Marguerite in the narrow back streets, with the two-foot wide sidewalks often blocked by parked motor scooters. I would lead her into the street, and then we'd hop back onto the walkway as the diesels and mopeds flew by. The racket stung our ears. Dust and fumes permeated the air, our lungs, and our clothes. The back streets of Florence seemed more Industrial Revolution than Renaissance.

Each block that we walked and each extra step down and up to bypass an obstructed sidewalk had to take away from Marguerite's stamina. There was weariness in her eyes but still no sign of an aching back.

I tried to admire the stonework in the palace walls and the herringbone pattern of the paving stones as Michelangelo had. He had grown up among the stone cutters and had seen their craft as art. On one of the rare walking streets, we came upon a man with a power chisel carving a design in the pavement. Here was evidence that Florentines cared deeply about the aesthetics of their city. I watched for a few moments and then turned to see Marguerite grimacing at the noise. What was she getting out of these cold, dusty days in Florence? There were no special meals and way too much noise, and the art was too enormous to touch. "Shall we head to the bus station?"

"Not so fast," she exclaimed. "Before we go, we can buy CDs."

I protested that I was tired and she should be, too, but I yielded to her enthusiasm—and my desire to add music to our collection. We'd been playing French CDs on our computer ever since Paris. They kept France fresh and alive, even in our cottage here among the olive trees and vines. If we found Italian music, it would nurture the good memories.

In the Duomo square, virtually beneath Brunelleschi's red dome, I spotted a music shop and we entered.

As the door closed behind us, the din outside gave way to classical music. Behind the counter a man of about twenty-five years greeted us. He had curly black hair and wore a loose, ruby Nehru shirt. His stature was far more modest than Michelangelo's *David*, but his fine-chiseled lips grinned easily. *"Buon giorno, Signora, Signore."*

We *buon giorno*-ed him back.

"What can I do for you?" Comprehensible English—a good sign.

"We're looking for music CDs," I said.

"Something *romantic,*" Marguerite amended.

"Ah, lovely . . . best kind of music. I play my favorite."

He whipped out a CD and showed me the cover—*Romanza* by Andrea Bocelli. "This singer, he is from near to Florence." The fellow on the cover looked much like our clerk, only with a scruffy beard and pouty lips. (And we had no way of guessing that this local talent was becoming a worldwide sensation.) The salesman slipped the disk into the machine and played parts from a couple of the songs. "And now is my best favorite." He caressed a button on the machine a few times and then swayed dreamily while a song played all the way through. "What you think?"

Marguerite's mellow smile accompanied her answer. "They were all lovely, but the last song was the most beautiful *and* the most romantic."

"So you understand the Italian?" He looked at her with new respect.

"No, it just felt full of passion."

"You perhaps not understand words, *signora,* but your soul, your soul it is most romantic . . . most Italian." He crooned the words, and I prepared to catch Marguerite if she fainted.

The clerk went on. "In this song, the man is wanting very much to come home from the city to see his love in their village, but he cannot. She loses hope and marries another. His heart, it is broken."

Suddenly, Florence resumed a gentler, more romantic spirit. This kind, poetic man had introduced us to a wonderful singer. We would take the special music home to cherish.

And his words confirmed something about the nature of Marguerite's soul that I'd felt since the first day I met her.

Extraordinary

November 22

> *It's the people, not the monuments, that make the travel experience extraordinary.*

*Spain—Not Just a
Plate of Paella*

Toledo—Dilemma of the Day:
Asparagus with Garlic or *Larry King Live?*

From Siena we drove northwest past the quarries of Carrara—a source of marble for mighty statues—to southern France. We lingered for a few days near Vence, then followed the arc of the Mediterranean to Spain. Pressing west and south into its heartland, we found rolling, dry grasslands guarded by solitary fortresses. Here and there set on hilltops were large, cutout silhouettes—a bull, a matador, a flamenco dancer—signs of the Spanish soul.

December 3

Here in Toledo, an hour south of Madrid, we're spending a whopping $65 a night–but how could we resist? Our hotel was once a cardinal's palace. We enter the grounds through an opening in the city walls to an expansive courtyard with bubbling fountains; marble lion statues; and rows of planters holding berry bushes, puffy evergreens, and the leafless trees of winter. Inside, salons are rich with paintings and antiques. Our suite includes a bedroom with cable TV, our own breakfast room, and two balconies overlooking the courtyard and ramparts.

In the hotel's parking lot outside the city walls, young and not-so-young toughs use fervent hand signals to guide guests into parking spaces. Their real plan is to extort protection money. For the safety of our Citroën, I gave them a couple of dollars—and felt crappy about it. If they decide I didn't pay enough, they'll take a can opener to Don Corleone and make off with our belongings. The hotel monitors the lot with closed-circuit TV, but the staff lacks enthusiasm, or courtesy, for that matter. How interested will they be if they spot a burglary in progress?

Toledo stands boldly atop its bluff in shades of brown and dashes of white. Surrounded on three sides by the Tagus River and fortified by medieval walls on the fourth, it is dominated by the blocklike Alcazar, with its four black towers piercing the sky. The city is an architectural treat, hardly changed since El Greco painted it in the sixteenth century. Its Arabic arches and towers were built by Moors, who controlled the city from 711 to 1085, and by their descendants, the Mudejars, who remained there after the Spaniards reconquered Toledo.

We wandered mazes of alleys lined with shops into still tighter passages past ancient churches. Palaces of brown stone rose into the air, with official seals of nobility carved over their doorways. At the far side of the city, I coaxed Marguerite to continue downhill, just a little farther, to the Tagus River. An arch with a bell-shaped flourish of marble and a carved, double-eagle crest above it led us onto the bridge. We paused in its center to feel the power of the coursing river. "Toledo really is a treasure. All the different architecture— that last church in swirling baroque, like something you'd see in Portugal—then this gate up ahead with patterned brickwork and little pinnacles, straight out of Morocco." I could see Marguerite's back was bothering her again. "You look pretty beat. We'd better rest."

"We still have to eat and get home to see Larry." She was off, and I had to lunge to keep her from colliding with the bridge's railing.

Just before two o'clock and not far from our hotel, we selected a plain-fronted restaurant named La Cancela. A twenty-year-old fellow in a white shirt and bow tie, and a middle-aged man in a brown tweed jacket showed us through the narrow room to a table decked out in gold linens. The young fellow wiped our stemmed glasses for water and wine with a white cloth, while the owner made a ceremony of opening a bottle of red wine from the Rioja region, pouring, and awaiting my approval. The two watched over us like mother hens as I did my best to interpret the menu. I understood the headings for meat, fish, and dessert, a few names of vegetables, and a couple of terms used to denote chicken.

"We need to leave here a few minutes before three o'clock," Marguerite reminded me.

"From the way they're bowing and scraping, it doesn't seem like it's going to be a hurry-up experience."

"What about Larry?" Alarm sounded in her voice.

"We could bolt and go to McDonald's up on the square, but I don't think we'd get the same treatment."

"We only have CNN once in a while."

"And we're in Toledo every day? I think we're in for something special here. Relax and enjoy it."

The owner asked for our order in patient Spanish. I tried my best in Spanish to ask for his recommendations. "The asparagus is very fresh today, and, of course, the partridge is the town's specialty, but the lamb is *excellente*." I recognized the word *perdiz* for "partridge" because we had read about local dishes in the guidebook. When our host used Spanish for *lamb*, our ignorance forced him to tap into his English vocabulary. This fellow was most cordial—a stark contrast to the staff at our hotel. He encouraged us to speak as much Spanish as possible, then a little more. He coaxed Marguerite seriously, but with a smile, saying it was *importante* to learn the language of the country.

We ordered the asparagus with bacon and garlic, mushrooms with garlic, and lamb Toledo style, which turned out to be heaped in garlic. Each dish was fantastic, as good as any other food on the trip, and with the excellent red wine, we all but forgot Larry. We made it back to our room just in time for his sign-off. We had lost, but not squandered, a day of TV.

That night, CNN was filled with stories about the movement to ban land mines—heavy stuff, important, and interesting for a while, but it had its limits. After an hour, we shut it off. The next morning, I clicked it back on—more land mines. I left Marguerite getting ready and walked to the Roman Circus, a big circle of vertical stone slabs in a park close to the hotel. There was no sign, no explanation of any kind.

At the tourist office we asked for information about the Circus, but none was available. "Back home they would capitalize on a thing like this," I told the agent. "Maybe build a mall around it and a couple of high-rise hotels." In a city so full of history, Roman ruins were apparently superfluous.

We explored a labyrinth of passageways to find the Santo Tomé church—unremarkable architecturally but for its majestic Mudejar tower with two levels of sculpted, keyhole windows high above the alley. Inside, we found what I was looking for—El Greco's *El entierro del conde de Orgaz*. I pondered the painting, so full of unique characters bidding farewell to the dead count of Orgaz. At the top of the scene, angels and kingly figures gazed down from a diaphanous world, as solemn nobles looked up to Christ for solace. Down on Earth, black-jacketed aristocrats with flouncy white collars looked on as a golden-robed archbishop supported the count's body in his arms. Set in the middle of the earthly throng, yet somehow apart, one of the characters seemed to be aware of me! A creepy, ten-year-old boy peered out from the canvas, making eye contact exclusively with yours truly. The work was inspired and stirring, intricate and articulate. (Not a chance I could explain to Marguerite the feelings the scene stirred up in me.)

Moving on to the city's cathedral, I left Marguerite listening to organ music while I visited more El Grecos and lots of other great art in the sacristy. All through France and Italy, I had seen so many crucifixions and holy births, so many dark chapels crammed with art, so many intricately carved choir stalls and golden statues that I was fairly well anesthetized. But then, by an entrance of the Cathedral, light from the heavens shone down on me. More accurately, I came to a very bright area in what should have been the darkest recess of the dim cathedral. I looked up to see floating angels and the Virgin ascending through the roof of the Cathedral into a cupola, bound for heaven. Some of the sculptures were made of marble, others alabaster. These works, the *Transparente*, filled the space with light. Light penetrated them, radiated, and shone into me.

Earlier we had stopped for lunch and enjoyed what was perhaps the best chicken of the trip. Was it truly better than Poulet à Go-Go back in Vence, or was it a case of "If I'm not near the chicken I love,

I'll love the one I'm near"? By 3:00 PM, we were ensconced in front of our TV in time to catch Larry, but did he catch us? No. CNN was preempting everything to cover the land mines.

"How could they do this?" wailed Marguerite.

"These big networks have no social conscience. They don't care that travelers around the world depend on Larry for their mental health." In my heart I knew it was important to cover the issue, but I couldn't help my disappointment.

Felicia was the only one who seemed unfazed. As I rested back against the headboard, she curled between my thighs and fell asleep.

December 6

I've been reading about Toledo—in brochures from the tourist office, a book I bought at the Cathedral bookstore, and our guidebooks. The glory of the city (besides the cooking) lies in the fact that Muslims, Jews, and Catholics lived and created here in harmony. Even though Toledo changed hands from the Spaniards to the Moors and back again by the late eleventh century, life apparently ran pretty well for a great many years. The Cathedral was begun during this period of harmony, taking over 200 years before it was completed in 1493. Synagogues were also erected during this time, including the Synagogue of Santa Maria la Blanca, which we visited today.

The synagogue's flat-ceilinged, Arabic interior contrasted sharply with the Cathedral's flamboyant, Gothic interior. It bore no famous paintings, statues, or jewels. The synagogue had been restored to good repair but, though eloquent, was very humble.

I described the rows of octagonal columns, the white Moorish arches, and the intricately carved designs in the beige plaster overhead. "High up on the walls there are pierced marble screens."

"You mean they had screens in the twelfth century?"

"Not screens for bugs. There must be a room behind them, where the Jewish women could have watched the services—like the synagogues we visited in Venice. What's weird is that it feels like a mosque in here."

"I like the way your voice echoes," said Marguerite.

"Does the sound tell you anything about the pillars around us?"

"The echo is complex . . . that's all I can tell." I set her hand on a carving at shoulder level on one of the columns. She fingered the cluster of little rams' horns, then frowned. "So it's a synagogue that looks like a mosque and is named Santa Maria?"

"According to the brochure, it was built in the twelfth century. Mudejars were the builders then. That explains the design. Later, the Spaniards expelled the Jews and turned it into a church."

"Catholics stole it and called it Santa Maria?"

"Pretty slick, huh?"

We stopped testing the echoes and contemplated.

December 6, continued

Christian buildings full of Moorish architecture and Jewish art. Although the Cathedral is a Catholic cathedral, Mudejar workmen created much of it, and its tower is like a jazzed-up minaret. Did Moors carve the statues? Did Jews paint portraits of saints or fashion gold medallions for the bishops?

Toledo speaks to me of synergies—Moors, Catholics, and Jews building, creating, and worshipping. Brochures from the tourist office and guidebooks confirm it. It must have been an uneasy calm after centuries of Spanish persecution against Jews, and then the Inquisition began in 1478. It summoned Jews and Muslims who had converted to Catholicism to test their faith. Not content with that, Ferdinand and Isabella issued the Edict of Expulsion in 1492 to send all remaining Jews packing. Their possessions, like the synagogues of Toledo, were forfeited.

It seems we're moving backward through a world gone mad, from Germany to Venice to Spain. How many of the Jews driven from Toledo found their way to the Venice ghetto, where oppression was less monstrous? Centuries later, Nazis rolled into that ghetto to finish the job.

Why am I fascinated with this tale woven in a sinister tangle through European history? Maybe because there had been such a marvelous blend of cultures here in Toledo until the crazy jackals of the Inquisition excised its heart. They killed its people, its culture, and its love. I am sick and furious.

Música Romántica

Though at night I pondered serious matters, the songbirds of morning—not to mention Marguerite—called for frivolity.

It was early December, and men climbed tall ladders to string lights across the city streets. These doings set off a primal urge in us for some serious Christmas shopping. We searched the shops for reasonably priced, gold-on-black jewelry—an ancient Toledan art from Moorish times. We found tie bars for a coworker and Marguerite's brother, and earrings for nieces, sisters, and her mom.

We sought out Spanish Christmas music for friends back home and *música romántica* for ourselves. That's what we called it, and the merchants seemed to understand.

In the second music store, a very sensual señorita in a nicely fitted, taupe sweater waited on us. "Where do you come from?" she asked in Spanish, her eyes shining into mine.

"*Los Estados Unidos.*" She was already approaching the limits of my *español* when she stepped close and approached the limits of my personal space.

"*Los Estados Unidos* is very nice, no?" She spoke soothingly and smiled to the accompaniment of her flashing brown eyes. "Someday I go *Estados Unidos.*"

I nodded, failing to find Spanish words to wish her success. She changed the CD in the player. Now a male singer crooned. Marguerite pulled me closer and spoke into my ear. "Nice music, but we asked for romantic tunes not a romantic salesclerk."

"She doesn't mean anything by it."

The señorita tried a couple of sentences that we didn't understand. Then she pointed at her boss. "He is my *blah, blah, blah,*" she said. She pointed at me. "You be my *blah, blah, blah?*"

"*No comprendo,*" was what I said, but the drift of her conversation was making me nervous. She wanted me to be her boss, or something more cozy? "I think she wants us to take her home and put her to work," I said to Marguerite.

"You're saying *us*, but are you sure I'm in this picture?"

"You may be optional."

"That's what we need, a Spanish maid to empty cat litter."

The young woman tried the same approach again, pointing at her boss and then at me. Marguerite eyed her a bit harshly, I thought. I stuck with "*no comprendo*" as my safest response. She stomped her foot, pouted, and shoved in the next CD.

We selected a mellow vocal, *Romances* by Luis Miguel, and she rang it up.

She asked another question, and I made a point of not *comprendo*-ing. A young man entered, and she took him aside. He told us, "She like to know how is possible a person go to work in United States."

"I don't know," I answered.

"It's very difficult," added Marguerite. I thought she seemed rather pleased about making this statement. "Maybe not possible."

The man forwarded our comments, and we bid *adios* all around.

Closing the door behind us, I caught a last glimpse of the señorita's soulful eyes following her lost opportunity out the door.

To make it home by three o'clock, we ate at McDonald's (not one of the better Big Macs I've had) and then rushed back for our appointment with the TV. We settled on the bed with Felicia, and the raspy melodies of Larry's voice came to us. "Today on *Larry King Live*—depression. Celebrities Art Buchwald, Mariette Hartley, and Margo Kidder tell about their experiences."

The TV went to commercial, and I muted it. "Want to watch this?"

"I came here to get *away* from my therapy practice, but it's English. Let's give it a try."

We did. It wasn't land mines, and it was definitely English. We loved it.

After Larry, CNN presented a weather map that was perfectly clear over Spain. Outside, wind rattled the windows. Clouds swelled and grew dark. Snow began to fall, catching on bare tree limbs and the walls of old Toledo. We stepped out on the balcony and let the snow tickle our faces.

That evening, my sweetheart dressed up in her red-and-green plaid skirt and her black turtleneck. She donned her new, black Toledan earrings and necklace with fine-gold, Arabian pheasants adorning each piece. We headed to the hotel dining room where we found a blazing fireplace; lots of empty, white-clothed tables with candles aglow; and bow-tied waiters. A pleasant man—tuxedoed and bald-topped—seated us by the windows, and I asked, "Would you open the drapes? I'd like to watch the storm." He seemed puzzled, as if no one would want to glance at the world while eating, but he complied.

Snow had accumulated to a thick cloak on the ramparts. Looking up, I saw a blur of flakes zinging sideways, but inside the city walls, they swirled, drifted, and settled peacefully into the courtyard. Snow amassed on cars and made little pointed hats on each post of the crenellated walls. As we ate trout and partridge Toledan style, Marguerite absorbed and reflected my joy at watching the tempest through the half-fogged windows. "Maybe we'd better stay another day," she mused.

"Is this about the storm or about your loving the palace life?" The idea sounded pretty good to me, too, but I didn't have to concede just yet.

"I'm only thinking of you. Driving could be difficult tomorrow."

I rubbed my chin thoughtfully. "The roads might even be closed."

A spark lit up in her eyes and then faded. "But the hotel is expensive. It could wreck our budget."

"Right. We'll move to a smaller room."

"But if we could afford it, Felicia really likes the suite."

"Okay. We'll stay in the suite."

Marguerite donned a grin of triumph and delight.

The waiters, who hadn't even planned to open the curtains, wandered to the window again and again. At one point, all three were lined up with their hands behind their backs, staring out at the scene. I had to peek between them. "Snow is rare here?" I asked.

"*Sí, señor.* It comes once in five, maybe ten, years."

After dinner we approached the hotel desk, pried a clerk from the little back room where they watched the parking lot on closed-circuit TV, and booked another night in the cardinal's palace. As we climbed the stairs to our room, Marguerite said, "Another day of *Larry King Live.*"

"And how about a rerun of the asparagus in garlic tomorrow?"

The slightest of smiles was her eloquent answer.

Seville—*Apartamento con cocina, por favor*

December 6

All these months in Europe have been like taking a course in life. Tomorrow we drive south to Seville. Although we don't go on to Paris until January, everything there has been arranged ahead of time. Seville will be our final exam. During the test we will seek our last apartment and our last cybercafe; explore new neighborhoods; and learn their secrets, resources, and specialties. Carry it off smoothly, and we get an A—but lower grades are possible. . . .

The search for lodging in Seville, like Spain itself, could not be rushed, so we began by getting a room in Alcalá de Guadaira at a handsome hotel called the Oromana, 15 kilometers outside of Seville. After negotiating a rate for three nights ($48 per), I told the clerk, "My wife and I . . . and our cat . . . seek an apartment in the city for three or four weeks."

"With two bedrooms," Marguerite added. "My sister is coming."

"Ah, *bueno*. Sonia work here tomorrow morning. She can find apartment for tourist."

After breakfast the next day, we found Sonia—a black-haired, petite woman with dark eyes and a ready smile—at the front desk. "Yes, yes," she replied. "I can arrange place for you in mountains outside Sevilla."

"Is it near the city?"

"Not too far . . ." We waited for more detail. "You must drive three hours." Sonia watched our faces droop and added, "But I find in Sevilla, too, if you prefer. I talk to my agency and telephone you tonight."

It was Sunday, and although most offices were closed, we drove to the city and spent the day searching. We followed lots of false leads from the tourist office and from helpful hotel clerks who thought that this or that hotel might have apartments for tourists. By the end of the afternoon, we had trudged four blocks here and two blocks there and seven blocks over yonder without any luck. Marguerite's back was holding up, thank goodness, but our feet had turned to pulp.

Back at our hotel outside the city, we awaited Sonia's call. I adjusted the wall heater several times, trying in vain to reach a sustainable comfort level. Marguerite called the hotel manager, seeking hot water to bathe our feet. His response was, "Yes, they have just this minute fixed the boiler. Try in an hour." We tested the water in an hour and then in two. Another inquiry brought the answer, "It is just now fixed. Try in an hour." Felicia was happy to lick my toes, which tickled and made me laugh, but it wasn't the kind of bath I had in mind.

We'll shower in the morning, and we'll find a place," I said. "There have to be loads of apartments in Seville."

Monday morning, without benefit of hot water, we tracked down Sonia and grilled her.

"Oh, yes. I didn't call last night. It was Sunday and, naturally, I couldn't get any information. This afternoon I will have something."

It was December 8, the Feast of the Immaculate Conception,

and Seville offices were again closed. We wandered the streets lined with orange trees, copious with fruit; passed the yellow and white bullring by the River Guadalquivir; and discovered a flamboyant church in mauve and blue with fine, tile crucifixion scenes on the walls. Since no apartments were to be found, we sought solace in a tapas bar with picture windows that beckoned and elegant gold letters that read *Robles Placentines*. We sat at a corner table, well back from the crowd forming near the dark walnut bar. Men and women, most of whom were in their thirties and wearing jackets or suits, stood at the taller tables, talked animatedly, tasted a series of wines presented by a waiter, and ordered plates of appetizers.

A bottle of excellent Rioja white wine and delicious little dishes—shrimp in a spicy tomato sauce, grilled vegetables in herbs, rosemary chicken—did wonders for our spirits. We called Sonia from a pay phone, and she informed us, "It is the Immaculate Conception, didn't you know? I couldn't possibly find anything. Tomorrow, for sure."

When we returned to the hotel—exhausted, discouraged, and without hot water—only Felicia purred in good spirits.

Tuesday's dawn bestowed hope. The hot water ran hot, and I found a sentimental, American, Christmas movie on TV. Sappy as it was, we glommed onto it. Real estate offices in the city would be open. Sonia would succeed. All systems would be go.

In the city, the tourist office produced a brochure showing *Residencias Turisticas* on this, our third, request. "Here it is," I said, waving the pamphlet. "Success—in my hand."

We hiked to three *Residencias* on the list. One was acceptable and very reasonable at $25 per night. It would do wonders for our budget. *Acceptable* is an English word meaning "livable for one or two nights but nothing special, and not a place Marguerite would introduce to her sister."

Walking narrow, shop-lined streets with Christmas lights strung overhead, we paused in a plaza by the city hall where a score of temporary stores sold nativity scenes of endless variety. I peeked into courtyards and church vestibules full of red poinsettias. A few blocks farther on, I described the blue-clad angels and their glittering wings on the El Corte Inglés department store. Would we find a place to call home for Christmas or still be wandering like waifs into the new year? And how would it feel to spend the holidays so far from home?

The first realtor we found quickly dashed my hopes. There were no short-term rentals in the city. Outside, I gazed up at all the apartment windows. "He's wrong," I said half-heartedly. "He just didn't understand my Spanish." We tried another realtor and another, but the man had been right.

"We still have the rest of this list from the tourist office," I told Marguerite.

"How many more places?"

"Plenty more."

"How many?" Her voice had that tone the no-nonsense lawyer Marcia Clark used on the woman who kept saying, *"No me recuerdo,"* in the O.J. Simpson trial.

"One more."

I popped coins into a pay phone, and Marguerite talked with Sonia. Partway through the call, she began to smile. "Sonia's found a great place by the river. She'll set up a meeting and call us tonight."

We visited the last *Residencia* on our list, the *Apartamento Turistico Los Angeles,* on a walking street in the shopping district. There we met Señora Limones, who was perhaps sixty, wearing a navy sweatshirt and matching leggings, with a dark complexion and deeply chiseled cheeks. Her twelve apartments were set on three floors of landings around a charming tiled courtyard, with her place on the fourth floor. We visited a studio and a one bedroom, both pretty and bright but too small to accommodate three adults and a cool cat.

Señora Limones invited us up to her apartment, seated us on a couch by a coffee table, and brought us a bowl of olives and a carafe of red wine. Her less-expensive apartments cost 8,000 pesetas ($54) a night. Señora Limones rattled on in Spanish and simultaneously in pantomime, and, remarkably, I got a lot of it. She used words like *gordos, California, niño, americanos,* and *no trabajan mucho* as she gestured with her arms to make a big round stomach.

"She says she has visited her son in California," I reported. "Americans don't work enough and are too fat." Señora Limones plucked an olive from the bowl, waved it in the air, and said some words I half understood. "She says we should grow more olives in California." She used the word *salud,* and I deduced, "Olives are healthy and keep you from getting *gordo.* "

"Is that what she's really talking about?" Marguerite asked. "I get a word here and there, but . . ."

"You know I don't speak that much Spanish, but this woman is a born communicator. You should see her acting. I *really* understand."

Between the two of us, with our limited abilities, Marguerite and I explained that Marguerite's *hermana* was planning to visit us for eight nights. We liked the *residencia,* but we needed a larger *apartamento.*

We returned to our hotel outside the city and to our devoted cat.

That night Sonia did not call. "What's wrong with her?" Marguerite fumed.

"Don't look at me. I'm ready to strangle her."

In the morning, Sonia was not at the hotel, and there was no message. The desk clerk reluctantly connected us to her home. Sonia would come to the hotel at 1:00 PM, and we would drive her into the city to meet the owner of the lodging at 1:30 PM.

With Felicia happily munching cat food back in the room, we entered the hotel lobby at 12:45 PM. Sonia fluttered in at 1:20 PM.

As I drove the three of us toward Seville, Sonia said, "I think it's very nice, this apartment. I have not seen it, but it's right on the river near the Expo." I conjured up the image of our picture window overlooking the Guadalquivir and the site of Expo '92.

Sonia folded and refolded her map as she directed us through numerous U-turns. We arrived at 2:00 PM, at a building a block from the river in a neighborhood we had rejected because it was seedy. As we got out of Don Corleone, a derelict asked us for money "to protect our car" (an opportunity I declined). At the apartment building, we found crumbling walls and litter in the hallway but no owner. He had given up when we were late.

I described part of the scene to Marguerite but reserved the details for later. "Time to have a serious talk with Señora Limones," I said.

"Maybe we can negotiate a better price and rent a second place for Patricia."

Sonia seemed mildly surprised that the owner hadn't met us, and she was unapologetic. On the drive back, she said, "I think it must be nice, this apartment, because they rent it to students."

Right, Sonia. I went to college in Boston. I knew what they rented to students. I could see the outside of the place and the level of upkeep.

"I will make other appointment for it and call you at the hotel," she added.

"No need for that," Marguerite said.

I watched in the rearview mirror as Sonia's mouth dropped open. "But this is very nice place. You don't want to see?"

"We have another prospect," I said. A yoke began lifting from my neck. We wouldn't have to deal with this woman again. I suddenly realized how much her incompetence had ground on my nerves.

Later that afternoon, Señora Limones served us wine spritzers and cheese and crackers in her tiny living room, and told us how Americans don't take care of themselves. "You should drink red wine and take siestas in the afternoon. You would live longer."

We settled on 7,000 pesetas ($47) a night for a nice studio with a glassed-in balcony—perfect for a Christmas tree—and 6,000 pesetas ($40) for Patricia's place, which was smaller but had a view of the square.

After finalizing the deal, our new landlady advised, "With all that land in California, you should grow more olives. And red wine, it is so much healthy." I couldn't disagree. (Hadn't I seen a piece about that on *60 Minutes?*) "But we have our problems, too. In Spain, it's the government. I show you." She took a notebook from her shelf. "Onto your room rate, I must charge the tax, you see."

"She's telling us about the room tax," I told Marguerite.

"How do you know?"

"First she said *impuesto*. When I didn't understand, she said *tarifa*, like *tariff*, get it? Now she's showing me a book with a listing of lodgers." Señora Limones rattled on and pointed to a section on the page with an official-looking stamp and a large signature. "She's showing me how the tax man comes to check her books, so she has no choice but to charge us the fee."

Señora L. mentioned *lástima, políticos, perlas, mujeres*, and *pero no están esposas*, all the while painting a visual picture with her hands. She touched both her ears and traced a curve beneath her throat.

"I get it!" I exclaimed. "She says it's a shame to charge us tax. The politicians use the money to buy earrings and pearl necklaces for their women . . . not for their wives."

Marguerite was skeptical of my translation, but I knew it was right. Marguerite added a good question, "So is the tax included in the price?"

"Tarifa está incluida?"

"Oh, no, *señor.*"

We negotiated some more and struck a new deal, bringing our price *with tax* to just about $50 a night, plus $42 for Marguerite's *hermana's* place.

We would have a home, and it would be a *feliz Navidad* after all.

Choosing Our Christmas Beneficiary

I have to confess—there's something I didn't mention about that first visit to Seville. It involved another memorable encounter, with a fellow I will call "the parking lot entrepreneur" (which was *not* my first name for him).

Maneuvering Don Corleone through the traffic chaos that is Seville, round and round a maze of streets, I grew increasingly frustrated. With each pass I began to see red, like a bull in a Spanish arena that just can't seem to nail the guy in spandex pants.

Marguerite sat silently in the passenger seat, stifling questions, understanding that a barrage of bewilderment was assailing my brain.

Spotting the Giralda, Seville's landmark cathedral tower, I homed in but was diverted again and again as lanes of traffic veered in the wrong direction. Finally, close to our goal, a sign for parking appeared, but I was in the wrong lane. The sign teased me, enticed me, and pissed me off. My inner voice cried out, "Do a bit of guerilla driving. They all do it." I stopped dead in the second lane. Horns sounded, but so what? The car to my right edged forward, and I nosed in behind it. A new horn joined in. A hand flashed crude gestures. I swung across the lane into the driveway. Tires squealed. The horns subsided. Relief!

A man stood in the alley ahead of us, wearing a dirty raincoat, a knit hat, and a rectangular badge on his chest. The guy needed a shave. He smiled and spoke soothingly in Spanish. "I show you where to park." At least that's what I understood him to say.

This grungy savior stood ready to show me a refuge for the Citroën—I would have followed him to the headwaters of the Guadalquivir. He walked ahead of our car to a spot where the driveway swung left between buildings, and I prepared to turn. "*Señor*, you park. . . ." He pointed to a spot at the bend in the driveway in front of a big, roll-up door. He guided me as I backed in.

"He wants me to park here. There's only one other vehicle."
"Is it okay?"
"I don't know. We're in front of some sort of garage. I'll ask him." I rolled down my window. "*¿Por qué no allí?* (Why not down there?)" I pointed along the driveway toward what I thought might be an actual parking lot around another turn.

The entrepreneur whipped out a few quick sentences that

sounded like *"loque noque, mejor aba saba, menos pesatas, blah, blah, blah."*

Marguerite asked, "Did you understand that?"

"Are you kidding? I *think* he's saying it's better to park here. We'll save money."

I got out, walked around the car, and took Marguerite's hand. In my pocket I found a hundred-peseta coin (70 cents), and handed it to him. *"Muchas gracias."* Marguerite and I headed toward the boulevard.

The man followed along, handing me back the coin. "No, *señor.* When do you leave?"

I conferred with Marguerite and came back with, "Three hours."

He leveled a serious look my way. "Three hours—one thousand." Was he just looking for a tip, or was it his garage we were blocking?

"He wants $7," I told Marguerite. "Too much," I said to him. He shrugged. "Okay. Better. Five hundred."

"You're not giving him seven bucks?"

"I'll tell you in a minute." I rummaged through my pocket and then my wallet. "I only have a ten-thousand peseta note," I told Marguerite. I waved the bill in the air. "This is all I have, *señor.*"

The man pulled a ticket from his pocket and handed it to me. He snatched the bill from my hand, mentioned *restaurante* and *cambiar,* and tramped off toward the boulevard. The ticket, like a theatre stub, bore a long number.

"What happened?"

"He's getting change." I led her to a safe place by the side of the alley. "Wait here. I'd better go along." A sinking feeling took hold of my stomach the moment he rounded the corner. It settled deeper and heavier each second as I hurried to the street and saw no trace of him. I entered a nearby restaurant, then another. I walked to the next street but then slinked back to Marguerite. "I lost him. He's not coming back, is he?"

"He will." She spoke hopefully. "You gave him ten thousand?

Seventy dollars?"

"How could I have been so dumb?"

"You weren't. He'll come back." We waited a few more minutes. "You're right," she said. "He's a *damned crook.*"

"We can't leave the Citroën here blocking this door." We climbed into the car, and I drove to the real parking area.

"We should tell them what happened," Marguerite said.

"What good will that do?"

"But, of course, we should. They'll call the police."

As Marguerite and I walked to the parking attendant's booth, I knew it could only be a humiliating mistake. As we did our best to tell the man at the raised kiosk about the rip-off, I felt a stupid, helpless, shame-filled smile crease my lips.

"Oh, no, never give them money," the attendant said.

"You have to help us." Marguerite insisted. "We gave him ten thousand pesetas." The man shrugged and gave me what I took for an *Americano-muy-estupido* look. I tried to sink into the pavement, but it resisted.

"A lot of money," he said, looking down on me.

As we trudged to the tourist office to begin our search for apartments, I tried to put my heart into describing the city squares, the orange trees, and the churches, but she could sense my mood. Finally, she asked, "Do you feel any better about the man in the parking lot?"

"I'm trying, but it's eating at me. This was the kind of thing I should have watched for. "

"Forget it. Look, we're in Seville!"

"I'll never forget it."

She stared at me. "What good will that do?"

"It's not that I'll want to remember, but I know myself. I won't be able to put it out of my mind, like the time I threw up on Eddie McClosky in second grade."

"I guess you really mean 'never.' It's just as much my fault as it is yours."

"No. You couldn't see how sloppy he looked. You didn't know

what was going on."

"How sloppy?"

"He . . . he was a damned derelict." Marguerite's lips turned up. She slapped hands over her mouth. Her body shook. "He did have a badge. How could I know how parking lot attendants dress in Seville?"

Giggles broke out from behind her hands, but she fought for control. "Look at it this way. His family will have that Christmas turkey this year."

"You mean he'll be drinking Old Turkey."

"No. He's sending his son through university. They'll use it for textbooks. Think of this. . . ." I couldn't help grinning just a little at her efforts to soothe me. "Every year we give a special gift to someone at Christmas, right?—someone less fortunate?"

"You mean we should make that thief our Christmas beneficiary?"

"Right! Who needs the money more? Now his crippled son, little Pedro, will get that tricycle."

"Hmmm. I hope he can pedal it with the leg braces."

"That's better."

It took me a couple of days to appreciate Marguerite's idea. Though logic told me our "beneficiary" would take the $70 to the nearest bar and become very popular, I pictured him instead presenting a great big box wrapped in red ribbons to his little boy.

The Seville bandito could have joined the ranks of the two crooked hotel owners in Germany and an unknown thief in Toledo who'd stolen Don Corleone's radio antenna. But instead, he was elevated. Weeks after the event, I came to refer to him as our Christmas beneficiary, the parking lot entrepreneur, the man who allowed us to keep our Christmas tradition alive with a little holiday giving in Seville. But I still felt bad about poor Eddie McClosky.

Finishing the Final Exam and Preparing for Christmas Company

December 14

Our apartment is one long room—from the kitchen area, past the sitting area and bed, to our glassed-in balcony, which hangs over a walking street of fashionable shops sporting pine garlands around their windows. In the evening, the street fills with couples out for the paseo, *while strings of Christmas lights glow overhead. The murmur here is different from Italy. It's lower-pitched and less passionate. Last night a South American band in colorful serapes played beneath our window— flutes hooting and bongos thumping. The whole picture is* muy agréable. *(Am I mixing Spanish and French?)*

Other great items in the studio include a table with an electric heater beneath; a shower that blasts consistent, hot water; and an actual double bed with a firm mattress and no crevice running down the center.

The overhead light in the bathroom works all the time; the lights over the medicine cabinet, once in a while. Illumination for the kitchen stove is also intermittent. I choose to believe the wiring isn't dangerous—I accept the need to shave by touch, and I sometimes move a bedside lamp into the kitchen.

Seville is a glorious mix of golds, whites, and cranberry-reds; lush, fountain-studded gardens; squares framed by fruit-filled orange trees; a magnificent cathedral; gems of pocket churches; elegant tiled courtyards full of poinsettias; and crowded tapas bars. To the east there's the Plaza de España, a fabulous, twin-towered, soaring tribute to the country, made of brown stone and tile tableaus depicting the different regions. But just a few short blocks west of downtown lies a section full of menace—run-down buildings, dirt lots, scroungy-looking men eyeing us sideways and asking for the time.

The basement grocery store at El Corte Inglés department store is the best of the trip. It has all sorts of deli items, premade dinners, and more types of cookies than we've seen in a year. At Marks and Spencer we buy crumpets and lemon curd. Why do things from Britain feel like things from home?

Since this is our final exam, let's see how we're doing.

Apartment hunting: The apartment hunting was arduous, but we scored high marks for selection and self-control. (We held out for the best in the face of disappointments.)

Cybercafe: The cybercafe we were referred to by the tourist office had Netscape in Spanish, and the staff wasn't able to tap into our e-mail. A college student we met, from Plymouth, Massachusetts, told us about two other cyberplaces. One is open only at the owner's whim, but the other one is great. We opened an account there, and the staff prints out our e-mail the moment we walk in the door.

We get A's for apartment and cybercafe hunting.

Finding the right parking lot: I lost points in this category due to the fiasco with the parking lot bandito, but I've redeemed myself. The tourist office has no clue about reasonable parking and referred us to the standard (and exorbitant) lots. Hotel clerks tell us that parking in the street is possible but that it is "not recommended unless the car is merely rented." Drug addicts and scrounges are everywhere, aspiring to "help us park" and "protect our car." Don Corleone may be a leased vehicle, but he's still part of the family. We will not put him in harm's way.

With no logical reason for doing so, we approached the information desk of El Corte Inglés and found the one English-speaking clerk—a commuter who had searched for a good deal on parking herself. We are now spending $90, one quarter the going rate, for a monthly pass at the Plaza des Armas parking garage.

Grade: C+

Christmas stuff: With the essentials behind us, it's time for some Christmas fun. Each day on our computer's CD player, we play Christmas music from Italy, France, and Spain. With our gifts from those countries gathered before us, we wrapped, boxed, and mailed them to our friends and family in the States. Now it's on to look for decorations.

For three days we sifted through neighborhood stores. A florist sold us a three-foot, potted Christmas tree for $7. In a stationery store, sheets of red and green construction paper set us back 40 cents. At a store advertising all items for 100 pesetas (70 cents), we picked out two sparkly garlands—one red, one gold; six-packs of miniature silver apples, red-glittered reindeer, and puffy white snowmen; masking tape; a string of flashing white lights; two plastic, 3-D wall Santas; and an extension cord. Total cost to decorate lavishly: around $15.

The hard part came next. We sat on the couch with Felicia sleeping between us and all of our recently purchased materials set out on the table. Between sips of white wine, Marguerite cut strips of red construction paper and lay them on the table in front of me. "This feels like second grade."

I made a green paper hoop, taped it closed, and then looped a red strip around that. "In second grade my fingers worked better."

"You're doing fine. I bet you got paste all over everything back then."

"Do you think Effie minds if I make her into a shelf?" As the chain grew, I piled it on her. Our kitty was dwarfed by a two-tone heap that mounded ever higher. Her head stuck out the end, and chains of red and green trailed onto the floor.

Next, I set the tree atop a stool on our balcony, where the citizens of Seville could see it on their evening stroll. We draped it with our dazzling, store-bought garlands, lights, glittered reindeer, snowmen, and silver apples. After looping a paper chain from one end of the apartment to the other, I stuck a plastic Santa over the center. We set Patricia's presents under the tree and saved the second chain and Santa for decorating her place.

"It reminds me of our first Christmas together, our apartment in Connecticut." Marguerite looked misty-eyed. "It was so exciting being married and on our own, decorating our own place. But I was sad, too. My family had just moved to California, and I missed them."

"Remember the pinecones we colored with sparkle paint and

the popcorn and cranberries we strung for garlands? Talk about budget ornaments. On Christmas Eve we drove to Mom's house, and my old high-school buddies showed up."

"You guys played penny-ante poker while your mom and I cooked dinner."

"That was only her second Christmas after Dad had died—her first after I'd moved out." I felt a tear slip down my cheek. "It had to be so lonely for her."

"But she never let it show."

"Nope. Not *my* mom. I wish . . . I wish we could have spent more time with her."

"We did our best, and she sure appreciated the times we visited."

I thought about the reminders of Mom I'd had this year—the women violinists at St. Médard in Paris, the bright birds that sang to me from a fruit tree on the farm outside Salzburg, cooking elbow macaroni in Holland. . . .

Marguerite interrupted my reverie. "Tricia's coming soon, and we get to spend Christmas in Seville. And then in January, it's home to see my mom."

Home. The word had a fine ring to it.

Christopher Columbus, Ben Franklin, Tricia, and Felicia

December 18

Patricia's here, and we're celebrating. She loves her little apartment with its paper Christmas chain and plastic Santa on the wall. And she brought us treasures—Starbucks coffee, See's Candy, a Christmas ornament from Marguerite's mom of a Felicia-colored cat sleeping in a suitcase, and multilayered cookies she and sister-in-law Joanne made for us. We gave her the necklace and earrings we'd bought for her in Toledo and then played our international Christmas CDs as we gabbed into the night.

The morning after Tricia arrived, the three of us ambled along a pedestrian shopping street in the heart of Seville.

"I'm so happy you guys invited me to Europe."

"We're the ones who should be glad." I said, patting her on the shoulder while dodging a mother with a baby carriage who seemed intent on ramming us.

"Christmas would be lonely if you weren't here," added Marguerite. "What do you want to see in Seville?"

"I have a list. There's Christopher Columbus's tomb in the cathedral, the Alcazar, and the Archivo General de Indias." Marguerite and I shot inquiring looks, and she explained. "Ferdinand and Isabella received Columbus in the Alcazar when he came back from the New World, and they have his letters about the voyages in the Archives . . . originals in his own handwriting."

"Good! You've been researching Seville." I yanked Marguerite's arm and whirled her past a teenaged boy who was walking forward but looking over his shoulder at a *señorita muy bonita.*

Marguerite glared at me as if I'd tried to kill her and then turned back to Tricia. "Why Columbus?"

"He's one of my heroes. Christopher Columbus and Benjamin Franklin. I always highlight them in my history lessons."

"You're a Columbus groupie," I said. "Is there a fan club?"

"Do you realize what a remarkable thing he did—to get King Ferdinand and Queen Isabella to finance the voyage, set off into uncharted waters, run out of provisions, and keep his crew from mutiny? He changed the world and the way people thought about it."

"Okay, okay. We'll go see his carcass," Marguerite laughed.

Ferdinand and Isabella—the initiators of the Inquisition—didn't hold a high place in my regard, but we were here with wonderful company on a lark. Why get serious? I steered a course toward the cathedral and asked, "So what is it about Ben Franklin—the kite thing?"

"He was an innovator, an inventor, and a diplomat. He . . ." She continued on about Ben and his statesmanship until we reached the immense cathedral with its flying buttresses, stained glass, and statues galore. We paid the admission fee and entered a courtyard of fruit-filled orange trees. We went inside the structure and moved slowly along the side wall, letting our eyes adjust to the dark. Tricia peered through an ornate metal grill into an alcove. "I can barely see back there, but all the pictures are framed in gold. The statues are gold, too."

"It's one of the side chapels," I explained to Marguerite. "Looks like they're all along this wall, and it's a *heck* of a long wall. Can you feel the enormity of this place?"

She nodded. "I hear the resonance of voices coming from all around and way up high."

"Wow, is it tall!" Tricia had finally looked up.

We wandered past several chapels, skirted a congregation of worshippers in folding chairs, and headed to the Columbus monument. There we found a bronze box mounted on the shoulders of four pall bearers—each a ten-foot-high king, with an alabaster face and bronze armor imprinted with either a castle or a dragon. "The tomb," Tricia said. "Can you believe we're here?"

"But is he really in there?" Marguerite wore an I-know-something-you-don't-know look.

Our guidebook made it sound like an iffy proposition, but Tricia shot back, "Of course he is." Then she took to silent contemplation of her hero's tomb.

I left Marguerite at her sister's side and returned to the altar, before which perhaps a hundred worshippers sat. For all the space they occupied in the enormous structure, it might have been a gathering of fleas. The priest—head of the fleas—stood in white robes before the golden altar screen, which rose many times his height and was adorned in intricate, jeweled sculptures. All that gold haunted me. The artisans of the ages, here as in other countries, had given everything to honor Christ. I thought about Columbus and the kings who financed his endeavors. Seville, a city with a large Jewish population, had been the nucleus of the Inquisition. This church, its heart . . . no, its center.

I located my two companions in the cathedral treasury, wandering between display cases of gilded Bibles, bronze statues, and jeweled crucifixes. The two of them were giggling like kids. From there we walked to the base of the Giralda, built as a minaret when the Arabs ruled the city. The ramps we climbed had allowed horses to carry men to the top. I imagined the Moorish sentries watching the approaching army of Spaniards that came to recapture Seville in 1248. From slits in the walls, we caught views of the outside of the cathedral, stained glass, buttresses, and bits of architecture. "Gargoyles," I pointed. "Man, they're ugly."

"I think they look cute," Patricia countered.

"She's right." As usual, Marguerite had the final word.

At the top, Tricia gazed out from one of the windows. "That's the Alcazar, isn't it?"

I nodded. "And I can see that great square with the huge fountain and all the horse-drawn carriages."

A breeze chilled the room, and Marguerite clung tight to my arm. "We still haven't gone for a carriage ride, Eddie."

"We will," I promised her. "That's the old Jewish quarter, the Barrio de Santa Cruz. It's full of narrow alleys, little pocket squares, and whitewashed buildings with balconies and beautifully tiled courtyards."

"He's leaving out the shops," Marguerite said. "Lots of pottery, lacy dresses, and mantillas."

I pictured the two of them drawing their credit cards from their pockets like old time gunslingers, but it didn't distract me for long. "Patricia, there's something you should know about your favorite king and queen who sent Columbus on his trip. That Jewish quarter was lively and thriving until those good Catholic monarchs banished the Jews and looted their homes."

"Eddie, they're her heroes!"

Tricia looked disconcerted. "*Columbus* is my hero, not the two of them."

It was time for me to lighten up. "Right. Columbus was a great guy, but he hung out with jerks."

❖

Back in our apartment, Patricia and Marguerite sat on the couch as I opened a bottle of Sangria. I handed each a glass and noticed Effie resting between them, her head against Tricia's leg. Tricia idly stroked our kitty. "And what would you like to drink, Felicia?" she asked.

"This is new behavior," I observed. "How long have you and Effie been so close?"

"She's sweet, isn't she?"

"I'd better take her on my lap." Marguerite reached for Felicia, but Tricia's hand blocked her.

"Let her stay. She likes me. She's my niece." She gazed down fondly at Effie.

"What about your allergies?"

"It's okay. I'll take a pill."

December 19

Some people are quicker and some slower, but Effie always wins them in the end.

Feeling History Deeply

Awake in bed that night, I brooded. Toledo . . . Venice . . . skulls in the foundations of churches . . . books about the Holocaust and Inquisition . . . crusaders killing and looting in the name of Christ. . . . The church in this city might have done more harm and sewn more hatred while amassing those treasures in its day than any other organization on Earth.

The year 1492 was a momentous one. Columbus sailed. Ferdinand and Isabella conquered Granada and ended the Moorish hold over Spain, expelling the Jews and confiscating their holdings. Now we tourists flocked to admire their stolen gems.

I couldn't sleep.

December 20

By day I walk the streets. I tread in the footsteps of Ferdinand and Isabella, strolling on the turf of the Inquisition. But where does the turf begin and end? Its spirit surely resides in the concentration camp in Dachau, Germany, which we visited in 1970; and in the crusader fortress of Bodrum, Turkey, which we explored in 1996. How close does the turf come to home? The Serbs and Croats, the Protestants and Catholics of Northern Ireland, the Dragons of the Ku Klux Klan. Catholic against Jew, Christian against Muslim, Protestant against Catholic, Jew against Muslim against Jew . . .

Though I've not killed a Muslim or looted a temple, am I heir to the perpetrators, those distant cousins in Germany to whom I bear some genetic link? I marvel and can't believe that my cousins would do these things. I stare at the skulls in the treasuries of cathedrals and cannot comprehend churches that bound their followers with fear, ignorance, and hatred. I gaze at the Mudejar masonry in a Toledo synagogue and the gold in Seville's cathedral, and plead for an answer. . . . Why?

Do I escape the guilt because I shun religion? What about wars fought for oil, territory, or vengeance? What about slavery? Does the fury lie inside of us all, waiting to be unlocked? When the finger points to the guilty parties, might it not reach to the hearts of all men and to the depths of our grubby little minds?

Oops . . . I think I just created "original sin."

I read over the diary entry, highlighted the words, and poised my finger over the delete button. We were on vacation. Why dwell on dark thoughts? But there was plenty of time for fun and great food. Our year's journey was also about pondering the depths of our souls. Instead of *Delete*, I clicked *Save*.

In the morning I made coffee and carried a cup to Marguerite. "Was it all right, what I said to Tricia yesterday about Ferdinand and Isabella?"

"Sure. You were just giving her the other side."

As she sipped coffee and rubbed sleep from her eyes, I turned on the computer and read to her what I'd written in the night.

I finished, and she frowned. "The Inquisition was horrible, beyond horrible, but you're not responsible, Eddie. Do you really feel so guilty?"

"Yes and no. At night sometimes, it bites into me, but by the light of day, I know the guilt isn't mine. I think it's good to explore the feelings, to make them a part of what history means to me."

"It's not ruining your visit?"

"No. I'm okay. But in the cathedral I look at a gold statue and think about how it came to be there. Someone mined the metal— maybe an Incan Indian in South America. Then those guys with armor and funny, boat-shaped helmets sailed across the ocean and beat the hell out of the Indians.

"Some of the conquerors died of malaria. Others died fighting pirates and hurricanes. But others came home with the gold. The king and church divvied it up, and they assigned an artist to mold it into something that would please God.

"Maybe this artist was the progeny of Jews who had been forced to convert to Catholicism. While he shaped his plaster molds, he worried that those soldiers with the funny helmets would burst into his shop and rip down the walls looking for the amulet he had hidden—a six-pointed star. Or maybe they would drag him away and torture him until he confessed that he didn't say his catechism every night. After admitting to that, the Inquisition could kill him, tear apart his home, and take all of his possessions, including the amulet and the share of gold he had received for performing his craft. The soldiers of the Inquisition would keep some of the gold and add the rest to the cathedral treasury. All of this would be going through his mind as he heated the gold and formed it into a crucifix with an agonized Christ nailed to it."

Marguerite pressed a palm against my shoulder, "They were *using* God, not *representing* Him."

Señora Limones Is One of a Kind

December 23

Though heavy thoughts weigh on my spirit sometimes, they don't keep me from appreciating our adventure, this apartment, and our landlady. Our home is called an Apartamento Turistico, *so we expected apartment living—no frills, do your own thing. But what's this? Cleaning service every day is spoiling us. Señora L. also does laundry for a reasonable price. When I went to pick it up today, we had a memorable conversation. The señora explained that she does the washing but won't do ironing because she has a bad back and feet. She conveyed this to me using Spanish and pantomime—she holds her aching back, then rubs her feet.*

Next, she points to the washing machine, to her eyes, and mentions su esposa *(your wife). I get the gist—she's only doing the laundry for us because my wife is blind. Otherwise, naturally, my* esposa *would wash it. I tell her she's very kind, but I'm thinking how happy I am that female chauvinism is alive and well in the south of Spain.*

With more eye pointing and esposas, *she asks how Marguerite went blind. I get the answer across with the French word* maladie. *And there's a lot of* Qué lástima *and* Lo siento *(What a shame and I'm sorry) talk. This culminates in her giving me a great big pot of vegetable soup and plates of crumbled egg and sliced scallions to add to the soup. She produces platters of olives and marinated red peppers with onions to go along.* Delicioso!

December 28

It's been another great visit with Tricia. She loved the shopping, Señora Limones, the cuisine, and all of the Columbus stuff, though not necessarily in that order.

We took day-drives to Carmona and Arcos de la Frontera, two peaceful and picturesque Andalusian towns with ancient churches and quiet streets to stroll along between whitewashed buildings. Arcos was once on the border between Catholic Spain and the last Moorish bastions in the south (hence the designation de la Frontera). *Another drive took us to Córdoba to see what was once the second largest mosque in the world (after Mecca). Rather than demolish this treasure, the conquering Spaniards closed the outside portals and built a cathedral smack in the middle of the mosque. Wandering through the maze of red-and-white arches and coming upon Gothic Spain in the center of the massive structure brought awe and another touch of sorrow for the tragedy of the religions here.*

Tonight our landlady came through with her second feast— chicken paella in honor of Tricia's last dinner—delivered right to our door.

December 29

We dropped off Tricia at the Seville airport very early this morning with far fewer tears than when we had left her outside Munich in August. I attribute the reduced water works to our promise to see her in the States within six weeks.

Back home from the airport, I stuck coffee grounds and water into the hourglass-shaped coffeepot and heated it on the electric stove, while Marguerite took a shower. From the balcony, I watched pedestrians in overcoats striding to work and shopkeepers rolling up their protective shutters, preparing to open for the day. An odor drifted to me—a mixture of burned coffee and scorched circuits. I scanned the buildings and sidewalk outside but saw no smoke. Turning back into the apartment, the smell almost gagged me. I rushed to the kitchen, where steam was rising from the burner, and coffee and grounds dripped from the stovetop onto the floor.

Marguerite's turbaned head popped out of the bathroom door. "What's going on? Should we evacuate?"

"The worst is over." I explained that the coffeepot had boiled over, and revealed that the stove seemed to be dead now.

"If we spill stuff on our stove back home, it doesn't cause a problem."

"Welcome to Europe. When you're ready, let's go out for coffee."

❧

Coming home from the day's adventures (Marguerite finally got her romantic carriage ride around Seville), we found a hot plate on the kitchen counter and a note taped to the stove: *No utilizar.* As I was reading it, a banging sounded on the door. Señora Limones entered, acting agitated. She gave me a long-winded explanation, speaking excitedly with lots of arm waving and fingers pointing at the stovetop and the oven, and lots of negative words. Apparently, our stove had been sensitive and had died a rather horrific death.

We Consider Life and Our Voyage

December 30

Señora Limones tells me that Felicia threw up today. To accomplish this communication, our landlady says, "La gata." I nod. She opens her mouth wide, makes a guttural sound, and jerks her head forward and back a few times—really pretty comical. "La criada limpia," she says. The maid cleans.

"Ella está gata vieja," I say. She is an old cat. Either that or she might have eaten needles off the Christmas tree. I hope everything's okay. When we get home to the States in a few weeks, we'll take her in for her 500,000-meow checkup.

December 31

On the table lies my envelope of receipts for December. Scribbled on it are credit-card expenses, ATM withdrawals, and items not considered part of living expenses (transportation costs, Patricia's rent, gifts we bought for ourselves and others). I could total, subtract, and divide this up, but I'm not motivated. Our rent for the month was a bit over the $50-a-day allotment, due to those days in the cardinal's palace in Toledo. Let's call it $52 a day. As for other living costs, we had some really great, cheap lunches here in Seville and some economical home cooking, but there were splurges, too, and that night *at the flamenco. I'll fix the grand quotient at $105 per day and call it good.*

It was New Year's Eve, and Marguerite sat close beside me on the couch, our kitty sleeping soundly in my lap. The table held a cold bottle of Cava (Spanish sparkling wine), dirty dishes from the appetizers we'd eaten (olive spread, crackers, cheese, and pieces of potato omelet, which the Spanish call *tortilla)*, and a bag of cookies. The electric heater beneath the table radiated warmth up our legs.

"I have a confession," said Marguerite.

I poured some wine, pressed her glass into her hand, and waited.

"You know that I'm excited to be going home in a couple of weeks. I can't wait to see my mom and speak English. But there's something I didn't want to tell you before. . . . It had me a little scared."

My heart pushed up into my larynx. "Something with your health?"

"No. I'm okay." She smiled and squeezed my leg. "It's just that when we were living in the vineyards in Tuscany and back in Brittany, when we were all alone out there in foreign territory, I worried something could happen to you—like a heart attack. I'd find you unconscious, and I'd have no telephone. I didn't know how to find help out there, though I knew I would somehow. Sometimes I worried so much I cried." Her eyes and voice displayed the horror of those thoughts, even as the relief of living in this apartment in Seville—where she could stick her head out the door and holler for Señora Limones—showed in her posture.

"Why didn't you tell me?"

"There was nothing you could do. Nothing I wanted you to do. . . ."

The image filled me: Marguerite rushing out of our Tuscan cottage, turning right instead of left, running down the driveway toward the forest with her cane flapping from side to side, smashing into a tree, groping, hitting more trees, desperate to find help, not thinking about herself, not rational.

I pulled her against my shoulder. "I'm sorry. You never . . . you should have told me. I could have taught you how to get to the road. We could have stayed somewhere else."

"Don't you see? I couldn't deprive you of those wonderful cottages away from everything. Anyway, from now on, we'll stay in hotels and the apartment in Paris, and then we'll be home, where there's 911."

"Did it ruin your trip?"

"*No*. This is the best thing we've ever done." She beamed at me.

"I have a confession, too—something I learned about myself this year."

"You mean how important it is to have toilets that work?" she teased.

"Ha-ha. No, it's not about plumbing or electricity. Look at this place. Our kitchen stove is dead, and we're fine. Think of the energy we're saving."

"You talk a good story about conserving, but you'll be glad for some conveniences. And I hope you see now that you can't handle everything yourself and make it all perfect." She held out her glass, and I refilled it with Cava. "It's touching that you want to take care of Felicia and me and protect us . . . like trying to distract me from the pain of menopause and going to several stores to find the right cat food for Effie. But it's been a lot of pressure on you." On cue our kitty rolled upside down, her chin turned up for me to scratch. "And then you got so mad at Felicia because she was waking me up."

"Maybe *I* was getting menopausal."

"You thought she would ruin my trip, but it was the opposite. She was my companion when you took all those hikes. She was warm and velvety comfort on a cold day, my contact with home, my stability. I would have quit if we didn't have her along."

After a quiet moment, I said, "Now here's *my* confession. . . . You know what I saw on this trip more than ever before? Your blindness is *really* hard, not just for you but for both of us."

"That's a discovery?"

"It's just that we both pretend sometimes that it isn't. I pretend to make you feel better, and you pretend back for me. Usually, I don't think much about it."

"When I'm cleaning dishes, and I break something, I know it's a hassle. You've cooked dinner, and you're tired, and you shouldn't have to help clean up my mess. It's not fair."

"It's all right. Or maybe it's not all right. It just is. Life isn't about fair." I opened the package of cookies on the table, making sure to crinkle the cellophane. She smiled and extended a hand. "The other thing I recognized," I said, giving her a cookie, "is how you want to please me—the way you ask what will make *me* happy each day and then try to do it no matter how you feel."

"That's why I continued on with this trip. I was feeling crazy, not sleeping. All my bones ached. I wanted to spend this time with you, yet I wanted to give up more than I wanted to go on. Your heart was so set on traveling, and you do so much for me."

"It's not the number of things, it's the love you show." I set my glass on the table, ran my hand around her waist, and pulled her close.

"Eddie, what about Felicia?"

"Time to get up," I cooed to our kitty. I scooped the wee ball of fur off my lap and set her on the bed. "There's some kissing your mother and I need to do to before 1997 ends."

Felicia, *Felicidad*

January 1—Wow, it's 1998!

Felicidad *means "happiness" in Spanish, and it's our kitty's seventeenth birthday today. We saved a generous portion of fish from our lunch, which she polished off as we sang "Happy Birthday." She accepted lots of kisses on her forehead and cheeks. We stripped the Christmas garlands off the walls and heaped them on top of her. She fell asleep there on the couch, well decorated and peaceful.*

*I know it's time to move on because our travel smoke alarm
has collected visible dust. We're packing it and everything else for
our run back to Paris, the city we look forward to with fondness. If
the roads are clear, and everything goes well, we'll spend a few days
in Chartres, forty miles outside the city, then move
on to our Paris apartment for the last eight days. I smell France like
a pig smells truffles. My taste buds sense the pastries and poached
salmon. I imagine electricity that works, my feet on clean tiles, my
bath towel heated and waiting as I come out of the deep tub of perfectly
warm water. I long to speak complete sentences and have them (mostly)
understood. After that, it's a welcome homecoming in California—to
friends and family, to our home and its backyard swing, to a land
where they'll really understand us.*

*Life has been pleasing in this convenient but quirky apartment,
with its easy access to sights and shopping, and its balcony so perfect for
our Christmas tree. Seville is a fine and beautiful city, its colorful
churches full of flowers and glistening Madonnas, its restaurants
excellent (including very reasonable Chinese places). Most memorable
of all is Señora Limones. We stopped by her apartment to deliver the
final rent payment and to receive her concluding dietary guidance in
support of olives and red wine. We hugged, praised her* paella
deliciosa, *and bid her a fond farewell. I thought I caught the hint of
a tear in her eye and in Marguerite's, too.*

*This place has been our last long-term rental of the journey.
The end of this most extraordinary voyage is at hand. I will miss the
adventure of seeking out unique experiences each day. And I wouldn't
give back one minute, not even from those down days in June. Still,
I'm not tempted to stay on. It's time for home.*

*By the way, the heater under the table is an SI (Spanish
Improvement).*

*A Bit of France and
Then Home*

Life Is a Croissant

January 6

Ah, France. Plumbing that works flawlessly (albeit without a shower curtain); immaculate floors; and great, reasonable meals. Supermarkets and pharmacies seem familiar after all of our sojourns in France earlier in the trip (and all the herbal remedies we bought in Brittany).

During the four days on the road from Seville, Felicia was the queen of traveling cats, a real pro. She split her car time between lolling in Marguerite's lap and lounging at the summit of the pile of luggage in the back seat, somehow managing to snooze and still keep an eye on everything.

Now we're settled for three days in Chartres, an hour from Paris. From our hotel window, I can view the striking cathedral with its two majestic, nonmatching towers and its world famous, Chartres-blue, stained-glass windows. Effie has a royal-looking velvet chair for napping, and we have wonderful croissants for breakfast at half the going price. To achieve this feat we simply decline the $10 petit déjeuner (breakfast) and ask for three croissants and café crème for two, $5. Voilà.

The real joy is being in this country with its familiar language and customs. French courtesy and a can-do attitude abound. I love the sound of the words bien sûr *(surely) or* certainement *(certainly) and* avec plaisir *(with pleasure). The French roll them out every time we ask for something. And there's nothing like a sweet* bonjour *from a* mademoiselle *in the morning.*

A disturbing note: While in town, we tried to pick up our tickets at Nouvelles Frontières, the travel agency for our airline, for our return flight to Los Angeles. Not only has the date of the flight been changed, but the tickets aren't available yet, and the flight from Paris will stop in San Francisco en route. Marguerite is beside herself. She sees an extra stop and more time in the plane as something akin to cat abuse.

We Love You, Paris

I drove into Paris, located a parking garage beneath the Champs-Elysées, and left "my women" in the car while I visited PSR for the keys to our new apartment. Returning, I found Marguerite stroking Felicia's tummy, and our kitty looking *très contente*. "We're all set. It was really neat to be walking the Champs-Elysées again, right past the front of our old apartment and the Brioche Dorée with those wonderful pastries in the window."

"I loved that apartment. How's Planet Hollywood? Still there, by the entrance to our building?"

"Yup, and they've got a new, geeky display in the window."

With a map spread across the steering wheel, I traversed Paris. My senses seemed sharpened now that I was a European driving vet. At the same time, part of my brain registered euphoria. Seeing the old landmarks brought me back to that first long walk on our second day in April. I had been so excited then, just beginning the adventure. Now we were about to end it. Paris had become a familiar city, one we knew and, yes, loved. Stopped at a signal, I scanned our surroundings. "We're by the Seine at the Alexander III Bridge. Remember the one with all the gold statues? The Eiffel Tower's back behind us and the Louvre ahead. What a great city!"

Marguerite hugged Felicia. "We'll be at our new home soon," she assured her.

After unloading Effie into the new apartment and bribing her with wet food, I hauled in the luggage. Marguerite and I jumped back into the Citroën and headed to the Gare de Lyon train station to turn in the car—all very direct and without a glitch. I had overcome my fear of Paris traffic. Compared to Athens, it was a piece of cake. After three months and nine thousand kilometers (about 5,500 miles) together, Don Corleone was no doubt sad to be losing us, but we weren't looking back, only ahead, to eight days here and then the trip home to California.

January 10

Again, PSR has provided an efficient package. Our apartment is a spacious, bright, one bedroom, with a comfortable living room and dining room and a well-stocked kitchen. I like to stand at the front windows overlooking the Avenue Daumesnil and gaze through the leafless trees to the boulevard below. We're in the eastern part of the city, a few blocks from two Métro stops and about a half mile from the Bois de Vincennes. The neighborhood is full of bakeries with gorgeous pastries, little restaurants, and rows of belle époque apartment buildings. An impressive, open-air market springs to life in the mornings with plenty of meats, seafood, and produce.

Later That Day

We stop at a Prisunic supermarket for omelet-making ingredients and pasta. Weighing beans in the produce section, we hear the market's jingle come over the store's loudspeaker, bringing back fond memories. We sing along happily. And we've rediscovered the joys of the French three-hour washing machine—a welcome appliance after days on the road.

Apprehension Joins the Holiday

January 11

Felicia seems bloated this evening, and we realize she's not doing number twos. We're giving her the French cat laxative we bought back in April. Maybe the rich Paris cuisine doesn't agree with her, not that we've offered her any.

January 13

Last time, the laxative worked within a day, but Felicia's problem hasn't gone away. We walk around Paris by day, taking in the sights and cuisine, but our kitty is always in our thoughts.

Tonight, I woke up certain I had lost the passports. I rummaged through drawers until I found them, but it wasn't about the passports. I awoke because I'm worried about my cat. Though I know she's deaf, I cradle her in my arms and talk to her.

Monday morning I gave Effie wet food, and she attacked with her usual gusto. Was she feeling better? No, she quit in less than a minute, leaving most of it in the bowl. I reported to Marguerite, and we decided to find a veterinarian. From the phonebook, I picked one nearby and made an appointment for later that afternoon. They promised an English-speaking vet.

After breakfast we headed to Nouvelle Frontières to (hopefully) obtain our plane tickets home. The agent informed us that not only would we have the extra stop in San Francisco, but we would also have to change airlines. Watching gloom shadow Marguerite's features, I knew she was worrying about all the time Effie would spend in her carrier, being shifted around the airport and having to wait so long.

The flight we would depart on would zoom from Paris to San Francisco and then continue on to Tahiti without diverting to L.A. This would be better, the agent asserted, because the flight could leave Paris later in the day and still get its passengers to Tahiti on time.

We were overjoyed for their Tahiti-bound clients but unhappy for ourselves. The agent assured us that they were responsible for getting us to L.A.—they would find a U.S. airline to fill in the missing link between San Francisco and Los Angeles, one that would let us keep our kitty with us in the cabin the whole way. Our tickets would be available that evening.

In the waiting room of the veterinarian's office, Marguerite unzipped the top of Felicia's carrier and petted our girl. "It'll be okay," she cooed. "We'll take care of you."

A dark-haired, mustached fellow in a white smock entered. Soft spoken with sympathetic brown eyes, he introduced himself as Dr. Rabot and led us upstairs to an examination room.

I explained Effie's symptoms, throwing in a French word now and again to make sure he understood. I told him about the cat laxative and showed him the pill bottle. He took her temperature, gently felt her stomach, and then spoke to us mostly in English with a few French words. "The laxative did no harm. What she has is liquid growing up in her, under the *peau* (skin). I will take some of the liquid out and do some tests." I wrapped an arm around Marguerite's shoulder as the doctor carried our kitty out of the room.

"She's going to be all right, isn't she?" Her voice trembled.

"He seems like a nice vet," was all I could manage.

Dr. Rabot returned, looking grim. He set Felicia on the steel table. I held our kitty against me and slid Marguerite's hand to her shoulder.

The doctor shook his head. "I removed this fluid from her." He showed me a thick syringe full of cloudy, pinkish stuff. "About ten cubic centimeters. It will make her more comfortable, but there is more inside. The white blood in the fluid is very high. She may have tumors. The body tries to fight them—this the white blood number tells me. Tumors, leukemia, perhaps tuberculosis. I don't know yet."

Not every word was understandable, but *tumor, leukemia,* and *tuberculosis* came through. Marguerite sobbed against my shoulder. I tried to stay strong for her, but tears ran from my eyes and dropped into her hair.

Dr. Rabot's sad eyes focused on Marguerite. "To be honest, I must say I think it is grave. *Grave*—it is a French word, but it means same in English, I think. You take this blood to the laboratory. They will give me more information tomorrow. Come back then."

Outside, it had begun to drizzle. As I waited for Marguerite to pull up the hood of her raincoat, I said, "We'll run home with Felicia and then go to the lab."

"It closes at five o'clock."

"I'm not dragging Felicia all over Paris. *We're taking her home.* Hurry."

Once our kitty was secure in the apartment, we hustled along the streets where we normally would have strolled. I would have described the quaint façades of shops, read menus to her, and mused about having dinner in one of the restaurants. Instead we focused on 5:00 PM. Neither of us spoke except for my reassuring, "We'll make it in time."

After delivering the sample, we strode uphill toward Nouvelles Frontières. I was aware of the deep breaths we both were taking, trying to collect our strength.

"We'll be able to take her home, won't we?" Marguerite asked.

"Yes." I found myself gritting my teeth with determination. We would take her home if it was at all possible, but, if necessary, we would stay in Paris longer.

"We'll insist she goes in the cabin with us?"

"Of course, but we can't say anything to them about her being sick. That could make them nervous." So we would avoid the subject, but we would insist. We would not cry, no matter what. We would get her home and deal with the disease with Doctor Lyon in California.

The Nouvelle Frontières representative still had not been able to arrange our passage all the way to L.A. She said we would receive our tickets the next day, and Felicia would be with us inside the plane all the way home, guaranteed.

January 15

Bad news about our flight turned into good fortune. Nouvelle Frontières could not find an airline that would let Felicia ride in the cabin from San Francisco to Los Angeles. They booked us instead on a direct flight from Paris to L.A. on AOM airlines. An American airline would never have done such a thing. Only the French understand the love of pets so well! We rejoice that Effie has only one flight to face, even as we mope.

Later That Day

We returned to Doctor Rabot, and he confirmed that Effie's condition is grave—probably tumors or leukemia. He gave us pills, which might help if it's leukemia. Maybe we're in denial, but we believe there will be a cure. Even if she is gravely ill, she can live a long time with the right medicine. If she has six months or a year, it's time to savor.

I'm still the leader of this expedition, and I must not let Marguerite get too upset. I must be optimistic and bring everyone home safely to the United States. Then we will put our kitty in Dr. Lyon's hands.

At the end of our visit with Dr. Rabot, he looked from Marguerite to me and back to Marguerite—two miserable faces. "She is a *lovely* cat," he said sorrowfully. Somehow that acknowledgment for our special girl comforted us.

A House Is Not a Homecoming

January 24

The peace of our California home is wondrous. To awaken this morning and to look out the bedroom window and see the eucalyptus trees along the street and the oaks on the hillside dripping wet from dew and sparkling in sunlight tickles my senses.

First, I recognized that I was in a beautiful place. Then, I realized we were home. Then, I remembered.

I remind myself that Sundays are just ordinary days, days that we don't go to work. Calling our time away "A Year of Sundays" does not exempt us from misfortune. But everything has happened with such terrible speed. Ten days ago Dr. Rabot in Paris gave us the news. It's been five days since Dr. Lyon confirmed.

Last night was our second night without her, the second night in all the time we've been in this house. The house holds memories. We hold memories. I am grateful she made the plane trip all right, thankful she survived to finish the journey we undertook together, and heartened that we were able to take her to our trusted veterinarian. There's a profound relief that she won't ever be suffering. When we made the decision, we carried it out the best way we could for her.

At night I wake to hear Marguerite weeping, or I wake expecting our kitty to nudge me for affection, to get as many caresses as she can, and then to settle, purring, against me.

We still have two months before we go back to work, two months of our Year. We try to focus on the good and familiar things—our reunion with Marguerite's mom and brother John; our home; the garments we haven't seen in ten months; washing our clothes after only one time of wearing them; and Marguerite not having to relearn her living space. All of it helps.

Marguerite says, "I never want another cat." I reply, "I want a cat now." Does that make me fickle?

I think it's a high purpose for a person to protect and nourish a soul that is in so many ways innocent and helpless in a world that we people have created. It was a privilege to take one who trusted me so much to meet her end. I think of her lifting her head that last moment at the vet. I said to her, "It's all right," and she rested her cheek back down on my arm in its gray-and-blue plaid flannel shirtsleeve.

January 31
We're in the dumps, but there's one piece of good news—Marguerite says she'll consider getting a cat. But she adds, "Not anytime soon." It's progress.

We had finished our errands for the day, but I was putting off the inevitable. I drove us to the beach in Ventura and parked facing the Pacific, our windows open to hear the surf. "It's too hard going home and feeling her absence," I said.

"She's gone, Eddie. I know it's hard, and it's going to hurt."

"It's like when we were in Brittany . . . all the grieving and sorrow."

"And it turned out for the best. You needed to grieve for your dad, and it made us both stronger. So we can face *this*. We have to let ourselves go through it, talk about her each day, cry, spend this time feeling lousy. . . ."

"But in Brittany we took steps to heal," I said. "We did everything we could to turn our grief around. The trip became something wonderful because we were determined to search for life. Right now, we're acting dead. We need to . . ."

"Eddie, it doesn't feel right to get another cat. It would be like we've forgotten her."

"Cats," I corrected. "I want cats, and I want them soon. I'll never forget her, so don't even think that. We'll get new cats because they're wonderful, because she was wonderful. I'm miserable, and this is my vacation, and we can't continue for two more months this way."

Afterward—Almost a Year Later

December 31

It's amazing to realize that these cats have been with us for more than ten months. Each day we look forward to coming home from work to see them. We are witnessing the cycle of life, springtime renewed after a long, cold winter. They thaw something in us every day.

It's 9:30 PM on New Year's Eve, 1998. I can still taste the garlic and hot peppers of the special paella we made in memory of last New Year's Eve in Seville. I pop the cork on the second bottle of champagne (the real stuff from France) and carry two glasses to our living room, which is in a cozy country style with a slate fireplace and lots of golden-oak paneling. I settle in the armchair to admire the blazing fire.

Marguerite, in her flannel pajamas with a print of cats in ballet outfits, kneels and holds her hands out to the warmth. "Nice fire."

"It's great to be home this New Year's Eve, don't you think?"

"Definitely."

"Because of all the American Improvements?"

"Partly. I love having my own clothes dryer, everyone speaking English, and Mom nearby." She slides backward from the fire, finds my ankle with her hand, and pulls herself onto my lap.

"And no smoking in restaurants is wonderful, but they had some improvements in Europe, too."

"Sure, that castle in Seefeld and the palace in Toledo for $60 a night," she says. "You can barely stay at a Motel 6 for that here."

"And strolling with the locals at night in Siena and Riomaggiore—just the warm vibrations of people and no machinery. We lived so simply and experienced so much more over there. Don't you think we're too spoiled in America?" I ask.

"We have too many choices, like entire aisles of jams and jellies and eighty-four different toothpastes to cure gum diseases we never heard of before."

"And we're always rushing and wasting energy like it doesn't matter."

She gives me one of her looks. "Am I in for a talk on fuel economy and global warming?"

"Well, no. How about the value of slowing down and taking time each day for ourselves?"

"We certainly did that last year, and it made us stronger, don't you think?"

"When it comes to feelings about my dad—yes. And our bond together has deepened."

"Being able to cry together. That's something we gained." She shifts on my lap and rests a hand on my shoulder. "And I'm a better therapist. With all that time away, I thought a lot about how your parents died and how lucky we are to have each other. And then we lost Effie. I see the crazy pace of life people live. My clients say they can't take a vacation because some other employee will gain an advantage, or they can't get out of an abusive relationship because they can't afford to. But next year, they say, it will be different. People have to see how vital it is not to surrender huge chunks of their lives, waiting for some right time that may never come. Life is *now*, not some hypothetical future."

"Don't leave out the past. The memories from our year—when I write about them, the writing seems important."

"I'm so glad you're doing that. In the articles you've written for the newspapers, you've shared part of your heart like you never did before. That's because you let yourself experience deeper feelings during the year. And I love the way your writing brings back memories." She wears a dreamy look as golden firelight flicks over her cheeks.

The kitties approach with their bells tinkling. Marguerite calls, "Hop up. Hop up." Jolie jumps up and settles in a white-and-orange ringlet on Marguerite's lap. Precious, our fluffy gray tiger, eyes my champagne glass on the end table, leaps up next to it, and watches us wide-eyed.

From the stereo, Andrea Bocelli's melodious, somber voice cloaks us. The CD is the one we bought near the Duomo in Florence. The song is a duet, and the part that's playing is in Italian. I'm not conscious of it yet, but my heart knows what's coming. My eyes anticipate. Tears stream down my cheeks. It's Bocelli's duet with Sarah Brightman, and the next phrases will be in English. *"Time to say good-bye. . . ."*

We sit silently for a few minutes. Then Marguerite says, "Remember taking Felicia into that supermarket, and when we carried her in the baby sling to visit the cows at the farm?" Tears moisten her cheeks, but she's smiling. "And sitting with her all day by the fireplace in Brittany, then putting on our heavy weather gear and marching out to face the storm? You were Torka, mighty Stone Age hunter of his people."

"With Lonit, my doe-eyed woman by my side." I caress her cheek and laugh. "You really were by my side when I needed you."

"The three of us, bound for adventure."

"We really seized the day, didn't we?"

"Oh, yes! We seized it, thanks to you, Eddie. You kept me on track when I wanted to quit."

"It was my dad. If he hadn't died young, I might not have been smart enough to take the year off in the first place."

"To Willard." Marguerite raises her glass, and I meet it with mine. "And to celebrating life!"